D1572562

A Future in Ruins

A FUTURE IN RUINS

UNESCO, World Heritage,
and the Dream of Peace

LYNN MESKELL

OXFORD

UNIVERSITY PRESS

OXFORD
UNIVERSITY PRESS

Oxford University Press is a department of the University of Oxford. It furthers
the University's objective of excellence in research, scholarship, and education
by publishing worldwide. Oxford is a registered trade mark of Oxford University
Press in the UK and certain other countries.

Published in the United States of America by Oxford University Press
198 Madison Avenue, New York, NY 10016, United States of America.

CIP data is on file at the Library of Congress
ISBN 978-0-19-064834-3

1 3 5 7 9 8 6 4 2
Printed by Sheridan Books, Inc., United States of America

For Jessica and Louise

Contents

List of Figures

Acknowledgments

A BOOK ON World Heritage necessarily conjures up a global itinerary, and I have been very fortunate over the past decade to be able to travel so extensively. Research for this book was greatly enriched by time spent in many countries visiting sites, conducting research and interviews, giving lectures, and learning about the UNESCO experience from my colleagues. In Australia I was fortunate to have generous interlocutors in Sydney and Melbourne, including Jennifer Barrett, Brett Bennet, Kristal Buckley, Denis Byrne, Elizabeth Gray, Duncan Ivison, William Logan, Glenda Sluga, Ana Vrdoljak, Andrea Whitcomb, and Tim Winter. Deakin University kindly offered me their Thinker in Residence Fellowship during the summer of 2014. In Brazil I was superbly hosted by Pedro Funari and Tobias Vilhena; for my time in Peru I am grateful to Luis Jaime Castillo Butters, Francesca Fernandini, and Grace Ocaña as well as government representatives in Lima and Cuzco. Ca' Foscari University supported my time in Venice, and I am grateful to Antonio Marcomini, Diego Calaon, and Krish Seetah for arranging site visits and lectures. In China Xingan Chen kindly organized lectures and field trips in and around Beijing and Xi'an. Over many summers in Thailand colleagues including Rasmi Shoocongdej, Paritta Koanantakool, Lia Genovese, Hahn Bich, and Thanik Lertchanrit took time to explain Thai archaeology and heritage matters. Part of this fieldwork in Asia was supported under the Australian Research Council's Discovery scheme (The Crisis in International Heritage Conservation in an Age of Shifting Global Power, DP140102991).

While working on World Heritage I spent many months in India over the past few years, which has proven compelling, so much so that it warrants its own distinct project. If anywhere could teach us about the monumental challenges of World Heritage, it is India. So for my first introduction to Indian archaeology and culture and for her long-term support I will always be grateful to Himanshu Prabha Ray. During my months in New Delhi and at research sites throughout Rajasthan, Gujarat, and Karnataka I am indebted to many individuals who shared their time, knowledge, and contacts: Pooja Agrawal, Andrew Bauer, Moe Chiba, Divay Gupta, Rima Hooja, Shikha Jain, Karni Jasol, Renu Khosla, Nyanjot Lahiri, Swapna Liddle, AGK Menon, Kathleen Morrison, Ratish Nanda, Vinay Sheel Oberoi, Rohini Pande, Shubham Prajapati, Krupa Rajangam, Indira Rajaraman, Nalini Thakur, and Mudit Trivedi. During summer 2016 I was a GIAN Fellow funded by the Government of India and based at Jawaharlal Nehru University, New Delhi.

This book was written on sabbatical during 2016–17 with the support of several fellowships and affiliations. In Paris I am indebted to Alain Schnapp and the University of Paris I Panthéon-Sorbonne, as well as Jean-Luc Lory and Nadia Chenour at the Maison Suger, part of the Fondation Maison des Sciences de l'Homme, Paris. Mary Beard, Enrico Bertacchini, Kimberly Bowes, Richard Hodges, Nicholas Stanley-Price, and Gamini Wijesuriya provided guidance and inspiration while I was based at the American Academy in Rome. As Visiting Fellow at New College, Oxford, in 2017 I shall always be thankful to the Warden and Fellows, but most of all to Caroline Thomas, who has supported me over the past twenty years, since my days as Junior Research Fellow in the late 1990s. Keble College, Oxford, hosted me in 2015 as Senior Research Visitor, thanks in large part to the generosity of my friend and colleague Chris Gosden. Oxford was made even more pleasant and productive by lively conversations with Paul Betts, Michael Burden, Jane Kaye, Ben Noble, Richard Parkinson, and Andrew Wilson. For her help with Sir Mortimer Wheeler's archive, now housed at the National Archives, London, I thank Katie Meheux from University College London.

At UNESCO's World Heritage Centre in Paris many people have been instrumental to my research over many years, but I especially want to mention Nada Al Hassan, Alessandro Balsamo, Tim Curtis, Lazare Eloundou, Feng Jing, Edmond Moukala, Kishore Rao, and Mechtild Rössler. Many months were fruitfully spent in UNESCO's archives thanks to the endless patience of Jens Boel, Alexandre Coutelle, Adele Torrance, Phan Sang, and Petra Van Den Born. From related institutions including ICOMOS and the IUCN I thank the good humor and generosity of Tim Badman, Gwenaelle Bourdin, and Regina Durighello. Moreover, ambassadors to UNESCO and members of national delegations from many nations have shared their expertise, experiences, and opinions. Some even read articles before publication, suggested lines of enquiry to follow, and, despite exposure to personal criticism, invited me to lecture at their national institutions.

A number of friends and colleagues read parts of the manuscript and offered their considered comments, including Paul Betts, Brett Bennett, Annalisa Bolin, Denis Byrne, Chiara De Cesari, David Edwards, Ian Hodder, Richard Hodges, Helen Human, Ben Isakhan, Eugene Jo, Sophia Labadi, Claudia Liuzza, Carrie Nakamura, Sabrina Papazian, Tamson Pietsch, Himanshu Ray, Simone Ricca, Trinidad Rico, Alain Schnapp, and Gamini Wijesuriya. William Logan deserves special note for his close reading of the entire manuscript and for sharing his many years of World Heritage experience. Christina Luke and Ana Vrdoljak were also especially wonderful. Other colleagues who have provided direction and inspiration in different ways from the start of this project include David Berliner, Nicholas Brown, Christoph Brumann, Brian Daniels, Chris Cleere, Henry Cleere, Brigitta Hauser-Schäublin, Michael Herzfeld, Morag Kersel, Richard Leventhal, Ian Lilley, David Lowenthal, Webber Ndoro, Gertjan Plets, Uzma Rivzi, and Helen Stacy.

At Stanford University I would like to acknowledge the Institute for Research in the Social Sciences. In my department I am fortunate to work alongside anthropologists who are attuned to the politics and materialities of heritage, especially Paulla Ebron, James Ferguson, Miyako Inoue, Sharika Thiranagama, and Sylvia Yanigisako. My graduate students, past and present, are always instructive and inspiring and hold the real promise for the future. My deepest gratitude is to Claudia Liuzza for the time we spent studying UNESCO both at Stanford and around the world from Paris to Phnom Penh. Her insights and expertise have undoubtedly made this a better book and my experience researching it much the richer.

This book would not have materialized without the vision and guidance of Stefan Vranka at OUP New York. He encouraged me to write a book about UNESCO in the first place and his insight and encouragement at every stage made writing it an unexpected delight. Finally, this book is dedicated to Jessica Pearson and Louise Martin with all my admiration and affection.

Paris 2017

Preface

The past rules us absolutely. These dreams—
—H. G. WELLS, 1905

ON NOVEMBER 16, 1945, forty-four nations gathered in London to forge an international body for educational and cultural cooperation under the aegis of the United Nations. Their project was no less than the intellectual and moral reconstruction of a world in ruins. At the San Francisco Conference that gave rise to the United Nations, President Harry S. Truman stressed the importance of a new international commitment to cultural and educational cooperation. This was in large measure inspired by his predecessor Franklin D. Roosevelt's conviction that "civilization is not national—it is international."[1]

When British prime minister Clement Attlee uttered those famous words that "wars begin in the minds of men," he captured what many had said already in the 1930s. In his speech at the Conference for the Establishment of the United Nations Educational, Scientific and Cultural Organization (UNESCO), he declared that "the peoples of the world are islands shouting at each other over seas of misunderstanding." Atlee recognized that in the future "we are to live in a world of democracies, where the mind of the common man will be all important."[2] However, it was the New Zealand delegate, Arnold Campbell, who made the linkage between peace, democracy, and education.[3] This became the chief objective of the new organization, to contribute to peace and security throughout the world by "promoting collaboration among nations through education, science, culture and communication in order to further universal respect for justice, the rule of law, human rights and fundamental freedoms set out in the Charter of the United Nations."[4] As the president of the conference, Ellen Wilkinson, saw it, "We need the organization of something positive—the positive creation of peace and the ways of peace."[5] But what philosophy would inspire such a venture and how international solidarity might be manufactured were just some of the concrete challenges they faced with the dream of peace.[6]

The foundational aspirations of UNESCO rest upon the modernist rhetorics of progress, development, and uplift that many critics consider its fatal flaw. Forged in the twilight of empire and led by the victors of the war and major colonizing powers, UNESCO's founders sought to expand their influence through the last gasps of the civilizing mission. Beginning as a program of reconstruction for a war-ravaged Europe, UNESCO soon set its sights on the developing world. Its aim was to formulate and disseminate global standards for education, science, and cultural activities.[7] However, it would remain a one-way flow, later to prove problematic, from the West to the rest. Within a matter of years the philosophical appeal for cultural understanding and uplift, a culture of peace no less, would be sidelined by the functionalist objectives of short-term technical assistance.[8] Nevertheless, it would be churlish to overlook UNESCO's achievements internationally, from the protection of refugees to freedom of expression and freedom from oppression, its confrontation of racism and apartheid, and its committed stance on education, rights and fundamental freedoms.[9] It would also be misguided to expect that one organization could effectively resolve all the problems of the world. Dag Hammarskjöld, the much-revered Secretary-General of the United Nations from 1953 to his untimely death in 1961, put it best when he said that such organizations were created not to bring us to heaven but in order to save us from hell.

It is not possible to fathom the creation of UNESCO's programs without understanding the history of UNESCO itself, its dystopian beginnings, and its utopian promise. In autumn 1942 the Allies set up a Conference of Allied Ministers of Education in London and assembled authorities from the field of education from eight governments then in exile.[10] They were there to plan the reconstruction of education systems in a liberated Europe. Libraries and books were needed, coupled with an ideological program to combat the fascist propaganda that had poisoned the continent.[11] Cultural reconstruction was also on the agenda in the face of international outrage at Nazi looting and the decimation of Europe's artistic treasures and heritage.[12] By 1943 the idea of a permanent organization addressing educational and cultural reconstruction began to take shape. In an attempt to sum up the vision and mission of UNESCO in a single sentence, one historian replied, "Following the catastrophes of the twentieth century, there is a need to reconstruct and above all to educate, in a scientific frame of mind, human beings that are equal and different, possessing the means to communicate, in order to protect and safeguard peace, the diversity of cultures and ultimately life itself."[13] There is still much in this explanation that remains relevant today.

Ruins were also on the agenda for reconstruction. But it was not simply that great buildings, museums, and art were affected by the war and required rehabilitation. It was the regulation of the past itself, and how it might be recovered, that was deemed part of a new world order. How archaeological excavations were conducted around the world and the resulting discoveries disseminated also required restructuring. Ultimately, archaeology's spoils were to be divided up for Western advantage, echoing earlier recommendations made by the League of Nations and its International Committee for Intellectual Cooperation. The past would be managed for the future. UNESCO capitalized upon an already existing momentum for a world-making project devoted to humanity's heritage. What followed was an inevitable progression from the vast conservation and restoration efforts needed in the wake of destruction after two world wars toward a more lasting project of rehabilitation and recovery.

Many critical accounts and analyses of UNESCO have been written, coupled with official histories and narratives by well-placed insiders.[14] Together they tell the story of an imperfect organization that began with midcentury optimism but rapidly devolved from an assembly of statesmen to a tyranny of states. Originally a globally oriented organization, UNESCO was transformed into an intergovernmental agency, a mere shadow of its former ambition for a world peace and mutual understanding between peoples. The overreach of powerful governments has come to permeate all aspects of its functioning. This is reflected in the workings of many of its high-profile programs, including World Heritage--the program that seeks to identify, protect, and preserve outstanding cultural and natural heritage sites around the world. While there are considerable problems, as this book reveals, they should not detract from UNESCO's achievements in creating a planetary concern for heritage preservation and its ability, however circumscribed, to exert pressure on its Member States to honor the treaties that they have ratified.

Entreating the world to conserve its cultural and natural places in the face of escalating industrialization and destruction can surely only be a positive step, yet how nations mobilize that call and at whose expense reveals a more complex dilemma. For example, the campaign to save the Cambodian site of Angkor is upheld by UNESCO as one of its greatest conservation achievements. Yet in conserving the temples the organization also legitimated the brutal Khmer Rouge, and in the decades to follow, harsh restrictions were placed on local communities by state authorities. These are the complicated stories of conservation, the underneath of things, that UNESCO cannot officially recount, since the nation-state is the ultimate arbiter of World Heritage. That tension between international aspiration and national machination on the ground constitutes a central strand that runs throughout this book, and while such statist self-interest has been there since UNESCO's beginnings, the politico-economic intercalations have multiplied over the decades. Given UNESCO's founding and purpose, the organization is required to tell the story of successful salvage; it cannot afford to dwell in the messiness of history.

UNESCO's major contribution may be its pioneering of international legal instruments such as the 1972 World Heritage Convention. Perhaps more subtle is its development of a body of general principles and customary norms of international law in the field of cultural heritage protection.[15] Its legal framing, resting upon an assembly of States Parties, provides its structure but also its limitation, premised on the goodwill and civility of states, both to each other and to their citizens. In a world where nonstate actors are now some of its most destructive combatants, the agencies of the United Nations have struggled to make adequate provision. UNESCO's inability to mediate during the destruction of religious sites in Mali and ongoing assaults in Syria, to name just two settings, remains a conundrum. Prosecuting one individual for war crimes against cultural property seems to lose sight of the larger impetus for attacks in the first place. UNESCO's failure to censure the illegal occupation in Crimea or the bombardment of Yemen, both perpetrated by its Member States in breach of various international treaties, reveals further fatal shortcomings.

Much valuable research on the World Heritage Convention has appeared since its establishment in 1972, from a range of different disciplines and perspectives.[16] Academics, activists, local communities, and indigenous peoples have, however, expressed dissatisfaction with UNESCO's philosophies, procedures, regulations, impacts, and exclusions. It is not only issues of nationalism and sovereignty that rankle, but the inability of today's World Heritage regime to incorporate the living aspects of heritage that necessitate rights of inclusion, access, use, and benefits. This view further bolsters the point that the organization cannot continue to privilege the technical, but must revisit its early commitments to creating a better world. In some cases that may entail not inscribing sites on a list but rather allowing groups to determine their own path for heritage. For UNESCO's part it may mean intervening more strongly when its Member

States attempt to forcibly relocate people, refuse to collaborate with them or include them in World Heritage processes, or fail to consider their needs for site use and management. For conservation to fulfill its midcentury promise for the future, it must strive to include the people who matter most, whose heritage it is, and to consider those who have most to win or lose in the fate of World Heritage sites. And finally, we have to be more attendant to history, to the actions of empires and nations that still influence the future of sites and regions, and specifically those conflicts that continue to haunt and recur. We forget that heritage at our peril.

A Future in Ruins was conceived and completed at New College, Oxford. During a sabbatical in 2010 I confessed to fellow archaeologist Chris Gosden that UNESCO would make a fascinating project for study, particularly its World Heritage program. He responded by laying out a paradox that I found compelling. While it was true that UNESCO status bestows a level of international prestige upon ancient sites, for archaeology as a discipline the organization means almost nothing. World Heritage might offer the only truly global platform to showcase the world's most famous archaeological sites to a global public, and yet Gosden was right that it had little impact upon the history of our discipline. I wanted to understand why.

He convinced me to undertake the project. I soon discovered that archaeologists, like many other scholars, had no great admiration for the organization and are more likely to summarily dismiss, misrepresent, or criticize UNESCO and its World Heritage List than to acknowledge its achievements. Educating ourselves about UNESCO then seemed to me the first step, and this project began as an exercise to understand the workings of World Heritage. It was nothing short of a discovery to find that the discipline of archaeology was originally part of UNESCO's early intellectual momentum and had even extended back to its illustrious predecessor, the League of Nations. And while there was an archaeological component to UNESCO's famous Nubian Monuments Campaign to save and study the sites and temples in Egypt and Sudan scheduled for submersion with the completion of the Aswan Dam, this was short-lived. In 1970 when the Tabqa Dam threatened the same fate for archaeological sites in Syria's Upper Euphrates Valley, UNESCO proposed an international appeal rather than a full-scale campaign, advising nations interested in excavation to enter into their own bilateral agreements with Syria.

The implications for archaeology in UNESCO's utopian, one-world mission for the future all but stalled after the 1960s. Some years ago, a senior UNESCO bureaucrat invited me to provide an official definition of an archaeological site, simply because it had never been adequately formulated by the organization. But the shift away from archaeology as a discipline marked a loss for UNESCO and its later development of a heritage program. That program would often be cast as conserving static sites and monuments, lacking active research agendas, and not infrequently overlooking living people and their practices. Quite the reverse was true for archaeology. Its historical development has increasingly incorporated and relied upon the perspectives and participation of local communities, indigenous groups, and other stakeholders that bring the past alive in the present.

As a modern discipline, archaeology effectively straddles the humanities and sciences, thus representing an administrative predicament for UNESCO's sectoral structure. Yet archaeology has the capacity to bridge disciplines, as Julian Huxley, UNESCO's first Director-General, immediately recognized, and to build international cooperation and partnerships in active and long-term ways. These are horizontal rather than vertical relationships, not simply captured in a single moment such as site inscription or at the level of the nation-state, but conducted over the long term and with many institutions and groups. In Africa, Asia, and the Middle East with their long histories of colonization, archaeological heritage projects can play vital roles in configuring new relationships and challenging negative legacies. Not simply a monumental exercise, archaeology today embraces and contributes to different heritage perspectives: it extends beyond a simple site-based focus and involves neighboring communities, training programs, academic and institutional linkages, scholarly exchanges, and so on. These struck me as some of the disciplinary dimensions that UNESCO's World Heritage program had failed to capitalize upon. How and why this unfolded as it did was tied to tensions over UNESCO's central mission—would it be promoting world peace or providing technical assistance?

A Future in Ruins focuses exclusively upon archaeology and cultural heritage, moving from the early salvage campaigns to the 1972 Convention Concerning the Protection of the World Cultural and Natural Heritage, commonly referred to as the World Heritage Convention or the 1972 Convention.[17] Other UNESCO conventions pertaining to intangible heritage, cultural property, and cultural diversity, while relevant and related, lie beyond the scope of this work. These conventions have their own structures, staff, statutory meetings, signatories, and legal formulations that do not precisely map onto World Heritage. UNESCO officials often see the treaties as having entirely different domains and philosophies: one high-ranking official described the development of the different conventions as like moving from solid to liquid to gas! Anthropologists, legal scholars, and heritage specialists have studied UNESCO's intangible heritage and diversity programs extensively, largely because of their implications for definitions of culture and their intercalations with indigeneity, rights and legal property. Alternatively, we have only recently begun to analyze the globalizing strategies of World Heritage, specifically concerning issues of governance, diplomacy, and bureaucracy, and the political economy of culture and rights.[18]

Given my own background and training in archaeology, the case studies presented are primarily cultural, often archaeological sites and excavations, rather than natural properties; the latter are a small fraction of the World Heritage List and their inscription, though perhaps not their conservation, is considered less contentious.[19] Cultural sites have always dominated the World Heritage List, and their tacit links to sovereignty, nationalism, territoriality, and identity are well documented. Yet I would argue that the processes, politics, logics, and consequences of World Heritage apply equally to both the cultural and the natural. My concern here is about the potentials of the past and the transition from an early focus on archaeological fieldwork to the broader remit of cultural heritage understood within a global frame. This requires paying attention to the shift from archaeology to monumentality and managerialism by asking what is at stake when the emphasis is placed upon monuments rather than multilayered places. Archaeologists too need to see their objects as embedded in these wider historical and sociopolitical contexts.

The book draws on archival analysis and long-term ethnographic research. I have been fortunate in gaining access as an official observer to UNESCO's World Heritage Committee meetings and events over the past seven years and have conducted countless interviews with ambassadors and members of national delegations, the UNESCO Secretariat, Advisory Bodies, and staff in UNESCO field offices from Brazil to Bangkok.[20] Hundreds of individuals from various countries and contexts took the time to share with me their views and experiences. My work has also benefitted from discussions with archaeologists and conservators, as well as site evaluators, consultants, and academics involved in all aspects of World Heritage. It has further drawn upon my archaeological fieldwork over many years in countries including Egypt, Turkey, and South Africa. Researching World Heritage has also taken me to India, Thailand, France,

Italy, China, Myanmar, Peru, and Brazil to follow UNESCO's mission in-country, asking how and why specific nations seek and later utilize World Heritage inscription. In the effort to protect global patrimony there is an ever-expanding number of actors with differing expertise, perceptions, politics, and agendas.

Alongside in-depth interviews and long-term participation, I studied documents in UNESCO's archives in Paris as well as UNESCO's extensive Web-based materials. Personal papers, such as those from the British archaeologist Sir Mortimer Wheeler (now housed in the National Archives, London), are also included. In other collaborative work with colleagues from cultural economics, we use statistical and network analyses to trace the international political pacting, economic interests, and voting blocs that shape today's World Heritage agenda.[21] Having been trained as an archaeologist, I am drawn to discerning long-term patterns and evidence of change that can be observed by calibrating documentary materials, historical accounts, statistical records, interviews with a wide cross section of players, and observation and participation. From the archives to my interviews to the international gatherings, all roads led back to politics, particularly to the motivations of the States Parties to the 1972 Convention.

During my first World Heritage Committee meeting in Paris in 2011 I remember being moved to see both poor nations and small ones raise their nameplates and take the floor on issues that were important to them. Naively I imagined a kind of equality was possible in heritage matters. My optimism was swiftly dashed as the interventions of powerful states, the pressure they exerted, and the extent of lobbying became evident as the days progressed. If we are to understand World Heritage, we have to acknowledge the array of institutional and international actors that ostensibly "make" heritage.[22] Anthropologists have written extensively about the difficulty of studying diplomats and the bureaucratic elite in agencies such UNESCO. Official credentials are required for access and one's movements are circumscribed by elaborate security measures.[23] Ambassadors and members of national delegations, as well as officials in the UNESCO Secretariat, require letters, emails, and calls before an appointment is granted. Many never respond. Others are happy to discuss issues, even sensitive ones like those described in the book, but do not want to be identified. Ethically I have respected those wishes. However, new appeals for transparency at UNESCO and extensive documentation, including Web streaming and posted transcripts from World Heritage Committee meetings, render most individuals increasingly identifiable.

Because I am an archaeologist researching World Heritage politics, this affords me an understanding of particular heritage sites and their issues, as well as the overall UNESCO system. But I am also distanced from the institutional politics that individuals routinely encounter and typically find burdensome, whether from their governments or from UNESCO itself. Researchers like myself are connected to the issues in such a way that navigating both closeness and distance entails a certain degree of loyalty and discretion. Some members of UNESCO's Secretariat, however, have expected a level of allegiance from me that is not possible to maintain if multiple viewpoints are to be represented, sometimes leading to antipathy and even threats. The stakes for heritage are indeed high. My intention throughout is to understand how and why the past comes to matter in the present, who shapes the political agendas, and who wins or loses as a consequence. It remains critical that we educate ourselves about the politics at work in cultural productions such as World Heritage and understand that we can never escape the past and are, in fact, too often doomed to repeat it. As that great utopian H. G. Wells wrote, the past "rules us absolutely."

I
———

Utopia

*There are many things in the commonwealth of Utopia
that I rather wish, than hope, to see followed in our
governments.*

—THOMAS MORE, 1516

IN NOVEMBER 1948 the British biologist and philosopher Julian
Huxley arrived in Beirut for the UNESCO General Conference. In 1945,
UNESCO had been established as an intergovernmental organization
aimed at fostering peace, humanitarian assistance, and intercultural understanding after the ravages of the Second World War, with Huxley appointed its first Director-General. In the wake of devastation and atrocity,
particularly across Europe, the agency's task was to promote peace and
change the "minds of men" through fundamental education, celebration
of cultural diversity, and a dialogue between different peoples of the world.
UNESCO's founders considered their mission to be no less than steering
the fate of civilization itself. Huxley was well qualified to direct the organization, being a lifelong internationalist and a utopian thinker with a particular vision for UNESCO that, in many ways, persists to this day.

Before and after the Beirut meeting Huxley traveled extensively
throughout the Middle East on a kind of archaeological odyssey that was
subsequently published in his popular book *From an Antique Land*. In
the book he described his international work with UNESCO as a "high-
speed business" packed with "endless meetings, working committees and
behind-the-scenes lobbying," while the bureaucratic work continued to
pile up in Paris.[1] His personal notebooks from the Middle East are filled
with ancient timelines, records of visits to excavations, sketches of prehistoric pottery, notes on Gilgamesh, and his characteristic ornithological
notations.[2] He found that the "rain of new impressions was sometimes
bewildering."[3] Nine countries later, he had visited some of the most

extraordinary archaeological sites in the Middle East, among them Byblos, Petra, Jerash, Palmyra, Memphis, and Giza. Perhaps more remarkable, given his background in zoology, was his zest for the epigraphic and excavation reports and publications from these ancient sites; he read the popular works of archaeologists Flinders Petrie, James Henry Breasted, Margaret Murray, Gertrude Bell, Austen Henry Layard, Henry Rawlinson, Henri Frankfort, C. W. Ceram, and V. Gordon Childe as background for *Antique Land.* Page upon page is devoted to the decipherment of ancient scripts, new discoveries of clay tablets, and the ongoing excavations at Jericho, Ur, Tel Halaf, and Ras Shamra, to name just a few.

Huxley was a polymath. Given his own remarkable lineage, it should not be surprising: his grandfather was Thomas Henry Huxley, known as "Darwin's Bulldog"; his father, Leonard, was a writer, like Julian's famous brother, novelist Aldous Huxley; and his half brother Andrew was a fellow biologist and Nobel laureate. He also knew personally and enlisted many of the great figures of twentieth-century British archaeology in his plans for the future of UNESCO: Leonard Woolley, Seton Lloyd, Mortimer Wheeler, Jacquetta Hawkes, Kathleen Kenyon, John Garstang, and V. Gordon Childe. Indeed, Huxley personally wrote to the renowned British geneticist J. B. S. Haldane recommending Childe as a "good man" for membership in the Royal Society, especially after the loss of the archaeologist Arthur Evans and social anthropologists Alfred Haddon and Charles Seligman.[4] This is not entirely surprising since Huxley, Haldane, and Childe all belonged to the Rationalist Association, whose members considered religion to be the main threat posed to society. Also included in its membership were H. G. Wells, Aldous Huxley, and Bertrand Russell.

When Huxley arrived in the Middle East in 1948, his directorship was coming to an end. His tenure had been prematurely shortened from six to two years, his radical philosophical views probably being in part responsible. The ultimate decision, however, had been orchestrated by the American delegation to UNESCO. Put simply, the Americans had failed to get their man, Francis Biddle, the top job. According to one well-placed observer, the British diplomat Gladwyn Jebb, they "had contemplated appointing Americans to all the key positions," and with the appointment of Huxley the Americans had unceremoniously reduced their funding to UNESCO by US$1 million.[5] The US delegate James Marshall had argued that art and culture could in no way contribute to peace and security.[6] The consequences of the American decision, though painful for Huxley personally, did not impede his intellectual commitment to the organization, his exhaustive travel schedule, or his prodigious literary output. Throughout *Antique Land* Huxley extolled the importance of "scientific excavation," involving "careful stratigraphic excavation, preservation and record of every kind of object, skilled reconstruction, [and] correlation of the results into a general scheme of dating."[7] He made further enthusiastic recommendations for site conservation, the construction of site museums, and the development of cultural tourism, all of which became the hallmark of UNESCO's international program of cultural heritage in the decades to follow.

Huxley said that to "write about the Middle East is to write something about history."[8] With a nod to the materiality of archaeology, Huxley called it "solid history." Like many of his contemporaries, he placed the beginnings of civilization in the Middle East, but he did so within a framework of evolutionary humanism. For Huxley, history was not merely irreversible but directional, and "the trend towards more knowledge," he asserted, must be capitalized upon.[9] Significantly for the time, he considered that archaeology was a science, knowledge of which formed an integral part of his intellectual vision for a global future. In his report of 1948 he noted that the immense archaeological wealth of the Middle East might be truly beneficial, for the rest of the world as well as for individual nations, if one considered its sites and artifacts "resources of the region as a whole."[10] He was surrounded by the great archaeological luminaries of his generation in Britain and had access to some of the world's most exciting archaeological sites and excavations, so it is no wonder that he saw a role for the discipline in this new international organization. "He who controls the past controls the future" could well have been his motto.

Huxley remains a fascinating figure who in many ways embodies a bygone age of belief in utopian social engineering, development and progress, cultural internationalism, and a voracious intellectualism that were all tied up with the end of empire. His is often called a "planetary utopia," nothing less than a global vision for an ideal polity through the creation of a united world culture.[11] The past constituted what Huxley would call "a unified pool of tradition" for the human species.[12] In reflecting upon the contribution of *Antique Land* and indeed Huxley's connections to the British archaeological establishment more generally, it is evident that the discipline of archaeology was firmly present at the very beginnings of UNESCO. A vision for the archaeological past in the present and future was deemed necessary in planning for the world culture to come. To achieve this goal Huxley drew upon the intellectual networks of empire and produced publications and broadcasts for an educated public. However, his programmatic vision for UNESCO was already losing ground by the end of the 1940s to expert-driven, technical, and managerial approaches to culture and development stemming from the United States. Despite its colonial and civilizing discourse, Huxley's distinctly British intellectual vision for the discipline of archaeology and its role in charting a new path for social progress would be short-lived.

The role of archaeology as a field science and discrete discipline in international planning and world-making extends back to the League of Nations and the International Committee on Intellectual Cooperation (ICIC). In light of this early history it is intriguing to trace how, in the arena of international governance and cooperation, archaeology was transformed in the decades that followed into the handmaiden of heritage. Archaeology employs multidisciplinary research in order to understand the total context of the human past; it draws from the natural sciences and social sciences. Its academic practitioners are typically based in universities and engaged in long-term field projects and international collaborations. UNESCO's understanding of cultural heritage in the material sense, on the other hand, has drawn from antiquarian, art historical, and architectural approaches to protecting the fabric of monuments, groups of buildings, and sites.[13] Archaeology within UNESCO, as both an intellectual discipline and a field practice, was replaced almost entirely after the 1960s by a preoccupation with monuments and monumentality.[14] While archaeologists also discover and excavate ancient monuments, much work on standing structures and buildings is the domain of conservators, architects, and engineers who are concerned with their recovery and preservation. Pompeii and Palmyra are good examples. This aspect of heritage conservation easily could be developed and promoted in ways that archaeological research could not: monuments were already existing icons, more readily embraced and mobilized by sovereign states than the uncharted territory of excavation and investigation. This shift from archaeology, with its focus on digging and context, to monumentality was predicated on prioritizing technical assistance instead of field research, and led to further tensions between technocracy and UNESCO's early commitment to peace-building.

This is part of the largely untold story of the formative role of archaeology and archaeologists in the founding years of UNESCO, their early presence during the massive international salvage campaign in Nubia, and then how they lost ground during the decades that followed with missions to Moenjodaro and Borobudur that were devoted largely to monumental preservation rather than to excavation and research. This shift away from archaeology had significant consequences, and not only for the development of global heritage. Lack of sufficient engagement with archaeology, as practiced and theorized, throughout UNESCO and specifically in what was to become the World Heritage program, has contributed to the alienation of various stakeholders who have deep attachments to ancient sites, to living heritage places and landscapes. Instead of the one-way flow of authority and expertise that still holds sway in the organization, research and collaboration could have provided greater possibilities for internationalism, exchange, and the co-production of knowledge. Therefore, it is necessary to consider more fully the early profile of archaeology at UNESCO, including its various international salvage and advisory missions, through to the flagship World Heritage program culminating in the 1972 Convention. By tracing its successes and challenges from the agency's foundation to the present we can also uncover, much as archaeology itself does, the politics of knowledge at UNESCO and what was at stake for a future in ruins. To understand the longer history and connection of the archaeological past we need to go further back in time to where issues of peace, conflict, a common heritage for humanity, and the dissemination of expertise were pressing for a world community in need of reconstruction in the aftermath of war.

One-World Archaeology

Telling this story requires an examination of how archaeology and internationalism played out in the lead-up to the formation of the United Nations, the political upheavals of the First and Second World Wars that formed the backdrop, and the emergent hopes for a better world that would captivate the "minds of men." Before UNESCO there was another intergovernmental agency established at the end of a world war in order to promote peace: the League of Nations (1920–1946). The League had grand ambitions for archaeological and cultural sites around the world, particularly in fostering research into ancient civilizations, the protection of selected sites, and the establishment of permanent museum collections. Through the Treaty of Sèvres in 1919, specifically its Article 421 and annex, the League sought to ensure equal treatment for archaeological research and excavations to the nationals of all Member States, although this was never ratified.[15] While much was made of the League's international representation of scholars in archaeology, the truth was a rather more European and North American affair, with scant if any mention of scholars from Africa, Latin America, Asia, and the Pacific or concern for their pasts.

During the expansive interwar period many international initiatives were forged under the aegis of the League of Nations when a group of European and North American academics, including the Oxford classicist Gilbert Murray and the physicist Albert Einstein, were involved in the establishment of a variety of committees and organizations that saw culture and heritage as a vehicle for international cooperation. The first of these committees, known as the International Committee on Intellectual Cooperation (1922–1939), organized the First International Congress of Architects and Technicians of Historic Monuments in 1931. What followed was the Athens Charter for the Restoration of Historic Monuments, which specifically focused on monumental preservation and embraced a one-world concept of cultural heritage by entreating states to assume a greater role in conserving the artistic and archaeological property of humankind.[16] The interwar decades were characterized by a new spirit of internationalism and global reach, not only with the establishment of international agencies but also with the increase in NGOs that resulted in the expansion of international organizations, councils, committees, and networks.[17] Saving the monumental past and ensuring the future of archaeological excavation were issues that were gaining international attention, albeit driven by Western intellectuals and guided by their national attachments and individual ambitions.

A further example of international scholarly cooperation, now largely forgotten in the discipline, is the International Office of the Institutes of Archaeology and History of Art in Rome. Originally established in 1933 by the International Institute of Intellectual Cooperation or IIIC (1926–1946), the office served as a nodal point and clearinghouse for all institutes and departments of archaeology and art history, an index of all archaeological excavations and exhibitions, and all related activities and publications, worldwide. While such an ambitious mission would be unimaginable today, at the time its remit was rather more restricted in scope, as it consisted largely of the eminent scholars and programs of Europe and the United States, with a few exceptions in British India and Japan. Humfry Payne from the British School at Athens was an enthusiastic supporter, helping to publish a bulletin from the organization. Significantly, the aims and ambition of the IIIC's International Office of the Institutes of Archaeology and History echoed the establishment of a much earlier office, the Instituto di Corrispondenza Archaeologica. Also based in Rome, the

Instituto, established in 1828, was a center of archaeological collaboration reliant on an extensive correspondence throughout the classical world: information pertaining to new excavations and monumental designs would be collated, archived, and published in its own periodicals. This too was a supranational organization bringing together scholars and diplomats, including Klemens von Metternich and Alexander von Humboldt, arranged over four European locations: Italy, France, Germany, and England.[18]

In August 1937 the League of Nations and the ICIC met in Geneva to discuss, among other things, the adoption of an internationally agreed upon System of Antiquities and Excavations. In March of that year a panel of largely European and American experts had met in Cairo for an international conference on archaeological excavations organized by the International Museums Office and supported by the Egyptian government. Harking back to the Treaty of Sèvres, their aim was to institute "a system of international co-operation in the matter of antiquities and excavations calculated to develop archaeological research, and to conduce to improved knowledge of ancient civilizations."[19] They envisaged a committee within the Department of Art and Archaeology at the ICIC that would advise on excavations and all forms of international collaboration arising out of archaeological research. This included creating an international register of members of archaeological expeditions and other experts, classified according to specialization, qualifications, and previous activities.

Eminent men including the conservator Harold Plenderleith, classical archaeologists Jean Charbonneux and Alan Wace, and Egyptologists Jean Capart, Etienne Drioton, and George Reisner were in attendance at the 1937 Cairo Conference. Many famous British archaeologists were notably absent. This was in part due to strained relations between the two countries after the Anglo-Egyptian Treaty of 1936, when the British had pledged the withdrawal of their troops from Egypt. British views, however, had been solicited via an extensive correspondence. For example, Sir Arthur Evans was requested to advise on the restoration and conservation of archaeological sites, a request that perhaps is rather alarming in hindsight given the results of his work at the Cretan palace of Knossos—in a scrawled handwritten letter Evans states that reconstruction was necessary at Knossos, just as at Pompeii, the alternative being "an unintelligible heap of ruins."[20] Sir Flinders Petrie, on the other hand, wrote that reburying sites was preferable, insisting that "the preservation of your site is a greater duty than the exposing of it to the present generation."[21] Archaeology and conservation were being considered here in tandem. Not content to establish a clearinghouse for archaeological excavations worldwide, the committee also dreamed of creating standardized lexicons and handbooks and coordinating all research across the globe. Their ambition was nothing less than the creation of a one-world archaeology.

A first step in this grand plan was the formulation of a treatise dealing with the technical problems of archaeology, its juridical aspects—particularly in light of foreign missions—and the development of standards for international documentation. The results were published first in French (1939) and then in English (1940). The *Manual on the Technique of Archaeology Excavations* was remarkable for its time, not simply because of the individuals involved but also because of the farsighted concerns for recording, conservation, publication, training, funding, and so on.[22] It was global in scope and grand in vision, unlike anything that had come before. There were less admirable goals as well, such as the provisions for dividing the spoils between host countries and the international excavation teams and museums. This too was depicted as a "wide scheme of exchange and co-operation."[23] There were also references in the introduction to the necessity of winning the "confidence of native populations," revealing the preoccupations and prejudices of the day as well as the tacit limitations of internationalism.[24] The *Manual* has been somewhat forgotten in the history of archaeology, although sections on the illicit trade and questions of sovereignty and ownership of antiquities are occasionally referenced by legal scholars.[25] But its claims for archaeology as a science and many of its recommendations remain relevant to this day. Its authors clearly felt that what was needed was an International Committee on Excavations, and while the League of Nations was replaced in 1946 by the United Nations, the international role of archaeological excavation would continue to command attention.

Amidst the turmoil of 1943 a remarkable document entitled *Archaeology After the War* was penned.[26] It proposed that the League of Nations' plans for archaeology be extended and made universal. Composed by three scholars based in Jerusalem, Nelson Glueck, Roland de Vaux, and Eleazar Sukenik, the report imagined a time after the cessation of hostilities when the archaeology of the Middle East would be carved up and apportioned to British and American institutions. The document proposed that because antiquities found within any modern nation-state would have both national and international interest, they should be subject to an international convention. Excavated finds would also be distributed between the host country and the excavator to enhance international cooperation and, of course, collections. These were sentiments that found their full expression in UNESCO's first salvage campaign in Nubia two decades later. Framed almost entirely around work in the Middle East, the document never stated whether such international agreements would be applied equally to excavations undertaken, for example, in European nations by other nationalities. *Archaeology After the War,* while initially presented as protecting the "origins" of "Western Civilization" through processes of enhanced internationalization, in true imperial fashion would be extended de facto to the rest of the world. Albeit premised on international cooperation and some measure of technical assistance, the document reveals the unidirectional and quasi-colonial imperatives of its drafters. This was, after all, the era of colonies and dominions. British statesman David Lloyd George exemplified the era when he declared with great enthusiasm: "I am for a League of Nations. . . . The British Empire is a League of Nations."[27]

Some forty experts met during June 1943 at the American School of Oriental Research in Jerusalem to discuss further these proposals and to set the agenda. At their Jerusalem meeting, Frank Brown from Yale argued that "the world at large has the right to oblige states" to protect and preserve their antiquities, encourage cooperation of international interests, and prevent wanton destruction or exploitation. But he was at a loss as to how to make it binding given a new world order and the unknown nature of postwar nationalisms. These discussions were taking place against the backdrop of unrivaled atrocities being perpetrated in Europe alongside the programmatic devastation of culture and heritage. Sukenik, from Jerusalem's Hebrew University, responded that, in the future, world conditions might indeed prove "utopian," but at present it was simply impossible for nations to accept that their antiquities belonged to all of humanity. In retrospect, the fact that a meeting to decide the fate of international archaeology was held in Jerusalem is striking.

Given the colonial conditions of the day, especially the carving up of the Middle East, it was easy for foreign scholars to argue in favor of international legislation and oversight, because the antiquities and heritage of their own nations were not under discussion. Emir Maurice Chebab from Lebanon, however, argued that his country would retain its antiquities, as it had the financial, scientific, and legal right to do so. Richard Barnett, an officer in the Royal Air Force and assistant keeper at the British Museum, recalled that since museums did not yet exist in some of the colonies, archaeological finds should be relocated so as to be accessible to "the world." By this he meant the Western world. Zaki Hassan, an Egyptian engineer who went on to play a major role in UNESCO's Nubian Campaign beginning in the 1960s, pointed out quite rightly that none of the proposals was actually binding. So what indeed was the purpose of such a discussion? British diplomat A. S. Kirkbride noted that "there has been some talk of compulsion" but that it was "not practical when applied to governments unless resort is had to war." Others felt that if their recommendations were attached to an international convention for archaeology, those proposals might acquire more leverage. In the meantime, if they could not impel nations to preserve and protect, they could attend to more managerial matters. Lady Hilda Petrie suggested they form small and large working committees in order to draft their recommendations.

As with the preceding ICIC Cairo meeting, the group that met in 1943 called for a standardized lexicon of archaeological terms, access to all excavation findings, the establishment of a Council for Near Eastern Archaeology, and a master plan for archaeology covering five to ten years. Their desires for a future world order, formulated in the midst of a world at war, were dismissed as "utopian" by some participants, including the Cypriot classical archaeologist Porphyrios Dikaios.[28] In retrospect, their recommendations constitute a precursor for the mission that UNESCO would ultimately inherit. But as the composition of the committee reflects, they were ineluctably shaped by colonial and Eurocentric concerns for maintaining control leading up to the endgame of empire: archaeology and global heritage were a high-profile part of that equation.

The League of Nations and the ICIC served as the model for UNESCO, and their ambitious programs retained an enormous influence on the later organization. The League's demise, the failure of multilateralism, and the outbreak of global conflict prompted a cycle of descent from utopian possibility to the dystopian reality of the Second World War. Preventing the brutal ideologies of fascism and Nazism from emerging in the future became a touchstone of UNESCO and, perhaps more so than the League, UNESCO placed culture front and center. A child of the Spanish Civil War, UNESCO Director-General Federico Mayor recounted with horror the Nazi slogan "Whenever I hear the word culture . . . I release the safety catch on my pistol."[29] Leading contemporary figures would once again try to "build the defences of peace in the minds of men." Education, culture, and heritage would have to be tethered in new ways at UNESCO in order to achieve a new world order. Throughout the war and immediately afterward there was an international frenzy to save and reinstate Europe's cultural treasures, artworks, and monumental architecture and to reconstruct its historic districts. World-making through the valorization of collective cultural achievements was deemed a priority. The heritage of humanity would require further international agreements, declarations, cooperative ventures, and salvage campaigns to fulfill the dream of peace.

One-Worldism

Although it has been five hundred years since Thomas More's *Utopia* appeared, many thinkers during the twentieth and twenty-first centuries have returned to the promise of lasting peace through world government by embracing what British Fabianist Leonard Woolf called the "internationalizing of laws, science, customs, thought, industry, commerce, and society."[30] More's *Utopia* was renowned for its welfare state principles, communalism, liberal views on divorce and euthanasia, six-hour workday, and singular lack of lawyers. The island society was founded on the principles of common property, good governance, social equality (with the exception of slaves), and even politeness. It is easy to see shades of the future UNESCO when one reads that in Utopia "all things are so regulated," "public lectures are offered every morning," and people are allowed "as much time as is necessary for the improvement of their minds."[31] Both Utopians and "Unescans" debated major issues in moral philosophy such as the nature of virtue or happiness and what constitutes the good. Indeed, of all pleasures Utopians "esteem those to be most valuable that lie in the mind," and what they detest most is war and violence. In Utopia everyone has a right to everything.

One-worldism extended the dream of world government and world organization writ large into a desire for unified disciplines, international cooperation and networks, and even global interdependence in academic spheres. UNESCO, like the UN, effectively globalized the imperial internationalism of the League of Nations.[32] H. G. Wells hoped for a permanent world commission of scientific men who might, despite their limited power, make recommendations, write reports, and to some degree control the fate of a global citizenry.[33] This was a vision of great statesmen rather than states. Julian Huxley's philosophies developed in this milieu. Despite the marked differences with his brother Aldous, author of *Brave New World*, in respect to population and eugenics, they shared the same notions of progress and the importance of biology, as developed by their grandfather Thomas Huxley. Both brothers formulated their ideas about human society and ethics through an understanding of the life sciences.

Politically, each was committed to a program of economic and social collectivism.[34]

Julian Huxley was a respected member of the British scientific establishment with his own impressive familial lineage. In an age of modern research and development, he argued that applied science would come to yield enormous power. Such power could not be enlisted in the service of superstition or political control: rational progress and individual freedom must triumph. He was a proponent of scientific humanism, a secular philosophy that advocates science, democracy, and compassion over religious or supernatural belief. Upon these principles both he and Wells hoped to engender international solidarity around a world state. The utopian philosophy of "scientific humanism" developed by Huxley, an idea of evolution that would encompass all human endeavor and provide the full integration of science and culture, continues to underpin UNESCO some seventy years later.[35] Support for the creation of a universal civilization could be seen as a direct product of this idea. Utopian ideology and the dream of peace are mirrored in UNESCO's early aspirations of one-worldism and world government, right through to its program of global citizenship. Indeed, Huxley would have championed the premise of a "shared global patrimony" that infuses all aspects of the 1972 World Heritage Convention, given the material evocation of an integrative cultural and scientific utopia coupled with a conservation agenda.

With his Cambridge companion Joseph Needham, Huxley proposed compiling a new history of mankind from prehistory to the present to reinforce his philosophical commitments; others had robustly challenged his views from within UNESCO. In 1947 he commissioned V. Gordon Childe, then head of London's Institute of Archaeology, to draft a report that could be presented to UNESCO's Member States.[36] Although a natural scientist, Huxley later initiated UNESCO radio programs on the ancient world featuring well-known figures in archaeology such as Jacquetta Hawkes and Sir Leonard Woolley called the *History of Mankind*.[37] He claimed that they were the first to be internationally planned and written. This four-part radio series designed for the general public began with an explanation of human evolution and traced human progress through to the Neolithic Revolution and the beginnings of human "civilization" in Iraq and Egypt. In England Huxley appeared on the popular *Animal, Vegetable, Mineral?* television program hosted by archaeologist Glyn Daniel, where experts attempted to identify obscure objects from museums. As part of his role in the Commission for the History of the Scientific and Cultural

Development of Mankind, Huxley worked with Henri Frankfort as well as Hawkes and Woolley. Historian Poul Duedahl has gone as far as to suggest that Huxley's *History of Mankind* and its particular format influenced UNESCO's crafting of the 1972 World Heritage Convention.[38]

Supported by Huxley, Jacquetta Hawkes became the main editor for the first volume, *Prehistory and the Beginnings of Civilization*, after Woolley's untimely death.[39] She had specifically chosen Woolley as "the Englishman best able to present the subject in a well written and imaginative form."[40] She invited some of the leading archaeologists of her day to contribute to the *History*, including Hallam Movius, B. B. Lal, Dorothy Garrod, Robert Braidwood, Louis Leakey, Gertrude Caton Thompson, and John Goodwin. The volumes took years to produce, partly because they were submitted to all the UNESCO national commissions and thus read and vetted by more than thirty scholars from around the world with decidedly different historical, theoretical, and political perspectives. Reading over the laborious comments on the manuscript, preserved today in the UNESCO archives, offers a daunting glimpse into the challenges of writing a world prehistory that would satisfy even a small portion of the globe. It was the Russians who posed the main opposition, drawing upon their own Marxist perspectives, as Huxley himself noted.[41] But there were also objections raised by the Chinese, not to mention the Pakistanis, who asked that the word "India" be removed. Along with the editors, Huxley too became the familiar recipient of a barrage of criticism premised upon religious or political orientation, "from Catholic sources, Western cultural sources, Capitalist sources, and communist sources, Russians and others."[42]

History for Huxley was to be conveyed as an evolutionary process, showing the increasing independence of peoples in cultural, economic, social, technical, and political fields that contributed to a common heritage. Huxley sought to treat the human species as a whole, but specifically from scientific and cultural perspectives. For UNESCO, imparting history was about the rise and fall of great civilizations and the factors involved, but it also stressed the necessity to overcome intolerance and underline the value of "human work which has slowly given men mastery of the world."[43] UNESCO's history projects advocated the equivalence of different national histories; narrating the idea of a one-world history was thus a story of the global connections and exchange that were instrumental to the very constitution of civilization.[44]

Balancing the politics of the past was central to Huxley's project of one-worldism. This was reflected in the establishment of another project under the aegis of the International Commission for a History of the Scientific and Cultural Development of Mankind, the *Journal of World History*, often referred to as *Cahiers d'Histoire Mondiale*. It was a major yet short-lived venture from 1953 to 1972 that included some familiar names from the British archaeological establishment, including Garrod and Childe. Huxley was also involved in discussions for a *Visual History of Mankind*, developed for nine- to twelve-year-olds, with Childe overseeing the archaeological components. Through UNESCO's archive of correspondence detailing personal networks and relationships we might begin to see how the lives of individuals "intersected in the corridors and correspondence" with larger historical and archaeological debates on origins and progress, as well as the optimistic vision for the past on a global scale.[45]

Huxley's connection to archaeology was almost exclusively a British one. He engaged the most famous individuals from the British archaeological establishment who had worked across the empire, from the British Isles to Palestine, from Iraq to India. The institutions of the United Nations were not simply built around British and imperial networks: they were envisaged as a way to shore up and extend imperial power. The personalities and nationalities involved at the UNESCO's foundation further underline the colonial connotations of holding on to the territories, peoples, and resources of empire.[46] Huxley had served as a colonial expert in Africa for the Advisory Committee on Education in the Colonies since 1930 and for the African Research Survey Commission in 1943. As an original member of Britain's Political and Economic Planning (PEP) think tank, his experience managing the empire made Huxley and other British elites ideally suited to lead the new international organizations, such as UNESCO, that shaped the postwar order.[47] He hired British colonial experts and put UNESCO funds into British development programs in the colonies at a critical moment when these territories were subject to greater UN oversight.[48]

Historian Joseph Hodge reminds us that such experts played a critical role in the growing institutionalization and globalization of colonial scientific knowledge and authority from the 1930s onward. Many experts of the empire like Huxley went on to become consultants and experts across the UN's special agencies, including the Food and Agriculture Organization (FAO), the World Health Organization (WHO), and UNESCO, bringing with them their particular vision of progress and uplift.[49] Colonial administrators and technical experts such as Huxley believed in a European superiority that necessitated the "improvement" of colonial lands and peoples—a view that implicitly informed their policies for social engineering and development. Huxley appealed for a "leveling up of educational, scientific and cultural facilities in all the backward sectors" in order to "let in light on the world's dark areas."[50] Science and technology not only could provide new possibilities for trade and industry, in a utopian sense, but also might contribute to the material advancement of colonized peoples worldwide.

Conservation in Huxley's terms thus represented a large part of the British colonial and postcolonial project, and he was instrumental in the foundation of the World Wildlife Fund (WWF) and the International Union for Conservation of Nature (IUCN). Indeed, Huxley's directorship of UNESCO exemplifies that, in the words of Hodge, "late British colonial imperialism was an imperialism of science and knowledge under which academic and scientific experts rose to positions of unparalleled triumph and authority."[51] Hodge describes this unbridled optimism as progressive and altruistic: conserving the natural and cultural wonders of the world for the future was to culminate some decades later in the 1972 World Heritage Convention and the creation of the World Heritage List. Yet there were clearly tensions and disagreements in such postwar visions, as Huxley's reduced term at UNESCO indicates, coupled with the institution's refusal to publish his manifesto *UNESCO: Its Purpose and Its Philosophy* in 1947.[52] In that book he argued that the UNESCO mission could not be founded on one religion, one politico-economic doctrine, or one particular philosophy. Its commitments were to equality and democracy and its concrete task was dedicated to education, science, culture, and the need for mutual understanding by the peoples of the world. If UNESCO wanted to attain the objectives of peace and human welfare, the organization must go further, he argued; there must be world political unity or world government. Again he proffered his personal view, that UNESCO's general philosophy should be scientific world humanism, global in extent, and evolutionary in background. The task was no less than to promote the emergence of a single world culture.

Monumental Potential

While the League of Nations saw a role for archaeology, managing its excavations and exhibitions, on what was then a limited world stage, UNESCO was the first organization to promote archaeological and cultural heritage on a truly international level. While its scope and projects would now stretch beyond the Mediterranean and Middle East, its initial deliberations on excavation, cooperation, and internationalism were framed almost entirely by earlier texts produced under the ICIC. The repetition and lack of novelty reveals a twenty-year stasis where the drafters relied so heavily on the texts, priorities and objectives from the 1937 Cairo Conference that they simply reinvented it under the mantle of UNESCO. Archaeologists customarily see the establishment of UNESCO as a point of departure, but as international history increasingly reveals, it simply continued interwar approaches to managing the material world.

At UNESCO's first meeting of the General Conference in Paris at the end of 1946, the Preparatory Commission stated that "we have to consider the whole range of pure science, both natural and social, from physics to prehistoric archaeology. . . . [O]ur great archaeological inheritance, which belongs also to the whole of humanity, has been damaged."[53] It was agreed that the past must be salvaged for the future as a didactic lesson in a lasting peace. There is reason to believe that it was both the scientific discipline and material legacy of archaeology that was identified from the birth of UNESCO at a time when scholarly research was still vital to the organization's intellectual vision. Huxley too had spoken of the twin functions of preserving the world's scientific and cultural heritage and making it accessible to the public. Addressing the nations of the world, he asked, "What have you done to preserve and make known your cultural heritage? Have you taken steps to preserve your historical and ancient monuments, to unearth further remains of your past history, to exhibit its treasures and make them known to the world at large . . . ?"[54]

But the real work began in earnest the following year in Mexico, when discussions very similar to those of the 1937 Cairo Conference concerning "securing every possible access by all countries to archaeological sites" prompted debate amongst its members.[55] Egypt and Greece, nations rich in archaeology, spoke out on the issue of sovereignty and their own national laws; Haiti too chimed in to support them. It should be remembered that in 1922 with the discovery of Tutankhamun's tomb the Egyptian authorities, tired of colonial occupation and loss of their antiquities abroad, fought to retain national control in the face of foreign domination. Archaeology had become a symbol of the Egyptian independence movement.

The timing, not to mention setting, of the Cairo Conference was critical. Arab nationalists in Egypt were agitating for independence. The 1930s saw the rise of many nationalist movements, culminating in the outbreak of a second global conflict and ultimately the failure and demise of the League of Nations and the ICIC. The League itself was crucial to the mechanics of nationalism and had failed to adequately respond to the "political challenges of the later 1930s, including the depression, the rise of fascism, and the regular resort by Member States to violence rather than arbitration."[56] By then utopian notions of "world government" and "world citizenship" were relegated to international activism focused upon institutions and the law. The tensions over sovereign control and international access at the Cairo Conference reflect nationalist aspirations in the political realm, yet in terms of cultural movements transnational intellectual networks were gathering momentum. However, internationalism took on a different hue after the Second World War, with the exuberance of victory, the challenges of reconstruction, the possibilities for new nations to have a seat at the world table, and the promise that peace must prevail. Archaeology was back on the agenda.

In Mexico in 1947, the French delegation had suggested that the International Council of Museums (ICOM) prepare a report on the issue of free access to archaeological sites in all countries to be presented at the third session of the UNESCO General Conference in Beirut.[57] The next year, in 1948, ICOM responded that they had consulted experts who knew the "situation in several European countries, the Middle and Far East, and in America." They had been instructed to look at examples of previous international cooperation, and so they found themselves again quoting from the *Manual on the Technique of Archaeological Excavations*, with the acknowledgment that despite its excellence it had failed to garner wide acceptance or great authority. The 1937 Cairo Conference was lauded for its attempts to "create a general doctrine which could supply a basis for enlightened legislation in different countries," but the international difficulties, namely those associated with overriding national legislation, persisted.[58] The resolution, now under the Museums Section at UNESCO, continued to languish for a number of years. At the Beirut meeting in 1948, the General Conference heard a proposal to establish an International Committee of Experts on the Preservation of Historical Monuments and Sites. A second motion, submitted by Brazil and Egypt, posed the possibility of establishing an international fund to subsidize preservation and restoration work.[59] While only an idea in 1948, financial aid certainly held appeal amongst the Member States, and Egypt itself was later to become the greatest beneficiary.

The following year, in October 1949, a committee of experts from just fourteen countries sat at UNESCO House in Paris to study the proposals for protecting historic monuments and archaeological sites. Their recommendations were to establish a permanent international committee, create a fund for preservation, and support the recovery of objects and protection of heritage in the event of armed conflict.[60] Quipped Euripide Foundoukidis, former Secretary-General of the League's International Office of Museums: "In view of the reluctance of 'excavating countries' to adopt an international convention to control excavations, it had been thought more expedient to encourage in museum circles the ideas of international fellowship and respect for the heritage of each country than to attempt the preparation of an official agreement."[61] Securing access to sites for archaeologists of all countries and the idea of an international fund for preservation were agenda items under a title, Archaeological Sites and Historic Monuments, that itself as a category was to have a limited shelf life. Then, as with so many other initiatives at UNESCO, there was a hiatus for some years and the committee on archaeological sites made little progress. Given the myriad of project proposals presented by Member States in the early years of the organization, this is not surprising.

By 1948 Jaime Torres Bodet had replaced Julian Huxley as Director-General. Deep philosophical ruptures were already emerging within the organization. By 1949 the US delegate and theologian Reinhold Niebuhr had recommended that UNESCO reduce its scope to the minimal common principles of justice based on pragmatism, tolerance, and cooperation. Establishment of a free world community, Niebuhr argued, could only take place in the Western world, specifically under American leadership. Further depriving UNESCO of its initial vision, Niebuhr proposed to focus instead on provision of economic and technical aid to countries falling under the US sphere of influence.[62] One example of this shift occurred after a massive earthquake devastated the historic city of Cuzco on May 21, 1950, leaving 30,000–40,000 people homeless. The following year, the Director-General authorized a technical mission of architects and art historians to advise Peru. This mission was largely advisory in scope and cost relatively little.[63] In fact, the entire budget for all technical assistance for cultural heritage in 1951 was only $10,000.[64] Like so many of these early projects, it had a demonstrable result: the inscription of the city of Cuzco on the World Heritage List decades later. That same year Syria had requested two missions, one for the preservation of archaeological sites already agreed upon for 1952. Afghanistan requested assistance with its museums and curatorial training the following year. Iraq also requested help in 1952 with preserving the archaeological site of Hatra. These all went forward as technical missions and became emblematic sites for UNESCO.[65]

In 1952 the United States proposed that technical assistance programs be included in UNESCO's ordinary budget, thereby curtailing long-term commitments to social, cultural, and educational missions. Torres Bodet opposed the US attempt to have technocracy as UNESCO's dominant profile, the expert-driven managerialism of international technical assistance. But since the US was a major contributor with widespread support Torres Bodet was defeated and subsequently resigned that same year.[66] He was succeeded by two Americans: first by John Taylor, then a year later by Luther Evans. Technocracy would gain a greater hold on the organization. Indeed, by the early 1950s European nations were more interested in developing technical centers of expertise such as the Centre for the Study of the Preservation and Restoration of Cultural Property. Belgium and Rome made bids and the latter won. There was also the French proposal for a Documentation and Study Centre for the History of the Art and Civilization of Ancient Egypt in Cairo.[67]

High-profile international missions made material the idea of collaboration between nations and were simultaneously projects that UNESCO could showcase in publications such as the *UNESCO Courier*. In 1952 UNESCO sent a mission to Lebanon to examine the monuments at Tripoli and Baalbek and in 1953 to Syria to examine the state of monuments and archaeological sites, including Aleppo, Palmyra, Basra, and the Crusader castles.[68] By 1955 the number of nations receiving assistance had grown to fourteen; another eleven were deferred for lack of funds. The missions were premised on imparting technical advice, although they were portrayed as an "exchange of information and experts." However, these were not exchanges of different worldviews, exploring questions of what constitutes heritage or how to best conserve it. Rather, such missions facilitated a one-sided exportation or information flow, typically from European specialists to their counterparts in poorer nations. Through technocracy and international assistance it was hoped that Member States, and thus UNESCO, could realize the potential of peace in the making. Given the postwar setting, a focus upon conservation rather than archaeological exploration took hold. It also provided a mechanism for countries to secure much-needed resources, develop infrastructures and cultural resources, and ultimately support cultural tourism.

Deliberations between UNESCO and its Member States over many years finally resulted in the 1955 publication of the *Report on the International*

Principles Governing Archaeological Excavations. The American archaeologist J. O. Brew, from Harvard University, headed a committee dominated by other Americans and Europeans. It was acknowledged that UNESCO was continuing the work of the League of Nations, and once again the report borrowed heavily from the original text of the 1937 Cairo Act. However, the same issues remained, among them "the reluctance of certain countries to accept foreign help in bridging the gap between their inadequate scientific and financial resources and their archaeological wealth; the differences between domestic laws on the subject in the various countries and special difficulties due to current conditions."[69] In light of UNESCO's global mission some difficult questions were raised, such as what would be done about the non-self-governing and trust territories. Belgium and Poland noted that in 1937 no one had considered archaeology in North and South America, Africa, the Far East, India, Indonesia, or the Pacific Islands. Egypt again intervened to ensure that international regulations were flexible enough to suit sovereign states. France wanted to ensure more extensive international exchanges of objects. Lebanon reiterated its inalienable rights of ownership over its archaeological sites. Many of the same arguments from the 1930s were rehearsed, accompanied by the familiar whiff of self-interest from colonial and other major powers. But there were also some notable additions to the document. The report specified that it was easier to work with institutions rather than governments. It also raised the controversial issue of prohibiting excavations in occupied territories. These may be some of the reasons why the *Principles* would only ever amount to a recommendation rather than attain the status of a convention.

UNESCO sent the report out to the Member States for their comment; for the most part, the states sought the advice of museum experts rather than archaeologists, which in itself is telling. So are the states' responses. Perhaps reconsidering what international cooperation implied domestically, the French only wanted to call upon foreigners when they deemed it appropriate. They also found difficulties with placing restrictions on any "occupying power" when it came to excavations. The Australians wanted to make sure they could fill their museums with their "fair share" of the objects found in the excavations. Ceylon didn't want to relinquish objects connected to Buddhism or Hinduism. The British found some aspects of museum repatriation difficult; moreover, they stated that excavation was often financed at home by voluntary organizations, not the state, thus adding further complication. And finally, the United States pointed out that the recommendations were purely voluntary and it suggested delaying any decision to allow time for further reflection. Despite the deep divides between Member States, the Recommendation on International Principles Applicable to Archaeological Excavations was passed in New Delhi in 1956.[70] Rather than being the beginning of a larger program of archaeological research and practice at UNESCO, however, it was the culmination of a 1930s-inspired international effort to standardize and secure access to the ancient wonders of the world. The shift from the discipline of archaeology to the site, or more specifically to the monument, had begun.

Although many of the general principles of the 1956 Recommendation remain salient, it found little traction within the discipline, and today it has largely been forgotten in archaeological and academic circles. While the recommendation is a normative instrument, it was not ratified by states parties like a convention and so did not translate into practice. In UNESCO's own account of its activities in 1956, archaeology had already become somewhat lost in an array of other cultural fields, glossed under the title "preservation of the cultural history of mankind," coming at the end after museums and collections, libraries, archives, and monuments, and alongside historic sites. The monumental shift to heritage preservation was well under way. Some nations immediately realized this "monumental" potential and appealed for international technical assistance: Indonesia, Jordan, Libya, Pakistan, Peru, and Ecuador each requested advice and/or training in historic preservation and restoration.[71] Director-General Jaime Torres Bodet, in addressing the committee, had already indicated the potential for states with newly achieved political independence that lacked qualified staff to benefit from the international exchange of technicians.[72] This fitted the largely American vision of UNESCO as being a technocratic, expert-driven, standard-setting agency that would disseminate "best practices" to less developed nations, rather than pursuing the more difficult and nebulous task of working together for world peace. This also accorded well with dominant Western European Member States who, while keen to export their skills and technicians abroad to nations where they hoped to extend their influence, were less willing to be subject to the same international interventions at home.

UNESCO's records show a gradual organizational shift toward prioritizing preservation and technical assistance in preference to supporting original research or excavation. Increasingly archaeology was subsumed under either museums or monuments, and heritage more likely to be considered architecture than archaeology. These categorical shifts reflect the international community's formative concerns about restoration of art and architecture after the war, rebuilding of museums, and the protection and preservation of monuments. This was reiterated in the first global treaty dealing with heritage, the Convention for the Protection of Cultural Property in the Event of Armed Conflict, signed in The Hague on May 14, 1954, and entering into force two years later. This treaty had its origins in the League of Nations and its International Museums Office, although its ratification was interrupted by the onset of war.[73] The Hague Convention addressed most fully the cultural devastation of the Second World War and "covers immovable and movable cultural heritage including monuments, art, archaeological sites, scientific collections, manuscripts, books and other objects of artistic, historical or archaeological interest" to ensure the cultural legacy and, by extension, the cultural property of nations, groups, and distinct members of a society worldwide facing armed conflict.[74]

Excavation and archaeological research was on the agenda from the League of Nations in the late 1930s through to UNESCO's efforts for a few years beginning in 1946. However, quite quickly the organization, often at the behest of its Member States, shifted toward technical and advisory missions rather than launching research projects. In June 1946 Mortimer Wheeler had written to archaeologist Cyril Fox to see whether there would be a place for him at UNESCO, because he had an "urge amounting almost to a fire within me really to do something worth while in a reasonably wide field."[75] He believed that the study of history must recognize the "nobility of man" and in doing so "save archaeology from the technicians."[76] That intellectual vision for archaeology and UNESCO soon took a backseat, transformed into the more routine practices of managing the remarkable.[77] Wheeler, like Huxley, was part of the British civilizing mission with its suspect concepts of improvement and progress, while their cultural fixations lay in the great civilizations of others in the Middle East or Asia.[78] As Mark Mazower contends, the formation of the United Nations was a British rather than American endeavor, ostensibly tied to the endgame of empire and the continuance of British colonialism and control over its dominions.[79] Yet British intellectual networks from Huxley's day, which included archaeologists, were gradually replaced by technicians and a development-oriented technocracy in which UNESCO would become an exporter of expertise developed in, and flowing from, Western Europe and the United States. The British intellectual vision for archaeological and cultural uplift would soon be passed over for more pragmatic and technical considerations as a new empire took the lead in global affairs.

In the decades to follow, with few exceptions, UNESCO would not routinely engage prominent archaeologists in major intellectual projects, nor in turn would the institution have a decisive impact upon the discipline. Archaeologists themselves remain largely unaware how the human past was woven into the core fabric of humanism during Huxley's time and how it assumed various roles in international instruments and programs. Huxley had an integrated vision for "constructing a history of the development of the human mind, notably in its highest cultural achievements" that included "archaeologists and classical scholars."[80] During his visit to the spectacular Nabataean site of Petra in Jordan, he wrote that it should be "one of the starred exhibits in a world museum of civilization," but for this to happen the site had to be "properly conserved, fully studied, and made accessible," and he noted that "scientific excavation has scarcely begun."[81] Huxley was enamored with the new techniques "of organized expeditions, careful stratigraphical excavation, preservation and record of every kind of object, skilled reconstruction, correlation of the results into a general scheme of dating."[82] However, without Huxley's interdisciplinary commitment, the techniques of survey, excavation, and material analysis would be difficult to situate between UNESCO's culture and science programs. Field archaeologists would be hired, however, as technocrats and consultants in the intergovernmental and preservationist sphere. Archaeology had become the helpmate of heritage.

Archaeology, as both a theoretical and methodological discipline to understand the past through its material remains, did not reach the status of anthropology, history, or philosophy at UNESCO—and the French influence on the organization, after its permanent headquarters was established in Paris, would see significant development around those disciplines.[83] The famous French anthropologist Claude Lévi-Strauss had a significant impact upon UNESCO and its early intellectual programs, along with Roger Caillois, Pierre Bessaignet, and Lucien Bernot.[84] With its adoption of Lévi-Straussian notions of cultural relativity and culture contact, UNESCO's programmatic anthropological position, encapsulated in *Our Creative Diversity*, has also sparked considerable controversy.[85] By contrast, mainstream French archaeological thought remained primarily positivistic and, with the exception of André Leroi-Gourhan, did not have a strong influence upon the organization.[86] However, the creation and operation of UNESCO afforded opportunities for the expansion of

French cultural imperatives and national diplomacy. France also became a major supplier of experts for UNESCO.[87] One early example was the French Egyptologists, art historians, and museum experts who secured the UNESCO-funded Centre d'Étude et de Documentation sur l'Ancienne Égypte (CEDAE) in Cairo.[88] In 1956 they were engaged in copying the architectural details of the rock-cut temples at Abu Simbel in Nubia. Considering the eventualities of the Aswan High Dam construction, they would be perfectly placed to consult on the beginnings, and the future, of world heritage.[89]

Conclusions

The cosmopolitan internationalism of Julian Huxley's UNESCO may have been short-lived, but its utopian aspirations continue to find resonance within the organization, waxing and waning with the politics of its Directors-General over the years. It was Huxley's intellectual vision for the organization and the possibilities of a one-world public sphere, rather than its bureaucratic shortfalls, that incurred the most resistance from powerful Member States such as the United States. Fearing an international revolution in political practices, the Member States demanded that UNESCO censor its more universalist and civilizational objectives and instead direct its energies toward purely technical matters.[90] Within just a few years an American-inspired program of technical assistance edged out the particularly British imperial vision for UNESCO, with its mantle of educational advancement, social progress, and an international civilizing mission. Like the League of Nations before it, the largely European ideal of world government and civilizational uplift masterminded by classicists and scientists would be replaced by the post–Second World War technocrats, economists, and engineers who were setting the development agenda. Notions of best practice prevailed rather than aspirations of world peace.

The future of the past would also be bound up with political agendas. Huxley's one-worldism embraced both the cultural and scientific aspects of archaeology, but it was imbued with the wonder, romance, and potentiality of the human past as well. The very notion that a turn to monumentality could be first universalized and then inculcated to anchor a future world peace is steeped in a particularly Western perspective. The deep past was appropriated from distant shores to serve the construction of a common humanity rather than a world of difference. With the rise of an intergovernmental rather than global UNESCO, archaeological research would be eventually narrowed down to the more technical aspects of preservation, salvage, and the shoring up of monumentality.[91] This gradual shift from archaeological *discovery* to monumental *recovery*, however, may have been less about a closure of certain futures than about a change in "colonizing" strategies, from the League's attempts to secure access through to a network of international excavations to UNESCO's monopoly on exporting expertise and controlling conservation. Regardless of the outcome, we should not overlook the role of archaeology as an intellectual enterprise early in the organization's history. Its waxing and waning fate mirrors the foundational dreams, challenges, and tensions within the organization: would UNESCO aspire to intellectual pursuits and world peace, or be a global standard setter fostering international networks, or be largely relegated to an advisory and technical agency? In considering these potential futures, the specificities of archaeology as a discipline, with its own history and politics, are also brought into sharp relief.

In Huxley's one-world agenda, archaeology provided a means to unite humanity while celebrating its diversity. Yet the crafting of his *History of Mankind* already foreshadows the difficulties of sustaining unifying narratives amidst competing worldviews. Moreover, the development of archaeology was intimately tied to territorial struggles, to empire and colonization. Many of those major colonizing powers were still at the helm of this new organization, just as they had been at the League of Nations. Material culture and monumental heritage had been for centuries embroiled in international politics and conflicts: Napoleon's campaigns in Egypt and Syria are prime examples. As history reveals, those claiming to bring knowledge and civilization are often ultimately the destroyers, looters, and beneficiaries of other people's pasts. Similar devastation wrought by the Nazis and Fascists during the Second World War was even closer at hand. Neither Huxley nor UNESCO fully acknowledged or sought to problematize the deeper roots of conflict when proposing their global projects. Conversely, archaeological practitioners and academics have continually sought to develop strategies to combat the colonial underpinnings of their disciplinary past. The politics of knowledge and critical self-reflection were not strategies readily taken up at UNESCO; rather, preserving the past was subsumed in the wonder and potentialities of monumental splendor.

UNESCO's own brand of heritage internationalism was also a very circumscribed sphere, typically comprised of "extraordinary gentlemen" from Europe and North America, although Huxley's choice of Jacquetta Hawkes was a momentary anomaly. But the directionality of information flows from the West to the rest and what constituted expertise, who had it, and who should be a recipient was an initial problem that continues to plague the organization today. Beyond Eurocentric perspectives, there have always been other ways of living with heritage, of valuing and conserving it across the globe: these too remain fundamental challenges for UNESCO. In bypassing archaeology as a multidisciplinary sphere in favor of monumental heritage—a place-based and object-oriented view of the past in the present—aspects of international research, collaboration, and the culturally specific experience of sites attenuated not only their management but also their ultimate future. Mapping the history of these developments underlines the practical and ideological impossibilities of managing the world's past, of managing the remarkable from a single global vantage. It also reveals the circularity of ideas and proposals that crystallized in different international organizations and committees over the past two centuries, confirming once and for all that there is ultimately nothing new and, given the lack of institutional memory and inertia in such agencies, we are destined to repeat ourselves again in the future. If governing the world itself has proven an impossible enterprise over the last two centuries, then so too has attempting to manage its material past.[92]

The shift from intellectual programs to assistance also presages what was to come for a future in ruins. UNESCO's first decades were spent entreating the world to unite to conserve endangered marvels as a common patrimony, what one might term a centrifugal approach, whereas later it devolved into disciplining states to list and conserve sites in their own territories, a centripetal approach. The managerial priorities of world-making took precedence, requiring a sophisticated bureaucracy that valorizes rationalized, scientific techniques as the primary means to ensure human progress and protect virtuous human endeavors.[93] Marx was right when he said that bureaucracy is the state that has made itself into civil society.[94] The centrality and decision-making power of the nation-state in a multilateral agency such as UNESCO has increasingly strengthened and, as we shall see in later chapters, is now the defining force for the future of global heritage. And with the entrenchment of the nation-state at UNESCO, like most other multilateral agencies, has come the dominance of political decision-making and politicians themselves. UNESCO has moved from being an organization of great statesman to being one of states.

At UNESCO's founding conference, British prime minister Clement Attlee, author of the statement that "wars begin in the minds of men," argued that the system of supranational cooperation in different fields such as labor, health, food and agriculture, and finance was incomplete without intellectual cooperation. Relying upon instrumentalism and functionalism—the idea that institutions emerge to address the logics of circumstance through practical utility[95]—the organization's founders believed that "the problem of our time is not how to keep the nations peacefully apart but how to bring them actively together."[96] UNESCO asserted that a peace based exclusively upon the political and economic arrangements of governments would not be a peace that could secure the unanimous, lasting, and sincere support of the peoples of the world, and that the peace must therefore be founded upon the intellectual and moral solidarity of humankind.[97] That utopian spirit and the commitment to future generations, coupled with the idealism of salvage and uplift, can all be found in UNESCO's most iconic and international cultural initiative: to save ancient monuments from the rising waters of the Nile. It should be no surprise, then, to find Sir Julian Huxley being invited back to UNESCO to serve on the Committee for Safeguarding the Monuments of Nubia.[98] For UNESCO, it would be no less than a victory in Nubia.

2

Internationalism

*With determined spirit, we dedicate ourselves once again to
the tasks of the future in the conviction that by unity and
faith we can move mountains.*

—UNESCO, 1962

IN THE TWILIGHT of empire, during just over a week in late 1956, Britain
and France followed Israel in invading Egypt. The three nations colluded
to wrest the Suez Canal from Egyptian control and remove Gamal Abdel
Nasser from power. After the occupation of Egypt in 1882 Britain had
assumed control of the canal. They had financed it with the French and
it was an emblem of empire. Often called Britain's lifeline, the canal was
vital strategically during the Second World War, both in the defense of
empire and for oil shipments. Nasser had nationalized the canal in July
1956, threatening British military and economic interests in the region.
Both British and French politicians drew parallels between Nasser in the
Egyptian situation and the rise of European fascism under Hitler and
Mussolini.[1]

Part of the issue for Western powers was the Soviet support for Nasser's
government in Egypt. Nasser's presumptive sympathies toward communism worried policymakers who sought to contain Soviet influence
in a geopolitical game of strategy, famously likened to a domino game,
where one state falling would impact neighboring nations. However, the
Soviets had stepped in to finance construction of the Aswan High Dam
after the United States and the World Bank had withdrawn their promise
of funding in an attempt to thwart Nasser's leadership. A few days after
that fateful American decision to withdraw their backing, Nasser turned
his attention to the Suez Canal and the opportunities it afforded to raise
much-needed revenues. The High Dam and its promise of electricity and
agricultural development was Nasser's great plan to rescue his people

from impoverishment and thus take their place in the modern world.[2] It reflected the nascent postwar ideology of development that was common to many newly independent states in the developing world, and it effectively combined expanding state power, centralized control over resources and expertise, and a vast infrastructural development project.[3] Coupled with the transformation of modern Egypt, the dam would also have profound effects on ancient Egypt and its wealth of archaeological sites. Infrastructure, development, colonialism, international politics, and archaeology would all be brought together around the issue and impacts of the Aswan Dam.

In the conflict that ensued after invasion, the Soviet Union threatened a nuclear retaliation in Western Europe and to send its own troops into Suez if Britain, France, and Israel did not withdraw. The British political elite was taken by surprise when the United States threatened economic sanctions against the three nations.[4] Following a US resolution, the United Nations stepped in to call for a cease-fire, the removal of all military forces, and reopening the canal. Finally, after the British withdrew from Egypt, through the efforts of UN Secretary-General Dag Hammarskjöld, the UN sent in its first emergency peacekeeping force (UNEF).[5] With the major powers again poised on the brink of war and set against the backdrop of the Cold War, Arab nationalism, and Arab-Israeli tensions, UNESCO attempted its most monumental project of global cooperation. The Rescue of the Nubian Monuments and Sites (1959–1980) fully realized UNESCO's central message of world citizenship from its very bedrock. It paired the ideals of the liberal imperialist past and its cultural particularism embodied in ancient Egypt with UNESCO's own inherently Western promise of a new scientific, technocratic, postnational future.[6] Archaeology was back on the agenda.

So much has been written about UNESCO's Nubian Monuments Campaign over the years: from the heroism and humanism promoted by the agency's own vast propaganda machine to the competing narratives of national saviors, whether French or American; from Nubia as a theater for the Cold War right down to individual accounts by technocrats, bureaucrats, and archaeologists. Therefore it would seem that there is little new to say. Yet if one recenters UNESCO's foundational utopian promise, couples it with its technocratic counterpart, international assistance, then adds the challenge of a one-world archaeology focused on the greatest civilization of the ancient world, we might produce a new slant on a future in ruins.

What crystallized in UNESCO's midcentury mission in Egypt was a material attempt to overcome the fissures that were already appearing in the postwar dream of a global peace. Portrayed as a vast international co-operation with unrivaled grandeur and romance, saving Nubia might potentially relegate the crisis of Suez to history, manufacture much-needed harmony in the Middle East, demonstrate once and for all that culture could contribute to a perpetual peace, and, acquisitively, recapture the materialities of ancient civilization for the West. Humanity as a whole could claim its inheritance from Egypt, thus reinforcing UNESCO's lofty ideals of world citizenship. A common humanity in the past would be paired with a common responsibility for the future.

Being poised for futurity requires a certain mastery of the past, as Utopians had long realized. Despite having no initial plan to do so, this meant that UNESCO had to embrace large-scale and transnational archaeology, bringing archaeological research into a monumental project with a technocratic conservation agenda. While only fleeting, and not entirely successful, this foray into field archaeology would mark both archaeology's apogee and demise at UNESCO and, in some respects, a wider intellectual landscape. Archaeology would soon become the hand-maiden of heritage, subservient to the more calculable metrics of physical preservation and restoration, the global rise of conservation ethics, and the marketable glamour of ancient monumentality. People too would be relegated by these grand designs: thousands of Nubians were relocated with the rising waters.[7] And this combination of infrastructural development, monumental preservation, and the secondary status of people with their own living heritage would become another hallmark of the modern conservation industry.

Sir Mortimer Wheeler regarded the rescue of Abu Simbel an "unparalleled and indeed almost frightening feat of engineering."[8] It was also a remarkable feat of bureaucracy, diplomacy, fundraising, international co-operation, and salvage archaeology. No single UNESCO initiative, before or since, has received so much media and scholarly attention as the Nubian Monuments Campaign. There have been many excellent recent accounts on various aspects of the rescue, from the vantage of internationalism and hydropolitics to that of architectural theory.[9] So much has been published and the archives thoroughly mined, yet the architectural and engineering aspects of uplift have almost entirely overshadowed the contributions of field archaeology, the teams of excavators who contributed their own monumental efforts and the discoveries that would change the way we look at Egypt and indeed Africa today. The technocratic achievements of Abu Simbel supplanted archaeological research not simply by scale and grandeur, but in terms of the heroic quest to save antiquity. It was the legibility and calculability of these engineering feats, whether dismantling and lifting the Abu Simbel Temples or transporting the entire Amada Temple on rails to its new location. These were measurable achievements, and there was an obvious finitude to coordinating these international efforts. Various technical options could be proposed, tested, and implemented, some with great success. Each temple relocation, and there were more than twenty, was made possible by a combination of money, metrics, and manpower. UNESCO too enjoyed bringing together science, culture, and education—its particular fields of competence within the UN system—within a single project. International engineering companies placed bids within a tender system and conducted their work in a professional and timely fashion as the world looked on in awe. Archaeological fieldwork, as we shall see, was neither smooth nor predictable, neither bounded nor finite in quite the same ways. Many nations were brought together, not always harmoniously, and still their teams accomplished extraordinary things. But the unknown elements of field archaeology—the number and extent of sites and finds, the implementation of new methods of recording, the funding and resources needed for a long-term, large-scale project—offered new challenges for UNESCO.

Engineering Internationalism

In the race to be UNESCO's first Director-General, Julian Huxley famously triumphed over the Oxford classicist Alfred Zimmern, another utopian thinker and a founding figure in the League of Nations. Zimmern's utopia was based on Greco-Christian spiritual values, and it had become a target of E. H. Carr's important book *The Twenty Years Crisis, 1919–1939.* Zimmern was thought unable to bridge the two cultures of arts and science.[10] His lasting legacy to UNESCO would be its official symbol and icon of civilization: the image of a Greek temple in blue on white. Another classicist, Oxonian, and internationalist, Gilbert Murray, believed that restoring postwar Europe was tantamount to restoring civilization itself: "Some great movement for unity and constructive reconciliation in Europe is an absolute necessity for civilization. . . . Of course Europe is not everything. There are other continents."[11] Murray was reflecting on the transition from the League of Nations to the United Nations. The League's

International Committee for International Cooperation was dominated by classicists like Murray and Zimmern, while UNESCO attempted to foreground science and technology, exemplified by the appointment of Julian Huxley. And it was the British delegation that had insisted on including the *S* for "science" in the title of the organization.[12]

UNESCO aspired to harness that movement to restore not only peace but also civilization in scientific, cultural, and educational spheres. This story of changing visions parallels the developments we see in global heritage, from an initial preoccupation with art and museums that was gradually reoriented toward technical expertise, preservation, and conservation science. In addition, between the late 1950s and the late 1960s other major shifts saw the majority of new members of the UN General Assembly representing Africa and Asia. Moreover, the 1960s were hailed as the United Nations Development Decade. Taken together, this made the efforts to save the Nubian monuments more vital and relevant in terms of both decolonization and development, and yet the technology that was brought to bear and the cultural claims on the project would continue to enhance European expertise and prestige abroad and at home.

Infused by idealism, the Nubian Monuments Campaign was inflected with UNESCO's formative utopian elements of one-worldism, world citizenship, and world community. But the Suez Crisis and the Cold War had already shaken that early optimism.[13] After a brief hiatus following Suez, Egypt and then Sudan requested UNESCO's technical assistance in the face of a drowning heritage.[14] Saving the temples, and the much-touted victory that accompanied their uplift, would be a perfect counterpoint to the massive flooding caused by the Aswan Dam, a similarly monumental project but of Egyptian, Soviet, and West German design. By the end of 1959 UNESCO's Executive Board had agreed to launch an international appeal and authorized preparatory work to begin on the two Abu Simbel Temples in Egypt and, as a matter of urgency, archaeological work in Sudan.[15] The fractious Middle Eastern setting was seen as crucial. Director-General Vittorio Veronese could not resist boasting that "from a land which throughout the centuries has been the scene of—or the stake in—so many covetous disputes should spring a convincing proof of international solidarity."[16] All of UNESCO's goals could be put into practice in one theatrical spectacle. While lofty in sentiment, the reality was sometimes more fraught, certainly amongst some of the archaeological missions, but also in the competing requests from Sudan and Egypt. In the end, Egypt emphasized that the victory in Nubia was theirs, first and foremost, symbolically etching the point into an inauguration plaque at Abu Simbel: the words "through co-operation with UNESCO" were added to the plaque only as an afterthought and following considerable pressure.

UNESCO's early utopian spirit briefly found new momentum in the achievement of peaceful multilateral cooperation. "Culture, an essential element of the intellectual and moral solidarity of mankind has thus been recognized by States, for all the world to see," Director-General René Maheu proclaimed, "as an important factor in their co-operation for the promotion of peace by the spirit to which the members of Unesco have pledged themselves. That is the significance of this event which will itself make history."[17] Making history entailed considerable financial commitment on an international scale hitherto unknown. UNESCO estimated the cost of the entire Nubian rescue operations (exclusive of archaeological excavations) at US$87 million. This entailed the dismantling and transfer of twenty-three temples, tombs, early Christian churches, and rock-hewn chapels in Egypt and the Sudan (estimated cost US$10 million), the preservation of the temple group on the island of Philae (US$6 million), and the preservation of the Abu Simbel Temples (US$70 million). Egypt had guaranteed US$20 million for Abu Simbel. Initially the United States pledged US$6–10 million to save Philae, US$2.5 million for the removal of temples, and US$1.5 million for archaeological expeditions and research in Nubia.[18]

The engineering feats conjured to save the Abu Simbel temples stood as a countermonument to the Aswan High Dam, funded by the Soviets. While the dam generated power, according to Lucia Allais, the colossi of Abu Simbel instead absorbed immense effort and resources.[19] And despite all the talk of internationalism, only four European nations would proffer architectural and engineering schemes to lift, or in one case submerge, antiquity. The French firm of Coyne et Bellier proposed leaving the temples in place surrounded by a rock-filled dam, while the Italian architect Piero Gazzola planned to cut and encase the temples in a concrete box, the modernist design of which featured on the cover of the *UNESCO Courier* for October 1961.[20] British architects suggested leaving Abu Simbel under water, adding tunnels, bubbles, and transparent walkways for submerged visitor viewing. A second French engineering proposal was to float the temples to a new site using shipbuilding technology.[21] A final Swedish plan, significantly cheaper, was adopted in 1963: the Ramesside temples would be numbered, then sawn into some 7,047 blocks. Each block would be mechanically lifted and transported to a holding area and then

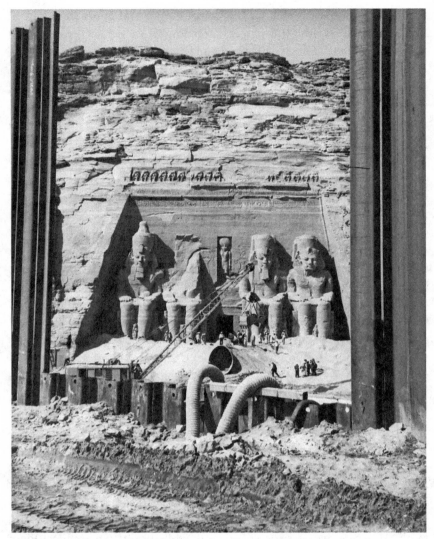

FIGURE 2.1 The Temple of Abu Simbel, 1965, © UNESCO/Nenadovic

later reassembled upon higher ground above the original site. Cutting, it was decided, was the only alternative to flooding, and by that time the Americans had secretly guaranteed funding.[22] The Swedish consultants Vattenbyggnadsbyrån (VBB) worked alongside other companies from Sweden (Sentab, Skånska), Italy (Impreglio), West Germany (Hochtief), France (Grands Travaux de Marseilles), and Egypt (Atlas) in what they called Joint Venture Abu Simbel. However, some commentators described the carving up of Abu Simbel as butchery. The face of Ramses II was sawn through, sheared from its body, then lifted by cranes onto trucks and driven to higher ground. During the "sawing, strengthening and transferring operations many small and very regrettable damages occurred" and "about 100 blocks or more were affected"; the consultants were worried that this might give "a wrong impression."[23] UNESCO likened it to a "surgical operation," and when the cutting and transplanting of the temples had been completed there would be the "further job of 'plastic surgery.' "[24]

The ancient temples were cast as remarkable examples of civil engineering, veritable mountains of masonry. Confronted by the achievements of the engineers of the New Kingdom, modern civilization could do no less than apply equally impressive science and resources to rescue their work. Though perhaps less reported upon, the Egyptian government had previously removed the three temples of Kertassi, Debod, and Taffeh. The Federal Republic of Germany pledged to remove the great Kalabsha Temple, and France the Temple of Amada. The Temples of Abu Simbel would be sliced from the mountainside into which they had been built three thousand years ago. UNESCO accepted this responsibility as the "trustee" of the "Future of the Past." On the other hand, determining how "perishable antiquities . . . will be explored and their stories deciphered before the waters rise, is a challenge which has been thrown to the archaeologists and the conscience of the world."[25] In this startling equation, science and engineering were advanced as an organizational commitment, whereas the archaeological remains were precariously "thrown" to archaeologists within a diffuse concept of worldly responsibility.

UNESCO appealed to its one hundred Member States for voluntary contributions, but this call also reached organizations, companies, and individuals, truly capturing the "minds of men" (and women), as the organization had so often proclaimed. Its archive in Paris reveals earnest letters from schoolchildren, Girl Guides, photographers, architects, engineers, and teachers from all over the world who wanted to assist in the rescue efforts. It is fascinating to see so many handwritten notes sent from countries as far away as Australia and New Zealand, from ordinary people in small towns like Tatura and Herekino, who enclosed a dollar or pound note. British schoolchildren from Wincanton, like their counterparts from Carcevelos in Portugal, raised money for the appeal. People sent modest funds acquired from bake sales and raffles through a trust fund established by *Reader's Digest* in 1966. Others wrote proposing alternative engineering methods to lift the temples from the rising waters. Many are touching offers to volunteer their efforts, and, for the most part, a staff member from UNESCO would respond gratefully and direct them to their respective national commissions, more than twenty of which were formed worldwide.

All the forces of media and communication were brought to bear on the rescue efforts. The most powerful were the numerous short films that were made for television and the journalistic articles that appeared in the *UNESCO Courier*, which was published in numerous languages and appealed to the general public in much the same way as *Reader's Digest* or *National Geographic*, which also covered the Nubian Campaign. Photography and film had formed part of the organization's mission to bolster universalism since its inception and the herculean rescue of ancient ruins proffered the perfect subject matter. The films captured the race against time, the looming threat of the waters drowning magnificent temples such as Philae, and the heroic efforts and expertise of the international engineering mission.[26] Trucks bearing the name *Joint Venture Abu Simbel* were captured moving an endless onslaught of sand to meet the ever-advancing waters of the Nile. Such sensational publicity materials were in great demand, and requests for copies poured in from as far afield as Guatemala, Haiti, South Africa, and Taiwan.

UNESCO produced its own films to document Abu Simbel's uplift that reveal a handful of European experts holding plans and directing operations amidst some seventeen hundred Egyptian workmen toiling in the harsh desert conditions. Impoverished Egyptian workers, both men and boys, haul sand, stone, and metal—an eerie reflection of new pharaohs amidst ancient ones and a concerted pride in the technical achievements of the former in saving the latter. More cynically, the chosen method of cutting the stone into blocks was labor-intensive and enabled the United States to pay its contribution in Egyptian pounds rather than US currency, whereas other experimental schemes did not. Those funds were held in Egypt as part of the costs of American grain shipments delivered as aid: the hard currency problem was solved.[27] Lucia Allais writes that while "the image of so many Egyptian laborers in direct contact with the monuments of Nubia suggested cutting was a native building method," the real logic was driven by American economics. In an altogether different form of international value, the techniques employed served to engineer a "technological bridge between two countries at a time when their diplomatic ties were strained."[28] The colossal reconstruction effort entailed not only cutting and lifting statues and temples, but also constructing a vast metal dome to simulate the original sandstone cliff and solar orientation, and then reproducing the original landscape. UNESCO was literally engaged in moving mountains.

Submerging Archaeology

"We are faced with the greatest crisis of our time," Egyptologist John A. Wilson explained to the US Senate in 1960. This "is going to be the biggest thing of our lifetime."[29] Yet UNESCO's intervention in Nubia did not initially include archaeological excavation: it was an afterthought that led to significant criticism.[30] Both Egypt and Sudan, however, had considered the fate of their ancient sites and what type of salvage operations would be possible before submersion. Discussions began with an urgent call for cooperation in 1955 when the Aswan Dam project was announced, then delayed by the Suez crisis. At that time only Italy and West Germany had responded.[31] Nasser himself was originally indifferent to the rescue project but soon rallied: "We pin our hopes on the preservation of the Nubian treasures in order to keep alive monuments which are not only dear to our hearts we being their guardian but dear to the whole world which believes that the ancient and the new components of human culture should blend in one harmonious whole."[32]

Perhaps more than the vast engineering feat accomplished by a consortium of European corporations, the archaeological campaign partly achieved the goals of one-world archaeology, harking back to the prewar ideas of the Cairo Conference with free access to all the nations of the world. Hundreds of archaeologists from more than twenty nations launched more than thirty survey and excavation projects across Nubia.[33] They were almost entirely European and North American projects but also included Egyptian, Russian, Argentinean, and Ghanaian teams as well as smaller contingents of Indian and Pakistani archaeologists. Solidarity was strengthened by an obligation toward another African state, in the case of Ghana, or another nonaligned country, in the case of India.[34] Archaeologist B. B. Lal, who headed the Archaeological Survey of India (ASI) team, further employed his discoveries to postulate connections between ancient Nubians and Dravidian-speakers in South Asia.[35] Nationalist deployments for the rescue effort could be packaged to prop up domestic politics. In Spain, for example, Franco's regime used the Spanish participation as political propaganda to counteract charges of isolationism, while at the same time the regime censored all newspaper coverage.[36] This international assembly was the utopian image UNESCO had dreamed of, uniting nations with different ideologies, religions, and traditions, and even those who were engaged in mutual hostilities.[37] On reflection it was "a congeries of field activities carried out by a multitude of persons and institutions at different times, in different places, under a variety of circumstances, and sometimes from very different motivations."[38]

The Nubian Monuments Campaign was remarkably interdisciplinary for its time. Many of the archaeological teams also included Egyptologists, art historians, epigraphers, architects, geologists, and bioarchaeologists. There was also use of aerial survey, photogrammetry, and geoarchaeology. Italians from the Lerici Foundation experimented with new geophysical methods.[39] Other newly developed techniques including radiocarbon dating, neutron activation, and palynology further enhanced methodological and technical standards, so much so that the Swedes considered that it revolutionized archaeology in the Nile Valley. William Y. Adams, an American archaeologist first employed in 1959 by UNESCO to work in Sudan, claimed it was the first campaign to involve the coordinated efforts of many different nations, and certainly the first in which an international organization played a major part in policy-making.[40] But he also complained that the project was "conceived almost entirely as a conservation rather than as a research program."[41] While UNESCO's use of the term "campaign" conjured up the notion of "some concerted plan and some overall coordination . . . nothing could be farther from the truth."[42] Adams was a key player in the Sudanese salvage operations, referred to in somewhat colonial parlance by UNESCO staff as "our man in Nubia." While having no expertise in Egyptian archaeology, Adams was a southwestern specialist who cut his teeth on salvage archaeology in the United States. Adams agreed with veteran Egyptian specialists like Torgny Säve-Söderbergh and John A. Wilson that the campaign ostensibly involved two unrelated operations: the removal and reconstruction of endangered temples, and the excavation of archaeological sites. The first was largely an engineering problem, the second a scientific one.[43]

As a result of this disjuncture between technical operations and field research, UNESCO had little idea of the priorities and scope of a major archaeological campaign. Instead, it regarded the archaeological program merely as an extension of the conservation mission. The two operations were "carried out under wholly different circumstances, by different organizations and under quite different financial arrangements."[44] Moreover, there was no uniform research strategy or even regular consultation

FIGURE 2.2 Excavation at Semna West, Nubia, 1964, © UNESCO/Rex Keating

between the two countries involved, so archaeological works in Egypt and the Sudan were undertaken as if unrelated. Some complained that the effects of "red tape" and nationalism further hindered collaboration. The Scandinavians argued that if they had waited for UNESCO to make decisions or recommendations for Sudan, little would have been achieved.[45] The only conference to discuss the scientific results throughout the entire eight years of the Nubian Campaign was held in 1964 at Bellagio, Italy, sponsored by the Society for American Archaeology.

Red tape is something that UNESCO has long been criticized for, yet managing the immense and multistranded project required a robust bureaucracy. Committees proliferated: there was the International Action Committee, the Executive Committee, various national committees, and committees to oversee engineers and archaeologists, not to mention the Honorary Committee of Patrons. Meetings were held in Paris, Cairo, Khartoum, The Hague, and so on. Some participants joked that the campaign would be flooded by paperwork before the monuments were by the Nile.[46] For the archaeological component, there was an elaborate bureaucracy starting with UNESCO Paris, then UNESCO's handful of employed archaeologists in Egypt and Sudan, one or two of whom conducted fieldwork, while others were engaged in administration. This was in sharp contrast with the thousands of laborers concentrated around Abu Simbel.

Another coordinating body was the French Centre d'Étude et de Documentation sur l'Ancienne Égypte (CEDAE), established by Christiane Desroches-Noblecourt in Cairo. There was the Sudanese Commissioner for Archaeology, the Egyptian Antiquities Service, Ministries of Culture and of Education, and high-profile government representatives in Egypt and Sudan. Tensions inevitably developed between UNESCO's adminis-tration and that of the Egyptian government. Georg Knetch, a German prehistorian, reported a "sort of 'contempt of UNESCO'" by what he called Egypt's "lower-floor-officials."[47] UNESCO further established an International Consultative Experts Committee to track the progress of ar-chaeological work, separate again from the major work of lifting the Abu Simbel Temples. Even with antiquities there were further divisions, seg-mented into the removal of "lesser temples," architectural survey, and ar-chaeological work. Temple dismantling was the domain of conservation experts such as Harold Plenderleith, based in Rome at the Centre for the Study of the Preservation and Restoration of Cultural Property, later to become the International Centre for the Study of the Preservation and Restoration of Cultural Property (ICCROM). Adams and his Scandinavian counterpart Hans-Åke Nordström oversaw prehistoric survey and excava-tion. UNESCO's records reveal the scale of the archaeological challenge, but also its incomprehensible nature for the bureaucrats charged with its management. Adams recounted how UNESCO subscribed to the "idea that a really detailed photogrammetric survey could actually take the place of on-the-ground exploration."[48] In a 1963 report the Executive Committee stated that "practically all the aims of the international solidarity cam-paign had already been achieved; all that remained to be excavated, of the 600 kilometres for the two banks of the Nile between Aswan and the Sudanese frontier, was some 50 kilometres between Sayala and Wadi es-Sebua."[49] To cover such vast areas in archaeological terms is quite simply unimaginable today.

In retrospect, the rescue mission elevated a nascent world heritage, just as it did the various pharaonic temples. But apart from some arti-cles in the UNESCO Courier, archaeological research was itself left out of the major spotlight. Thousands of new sites were recorded and many excavated and documented, providing the basis of entirely new accounts of the vast human history of Nubia spanning an enormous timescale from human origins to modern times. For archaeologists, Wendorf's The

Prehistory of Nubia demonstrated the region's rich prehistory and its role in developments north and south of the Sahara.[50] At the other end of the timescale research, archaeologist Peter Shinnie, leading a Ghanaian team, shed light on the Christianization of Nubia.[51] Most of the excavation and dismantling of temples took place in Egyptian territory, whereas the bulk of the survey and site excavation occurred in Sudan. To give an idea of one team's working methods, in one five-month season 53.8 kilometers were surveyed and 101 sites investigated by one UNESCO employee, A. J. Mills, his wife, a technical assistant from the Sudanese Antiquities Service, thirty-five local laborers, and four supervisors.[52] Despite the limitations, by 1962 UNESCO reported outstanding discoveries from various expeditions, including the Old Kingdom town of Buhen, the archaic cemetery at Ashka, the Middle Kingdom town near Mirgissa, excavation of C-group cemeteries, fossilized human remains from Paleolithic times, the discovery of the large Christian town at Debeira West, the Christian frescoes of Faras, the uniquely decorated rock shelter at Korosko, and numerous rock inscriptions and stelae.[53] These were featured, but to a much lesser degree than the famous temples, in postcards, books, magazines, slides, radio programs, films, and numerous press releases. Ultimately, the survey and excavation of settlements, cemeteries, fortresses, and traces of prehistory left on the landscape were also partly submerged against the dramatic backdrop of Abu Simbel.

Reticence on the part of UNESCO to fully embrace archaeology is in some ways understandable. Archaeological expeditions might have detracted from the main aim of rescuing the monuments, specifically the two Abu Simbel temples. Quite rightly, UNESCO may have feared setting precedents whereby other Member States could petition for financial, technical, and expert assistance for salvage archaeology in the face of infrastructural development projects.[54] But if UNESCO as an institution failed to grasp archaeology, the archaeologists also struggled to work within UNESCO's operational framework, being strongly tethered to their own governments, funders, and institutions. National interests routinely trumped internationalist efforts. The archives reveal that American archaeologists were the most egregious here, in both their professional behavior and their rivalries over areas granted as concessions. There were complaints about Fred Wendorf and his conflict with the joint Yale-Toronto project headed by Charles Reed over archaeological concession.[55] Remarkably, Wendorf would continue to rehash the same tensions twenty-five years later.[56] There was also duplication between some projects and overlaps in the territory covered. Some teams sought to acquire field permits directly through UNESCO, thereby eliminating the Egyptian Antiquities Service from the equation—possibly out of ignorance in working abroad rather than political motivation. UNESCO's representative in Cairo, French Egyptologist Louis Christophe, likened it to a "rat race" and questioned whether they were all working for the same goal.[57]

The Americans expected to lead the International Action Committee and bemoaned the Swiss appointment, blaming the political situation and need for neutrality at UNESCO.[58] Committees were political bodies and often debates over technical issues were subsumed by national agendas.[59] Other problems arose when some archaeologists failed to publish their findings in line with the commitments they undertook with UNESCO. Others failed to publish at all yet expected to have their contracts renewed and were constantly asking for more money.[60] Twenty-five years later Torgny Säve-Söderberg urgently appealed to his colleagues "who had not yet fully honored their regulations of their concession contracts to publish their Nubian results."[61] This further highlights the disciplinary differences between the archaeologists and technicians, academics and consultants. Other routine problems included the USSR joining the venture at a late stage, the unreliability of the Polish mission at Faras, lack of proper recognition for the joint Scandinavian team, concerns over the Spanish work at Debod Temple, and various financial irregularities.[62] While the archives also reveal certain issues and intrigues with the engineers employed in Nubia, the scope and number of incidents reported in the documents and correspondence pertaining to the archaeological missions is unmatched.

There were further predictable tensions between archaeological, Egyptological, and philological approaches to research in Nubia. British Egyptologist and architect Walter Emery felt some highly qualified field archaeologists were brought in de novo and essentially knew nothing about Nubia.[63] In return the Americans were keen to privilege the position of "science" within UNESCO's mission. Professor J. O. Brew, already familiar to UNESCO through his involvement on its International Principles Governing Archaeological Excavations, asked Director-General René Maheu specifically about "science." He enquired "if it could be true that UNESCO was not interested in scientific work."[64] Brew cautioned Maheu that "academic people in the United States are by no means solidly behind the schemes for moving and preserving monuments." In a striking blow, American Egyptologists and curators including Bernard von Bothmer and William Hayes were openly apathetic or even hostile to the salvage project and the Egyptian government, considering the work pseudoscientific and that the Egyptian treasures on offer were instead ordinary items with no merit at all.[65] Despite the bickering, the research impact of the archaeological fieldwork is immeasurable. Some forty expeditions had explored 500 kilometers of the Nile Valley. Already by 1977 Louis Christophe had recorded well over seven hundred archaeological publications stemming from the campaign. In terms of new discoveries, since neither Egypt nor Sudan has maintained archaeological site registers we shall never know for certain; however, the number of sites uncovered is inestimable, but must count well into the thousands.[66]

Overlooking UNESCO's own 1956 Recommendation on International Principles Applicable to Archaeological Excavations, Swedish archaeologist Säve-Söderbergh applauded UNESCO's internationalist spirit for rescuing the common heritage of humanity. He drew attention to the need for "an international convention or recommendation which underlined their moral duty to allocate economical and personal resources on rescuing temples or on excavating antiquities."[67] But it was the precise nature of the international call and the coordinating United Nations agency that ameliorated sovereign tensions. UNESCO transferred these national patrimonies into an international realm, rendering them supranational and above the exclusive property of Egypt or Sudan. UNESCO's Nubian mission ultimately challenged state sovereignty in subtle ways, according to historian Paul Betts.[68] Before the campaign, all monuments within states were exclusively the concern of those nations; now they were elevated to a global concern. The change in the Executive Committee from a panel of experts on Nubia chosen by the Director-General to fifteen Member State representatives elected by the General Conference was also a sign of the changing national stakes in heritage on the international stage.[69]

Addressing the United Nations Development Programme (UNDP) in 1966, UNESCO's Deputy Director-General, Malcolm Adiseshiah, explained how the two agencies should work together on three fronts: the intellectual, the operational, and the ethical. Indeed the UNDP had offered aid through UNESCO's auspices during the Nubian Monuments Campaign. The Indian development economist proclaimed, "You have to teach cooperation, you have to research for peace, you have to communicate cultural understanding."[70] These ideas were all rehearsed in the Nubian arena: the cognitive (acquiring knowledge), the socioemotional (engendering belonging), and the behavioral (acting responsibly). The international collaborative work, both engineering and educational, would ideally forge a sense of world community and a shared past which would instill a greater global responsibility for future generations. The past was a burden to be collectively shouldered, but there were also potentials in terms of knowledge, development, and socioeconomic and political benefits, albeit unevenly distributed. Cultural heritage provided the seemingly neutral shared resources for fashioning new world citizens, through technocratic networks, supranational heritage and stewardship, and mutual understanding of each other's cultures.

Salvage Mentalities

Never one to miss an opportunity for grandiosity, French minister for culture André Malraux claimed that with Nubia one "could not too highly praise your having conceived a plan so magnificent and so precise in its boldness one might say, a kind of Tennessee Valley Authority of archaeology."[71] This was a reference to the federally owned corporation formed by an act of Congress under President Roosevelt in 1933 and tasked with constructing and running infrastructural development projects across several American states. Ironically, in 1943 Julian Huxley had written a book praising the authority and its potential for enhancing development, education, research, and conservation.[72] At the time of the Great Depression, the Tennessee Valley Authority (TVA) was a powerhouse of employment not only in construction but also in archaeological salvage operations. Cultural resource management in the United States, as well as in Egypt, was required for the hundreds of sites and thousands of artifacts submerged by dams and threatened by large-scale infrastructural development. The Egyptian minister for culture, Sarwat Okasha, described how the "modern world of machines and technicians invaded, en masse, the world of Rameses II."[73] Not surprisingly, the TVA was also influential in the original proposal for construction of the Aswan High Dam and its cost-benefit logics were followed, even if the project was completed in collaboration not with the Americans but with the Soviets.[74] Classicist Gilbert Murray and other British diplomats had mocked the American "New Dealers . . . and their Tennessee Valley Authority nostrums for the organization of international society."[75] Yet despite the commercial contracts and competitive tendering around Abu Simbel, the Frenchman Malraux saw the task as noble, "the antithesis of the kind of gigantic exhibitionism by which great modern states try to outbid each other. Nor should the well-defined object of your scheme conceal its profound significance. If UNESCO is trying to rescue the monuments of Nubia, it is because these are in imminent danger."[76]

J. O. Brew, the director of Harvard's Peabody Museum, demonstrated that formal salvage archaeology had been developed in Egypt in 1907, with the first Aswan Dam, rather than being a distinctly American innovation.[77] The original dam, engineered and constructed by the British, inundated Philae Temple for part of each year. The proposed increase in the dam's height meant that portions of the Nubian valley and its archaeological sites would similarly be drowned. The Egyptian government funded an archaeological survey and excavation led by British and American archaeologists George Reisner, Cecil Firth, Aylward Blackman, and Oric Bates. A second salvage effort began in 1929, directed by British archaeologists Walter Emery and Lawrence Kirwan, that extended to the Sudanese frontier, when the British ostensibly controlled Sudan.[78] These projects were echoed two decades later when the height of the dam was raised a second time, but this time directed in part by American field archaeologists who had no expertise in Egyptian archaeology. Some archaeologists complained that this earlier salvage archaeology in Nubia was so successful that it influenced later work and sometimes hindered the implementation of newer approaches.[79] In a twist of fate, Adams, Wendorf, and Brew were all, in one way or another, involved in the TVA scheme in the United States before transferring their expertise to Egypt. While the first Nubian salvage campaign is less well known, the second would have significant impact on world opinion and change the general attitude toward salvage programs. In line with UNESCO's programmatic vision, monumental salvage would be constituted as a moral duty for future generations. And like the TVA, there was recognition that preservation of monuments, and even entire landscapes, could further have importance in the realm of socioeconomic development.[80]

Rex Keating, who worked for UNESCO publicizing the Nubian Monuments Campaign and was known for his broadcasts on archaeology, wrote that the campaign was both the first of its kind and a signal of what was to come. Given "industrial expansion going ahead on all sides the threatened destruction of ancient sites increases month by month with its corresponding increase in demands on what has come to be known as salvage archaeology." Recognizing the urgent need for salvage, archaeologists from Yale University found rich Upper Paleolithic sites near Kom Ombo being destroyed by earthmoving equipment in preparation for the resettlement of the Nubians.[81] And while this might seem to be a boon to archaeology, "our man in Nubia," Adams, lamented, "it will be indeed an evil day for archaeology if it becomes entirely salvage and we have no more option to choose and follow problems as we would like."[82] Keating predicted quite rightly that UNESCO would be increasingly drawn into these campaigns since it was the only institution with the necessary size, prestige, and experience to organize archaeology on an intergovernmental scale. He suggested then the formation of an association of professional field archaeologists for salvage operations, liaising with UNESCO, to work in partnership with governments, funding bodies, and publicity agencies.[83] While an admirable proposal, it never came to fruition, and one can only speculate how such synergies could have transformed what later became variously known as contract archaeology, commercial archaeology, preventive archaeology, or rescue archaeology.[84]

What was produced was yet another recommendation, the 1968 Recommendation Concerning the Preservation of Cultural Property Endangered by Public or Private Works. It recommended that the costs of preserving cultural property endangered by public or private works, including archaeological research, be included within construction costs.[85]

FIGURE 2.3 Archaeological encampment on the Nile, 1964, © UNESCO/Rex Keating

This impacted the role of contract archaeology in Europe and North America, though few practitioners would trace its genealogy back to UNESCO and the Nubian Monuments Campaign. At the same time there were real complications for the position of archaeology back in Paris, and more specifically salvage archaeology, since it qualified as neither a social science nor a cultural activity in UNESCO's definitional terms. This goes some way to explain why the Nubian Campaign began and remained an extradepartmental program with little initial support, and why it left almost no mark upon the long-term organizational structure of UNESCO.[86]

The specifically salvage component, the race against time, the fact that most teams had few professional archaeologists to oversee legions of workmen working in the quasi-colonial style, some led by archaeologists with no expertise in Egypt or Sudan—all of this further curtailed the long-term impacts of this vast contribution. Again it would be technical work, rather than a fully integrated research program, that would take precedence. Regarding the North American contribution, the 1960s marked the height of positivism in archaeology, moving the discipline closer toward science, secured by National Science Foundation (NSF) funding, and away from historically, socially, or culturally contextual fields. Perhaps in Huxley's time these developments might have been capitalized upon, yet only if scientific approaches could effectively connect to wider social and cultural imperatives on a global scale. Americanist archaeology in the 1960s had its sights on developing lawlike generalizations about culture, rather than writing particular and diverse histories for humanity. This also would serve to limit the broader intellectual potential of archaeology at UNESCO yet accorded well with the aims of exporting technocratic prowess to undeveloped nations. There were other resonances too with the organization's split mission privileging science over religion, preservation over politics, and technocracy rather than the dream of a global peace.

The Nubian salvage operations mark a turning point when great swaths of the world were presented with ideas that aspired to universal acceptance: a common humanity premised on a shared global past, shared responsibility for heritage protection worldwide, and the dissemination of Western technical expertise. This system of presumed universals would require novel legal and bureaucratic structures for the management of cultural heritage worldwide. Though it was not specifically stated, we might also see the initial stirrings of a language of rights to heritage and rights to culture in UNESCO's mission. This is not to say that other movements, organizations, and individuals were not major contributors, but rather that UNESCO galvanized and institutionalized those sentiments and practices and set them in stone during the Nubian Monuments Campaign.

The French Connection

Saving Nubia involved many stories and actors, not simply Nasser's Egypt and relations with the West, or even East and West relations during the Cold War. It reveals many of the intersecting twentieth-century histories of politics, empires, nations, and international institutions.[87] For instance, there was the declining position of Britain following the extended colonial occupation of Egypt that led to the failed invasion of Suez. Despite their own participation in the conflict, the French, by comparison, strategically forged even greater ties with Egypt throughout UNESCO's mission. They often claimed to be at the forefront of the Nubian Campaign, a position bolstered by their long-standing dominance in the field of Egyptology. The major contribution of Egyptians themselves in archaeological salvage over many decades has only recently been fully appreciated.[88] The United States too emerged as a key player, after withdrawing funds for the dam that ultimately precipitated the nationalization by Egypt of the Suez Canal Company. The Americans supported the withdrawal of foreign troops and threatened sanctions within the wider arena of the UN. To balance Soviet economic support for Nasser's dam, the Kennedy administration offered major backing for the cultural salvage in Nubia. Indeed, there were many national agendas at play even before the project got under way, including tensions between Egypt and Sudan and the perceived prioritization of the former over the latter in terms of aid and salvage.

Teams of archaeologists from East and West, North and South worked within UNESCO's framework: Russians, Americans, Finns, Hungarians, Czechs, and East and West Germans, as well as Indians and Pakistanis, who had been embroiled in numerous conflicts beginning in 1947 with Partition to the Indo-Pakistani War of 1965. The Soviet Union offered a team from Leningrad University that would integrate into other expeditions. The Egyptians felt they could not press for more support given the Soviet Union's extraordinary efforts constructing the dam.[89] But the Russians were keen to monitor the progress of other missions in Nubia, and UNESCO used this to their own advantage. In 1961 an internal memo advised that "Mr. Tolstov and Mr. Petrovitch should be kept informed more frequently on developments in the Nubian Campaign.

For instance, a letter from Mr. Van der Haagen giving details of the recent American archaeological discoveries would be opportune."[90] As part of the Soviet bloc, the Polish mission at Faras might have been regarded as participating in an expansive Soviet international agenda. However, under the expedition leadership of archaeologist Kazimierz Michałowski the Poles were keen to establish their neutrality in Sudan and avoid deep political divisions, despite the fact that all diplomatic relationships were framed by the USSR. Irrespective of the prevailing communist ideology at home, the Polish discoveries from Faras were the subject of a vast media outpouring, their international character standing in direct contrast to the political restrictions on ordinary Polish citizens traveling abroad.[91] Given these interwoven histories of economic, territorial, military, and colonial hostilities, the Nubian Campaign, itself rather military-sounding, was not always conducive to the utopian mission of rescue and uplift. In this instance it may be one successful example of UNESCO's technocratic focus ameliorating, or papering over, the international political tensions between nation-states.

Beginning with the French, the antiquity of Egypt has been of importance since medieval times, and the relationship only deepened after Napoleon's expedition transported 160 scientists and artists to Egypt.[92] It is said that his expedition and its discoveries, including the famous Rosetta Stone, created the field of Egyptology. Significantly, Nubia was the site of nineteenth-century French archaeological expeditions made famous by Jean-François Champollion.[93] French archaeologist Auguste Mariette founded the Egyptian Antiquities Service, which was then continuously administered by Frenchmen including Gaston Maspero, Pierre Lacau, and Étienne Drioton until 1952. Cultural exchange between the two nations was always firmly felt, and it was André Malraux, the French minister for culture, who chaired the UNESCO session that first announced a global appeal for Nubia. In his rousing speech, much cited, he declared that "all nations, though many of them even now are engaged in covert or open conflict, have been summoned to save by a united effort the fruits of a civilization on which none has a pre-emptive claim."[94] The Egyptians and Nasser himself may have had other ideas. In closing, Malraux famously likened the quest to the "action of a man who snatches something from death." His endorsement was entirely in keeping with UNESCO's profile and setting. As Betts recalls, UNESCO was, after all, based in Paris, with the privileged use of the French language, and continues to be seen as a particularly French institution in terms of its crusade of defining and defending the idea of universal civilization.[95] France certainly benefitted from UNESCO's location, whether in terms of language privilege, expanded cultural influence, or aligning the organization's activities with French cultural policy.[96] Ever the orator, Malraux embodied UNESCO's one-world and civilizational ambitions: "You are proposing an action which all men together to defy the forces of dissolution. Your appeal is historic not because it proposes to save the temples of Nubia, but because through it the world civilization publicly proclaims the world's art as its indivisible heritage."[97]

In reality French claims sought to reconfigure ancient Egypt as part of France's own heritage, not least because the French claimed to have initiated the project. In 1955 UNESCO had created the Centre d'Étude et de Documentation sur l'Ancienne Égypte in Cairo to document some four hundred private tombs of the Theban Necropolis along with hundreds of other sites. Louvre curator Christiane Desroches-Noblecourt was instrumental in establishing the center, calling it a new collaboration in Egyptology. She was similarly credited as the driving force behind the rescue campaign, although Egyptian officials have refuted her claim.[98] She famously persuaded President Charles de Gaulle to commit additional funds after having pledged French support without his authorization. Additionally, the French Institut Géographique National carried out an early photogrammetric survey of the area to be flooded, aided by the Egyptian armed forces.[99] All of these endeavors facilitated France in maintaining and improving its relations with Egypt after Suez, while simultaneously increasing its national claims to Egyptian patrimony and securing archaeological permits for its researchers.

Archaeological ambitions and national rivalries in Egyptian archaeology have had a long and bitter history.[100] This particular Anglo-French rivalry was just one facet of the two nations' wide-ranging competition throughout the Middle East.[101] Historian Donald Reid explains that Lord Cromer conceded archaeological predominance to the French in "about 1889 and the French thought the matter important enough to have it confirmed in the Anglo-French entente agreement of 1904. English Egyptologists never forgave their government."[102] The British humiliation after Suez would further reverberate in archaeological circles, and again the French capitalized upon their influence in Egypt.

The British government had made it a policy not to fund UNESCO's mission in the wake of Suez. In Parliament, Labour Party politician William Warby reasoned that "we cannot really have a future for mankind unless we have a sense of the past." More, he argued, must be done, and "while we are glad that individual British archaeologists and Egyptologists are lending their support, we would like to feel that support is being given by this country as a whole."[103] Though not an Egyptologist, Sir Mortimer Wheeler was selected by the minister for education to represent the United Kingdom in the Nubian Monuments Campaign and was put on UNESCO's International Action Committee. Funding remained an embarrassment. Wheeler bemoaned, "If only the crisis had occurred two years ago, things would have been a good deal simpler."[104] He worked closely with Walter Emery and the Egyptian Exploration Society (EES), who were already excavating at the Sudanese sites of Buhen and Qasr Ibrim. The British were prepared to move one dismantled temple to a safe distance with the help of Sudan, but not to reconstruct it in Khartoum. Indeed, letters from the U.K. National Commission to UNESCO were clear and their position not particularly savvy: they were focused on the division of archaeological finds and attaining permits for excavations beyond Nubia.[105] Desperate to play a leading role, Wheeler used British self-interest shamelessly, hinting that British Egyptology would suffer. He showed films about Abu Simbel sent from UNESCO and wrote impassioned letters to *The Times*, all to no avail. "I and my colleagues remain bitterly ashamed of the British Government's negative action in the whole business."[106]

The European civilizational dimension was significant in the international profile of the funding campaign signaled by the constitution of the Honorary Committee of Patrons. Chaired by King Gustav Adolf VI of Sweden, it included Queen Elizabeth of Belgium, Queen Fredrika of Greece, Princess Grace of Monaco, Princess Margrete of Denmark, the Duke of Devonshire, and statesmen Dag Hammarskjöld, Julian Huxley, and André Malraux. Many European nations saw much to be salvaged, not simply for Egypt and Sudan but for themselves. Foreign gifting profitably secured all manner of artifacts in return, and even entire temples, for Western museums. Catalogues advertised Egyptian antiquity as means of payment in return for foreign aid: a colossal head of Amenophis IV, the New Kingdom sarcophagus of Kheruef, and alabaster vessels from King Zoser's pyramid were all presented in *A Common Trust*.[107] Much like the operations of Sotheby's or Christie's, Egyptian objects and temples were auctioned off in a highly acquisitive atmosphere: the Temple of Debod to Spain, Taffa to the Netherlands, the Temple of Ellesyia to Italy, and Dendur to the United States. By comparison, the Sudanese lamented that they did not possess the same important museum reserves to cede, the temples and chapels to be transported to other countries, or attractive sites like Saqqara to offer as favors in return for aid.[108]

In such an extractive economy European and North American museums, academic institutions, and researchers themselves would benefit not only materially but also in terms of access to new research and field sites. Through quasi-colonial concepts of enrichment, Western nations could argue that they were the rightful inheritors of ancient Egyptian civilization, and many continue to do so today in the guise of the "universal museum."[109] There was a calculated rationality to the nationalistic and ideological carving up of Nubia. For example, the Holy See was only concerned with rescuing Christianity from the floodwaters, and other predominantly Christian nations like Poland and the United States were tasked with saving Christian sites and Coptic churches. The French, Germans, Belgians, and other Europeans possessing the longest traditions of Egyptology secured the most important archaeological and architectural concessions. And the Americans considered that they excelled in the scientific and salvage aspects of prehistoric archaeology, their efforts being underwritten by the NSF. The NSF made their intent, and historical bias, crystal clear: "We feel that the preservation of monuments of the Dynastic period and other problems of classical Egyptology do not fall within the accepted range of the Foundation's interests."[110]

From the American perspective they were really driving the campaign. The United States was the largest single contributor and they had prestigious universities involved on the ground, plus many active players at UNESCO, and an energetic national commission busy raising substantial funds through a voracious public relations campaign. The American expeditions, as Adams himself purported, "were more or less frankly 'in it for the money'; that is they came to Nubia simply because money was made available to do so."[111] Back in 1955 it was the new American Director-General, Luther Evans, who had visited Abu Simbel and formalized the agreement with Egypt to offer technical assistance.[112] Evans believed UNESCO was a technical agency and that advancing peace need not be accompanied by ideological or philosophical positions. Directed by the Americans, UNESCO would become an intergovernmental agency more concerned with technical assistance than cultural or educational reform of the mind.[113] As they would do with Afghanistan's Bamiyan Buddhas many years later, some Americans thought they could simply buy the temples and ship them home. This understandably caused great affront to the Egyptians.[114] They were similarly eager to acquire objects for their national collections, making frequent mention of the outstanding US contribution.[115] Chicago's Oriental Institute requested one of the major pieces, the colossus of Amenophis IV, even before embarking upon major field-work. Letters of complaint to UNESCO officials describe how American academics flaunted their national wealth, suggesting that given their thousand colleges at home, they could easily pay to save the Abu Simbel Temples.[116] Archaeologist William Adams wrote wryly to his collaborator Ralph Solecki that "our proposed contribution to the Nubian project is not really costing us a cent, since we are merely earmarking money which Nasser owes us, and which would probably otherwise never get repaid!"[117] This pervasive attitude did little to endear them to their foreign colleagues, UNESCO representatives, or the Egyptians.

These attitudes should not be too surprising given the 1962 official US Senate hearings where the national motivations behind competitive gifting were laid bare by politicians such as Senator Roman Hruska from Nebraska: "Here Russia builds the dam. They get all the glory and the credit, and the Egyptian people think the Russians are fine. And then, under the guise of a United Nations suborganization, Uncle Sam furnishes the bloodstream financially and gets no credit whatsoever."[118] Other politicians stated publicly that without US support the Nubian scheme was doomed to failure. A more moderate view, albeit one of cultural appropriation, was that rather than offering Egypt any favors, these "monuments are great historical roots of all Western civilization. We are doing our own future generations in this country a favor, insofar as we are helping preserve their own historical roots."[119] For America and its increasing vigilance in Middle Eastern affairs, participation was paramount, and the archives reveal that they did not want to be shown up by the Dutch, Germans, or Russians: "During a period when the United States is attempting to improve its relations culturally with other peoples, the denial of support for a project of acknowledged great cultural significance would result in a serious setback in this important arena of foreign relations."[120] President John F. Kennedy expressed it more diplomatically when he said that as one of the newest civilizations, the United States had a deep regard for the study of past cultures and a concern for preservation, especially "ancient Egypt from which many of our own traditions have sprung."[121]

Edmundo de Lassalle, the flamboyant leader of the US National Commission campaign, *Save the Temples on the Nile*, tried to repackage national economic and political interests through postcolonial propaganda.[122] In colonial times, Lassalle suggested, archaeologists and art historians carried away whatever they pleased from other countries. With the demise of colonialism, that policy was now bankrupt and one should adopt "an anthropological point of view as things are really better in their normal environment." From time to time, however, some new, small nations may neglect their antiquities and call upon "stronger and more advanced nations," thus providing further justification for US technical intervention. Lassalle's vigorous campaigning helped secure a stellar national committee that included academics, business tycoons, bankers, and writers, not to mention Cary Grant, Joan Crawford, Gene Kelly, and Richard Nixon. Yet, as outlined above, there were deep ambivalences and some astonishing hostilities toward the rescue mission from major American Egyptologists and museum curators that could not be ignored and further complicated funding requests in the US Senate. The detractors believed the funds requested were out of scale with the value of Abu Simbel. Froelich Rainey, head of the University of Pennsylvania Museum, tried to close the chapter on excavations in Nubia altogether. Lassalle likened it to a "blackmail operation" by which American Egyptologists hoped to discard Nubia and move into more coveted excavations further north.[123] UNESCO's bureaucratic methods also came under attack as "arcanum bureaucrationen"—an attitude that has long held sway in the United States, with disastrous consequences for the organization.

UNESCO aspired to "create a psychological climate conducive to moral, technical and financial co-operation both by the public and governments." In the United States this notion took on decidedly corporate, consultant-driven, and even cinematic proportions. American business interests were front and center with Westinghouse, Singer, Bank of America, Ford Motor Company, Getty Oil Company, and Socony-Mobil Oil Company, to name a few. Public relations giant Hamilton Wright Organization Inc. regularly petitioned UNESCO, marketing itself as the American firm that could promote the Nubian Campaign and indeed the nation of Egypt. It counted amongst its clients many governments, states, and cities of the world, not to mention corporations. Its motto was "Serving government and industry since 1908." Private individuals such as architect Harold Simpson also saw the colossal corporate potential: he contacted the US National Committee proposing to lift the temples in a single piece for $25 million, one-half to be paid in hard currency.[124]

The rise of consultancy culture in the global heritage arena has a long history. Lassalle saw the immediate possibilities for the touring Tutankhamun Treasures exhibition (1961–1966), although it was refused by the Metropolitan Museum in New York. He also saw great potential in marketing Egyptian-inspired fashion items.[125] Even serious academics such as J. O. Brew sought to tie the campaign to the premiere of Twentieth Century Fox's film *Cleopatra*, starring Elizabeth Taylor and Richard Burton. Finally, and rendering another blow to the role of archaeology, the US public relations machine with the help of Brew thought it best to approach Abu Simbel "not as an archaeological problem but as a 'cultural' project emphasizing the international cooperation angle, the technically challenging engineering aspects."[126] Together with UNESCO, some of the key archaeological players sought to minimize the status of the discipline within the overall mission. In this respect, the American contingent played a significant role.

Lastly, one cannot overlook the competing national interests and agendas of Egypt and Sudan. The hydropolitics of the Aswan High Dam were very much in Egypt's favor, and Nasser had to pay US$43 million in compensation for dislocating many thousands of people in Sudan and flooding their land. Technological, agricultural, and heritage assets would all favor Egypt. Jean Vercoutter, the first post-independence commissioner for archaeology in Sudan, insisted at the outset that purely archaeological investigations should not be forgotten in favor of the more glamorous program concerning the great monuments. Egypt should not overshadow Sudan as it had done with the control of the Nile. This was reiterated many times in letters from Sudan's education minister, Ziada Arbab, to UNESCO representatives. Bringing his archaeological experience to the fore, Vercoutter outlined in great detail the striking disparity between the support from and interest of UNESCO in Egyptian Nubia and that in Sudanese Nubia: he felt it heavily biased toward the former. While he admitted that the largest part of the submersion was in Egyptian Nubia, Sudanese Nubia had scarcely been explored archaeologically. Meanwhile in Egypt, unnecessary and duplicate work was conducted, including plans for yet a fourth survey covering exactly the same area.[127] Quoting Wheeler, a prominent member of UNESCO's Action Committee, Vercoutter pleaded the case for Sudan: "We, as individuals or as nations, all suffer from an unusual anxiety as to the future, yet curiously enough, as a counterpart to that anxiety to the future, there is throughout the world an increasingly intelligent interest in the past. The two things go together . . . and that sense of security and stability which an understood tradition and history give to a nation is an essential contributory factor to its capacity to make good in the future."[128]

Amidst the carving up of territories, historic rivalries, and competing colonialisms, UNESCO entered Egypt with the idealistic spirit of international collaboration and heroic rescue of the heritage of humanity. Yet there was much less to celebrate for the living people of Nubia, who would have to be relocated and their own modern heritage submerged. Their eventual resettlement was far from their ancestral home, further alienating them from their traditional lifeways and means of subsistence.[129] Archaeologists such as Frederic Gysin and J. O. Brew were similarly interested in the ethnology of these populations. And along with the International Union of Anthropological and Ethnological Sciences and the Austrian delegation to UNESCO they proposed that 2 percent of the international funds be used for complementary studies.[130] UNESCO declined, stating that resources were limited and such research was not a priority. Some 100,000 people were affected and "despite the emotional upheaval forced upon them by the exodus, the Nubians became an essential element in the salvage operation."[131] The organization could claim no great achievements there, no uplift, despite being the agency charged with social and cultural issues within the UN system. The UNESCO archive contains little on the evacuation, whereas other sources captured the upheaval of the Nubian people in considerable and depressing detail.[132] Even with the inscription of the Nubian monuments on UNESCO's World Heritage List in 1979, the Nubians themselves would be once more cast as victims of conquest and colonization. In 2008 Nubian heritage would again be sacrificed to the hydropolitics of the Meroe Dam, accompanied by yet another archaeological salvage campaign and its international politics.[133] UNESCO would play an even smaller role.

Conclusions

The arena of Abu Simbel highlights a time of dramatic change from Huxley's and Torres Bodet's vision of UNESCO as a globally oriented humanist organization to the intergovernmental organization Luther Evans promoted, more interested in technical assistance than in cultural and educational reform. This marked a shift from the utopian ideology of scientific humanism to one of technocracy and functionalism.[134] Following political scientist Vincenzo Pavone, the intergovernmental UNESCO that emerged during the Cold War supplanted an earlier global UNESCO that concerned itself with creating a lasting peace after the Second World War. The model of international cooperation had changed too. UNESCO in the

1950s and 1960s had more modest aims to establish a common practical ground where science, education, and culture might assist in resolving and negotiating particular conflicts. Concerned primarily with short-term objectives, the organization was then subordinated to the UN and, more implicitly, to US liberal ideology.[135]

The rise and consolidation of UNESCO's technocratic profile was evidenced by the burgeoning requests by Member States for technical conservation missions, particularly after the success of Nubia, to sites such as the ancient Indus Valley city of Moenjodaro in Pakistan or the Buddhist site of Borobudur in Indonesia. By officially labeling it the "International Campaign to Save the Monuments of Nubia," UNESCO not only signaled the scope and urgency of the challenge but implied that the entire enterprise was about conserving temples rather than rescuing the past.[136] Even at the archaeological excavations of Moenjodaro, where a familiar set of engineers and other experts from the Nubian Campaign were assembled to face a similar set of problems (salvage, water, hydraulics), there was a notable absence of support for archaeological research. Inscribing it as the "Archaeological Ruins at Moenjodaro" only served to further fossilize research and future investigation: it became about monumentalizing and conserving a ruin. Moving toward technical assistance entailed a firm focus on preservation, often in tandem with UNESCO's development agenda to promote cultural tourism, rather than archaeological exploration or support for research.[137] Technical assistance programs inevitably involve some element of cultural assault. And whilst UNESCO's communications programs were charged with "cultural imperialism," its technical transfers on the scale witnessed in Nubia were laden with what has been termed "development imperialism."[138]

Along the Nile one could almost see reflected the desire of the postwar powers for the United Nations: the construction of the Aswan Dam and rescue of the temples combined the scientific technocracy of the New Deal with the political reach of the nineteenth-century alliance system.[139] The campaign effectively united, on a grand stage, development and large-scale infrastructures with international economics and politics while playing off former colonial and Cold War tensions within a peopled landscape where the past held ambivalent connotations. We can witness in Egypt's efforts, alongside those of France, the United States, the USSR, and every other nation involved, the performance of an intense nationalism within the sphere of internationalism. There were considerable economic, political, and cultural gains of global proportions to be harnessed in Nubia.

Archaeology as a discipline was no stranger to the manipulations of the nation-state. Indeed, it had always been particularly malleable given its orientation toward the material presencing of putative origins and deep histories. Napoleon and Nasser understood its myriad possibilities. With Egypt, the full force of its civilizational potentials could be unleashed on a waiting world, as Western nations vied with each other to claim their inheritance and ownership of ancient Egypt. The competitive gifting of pharaonic temples to New York, Berlin, Turin, Madrid, and Leiden, along with artifacts and excavation permits exchanged as partage for foreign assistance in the mission, only served to materialize those imagined connections.

For a brief moment UNESCO's utopian promise was resurrected by a pharaonic past. Multilateral cooperation instantiated, albeit briefly, the ideal of a common humanity in tandem with the ethic of collective responsibility. In this chapter of UNESCO's history archaeology as a field practice would reach its apogee. Yet the episode highlights the tensions and ambivalence surrounding the discipline within the organization that was also mirrored, at least in America, in the academic establishment. In Nubia, UNESCO had moved into uncharted waters.[140] If UNESCO struggled to align archaeology's cultural and scientific approaches within the bureaucratic structure of the agency, the archaeologists similarly struggled to see the relevance and merit of UNESCO's international salvage mission. There were misunderstandings on both sides that have had lasting consequences. In this great amphitheater of archaeology it would be the developmental schemes of the TVA, the principles of salvage, and the science of conservation that ultimately gained ground, with America's particular brand of internationalism casting a long shadow. Conversely, the science and potentials of archaeological research would be relegated to the wings, in stark contrast to Julian Huxley's assertion that the TVA might embrace all. The campaign would mark the rise of consultancy culture, however, which has become integral to UNESCO's programs, and the ascendancy of entrepreneurs and experts alongside economists and engineers. Here too recovery would be privileged over discovery.

3

Technocracy

*They are cut off from serious political impact by a technical
cordon sanitaire. Technical co-operation has had so far
virtually no impact on foreign policies.*
—RICHARD HOGGART, 2011

THE ACCLAIMED SUCCESS of the Nubian Campaign inspired many new
monumental requests for UNESCO assistance in the field of cultural
heritage. Wonders of the ancient world such as the Athenian Acropolis,
the vast temple compounds of Borobudur in Indonesia, the capital of
the Sukothai Kingdom in northern Thailand, and the great Phoenician
city of Tyre on Lebanon's southern coast all required saving. In the
raft of safeguarding missions between the 1960s and 1980s UNESCO
launched various appeals to secure both financial aid and technical expertise for these remarkable sites. While these later projects were strictly
monumental ventures that lacked an archaeological field component like
in Nubia, the "Save Moenjodaro" international appeal was directed at
salvaging a five-thousand-year-old archaeological site in Pakistan and one
of the world's earliest and most extensively planned urban settlements.
A vast metropolis extending over a hundred hectares, there is evidence of
a large granary, public baths, an elaborate drainage system, wells, and a
sewage system to accommodate an estimated population in excess of forty
thousand people. It is considered one of the largest cities within the Indus
Valley civilization, possibly the most advanced of its time, having elaborate
international trade networks, civil engineering, and town planning.

Sir Leonard Woolley had written about Moenjodaro for Julian Huxley's
controversial History of Mankind, published in 1958. The Indian archaeologist R. D. Banerjee first discovered and excavated the site in 1922 under
the watchful eye of British archaeologist Sir John Marshall, then Director-
General of the Archaeological Survey of India (ASI). Later in the 1940s

Marshall's successor at the ASI, the irrepressible Mortimer Wheeler, continued excavations and, in his own flamboyant style, described the demise of the prosperous city at the hands of Indo-Aryan invaders.[1] The site had a colonial pedigree dating back to pre-Partition times. In 1964 excavations were taken over by the American George Dales, at which time impending threats to Moenjodaro's long-term preservation were identified. UNESCO was the obvious organization to turn to and, with the visibility of the Abu Simbel rescue, which was still underway, its expertise in saving archaeological and architectural heritage had been successfully showcased on a grand scale.

In 1964 Harold Plenderleith, founding director of ICCROM and a major figure in the Nubian Campaign, was sent by UNESCO to examine Moenjodaro and compile a conservation report on the archaeological remains. Two years later UNESCO engaged NEDECO, a Dutch engineering consultancy specializing in water management that had previously worked in Nubia, for another expert mission.[2] Then an international team of archaeologists was dispatched to the site for a grand total of two days in October 1968 and another two days in February 1969. The team included some familiar faces from the Nubian Campaign: J. O. Brew, Louis Christoph, Kazimierz Michałowski, and Sir Mortimer Wheeler. Their mission report took issue with UNESCO's technocratic approach to Moenjodaro as being too heavily reliant on "technological science and engineering," rather than research and excavation. They proposed "an equal concern with the demands of archaeology," arguing that the methods of conservation for Moenjodaro could "only be adequately appraised if applied through a considered phase of excavation."[3] Wheeler and the Pakistani authorities both stressed that the integration of excavation into any future Moenjodaro project was vital, digging deeper into existing excavations and opening up new areas of the site for exploration. The team recommended that nothing short of five consecutive excavation seasons would be satisfactory. It would cost around US$95,000 per season. As with the invitations to conduct salvage work in Egypt and Sudan, the report suggested that Pakistan consider a system of partage, offering foreign teams a share of the finds if they assisted by sending teams to join the excavation effort. But as the Dutch engineers pointed out, ongoing excavations might be considered "extremely important from an archaeological point of view, but have no bearing on the preservation of the existing ruins."[4] Ultimately no funds were allocated to archaeological survey, excavation, or research, and only a portion was designated for conservation.

Today Moenjodaro reveals a vast city constructed in brick, with major buildings and streets laid out on a grid, drainage systems, and evidence of craft specialization and an impressive transnational trade network. It is estimated that only one-third of the site has so far been uncovered. Running parallel with the story of Abu Simbel, the fate of Moenjodaro was tied to crafting new national histories, state projects of development, and desires for modernity stretching over many decades. All such future-oriented decisions would have impacts on the past. In 1932 the Sukkur barrage and its vast network of canals opened to provide irrigation for rice cultivation, resulting in a dramatic rise in the groundwater level. High rates of soil capillarity drew salts to the ground surface and into the ruins, causing the baked clay and mud structures to disintegrate.[5] Media coverage warned that the site was "facing extinction" and would crumble in a matter of years. It was threatened by exposure to harsh climatic conditions, including flooding, deterioration from the rising salts, and waterlogging. Even during Wheeler's excavations in 1950, his attempts to reach the lowest occupational levels were hampered by "subsoil water oozing from the trenches," as Qudrat Ullah Shabab, secretary in the Ministry for Education, informed an international symposium in 1974, with Wheeler himself in attendance.[6] That same year, after an appeal from the Pakistani government, UNESCO launched its official International Safeguarding Campaign for Moenjodaro.

In that appeal Director-General Maheu explained that only the upper site of Moenjodaro had been exposed over the last fifty years, revealing an "archaeological site of unusual importance." Hinting at its potentials for multicultural dialogue and cooperation in his appeal, he added that the site's influence once extended across India, Iran, and Pakistan.[7] But instead of cultural cooperation, what was now being sought was primarily technical and financial assistance. Likening it to the salvage campaigns of Nubia and Venice, Maheu said, "We have called upon modern technology to supply the means of remedying the disturbances that its own action in the service of hurrying progress has produced in particularly delicate states of harmony or balance."[8] Unlike Nubia or the salvage efforts in Tabqa, Syria, that both faced peril from flooding, Save Moenjodaro focused tightly on hydrological, engineering, and conservation techniques rather than a broader raft of cultural projects, and in doing so attenuated the possibilities for international participation and scholarly development. By seeing the site as a ruin rather than an archaeological site, unsuccessful

FIGURE 3.1 Laneway at Moenjodaro, Pakistan, taken from M. Wheeler, *Early India and Pakistan* (London: Thames and Hudson, 1959)

preservation programs were instigated over many decades and cost millions of dollars, only to ultimately fail.

The formula of an international campaign, an appeal, committees of experts, and the developing-world context followed the same trajectory as Nubia, yet without the archaeological fieldwork or collaborative research. Significantly, Moenjodaro's illustrious past and the achievements of its inhabitants were to be resurrected only in public speeches and pleas for funds, while kept silent in much of the project planning and documentation. Conserving the ruin became the monumental challenge. And it was UNESCO, rather than Pakistan, that decided to pursue a singularly

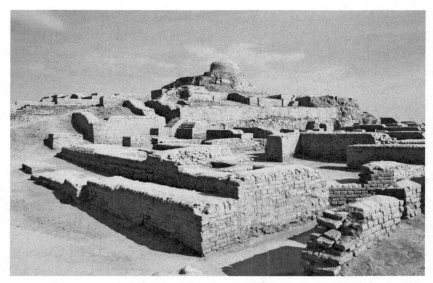

FIGURE 3.2 Moenjodaro archaeological site, Pakistan, courtesy of Shutterstock

technical solution, following the lead of consultant engineers. NEDECO
had proposed digging a vast canal removing 475,000 cubic meters of soil,
whereas the archaeologists understandably were aghast at the destructive potential of this scheme upon the ancient remains. Under UNESCO
auspices safeguarding Moenjodaro would comprise three phases: diverting
the river Indus from the site, at a cost of US$3.15 million; lowering the
water through tube wells, estimated at US$1.78 million; and desaliniza-
tion and consolidation of the site, costing some US$2.07 million. There
would be neither funding nor a systematic plan for archaeological excavation and further research. Irrespective of this decision, UNESCO touted
Moenjodaro as "one of the human race's pioneer cities" that "should provide a fascinating attraction for culturally interested tourists from around
the world."[9] To pursue that goal, Director-General Maheu included a
landscaping component in the proposed project in order to develop the
site as a tourist attraction. By the 1970s the project cost was an estimated
US$7.5 million and its completion was expected in five years.[10] A new con-
sultative committee of experts was subsequently formed of hydrologists,
engineers, archaeologists, and landscapers. The one "archaeologist"
suggested was Paul Perrot from the Smithsonian Institution; with a lifelong career in art history and museum development, he was neither a field
archaeologist nor an expert on Pakistan.

Selling Pakistan was an altogether different proposition from Egypt. Maheu regarded the appeal for international financial aid as "a question of conscience." However, with Moenjodaro the international community was less forthcoming, perhaps because Moenjodaro lacked the pharaonic charisma of the Nubian Campaign or perhaps as a result of "assistance fatigue." Participation by foreign universities and museums was not on offer either as it had been with Egypt and Sudan. The archaeological mission in its 1969 report posed a difficult question: "In the present climate of world-opinion," could the "sociological importance of Moenjodaro in the protohistory of mankind present a comparable international appeal?"[11] Certainly without new findings and research programs, in comparison to the strategy being implemented in Nubia, one might argue that this was less likely. By 1976 there were serious concerns about the lack of funding and the United States had not offered support. There was also an economic recession in the West. A different suite of donors stepped up, including Australia, Bahrain, India, Nigeria, Iraq, Sri Lanka, Egypt, and Saudi Arabia. The Federal Republic of Germany and Japan were the largest contributors, while other Western European nations, the United States, and the United Kingdom were initially absent.[12] By the end of 1980 it was decided that the figure needed for the project, given inflation, was more likely US$13 million.

Through 1997, UNESCO dedicated US$23 million to large-scale measures to save Moenjodaro. Yet the ultimate failure of UNESCO's salvage mission was compounded by the fragility of the ancient remains, the hostile environmental conditions, rivalry between government authorities, and an inappropriate technical approach. The annual electricity costs for running the tube wells rose to US$400,000 and absorbed most of the budget for Moenjodaro, constraining any real conservation efforts.[13] One internal World Heritage Centre memo conveys the situation with great candor. In the final analysis, after more than twenty years of support, and "despite large sums of funds (national/international) used for this campaign it was poorly managed without sufficient national capacity building and a mistaken strategy focused on trying to lower the water table (pumping etc) which amounted to nothing." Another rails that despite "UNESCO's involvement in the campaign and some US$ 24 million investment, the most essential aspect of UNESCO's work, which is national capacity building has not been achieved." The project lacked overarching scientific control, the site interpretation program was insufficient, the inventory was inadequate, and the archaeological remains still faced major conservation problems.[14]

Decades on, the cultural and research aspects were still sidelined. As one heritage expert noted, an "archaeological site of such universal significance as Moenjodaro should be the focus of various forms of international scientific co-operation."[15] As an exercise in repetitive failure and redundancy, the World Heritage Centre developed a postcampaign strategy in 2004 to address, yet again, problems with conservation and stabilization, management structure, training, and site and tourism development.[16] Unlike the acclaimed victory in Nubia, Moenjodaro signaled a technological defeat for the organization and a lapse into futility. Fifty years after UNESCO's first forays at the site, continued flooding, poor conservation work, and further deterioration, coupled with the lack of a comprehensive management system, all indicate today that the site's future is at risk.[17] Currently discussions are under way to determine whether the site should be reburied to preserve what remains for the future.

After successes and setbacks UNESCO emerged from these early salvage missions with a more technocratic focus to embark on a global program of saving the world's greatest sites. It embraced its technical, advisory, and reporting priorities and moved further away from supporting multidisciplinary, research-oriented programs in archaeology. An elaborate bureaucracy evolved to shore up this institutionalization, providing detailed reporting and oversight on international collaborations, financial contributions, expert evaluations, mission reports, and an ever-expanding consultancy culture. The high-profile Nubian Campaign had captured the world's attention and prompted further appeals for emergency assistance, and UNESCO found itself entangled in another major mission, this time to Borobudur. Like the work in Pakistan, the restoration of the Buddhist temple of Borobudur, dating to the eighth–ninth centuries CE, represented a primarily technical and managerial mission with fewer resources, time, and money to coordinate the work of engineers, conservators, and experts, hire consultants, set up field offices, and staff them. UNESCO was providing technical solutions, retreating further into its bureaucratic, managerial, and expert-driven functions.

At Borobudur the challenge was also environmental, countering the effects of Java's tropical climate and volcanic eruptions on an already fragile stone temple.[18] As with Nubia and Venice, it was the participating nations rather than UNESCO that directed the specific conservation techniques employed. Unlike the strictly European dominance during those earlier campaigns, in Indonesia it was the Japanese who provided both funding and expertise and thus directed the conservation strategy.

More than one million stones from the gigantic Buddhist temple would have to be dissected, dismantled, cleaned, catalogued, preserved, and restored to their original positions. Operating as a vast testing ground for new scientific techniques, at Borobudur engineers, chemists, biologists, and conservators would battle the deterioration caused by water, known as "stone cancer," for eight years. Here too this was intergovernmental UNESCO at work rather than global UNESCO, saving imperiled sites from natural or human intervention through the technocracy of "best practice."[19]

Managing the Remarkable

The great legacy of Nubia, and to some extent the International Safeguarding Campaigns to save Moenjodaro, Borobudur, and Venice (see Chapter 4), was the institutionalization of a global program to conserve the world's greatest sites. Unlike the 1956 Recommendation on Archaeological Excavation, the normative instrument for this global program would be enshrined and elevated to the status of a convention. The formulation of UNESCO's 1972 Convention Concerning the Protection of the World Cultural and Natural Heritage created the ultimate inventory and furthered the agency's technocratic goals of listing, standardizing, monitoring, and conserving the past. The routine of managing the remarkable, the register of the world's outstanding sites, required a vast bureaucratic machine: formation of an international legal instrument, a Secretariat for managerial matters, Advisory Bodies composed of technical experts, internal and external committees, auditors, independent evaluators, experts and consultants, States Parties and their national bureaucracies, and so on. By the late 1970s UNESCO was already shifting from an agency able to mobilize a world of salvage projects as Nubia, Venice, Moenjodaro, and Borobudur to a standard-setting agency and the world's clearinghouse for culture. UNESCO generated handbooks, manuals, guidelines, and other documents in multiple languages to accompany its burgeoning programs. What remained central was the midcentury commitment to global conservation of the world's treasures, embraced as a collective responsibility and afforded through technical solutions.

Under UNESCO's leadership the international community manufactured "world heritage," a conservation regime that combines abstract concepts like universalism with the practical experience of global Safeguarding Campaigns, thereby oscillating between utopianism and empiricism.[20] On November 16, 1972, the members of UNESCO's General Conference adopted the international treaty enshrining a system of collective protection, based on modern scientific methods, for the protection of cultural and natural heritage deemed as having "Outstanding Universal Value."[21] Combining the conservation of nature and culture in one treaty is often considered the most innovative achievement. At the time of its formulation, the Convention's main concern was the increasing threat to heritage sites worldwide. New and proliferating forms of danger, destruction, and deterioration signaled not only a loss for respective nations but also a harmful impoverishment of the heritage of all nations. Given their outstanding interest, these masterpieces in terms of history, science, conservation, or aesthetics should be "preserved as part of the world heritage of mankind as a whole."[22]

Originary accounts of the Convention, according to UNESCO insiders, reveal a complex story involving drafts, counterdrafts, fierce debates, and institutional rivalries.[23] Some claim that the Convention was largely an American invention focusing on natural sites, spearheaded by Russell Train and the US environmental lobby, and later endorsed by President Richard Nixon.[24] UNESCO's own institutional histories credit René Maheu and regard the Convention as the culmination of international projects to save heritage in danger, like those for Nubia and Venice.[25] From the beginning UNESCO had assembled expert committees for managing monuments, historical sites, and to some degree even archaeological excavations. Others posit that the Convention was the result of an encounter between two distinct, largely autonomous movements to save nature, on one hand, and culture, on the other.[26] Here too, the politics is in the telling.

UNESCO sought to select the unique and irreplaceable wonders of the world and to categorize, inventory, and monitor their management according to uniform technical and managerial standards. In doing so, they transformed the miraculous into the mundane. By creating a list, the oldest form of written record and similarly the foundation for the most advanced documentation, it inadvertently created a system for the routinization of charisma.[27] While UNESCO's technocratic interventions did not necessarily impinge upon the intrinsic aura of sites, they did produce a parallel landscape of paper and a cumbersome bureaucracy, all fashioned in its quest to manage the remarkable. Conceptually, developing a heritage of the world is tethered to the other globalizing processes, including the idea of an interconnected world polity, that UNESCO had been instrumental in inculcating. The invention of World Heritage further extended the utopian notions of one-worldism and world governance, stressing universal application, since "World Heritage sites belong to all the peoples of the world, irrespective of the territory on which they are located."[28] Alternatively, the List showcases the world's great diversity of cultural achievements and natural wonders that are particular to, and rooted in, nation-states and their sovereign territory: properties can only be nominated by the relevant State Party. UNESCO navigates this tension by attempting to peacefully balance cultural particularity, difference, and diversity, on one hand, with collectivity and universalism, on the other. UNESCO's rationalization of virtuosity evinces all the hallmarks and wider effects of a globalized present.[29] Enlightenment thinking may have provided the basis for this universally prescribed intellectual, cultural, and moral solidarity, unsurprising given UNESCO's historical context.[30] Yet its philosophical underpinnings have proven problematic when the program expanded to embrace a truly global heritage.

The 1972 Convention came into force in December 1975 following its ratification by twenty Member States. It marked the culmination of many different national and international initiatives over several centuries, many of which were formulated in Europe. However, there were also well-documented conservation philosophies developed in South and Southeast Asia that have received comparatively less attention.[31] For example, an Indian treatise called the Mayamatha from the sixth century CE describes the proper restoration of temples.[32] There is also the Indian concept of *jeernodharanam*, an indigenous philosophy linking tangible and intangible heritage concepts within heritage conservation. In Thailand from the mid-seventh century CE onward there have been various efforts to protect and conserve monuments, with royal personages such as King Mongkut (Rama IV) actively sponsoring heritage restoration programs from the nineteenth century to the present.[33] Every society has a relationship with its past, and heritage processes are produced in the context of contemporary concerns and experience.[34]

Most accounts of the rise of global heritage begin with the nineteenth century, when various forms of state and nongovernmental organizations attempted to formalize the value of artistic and cultural works and devise common standards for their protection.[35] Some focused largely on national patrimony, while others were already considering a more international ambit. By the end of the nineteenth century almost every European state, from Denmark to Greece, had a Monuments Act to ensure the protection of its patrimony.[36] For example, in 1877 the Society for the Protection of Ancient Buildings was founded in England. Led by William Morris, the society sought to preserve rather than restore ancient buildings in their original state for the benefit of future generations. In 1879 it led an international campaign to preserve St. Mark's Square in Venice. The French established the post of Inspector of Historic Monuments in 1830 followed by a Commission of Historic Monuments in 1837.[37] In only a few decades after the fall of Napoleon "France managed to swap her reputation as the fatherland of vandalism for the role of vanguard in the protection of the past."[38] Over just a few decades architect Eugène Viollet-le-Duc restored—some might even say rebuilt—some of France's most famous monumental buildings, including Notre Dame in Paris and the fortified medieval city of Carcassonne; both are now World Heritage sites. Protected sites such as these were often isolated and stripped of their wider urban context through "civic cleansing."[39]

Precipitated by the Napoleonic Wars, international attention became focused on plunder and destruction during conflict, necessitating formalized rules between nation-states. This resulted in the 1874 International Declaration Concerning the Laws and Customs of War. Similar to what occurred with UNESCO's own treaty, concern was raised in the nineteenth century over whether cultural properties were part of the national estate or a collective good that all nations were obliged to respect. Then in 1904 the Sixth International Congress of Architects met in Madrid, with representatives from Europe, Russia, Mexico, and the United States, and adopted principles to preserve the original style of historic and artistic monuments. They also proposed the establishment of restoration societies in each nation to prepare an inventory of architectural treasures.[40] Diplomats and state bureaucracies as well as professionals and associations drove many of these transnational heritage networks.

In the twentieth century the League of Nations launched its International Institute of Intellectual Cooperation in 1922 and International Museums Office in 1926, which dealt with art, archaeology, and monuments. The Inter-American Treaty of 1928, known as the Roerich Pact, recognized that institutions of education, the arts, and science "constitute a common treasure of all the Nations of the World."[41] The 1931 Athens Conference followed with the protection and conservation of monuments of art and history, driven by technical concerns that necessitated international collaboration.[42] Then in 1945 UNESCO's constitution mandated "the conservation and protection of the world's inheritance of books, works of art and monuments of history and science." UNESCO's first heritage treaty in 1954 was the Convention for the Protection of Cultural Property in the Event of Armed Conflict, known as the Hague Convention. This was followed by the Recommendation on International Principles Applicable to Archaeological Excavations in 1956 and the Recommendation Concerning the Safeguarding of the Beauty and Character of Landscapes and Sites in 1962.

Early heritage initiatives, particularly those in Europe, were formulated in the wake of conflict and destruction with a focus on preservation efforts that straddled both national and international patrimonial claims. They serve to remind us that the fate of heritage in times of war and devastation is an age-old crisis and, despite the efforts of global institutions, binding international treaties and utopian philosophies remain unresolved. Isabelle Anatole-Gabriel suggests that between the 1940s and 1960s three developments broadly redefined international heritage protection and state sovereignty: the regulation of excavation, the compilation and comparison of national laws, and recovery of illegally acquired objects. Through these imperatives the international community reformulated the rights and obligations of nation-states in an emergent multilateral arena and in doing so inadvertently limited the scope of international organizations such as UNESCO to govern national patrimony.[43]

Creators of the 1972 World Heritage Convention hoped to instill in all nations a set of obligations to conserve particular places for future generations. An initial draft document can be traced back to 1966, when the General Conference requested the Director-General "to study the possibility of arranging an appropriate system of international protection, at the request of the States concerned, for a few of the monuments that form an integral part of the cultural heritage of mankind."[44] The resulting report, drafted primarily by European experts, called for a national and international system of protection for sites of universal interest with corresponding technical and financial provisions. It further explained the existence of the little-known 1972 Recommendation Concerning the Protection, at the National Level, of the Cultural and Natural Heritage that was adopted at same time as the World Heritage Convention yet has been largely forgotten. The report also advised that an international body, possibly UNESCO, oversee the implementation of an international protection system, consisting of experts and technicians drawn from the Member States as well from a permanent staff.[45] A fascinating shadow history, this episode also serves to underline the redundancy, duplication, and time lag between critical ideas and action that permeate the organization, past and present.

Over three weeks in April 1972, with twenty-seven plenary sessions at UNESCO's Paris headquarters, sixty Member States argued over much the same issues that captivate the World Heritage Convention today: concepts such as authenticity and integrity, definitions of natural and cultural heritage, and the funding formula. The head of UNESCO's Culture Sector, Gerard Bolla, described the drafting process as tense and arduous, with moments of "violent" debate.[46] The technical process of drafting the text became a proxy battleground where geopolitical power was both exercised and disputed. The United States, for example, proposed a seemingly innocent semantic modification to a draft section on financial contributions that, in reality, masked a highly political agenda. Moving between French and English texts, the American delegate suggested that since the French word *doivent* was used, the more correct English translation was "ought to" rather than "shall." He offered this "small translation correction" to the English text, professing that his intent was not to affect the meaning of the provision. This intervention, he claimed, would enable the United States "to vote with enthusiasm in favor of the Convention." The United Kingdom, West Germany, and Canada endorsed the US proposal. However, this textual sleight of hand was deftly challenged by Algeria, Tunisia, and Sudan. Perceptively, Senegal and Nigeria retorted, "The problem that arises is not semantic, but political."[47] As a result of the rebuff, powerful Western states and the Soviet bloc failed to impose their agenda over the level of financial contribution to the World Heritage Fund and the voluntary application process. These two key features, determined by delegates from the developing world, meant that the major funders lost direct control over both the List and the Fund.[48] In UNESCO's international arena it has been said that "sovereign States are easily resentful," and there would be financial repercussions in the decades to follow.[49]

Although the Convention was adopted in 1972 and entered into force in 1975, implementation only began in 1977, when more than forty States Parties had ratified it and paid their contributions to the World Heritage Fund.[50] Before that time the List was but an idea. The Convention was primarily conceived as an instrument for conservation, where each country pledged to conserve not only World Heritage sites within its territory but all national heritage. Then in 1978 a dozen sites were inscribed by the World Heritage Committee, consisting of both natural and cultural sites from various regions of the globe. Famous sites such as the Galapagos

Islands, Yellowstone National Park, the Old Town of Quito, and Gorée Island were some of the first enshrined, with scarcely any justification or documentation. When the Giza pyramids were inscribed in 1979 it was claimed that "the exceptional historic, artistic and sociological interest of these monuments . . . needs no commentary."[51] Yet even with the first few inscriptions, concerns were raised that the workload and evaluation processes might outstrip the capacity of the Advisory Bodies and Secretariat.[52] These two groups of professionals coupled with the World Heritage Committee form the Convention's three main pillars, enabling it to function as an international legal instrument.

As set out in the 1972 Convention's Operational Guidelines, technical and managerial expertise is drawn from three expert advisory organizations.[53] The International Union for the Conservation of Nature and Natural Resources (IUCN) was Julian Huxley's initiative during his time as UNESCO Director-General. Based in Gland, Switzerland, it was founded in 1948 to promote international cooperation in natural conservation efforts. The International Council on Monuments and Sites (ICOMOS), established in 1965 and located in Paris, is a nongovernmental organization of experts on site management and conservation methods stemming from a proposal by the Second Congress of Architects and Specialists of Historic Buildings in 1964. Lastly, the International Centre for the Study of the Preservation and Restoration of Cultural Property (ICCROM) was created by UNESCO in 1956 and came into effect in 1958. Based in Rome, it is an intergovernmental agency for the study and restoration of heritage sites. Taken together, these three bodies, all based in Europe, reflect the international professionalization and bureaucratization of heritage as a scientific field and remain essential to the operations of World Heritage making. They produce technical evaluations, monitor conservation progress, and provide training. In tandem with changing political orientations at UNESCO, their development evinces how the organization has shifted from a globally oriented humanist organization toward a pragmatic, intergovernmental organization focused on technical assistance rather than cultural and educational reform.[54]

During the first decades of the Convention's operation, UNESCO officials credit the success of the Committee to the presence of "high-level" specialists and the professionalism of the Secretariat and Advisory Bodies.[55] In 1979 another twenty-five properties were added to the list, including the Nubian Monuments from Abu Simbel to Philae, and the first site was inscribed on the List of World Heritage in Danger.[56] During these meetings the Committee also formulated procedures for deleting a property from the List. In 1980 Moenjodaro was inscribed; as with the inclusion of the Nubian monuments a year earlier, its listing served to further reinforce and validate UNESCO's long-term institutional efforts. More controversially that year, Jordan proposed the Old City of Jerusalem and Its Walls for inclusion on the World Heritage List and the List of World Heritage in Danger. Some 220 historic monuments were included in the dossier, among them the Dome of the Rock, built in the seventh century CE. The nomination was held over until 1981. In the first extraordinary session of the Committee a vote was taken and the Old City of Jerusalem was inscribed on both lists.[57] The US reaction was to withdraw its financial contribution to the World Heritage Fund on the grounds of politicization. For the United States, "politicization," the Australian ambassador to UNESCO, Gough Whitlam, told his British audience, means "the introduction of issues which they no longer have enough votes to exclude."[58]

In 1982 Jordan proposed hosting the World Heritage Committee meetings in 1982, but its offer was politely declined. The veiled reason was the "political sensitivity of issues related to Jerusalem and aware[ness] that any action which tended to increased politicisation of the World Heritage Convention could have adverse repercussions."[59] Throughout 1983 the Reagan administration continued to accuse UNESCO of politicization, financial mismanagement, and having an unworkable bureaucracy. The United States had previously suspended funds to UNESCO in 1977 when Israel's petition to be considered part of Europe was denied, costing the organization US$43 million in lost revenues.[60] Another point of contention was UNESCO's resolutions over Israel's illegal excavations in Jerusalem, an issue that has spanned decades, leading the organization to adopt something akin to "impasse management."[61]

The next major development, celebrating the twentieth anniversary of the Convention, was the establishment in 1992 of the World Heritage Centre.[62] Under Director-General Federico Mayor, cultural heritage was prioritized as he sought to renew the organization and "build a bastion of peace in the minds of all people."[63] Now with a unit of its own, World Heritage became the flagship program of UNESCO. Intercultural dialogue, cultural pluralism, and the universal culture of peace were again in the spotlight. However, the new Centre was immediately confronted with the Balkan crisis, the shelling of Dubrovnik's Old Town, and threats to other World Heritage sites.[64] This further underlined the failure to implement UNESCO's 1954 and 1972 Conventions as well the Geneva

Protocols.[65] Additional challenges included the lack of global diversity amongst sites inscribed as World Heritage, and in response the Global Strategy was launched in 1994 to ensure a more a representative, balanced, and credible list. In subsequent years, however, those inequities further deepened.[66] Despite the good intentions of global solidarity around recognition of a common, universal heritage to which all societies contribute, the limitations of an operationally effective and conceptually coherent regime produced, according to former French ambassador to UNESCO Jean Musitelli, a "mediocre result." Another growing concern was the burgeoning global tourism industry that UNESCO had once promoted as a means of linking culture and development. Now tourism was taking its toll on World Heritage sites such as Venice.[67] With a profoundly changed context in the decades following 1972, World Heritage was also expanding beyond the realm of conservation and was being called upon to shore up cultural identities, drive development, foster cooperation, promote rights, and generate tourism.

The 2000s were marked by escalating global conflict in which heritage sites were more ideologically and politically entwined, paralleled by further internal dissent among the states parties about the direction of the Convention. The year 2001 marked UNESCO's great failure to save the Bamiyan Buddhas from intentional destruction, although the fourth–fifth century CE monumental carved statues had not been inscribed on the World Heritage List.[68] They were subsequently destroyed despite the fact that UNESCO had a long history of involvement in Afghanistan and Bamiyan itself, supporting museums and conservation training.[69] Other failures included the Global Strategy described above, prompting growing tensions between Member States over the imbalance of the List: more than half the properties listed were in Europe and almost none were in the Pacific, in the Caribbean, or in parts of Africa. Despite the lack of representation and equity, more and more properties were being nominated and inscribed each year, often by the same small subset of nations. This brought the larger issue of credibility to the fore. At the same time, there were efforts to establish a more expansive understanding of World Heritage, moving from a purely monumentalist, "wonders of the world" perspective to a more anthropological conception based on a representative or comparative "selection of the best."[70] Collective decision-making and the overarching responsibility for the conservation of sites, once the remit of national delegates with heritage expertise, were gradually replaced by excessive backstage lobbying by politicians and the bargaining power of nations with geopolitical alliances based on geography, religion, or trade partnerships.

Structurally, most of the Member States had already ratified the Convention, and while signaling the treaty's success, its ratification also marked the end of new funding sources leading to pragmatic concerns over sustainability. More disastrous still was the third halt to US funding in 2011 after the admission of Palestine as a Member State to UNESCO. The assessed contribution of the United States is around 22 percent of UNESCO's total budget, yet with inflation and statutory increases, the accumulated loss is equivalent to 30 percent. In 2017 its unpaid dues amounted to almost US$550 million.[71] Additionally, the United States ceased all extra-budgetary funding to UNESCO, including its voluntary contribution to the World Heritage Fund.[72] Today that fund is operating with only US$4 million for all requests of international assistance. However, since the United States did not officially withdraw from the organization in 2011, only from its financial obligations, it was elected to the Executive Board in 2015 for a four-year term and continued to nominate sites to the List.[73] While not wanting to pay for the privilege of membership, the United States was intent on exerting influence across the organization and benefitting from the recognition that World Heritage listing bestows. Then in 2017, President Trump announced the US decision to the withdraw from the organization, while still retaining a permanent observer mission to UNESCO, to take effect on December 31, 2018.

Today the current financial shortfall negatively impacts the conservation and management of World Heritage properties, evaluation and monitoring missions, assistance with nominations, capacity-building, educational materials, information systems, and annual meetings. In view of the crisis, Director-General Irina Bokova made an appeal for further allocation of emergency funds to support the statutory functions of the Convention. Klaus Hüfner, who served on the German Commission to UNESCO, regards the financial crisis as a political issue.[74] He underlines that while European nations largely ignored the appeal, save for Scandinavian countries, the Arab states, including Algeria, Oman, Qatar, and Saudi Arabia, have responded positively. So too have African nations including Benin, Chad, Congo, Mauritius, and Namibia. Right from the beginning, when Julian Huxley's original budget was axed by the United States and his successor Jaime Torres Bodet faced a budget crisis, powerful Western states have acted unilaterally, effectively holding UNESCO to ransom over political issues where they cannot build consensus and thus ultimately cannot exercise control.[75] Thus the principle of collective responsibility, both ethical and fiscal, that was observed in the Nubian Campaign and was once so central to UNESCO's ideals has lost significant ground.

The Routinization of Charisma

During the early missions to Peru, Afghanistan, Syria, Egypt, and Pakistan, prior to the adoption of the 1972 Convention, UNESCO regularly called upon universities and academics from around the world for their expertise and collaboration. Gradually consultants, bureaucrats, and politicians replaced the contributions of intellectuals, particularly after World Heritage became an international arena for showcasing the outstanding sites of particular nations, rather than summoning all nations to save a handful of charismatic but endangered sites. Whereas Huxley envisaged an Executive Board of outstanding intellectuals, what he called the "leaders of civilization," without recourse to national provenience, others, such as the US delegate Reinhold Niebuhr, would only contemplate an assembly of state officials representing and answering to their respective Member States. The latter view has prevailed, and deliberations over global heritage from Abu Simbel to Bethlehem have since been susceptible to the whims of governments. The two developments went hand in hand: the internationally competitive process of listing sites and the ever-expanding national inventories with the rising prominence of governmental representatives who promote statist agendas and the decline of intellectual and research-driven contributions. Academics and universities would play a less prominent role than in Huxley's day, especially in archaeology, the result being that original research was replaced by report writing: discovery was supplanted by recovery. The international ties that bind, the moral obligation and fiscal responsibility to preserve heritage in all nations of the world as part of humanity's heritage, had also been sacrificed for national ambitions.

The creation of global patrimony has culminated in the routinization of charisma, in the sense of both UNESCO's own normative and technocratic trajectory as well as an international bureaucracy advancing its own agendas for World Heritage. Manufacturing and managing that global inventory, accompanied by the increasingly complex concomitant processes it generates—planning, nominating, upstreaming, monitoring, reporting, and updating—necessitates an equally complex and resource-hungry bureaucracy. During the 1970s and 1980s it still could have been said that the Convention was a mechanism for conservation. Yet in the last two decades the greatest shift has been away from preservation and toward a singular fixation on inscribing more and more sites on the List.[76] The States Parties to the Convention are the most powerful decision-makers in setting the World Heritage agenda, and with the implementation of their policies has come an escalating number of heritage disputes and disagreements. In response to this escalation, and in keeping with the conduct of diplomacy, UNESCO and its World Heritage program have increasingly advanced technocratic solutions, not only for conservation problems but also for political ones. In fact, each pillar of the Convention—the Secretariat, the Advisory Bodies, and the World Heritage Committee—routinely retreats from controversy through recourse to textual formalism and technical proceduralism.

Members of the Secretariat and the Advisory Bodies claim to have a superior normative and technical authority in World Heritage matters based on their knowledge and experience. UNESCO and its chosen experts have gradually extended their reach beyond the role of an intermediary in the World Heritage arena to that of "strong broker" or "objective broker."[77] Governing the world's heritage represents something both larger than the academy and also familiar and quotidian, the product of endless administration, site visits, report reading and writing, publications, and assessments.[78] Neither faceless nor neutral bureaucrats, members of UNESCO's Secretariat have advanced degrees in economics, law, or architecture. Some are perfectly aware of the academic critiques launched at the organization. Together they represent a group of people with very different backgrounds, national and disciplinary attachments, and levels of experience and commitment, loosely bound together for a single, global, and imagined mission.

Tracing how bureaucracy and routinization has shaped and constrained UNESCO's mission, the sites of social production, local interaction, and expression of norms requires access to archives and documents, meetings, and events, as well as individual accounts drawn from many avenues of World Heritage. Ethnographic studies of UNESCO's Secretariat suggest that high-level staff in Paris resolutely support the organization's mission and see themselves at the center of a vital global project. Yet many are critical of the bureaucratic logics at work, frustrated by the lack of funding, and worn down by political pressure applied from all sides. They express hope and cynicism simultaneously, asserting that UNESCO's principles help to create a better world while also recognizing that their ability to act is severely curtailed by bureaucracy and politics.[79] A less sanguine view, expressed by one long-serving official, was that "it's the bureaucrats that are the problem, not the politicians." Bureaucrats are invested in keeping their positions within the organization given the significant benefits, and so they are promoted or transferred but rarely ever fired—a situation that many States Parties find problematic. This, coupled with a resilient Eurocentric bias in staffing, constitutes a constant source of tension that is expressed by most delegations from Scandinavia to Latin America.[80] There are issues with the Secretariat's rule by expertise, which can be closely sutured to its members' national attachments. As anthropologist Michael Herzfeld observes, all bureaucracies hold the potential for caprice and no system is proof against self-interested manipulation.[81] Many States Parties would concur; the premise of a neutral international civil service committed to objectivity is pure fiction. The United States has made such indictments since UNESCO's founding, claiming that the agency was top-heavy; mismanaged and inefficient; mired in elitism, favoritism, and cronyism; and generally suffering from low morale.[82]

If "any international organization needs to be in a permanent state of rethinking and relearning," Mayor said, "it is UNESCO. It cannot be a faceless, thoughtless, insensitive and routinized bureaucracy."[83] However in light of the myriad complexities and conflicts involving heritage properties and the States Parties, World Heritage Centre officials defend and legitimize their priorities but rarely engage in substantive reflection upon their own role in such tensions. One unit chief described "suspending my academic side" while employed at UNESCO so as "to be objective," thus preventing her from speaking as an individual; instead she could comment only from "my position in the organization." Many senior employees tend to fall back on their neutral role as international civil servants, subservient to the whims of powerful nations, having little or no power to curb those nations' infractions or solve the broader problems of world peace in which World Heritage is increasingly entangled. "To work in UNESCO," Richard Hoggart wrote, "is sometimes to feel as though you live in an unprotected territory of boundless good intentions, pressed in from all sides by bodies with other, more practical, forceful and precise purposes."[84] Those purposes today are, more often than not, political and economic, generated by States Parties using conservation and cultural diplomacy to mask other high-profile agendas in ever-increasing circuits of geopolitical intrigue.

In recent years, with the growing number of sites being listed as World Heritage, the ability to conserve those sites and implement real programs has proportionately declined. On one hand, the Convention is a victim of its own success; on the other, it is a victim of geopolitics. That shift has been accompanied by another dramatic transformation through time, from its internationalizing and collaborative efforts to a heritage regime that serves distinctly national goals. Efforts to mobilize global attention upon sites in danger that required international assistance were significantly reduced, devolving into an exercise in branding within an ever more acquisitive heritage economy. Jean Musitelli argued twenty years ago that the World Heritage Centre lacked both the means and political authority to ensure that the spirit of the Convention was applied.[85] Suffering from "institutional anemia," the Centre is powerless to provide a regulatory regime, while states parties continue unhindered to erode the legitimacy of the Committee through their political maneuverings.

Of the 193 States Parties to the Convention, Musitelli claims that more than 100 had never held a seat on the World Heritage Committee, while a dozen nations had dominated from the outset. The distribution of seats on the Committee has also been biased toward Europe, coming to a head in 2013 when no African nation was selected, despite UNESCO singling out the continent as an agency-wide priority. Western European nations have the funds and capacity to pay consultants, prepare more professional dossiers, nominate more sites, and send more delegates to meetings to lobby. They deploy their resources and influence to mobilize their cultural wealth, achieving disproportionate representation on the list. For example, in one year Italy managed to inscribe ten sites (and continues to nominate sites each year). This is striking, since 166 out of the 193 States Parties to the Convention have inscribed fewer than ten sites in total.[86] As a general rule, one can also say that countries making the largest contributions to UNESCO tend to exert more influence on UNESCO's budget and programs.

Because UNESCO is an intergovernmental agency, states parties that are signatories to the Convention, and especially those with a seat on the World Heritage Committee, are the most powerful players. The Committee is made up of 21 States Parties, elected at a General Assembly, that currently serve a four-year term. Today state-appointed ambassadors and politicians, rather than cultural or natural heritage experts, dominate the national delegations. The Committee is the body responsible for the implementation of the World Heritage Convention; it oversees the use of the World Heritage Fund and allocates financial assistance as requested by states parties. Significantly, the Committee makes the final decision on whether a property is inscribed on the World Heritage List. It examines reports on the State of Conservation of inscribed properties and makes recommendations when properties are not being properly managed. It also decides on the inscription or deletion of properties on the List of World Heritage in Danger.[87] In light of its decision-making power, the stakes for Committee membership are high. Moreover, there is an acknowledged correlation between the countries represented on the Committee and the location of properties successfully inscribed on the World Heritage List. From 1977 to 2005, in 314 nominations, 42 percent benefitted those countries that served as members of the World Heritage Committee. This is striking when one considers that the twenty-one Committee members account for only about 11 percent of the total number of signatories to the Convention.[88] World Heritage status has increasingly become a capitalized commodity in a decidedly transactional sphere.

The annual World Heritage Committee sessions take place over ten days each year, days filled with meetings, side meetings, events, and receptions as well as endless diplomacy, lobbying, and negotiation.[89] In today's deliberations over World Heritage the conduct of conduct, to paraphrase Michel Foucault, has visibly changed.[90] Many hundreds of delegates, year after year, sit in dark, windowless, overly air-conditioned auditoriums in Phnom Penh, Doha, or Krakow, staying long into the evening. For those ten days they listen to repetitive bureaucratic procedures, shuffle papers, and respond to pressures from their governments or other nations, lobby groups, NGOs, the media, and observers. Perhaps it is not surprising, then, that many politicians and diplomats are not interested in the presentation of World Heritage properties and their concerns, as prepared by the Advisory Bodies and the Secretariat. As Bruno Latour argued for the law, the "relationship between appearances and reality . . . is meaningless here: appearances are everything, the content is nothing."[91] State agendas now eclipse substantive discussions of the merits of site nominations in tandem with issues raised over community benefits, the participation of indigenous stakeholders, or threats from mining, exploitation, or infrastructural development. Since delegations are now populated by politicians, not heritage experts, many are uninterested in conservation issues and the specificities of site borders, buffer zones, and management plans. One Brazilian representative put it succinctly when he rebuked the overly technical priorities of the Advisory Bodies, saying that the Committee "evaluates sites, not management plans."

Much of the utopian sentiment of intercultural exchange, cooperation, peace-building, and even global conservation through heritage has been replaced by international competition, conflicts, and politics that have little to do with the materiality of the past and much more to do with the economic, religious, ethnic, and territorial struggles of the twenty-first century. Over time, however, the aspirational aspect of this international treaty evaporated into a mechanism primarily for national accreditation of, branding of, and capitalizing on historic sites, rather than their protection. The entire arena of World Heritage has become more political and contentious, and in a parallel development, a landscape of paper is required to evaluate, monitor, and advise the States Parties, the Committee, and the world about the fate of the Convention and the List.

A *Landscape of Paper*

Given UNESCO's Parisian setting, there is some irony that the word "bureaucracy" is French in origin. It combines the French word for "desk" or "office" (bureau) with the Greek word for "rule" or "political power" (*kratos*). Rule by the writing desk, in the Weberian sense of domination through knowledge, encourages attention to the place and power of paperwork, together with its logics, language, and legacy.[92] Describing the vast quantity of texts UNESCO produces, one historian admitted it induced "a sense of vertigo" where one had the "feeling of being crushed."[93] British academic and former UNESCO Assistant Director-General for Culture Richard Hoggart was one of many to critique the organization's overly bureaucratic, paper-producing practices. Although an expert on literature and literacy, he had a loathing for much of UNESCO's penchant for paper. In his revealing yet scathing book, *An Idea and Its Servants: UNESCO from Within*, he wrote that in the basement of the Paris headquarters resides "a huge steel machine which grinds remorselessly. Its job is to shred the mountains of paper which UNESCO produces and discards each week. Lorries wait in the nearby loading bay to take the bales to some paper Valhalla or recycling Heaven. If an atom bomb destroyed UNESCO, that massive machine would be likely to survive. There would be some truth in what it would suggest to the survivors who came upon it: that this building had been a sort of temple to paper, to words; and that here, in this great stark machine, was the godhead."[94]

UNESCO, once described as the laboratory of ideas, is today less a think tank and more an international standard-setter and agency for branding, World Heritage being its most sought-after label.[95] One of its enduring missions is to collect facts from all over the world, in all aspects of its "areas of competence." Federico Mayor said that UNESCO "teaches us how to "swim" in an "ocean of facts."[96] Those facts are then circulated in a vast outpouring of publications: comparative statistics, periodic reports, audits, monitoring reports, and an endless succession of meetings where this information is analyzed, interpreted in new ways, and then set in motion across the globe.[97] They emanate not just from the World Heritage Centre in Paris but also from UNESCO regional offices, whether in Venice, Rio, Delhi, or Bangkok, or from its Category 2 Centers, established by host countries in Shanghai, Oslo, Milan, and Zacatecas, that are dedicated to capacity-building. Such tentacular bureaucratic mastery combines the extraordinary power of technical knowledge with the added knowledge derived from experience. This monopoly of administrative control has remained remarkably stable, withstanding political scandal, financial disaster, and changes of regime, "creating heavy technological and bureaucratic structures driven by pure inertia."[98] UNESCO's stability is partly due to the pervasive "system of files" that props up programs such as World Heritage, plus the effect of norms inculcated in its bureaucratic functionaries. By retreating into the circularity of referential chains UNESCO officials superimpose layer upon layer of documents, reports, plans, graphs, and statistics, much like archaeology itself, thus keeping information standard and intact across a play of transformations.[99] After the debilitating financial withdrawal by the United States in 2011, the World Heritage Centre continues its prodigious technocratic output, often at the behest of its Member States, to generate more reports, statistics, guidelines, and audits even on its own dwindling finances, thus utilizing more and more funds to demonstrate that it actually has less and less.

As an example of the proliferation of paper, the 1972 Convention's Operational Guidelines began as a 16-page document, while its most recent iteration stands at 170 pages. The guidelines cover different aspects of the articles of the World Heritage Convention, including instructions for completing nomination, reporting, and assistance request forms. Sophia Labadi describes it as a flexible, working document that can be revised at any time by the World Heritage Committee, and this has been done more than twelve times over the last forty years. This flexibility illustrates how interpretation might also evolve in light of current legal and social contexts, rather than strictly reinforce the original intent.[100] One positive example of changing interpretation by states parties involves the introduction of the "5Cs," or priorities for the World Heritage Convention (credibility, conservation, capacity-building, communication, and, added later, communities).[101] A more critical example is a recent revision to Paragraph 68 of the Operational Guidelines, a seemingly innocuous section on fact-checking and compliance in preparing World Heritage Tentative Lists. Committee debate in 2016 over wording and terminology, fact checking, map references, Web publication, and other technical matters masked a number of unspoken but deeply antagonistic territorial struggles between States Parties. One was China's strong objection to Japan nominating four islands in what they consider Chinese territorial waters.[102] The second was Palestine's opposition to Israel's listing of Jerusalem as an extension of the Old City of Jerusalem and Its Walls, proposed by Jordan and inscribed in 1981.[103] The neutrality of technical language, the proceduralism of drafting, and the cloak of diplomacy all serve to obfuscate the political breakdown and failures of multilateralism. On the other hand, with Israel and concerns over the State of Conservation in Jerusalem, many Western European nations refuse to address the technical, expertise-driven aspects of draft documents, considering them too political to touch. In this case, the political masks the ability to perform their statutory role on the World Heritage Committee.

States Parties have also contributed to the landscape of paper by generating massive dossiers for site nominations with thousands of pages that Committee members complain are impossible to read. Such nomination files for individual sites evolve over many years and cost millions, sometimes many millions, of dollars to produce. This is one response to deflect criticisms from the Advisory Bodies: they include more and more papers, files, and maps so as to stave off further unwanted revision, given the escalating expectation that every dossier will inevitably lead to inscription. The scale of these national resources indicates just how much the stakes have changed. States Parties petition other members aggressively for support before and during the meetings, especially in their efforts to have sites inscribed on the List. International alliances are cemented prior to properties being presented for debate, often through the prohibited practice of circulating signature sheets for countries to pledge their support in writing. Garnering signed amendments before the opening of the debate was officially prohibited in 2010.[104]

Specific texts are also prepared by nominating states and pre-circulated for verbal presentation by willing (or sometimes coerced) Committee members. Such speeches tend to be singularly effusive and elaborately orchestrated. Listening to the speakers in turn, it often sounds as if a single text has been crafted and then divided between delegations to read out in order. During such "illegal" performances, as when the United States prepared a statement for Zimbabwe to read out, delegates often struggle to make sense of, and to read aloud, the typed script before them. The intense scripting of statements of support now involves the complicity of almost all Committee members, guaranteeing a positive decision and ruling out all possibility of discussion about substantive heritage matters. World Heritage meetings now resemble a "market-place, an elaborate machine contrived to present, on a succession of concurrent stages, almost all the nations of the world addressing each other, at great length, but by procedures which ensure that genuine dialogue is ruled out."[105]

While States Parties script responses, endorsements, and rebukes in a self-serving fashion to ensure that their sites are listed and not endangered, their development agendas are retained, and their political positions and alliances are shored up, the Secretariat's own landscape of paper far outstrips them. Towering columns of drafts and documents produced by the World Heritage Centre, prepared and paid for by the host nation, can be seen on every delegation's desk during the meetings. In 2013 the cost of producing these texts for the Committee meeting in Qatar, including the reports themselves, translations, and technical assistance, was some US$600,000. The Secretariat spends the first few days presenting and presiding over exhaustive reports from the Center and the Advisory Bodies on the Convention, thematic programs, Category 2 Centers, the Global Strategy, periodic regional reporting, site-specific State of Conservation reports, sites in danger, site extensions and buffer zones, retrospective statements of Outstanding Universal Value, revision of the Operational Guidelines, policy guidelines, audits, working groups, financial reports, and requests for international assistance. Through the sheer weight of these pronouncements, documents are endowed with their own institutional power. Crafting a report often substitutes for work on the ground, just as the constitution of yet another "working group" during the Committee meetings substitutes for a decision or action taken, preventing change or progress within the organization and prolonging the status quo.

The weighty production of reports, which no delegation can fully digest, makes them appear less contestable, more expert, and technologically objective, masking the fact that they are products of social and political processes.[106] No document is innocent, Mayor wrote, still less those of an organization such as UNESCO. Instead one "needs to know how to read them in order to sense their inner meaning, how to select and classify them and see beyond the inevitable abridgements and rearrangements dictated by present-day reality."[107] The techno-politics of "guidance culture" at the World Heritage Centre relies on many layers of referential chains that prevent its employees from envisaging any real alternative.[108] The persuasiveness of form, correctness of language and logic, and referential deference to previous texts are all measures of drafting success. Neutral, even vague language and sentiment render organizational decision-making impersonal and generalized, in contrast to the politicized decisions taken by the Committee and individual States Parties.

These long-standing formulas for fashioning patrimony have global impacts, albeit in often unexpected and unpredictable ways that are typically occluded in official transcripts. While many World Heritage documents might bear the imprimatur of UNESCO, they are in fact crafted and edited by numerous national delegations, sometimes over days, with suggested language from the Centre, legal advice, further revision, and so on, all leading to a kind of textual schizophrenia in form and content. Deliberations over the destruction caused by the militant Islamic group Ansar Dine in the World Heritage sites of Timbuktu and Askia in Mali during 2012 provide a telling example. Preparing a draft declaration of condemnation of the attacks continued over several days at the meetings in St. Petersburg. Committee members wrangled for hours over wording such as "rehabilitation and reconstruction" and were plagued by problems of translation between the English and French terms for "safeguarding."[109]

Mexico asked for harsher wording, perhaps by using the word "repugnant'; Senegal suggested "barbaric"; Germany then asked to add "depriving young Africans and future generations." After so many drafts and amendments from the twenty-one-member Committee, the Russian chairwoman gave up in frustration, saying, "I understand how touched we are of all this sad event which happened in Mali . . . but we can't work like we work now." All of this was captured fleetingly on vast screens with bilingual track-changes documents running concurrently. The Malian delegation appealed to the Committee for assistance, albeit without specifying exactly how UNESCO might respond given the continuing violence. And while members were eager to find a solution, they were quickly frustrated by their inability to act or offer concrete solutions on the ground. Some delegations complained that such inaction called into question the Committee's integrity, while others were absorbed in debating the text of the draft statement. France quipped that since they were not addressing a State Party, they could be fairly sure that the perpetrators would neither read nor follow the declaration. The Russian ambassador vividly captured the predicament: "All we have are computers, papers and pens . . . you're dealing with bandits and criminals and we only have paper and pens."

Conclusions

From Mali to Moenjodaro, saving historic sites underscores the vast challenges for UNESCO's global conservation program. The slow pace of change documented for Moenjodaro followed by repetitive failures conjures up other spectacular failures of postwar development, such as the British-led East African Groundnut Scheme to cultivate peanuts in Tanzania despite inadequate rainfall and conditions. Sir Mortimer Wheeler wrote to his colleagues in exasperation that UNESCO was "a slow working organization" having "the most inefficient staff in the world."[110] Scientific missions were sent in 1964 and 1968 without archaeological consultation, he complained, the result being that all the time and energy involved were wasted. Complaining to J. O. Brew about the lack of progress on Moenjodaro, he retorted, "I do wish someone would inject a strong chemical under the tail of UNESCO."[111]

Tracing these international heritage projects over several decades allows us to follow their fate and funding and how this is often tethered, at the national level, to state objectives, understandings of modernity, and projections for the future. Internationally, the techno-politics of conserving Moenjodaro or Borobudur have been susceptible to the whims of specific nations and the global positioning of sites in international circuits of power and strategy. Managing the remarkable has involved constructing a vast apparatus of recommendations and conventions, listing and monitoring mechanisms, reports and audits, which themselves have produced the prodigious landscapes of paper of which Richard Hoggart wrote. Its culmination is unquestionably the 1972 Convention Concerning the Protection of the World Cultural and Natural Heritage, UNESCO's flagship program. Making World Heritage, or turning the mundane into the miraculous, has required from UNESCO considerable resilience and reinvention, balancing a presumptive universalism with myriad sovereign agendas while straddling its technocratic and sometimes utopian ambition.

Cultural heritage projects such as the Safeguarding Campaigns or the various heritage conventions have been housed and managed in many different units throughout UNESCO's history. Over the history of the organization, beginning in 1948, there have been no fewer than twenty different configurations: the Museums Section, Division of Museums and Historical Monuments, Monuments and Museums Section, Division of Cultural Heritage, Museum International Unit, and so on. This dizzying array of institutional arrangements also lends some insight into the perception of heritage at UNESCO throughout its history. There have been at least two types of technical managerialism: the first arose with UNESCO's international salvage campaigns and the second with the World Heritage List. With regard to the latter a further two moments remain key, the adoption of the World Heritage Convention in 1972 and the establishment of the World Heritage Centre in 1992. Through the history of the World Heritage Convention and its technical and normative functions, particular modes of conservation and management have been formalized alongside the global recognition of sites inscribed on the World Heritage List.

In tandem with these developments was the recognition that UNESCO's professionals and consultants similarly "reproduce their own status, identity and legitimacy in the technical order of conservation work."[112] As in other multilateral contexts, this is often achieved through something dull but respectable called "best practice."[113] So-called experts are not always capable of standing above the political fray and can easily end up representing their own governments. As we saw in the Nubian Monuments Campaign, the deployment of expertise in international projects is always inflected with a political valence, though typically masked by technical neutrality.[114] Jan Turtinen, an anthropologist working within UNESCO's Swedish delegation, argues convincingly that UNESCO not only organizes and disseminates culture but creates culture in its role as an influential international actor with the expertise to define and frame conditions, problems, and solutions.[115] Through technocratic means, members of the World Heritage Centre possess the power not simply to mobilize other specialists for conservation and restoration goals but also to direct the representations of particular historic sites, as we will see in Chapter 4.[116]

A recent challenge to their technical direction has come from the States Parties and the World Heritage Committee. Conservation has increasingly been supplanted by the lucrative potentials of World Heritage inscription and branding for tourist revenues and infrastructural development, continued challenges over territory, and reignited conflicts between states. Political problems such as these are often concealed as technical issues, and now all parties from the Secretariat and the Advisory Bodies to the Committee itself retreat into the bureaucracy and supposed neutrality of the organization to make any headway in achieving their goals. Managerial interventions are effectively used to "greas[e] the wheels of tired machineries and conflicting state positions."[117]

A further challenge has followed in the wake of the 2011 financial crisis, with program and staffing cuts. Today with a budget that amounts to little more than US$250 million annually (one-sixth of Cambridge University's, for example) and a dwindling staff, UNESCO is stretched.[118] This shortfall negatively impacts not only conservation and management of World Heritage properties but also evaluation and monitoring missions, assistance with nominations, capacity-building, educational materials, information systems, and annual meetings. By 2017 there were some six hundred unpaid interns from the elite corners of the globe offering their services at UNESCO's Paris headquarters. It has become an institution of volunteers, as well as temporary staff on short-term contracts, consultants, retired employees staying on, and a reduced regular staff trying to manage two or three posts each. Amidst financial ruin and harsh criticism from independent reviewers, bureaucracy continues to proliferate, as demonstrated by Director-General Bokova's Reform for Innovation @ UNESCO program. Bokova is no stranger to harsh criticism, whether from the British government or from her own native Bulgaria, and her proposed reform is made manifest in a two-meter-long display panel displayed in Paris: it is covered with minuscule, unreadable script, linked by scores of lines, arranged in a bewildering organogram.[119] UNESCO is less an ideas factory and more a matter of just managing the factory.

The charisma of World Heritage, and certainly its routinization, is being questioned from divergent quarters, from the states parties to NGOs, indigenous communities, and residents who live amidst the ruins. In the early campaigns, such as Moenjodaro, decisions were formulated around technical and technocratic goals, often at the expense of collaboration and the co-production of knowledge with researchers, local experts, and other stakeholders. By privileging conservation, with its myriad consultants and training schemes, UNESCO reinforced its own technical assistance and participation programs and its own structural raison d'être. After the Nubian experience UNESCO advanced its postwar conservation logic whereby recovery would replace discovery, so neatly demonstrated at Moenjodaro. Mayor claimed UNESCO had saved "this fabulous work of the creative imagination from the 'deadly embrace' of the River Indus."[120] The trouble was that if, after decades of foreign expert-driven preservationist programs, the recovery itself failed and there was no parallel advancement of knowledge or discovery, then UNESCO's efforts were similarly in ruins. Another problem was that the flow had become too one-way. Western preservationist ideologies and methods dominated, as did those same European nations when it came to the inscription of World Heritage sites and their own ambitions. The technical assistance offered to Egypt, Syria, Iraq, Afghanistan, and Pakistan, in Hoggart's words, created a technical cordon sanitaire, but its long-term promise of peace could not prevail.[121] The Upper Euphrates Dam project at Tabqa, where UNESCO at one time supported a salvage project, is near Raqqa, once an ISIS stronghold, and all six of the Syrian World Heritage sites are now endangered.[122]

4

Conservation

*Just as ensuring that archaeological monuments with-
stand the ravages of the elements, societies must also be
helped to conserve their songs and stories. Inculcation
of an instinct of conservation is the best antidote to the
exploitative tendency.*

—RAJIV GANDHI, 1985

ON NOVEMBER 6, 1966, floods ravaged Venice in what many claim was an
early warning of global climate change, presaging other disasters to come.
It was the perfect storm of high tides, rain-swollen rivers, and a sirocco
wind that filled the Venice Lagoon to bursting, sending a torrent of dirty
water through the canals. Floodwaters rose almost two meters above the
usual fluctuations to which Venetians had become accustomed. Thousands
of people were trapped, their homes and livelihoods ruined, along with
cultural treasures valued at US$6 billion. The flooding was not simply a
natural disaster: human interventions, including the industrialization of
the lagoon, destruction of sandbanks, and dredging the canals to allow
for large ships, played a role.[1] UNESCO rallied quickly with numerous
appeals. It constituted an advisory committee and a system of international contributions, and it mobilized teams of experts from other Western
nations to assist in the restoration effort. National committees were also
established; the United Kingdom and United States felt compelled to contribute when it came to Venice.[2]

During the 1960s and 1970s UNESCO was engaged in numerous
major safeguarding campaigns, often simultaneously, with an almost
military zeal against a world of destruction in Egypt, Sudan, Pakistan,
Tunisia, Syria, Indonesia, and Italy. As a preservationist war waged on
many continents, UNESCO launched conservation offensives, often in the
face of rising waters. Gaston Palewski, the French politician and Charles

de Gaulle's *homme de confiance*, was enlisted in what became known as "the struggle for Venice" and by 1972 was addressing his audience with Churchill's famous phrase, "This is not the end. This is not even the beginning of the end. But it is, perhaps, the end of the beginning."[3] The former French ambassador to Italy realized that any "isolated and small-scale action was insufficient" and convinced his "eminent friend" and fellow Frenchman René Maheu to recruit UNESCO for the task, and in doing so took credit for the entire international operation. Cementing their bilateral relationship further, Palewski claimed "it was the French who as a whole have voted for Venice." Being both a decorated soldier and member of the Académie des Beaux-Arts, Palewski could not resist a final flamboyance, stating, "Nor will it be in vain that the buffoons and dwarfs, the harlequins and masks of Venetian comedy have mocked the inadequacy of our efforts and the futility of our disagreements. Once again Venice will have conquered; once again its victory will have been universal."[4]

In 2016, fifty years after the floods, the World Heritage Committee was again intensely debating the State of Conservation of Venice and its lagoon. But this time it was patently the work of humans, rather than nature, that was the problem. The Secretariat and Advisory Bodies outlined the myriad threats to Venice: the presence of oil tankers and enormous cruise ships, a new airport, large buildings and other construction, infrastructure projects, the touristic transformation of historic buildings, and the massive scale of tourism and its impact on every aspect of Venetian life. The conservation report laid the blame squarely with the Italian authorities; they had overexploited both cultural and natural resources, uncontrolled tourism had weakened the resilience of living communities, and the many additional proposed infrastructure developments would lead to further irreversible changes. The authenticity and integrity of Venice were considered highly vulnerable. A reversal would be neither quick nor easy, ICOMOS warned, and a new vision with new approaches and strategic planning was urgently needed. Many members of the World Heritage Committee were dismayed. Venice was clearly in danger and yet the Committee had studiously avoided discussion of the site for decades. Europa Nostra, a recognized NGO partner of UNESCO and the leading federation for cultural heritage in Europe, was founded in response to the 1966 Venice floods.[5] Its representatives told the Committee that Venice was the most endangered site in Europe and, for all the reasons presented, UNESCO should place Venice and its Lagoon on the List of World Heritage in Danger. Many speakers emotionally described the site as iconic in UNESCO's history, and its sustained preservation was at the very heart of the World Heritage Convention. And there was also the issue of financial assistance. UNESCO's program for Safeguarding Venice has included more than 1,500 projects and cost more than €50 million.[6] Even more remarkably, UNESCO has over the years established not one but two offices in Venice, one a regional bureau, the other dedicated to Venice itself. I had recently visited both offices while witnessing for myself the effects of rising waters and pollution: gigantic cruise ships looming over St. Mark's Square, uncontrolled tourism coupled with the mass exodus of residents, and angry Venetians protesting against their local officials.

Members of the World Heritage Committee voiced their concern: Venice was indeed in danger and would require a new safeguarding campaign. Jad Tabet, the Lebanese delegate, argued that the Committee could not keep giving Italy more and more time as the situation worsened year by year. Privately he had been pressured from various quarters not to pursue publicly the issue of Venice, but he had steadfastly resisted. Toward the end of discussion Francesco Bandarin, Assistant Director-General for Culture and former director of the World Heritage Centre, took the floor to make an impassioned speech. He began by saying, "I am a citizen of Venice, this is the place where I was born, this is my city. As such, I should

FIGURE 4.1 St. Mark's Square, Venice, Italy, courtesy of Shutterstock

not dare making any comment, because, as the proverb says: *Nemo Propheta in Patria*."[7] He recalled vividly the 1966 floods when "the people of Venice and Italy, massively supported by the world's public opinion, raised their voice, and a major safeguarding program, spearheaded by UNESCO, largely financed and implemented by the Italian Government and supported by many international organizations and committees, was launched. Venice became one of the symbols of the international cooperation for heritage conservation, a star in the UNESCO constellation of safeguarding campaigns." Bandarin then went on to describe the current risk, saying, "Venice seems to have lost its capacity to define its future, and can become the prey of sectorial interests, be they called mass tourism, the harbour economy, infrastructures, boat and ship traffic, the exploitation of the natural environment . . . This is why it is again time for the International Community that you represent in this moment—obviously jointly with the Government of Italy and the City, and the National and International NGOs concerned for its future—to help Venice finding its directions for the future." As we watched and listened, a carefully scripted endorsement and plea for further assistance and cooperation unfolded, coming directly from UNESCO's highest levels. Venice was given a year's grace.

The example of Venice underscores how national prestige, economic revenues, and the international bargaining potential that World Heritage bestows now eclipse the conservation of historic sites. UNESCO is largely synonymous with a vision of global heritage encapsulated by the World Heritage brand, and once that status is achieved for a given site, States Parties will go to considerable extremes to stave off any curtailment. The Convention's original mandate to protect and conserve the world's most important heritage places has gradually been replaced by an international desire to secure and mobilize that brand. For UNESCO conservation "is not only 'words on paper' but is above all a useful instrument for concrete action."[8] That action is largely overarching and managerial, setting the framework by which states parties ensure the "identification, protection, conservation, presentation and transmission to future generations of the cultural and natural heritage situated on its territory."[9] Each country is required to adopt effective measures that include planning, policy-making, protection services, technical studies of conservation, training, and implementing the legal, scientific, technical, administrative, and financial measures necessary for protection and presentation.

Conservation is thus systemic and relational, premised on the management and monitoring of sites, rather than simply the techniques of conservation science employed on the ground. It operates as a "total social fact" because UNESCO's understanding of conservation has ramifications throughout society, in economic, legal, political, and religious domains.[10] The Convention's position on conservation is heavily technocratic and tethered to the principles of the safeguarding missions, namely, managing risk.[11] Saving threatened sites such as Venice is now extended on a global scale to include Angkor Wat, the Giza Pyramids, and Delphi in Greece. These are just some of UNESCO's self-declared success stories. Those listed sites, now more than one thousand, and their attendant protective systems must be then routinely monitored and reported upon.[12] However, this ethos of salvage is not necessarily paramount for the Member States that view the Convention instead as a prestigious contest of selection, inventorying, accrediting, and promotion.

UNESCO's early campaigns were directed at outstanding sites facing imminent danger, such as Abu Simbel or Moenjodaro, warranting both rescue and sometimes research, premised upon assistance and coopera- tion under the framework of internationalism and multilateralism. The or- ganization was responsive to conservation threats wherever they occurred in the world rather than privileging any particular region. When the con- cept of the World Heritage List took root it created a competitive process of inscribing sites, and European nations dominated, having greater re- sources, capacity, and political leverage. Sites are now enshrined on the list for purely national reasons, albeit premised on the putative international value of these places and the already receding concepts of a common hu- manity and one-worldism. From the very start of the list, sites such as the City of Quito, the Island of Gorée, and the Galápagos Islands were listed regardless of their conservation status, and some of these emblematic sites would later become endangered, in that way reversing the previous trend of the Safeguarding Campaigns, where protection was the first priority. The foundational principle of conservation has been gradually sidelined, just as the time devoted to conservation issues in World Heritage sessions has decreased.

On the positive side, the status the World Heritage label bestows ensures that a global public is more aware of conservation issues. It is easy to imagine that without the Convention, industrialized development would have proceeded unchecked. On the negative side, the List creates a com- petitive arena for nationalist aspirations and rivalries where conservation priorities are increasingly outstripped by the potential developments that accompany the World Heritage brand. In the past decade it has also been about securing and keeping the label in tandem with development, exploitation, and commercialism, as in Venice, Vicenza, Vienna, Kiev, London, and Bordeaux. European nations are particularly egregious in this regard. Countries such as Italy, France, Germany, Spain, and the United Kingdom have relentlessly marketed the UNESCO brand, taking full advantage of their long experience within the World Heritage system, at the expense of the conservation principles it represents. Poorer, less powerful nations are more readily criticized and have less bargaining power to fend off censure. Conservation, once so central to UNESCO's mission and the raison d'être of the 1972 Convention, is now itself in danger.

Reversals of Fortune

In the aftermath of the 2016 World Heritage Committee meetings in Istanbul many delegates were shocked that the outcome for Italy was so different from that for nations in the developing world. The dominance of Europe in World Heritage and, within that, the dominance of Italy, which has the most sites on the List, is a point of contention. Venice was supposedly the "jewel in the crown" of World Heritage, inscribed almost uniquely on all six cultural criteria. Less glittering, however, were the EU reports accusing Italy of mismanagement of heritage funds and poor conservation in its other World Heritage sites.[13] With Venice the twenty-one official bodies that are involved in its overall management are poorly coordinated and have no binding power, thus signaling their technocratic failure. One Italian official at the UNESCO office in Venice bemoaned that it had taken her two years to arrange a meeting with just nine of those representatives.

The state has also been criticized for its unwillingness to provide the necessary funds for preservation and for excluding NGOs and civil society organizations. Thus further scrutiny into Venice "would not only be embarrassing for the Italian government, which regularly uses its cultural assets and conservation know-how as an instrument of foreign policy, but would also lead to the close and potentially unwelcome monitoring of Venice."[14] On exactly that point, diplomats from Kuwait, Azerbaijan, and Tunisia recalled the aid provided by Italy along with its participation and competence, as if these initiatives might allow the State Party a free pass. They "seemed to confuse Italy's visible support of world heritage (for example, the 60 carabinieri now in training to protect monuments in war zones) with the capacity of decentralized government to deal with the complex, long-term problems presented by Venice and its lagoon."[15]

Undeterred, other members of the Committee called upon the Italian government to pledge that conservation issues would be addressed.

What unfolded before us during the Istanbul meetings was a display of European exceptionalism. Director-General Maheu confronted the same issue of Italy's fiscal and moral responsibility with similar recourse to exceptionalism when he addressed Member States during the first international appeal for Venice. This was particularly stark in light of salvage campaigns launched in developing nations. In 1973 the developed, urban, and romanticized context of Italy stood in stark contrast with UNESCO's rescue missions to Egypt, Pakistan, Syria, and Tunisia. "Perhaps some people will say, have said, that Italy has the intellectual and material resources to provide on her own for study of the natural phenomena and the human environment, for the necessary work for physical defense of the city and the lagoon, even for preservation of the historic heritage. They will say that the funds available under the law will amply cover the work that can actually be carried through in the next five years. They will say, they are saying, that there are other crying needs in the world, other cases of distress, and that the energies and generosity of foreign countries could more usefully be directed elsewhere."[16] Talking of "aid or assistance" would be "an insult to Italy . . . a country as developed and richly endowed"; instead it was a matter of cooperation and of course an "association to the mutual advantage of the parties concerned."[17] Thus the benefits of cooperation would flow from Italy to other Western nations affording the latter access by means of their technocratic and financial capacity: France, Sweden, Switzerland, Germany, Australia, the United States, and the United Kingdom. Eager to dispel further misinformation, Maheu exhorted, "The safeguarding of Venice is not a work of charity in aid of a princess fallen from high estate. It is an undertaking that may serve as an example for the solution of certain essential problems of the urban civilization of our time. It is not a mummification of the past but a field for construction of the future."[18] Maheu, like the Advisory Committee for Venice, was at pains to uphold Venice'sexceptional standing in the face of "the excessively widespread ignorance of the real Venice"; focusing on the dangers might convey the erroneous impression that Venice is "sick and dying."[19]

Thomas Mann had famously written that "the city was sick and was disguising the fact so it could go on making money" in his 1912 novel *Death in Venice*. Perceptively, he portrayed Venice as "half fairy tale, half tourist trap."[20] The city's problems were indeed systemic. As British art historian

John Pope-Hennessy insisted, "It was not just a matter of the flood; rather it was a matter of what the flood revealed, of the havoc wrought by generations of neglect." In the 1960s experts warned that Venice had "lived off tourists, and almost none of the money they brought into the city was put back into the maintenance of its monuments. And that had been aggravated by problems of pollution, an issue of the utmost gravity."[21] Gaston Palewski was correct in describing the situation as a "permanent disaster and one which is developing with frightening rapidity."[22] Corporatization and corruption have also been increasingly entangled with the fate of such sites. Such are the long-term conservation crises facing celebrated European settings including Pompeii and Venice, two of the most famous and critically endangered properties on the list that have miraculously escaped World Heritage Committee censure.

Pompeii was a bustling Roman town till it was engulfed by the eruption of Vesuvius in 79 CE; today it is one of the world's most famous archaeological sites, progressively excavated since the eighteenth century. Classicist Mary Beard, in appealing for some proportion over Pompeii, describes it as "a jerry-built town, destroyed by a volcano, fairly roughly excavated for many years, then bombed by the allies in World War II."[23] It has received many millions of euros over many years to support conservation and restoration, and yet little of the sprawling settlement is actually open to the public. Entire buildings are covered with rusty scaffolding, joined by a sea of unnecessary fittings or couplers, since contractors base their quotes on the number of couplers supplied. Pompeii's villas with their deteriorating mosaics and wall paintings are propped up by ugly wooden and metal supports. Walls frequently collapse, modern cement is used everywhere, and vegetation has overrun the ancient buildings, causing further decay. Overrestoration in the amphitheater, which resulted in further damage to the site, cost the astonishing sum of US$8 million—which was in large part siphoned off by the contractor.

Like Venice, Pompeii has had widespread international media coverage of Mafia corruption.[24] UNESCO's 2014 State of Conservation report for Pompeii listed key threat areas in a seventy-page report: financial resources, housing, human resources, tourism impacts, poor site management, insufficient monitoring and provision of guards, poor drainage and solid waste management, ongoing structural collapse, and the lack of an effective management plan. Of the many famous frescoed villas at Pompeii, most are closed and many are neither restored nor even protected but simply left open to the elements and therefore to risk.[25] Yet within the

FIGURE 4.2 Pompeii archaeological site, Italy, courtesy of the author

World Heritage Committee there has been scant discussion of Pompeii, much like Venice. On the other hand, some sites that are routinely criticized in World Heritage circles, such as Machu Picchu, are adequately managed, employ indigenous conservation strategies, and maintain good relationships with local communities. What accounts for such inequities?

Given UNESCO's multilateral setting, it is during the annual World Heritage Committee meetings that lobbying and decision-making about individual properties and their conservation take place. A handful of countries are immensely influential. Many others cannot afford to send their representatives to participate. Certain indices divide powerful nations from poorer ones: international profile and perception of the State Party; candidature on the World Heritage Committee; influence within the Committee, within the World Heritage Centre, and across UNESCO and the UN; nomination activity; perceived level of (Western) expertise; record of donor aid abroad; and corridor diplomacy and capacity to send national representatives to international meetings, with other tactics of political leverage.[26]

To take an example of the influence that profile and perception exert, sociologist Victoria Reyes has shown how, in World Heritage, "symbolic wealth is heavily dominated by just two countries: Italy and Spain," and to a lesser extent by France. Coding each inscribed cultural site's description for words referencing Italian, Spanish, and French influences, and excluding those sites within France, Greece, Italy, and Spain, she found that "31% (166 of 536) of the remaining cultural sites indicated an Italian influence in their site descriptions, while 10% (51) were influenced by Spain." For Reyes the "distribution of World Heritage cultural sites across both cultural regions and countries masks their content, since two or three countries have a worldwide impact on local cultural values. Sites considered to have 'Outstanding Universal Value' are those inspired by Italy, Spain, and France."[27] Given Italy's exceptional standing and having the greatest number of inscribed sites on the list, conservation criticisms have been muted, if not silenced. However, with emerging nations such as India, South Africa, or Panama, threatened sites are brought forward to the Committee for debate but then expeditiously tamped down and their detractors suppressed through coordinated and strategic alliances. While the suppression of detractors involves covert maneuvers, strategic alliances operate more overtly and occur during Committee sessions that can now be traced and live-streamed for the world to see. Jad Tabet from Lebanon said it best: "Millions of people throughout the world are following what we are doing here, what are they going to say. They are going to say what these people are interested in are their own interests."[28]

A salient example of expert maneuvering, captured in the media spotlight of World Heritage meetings is the political pacting of Brazil, Russia, India, China, and South Africa. The solidarity of this group, known as BRICS, hinges on advancing their own emergent politico-economic power in opposition to the older-style developed G8 countries, rather than any particular regional or religious alliance. In multilateral organizations blocs are typically forged around continental, regional, religious, economic, ideological, and even former colonial relationships to achieve certain shared objectives. BRICS nations deploy both formal and informal influence to enhance the international recognition of their heritage, enabling unhindered development regardless of the constraints of conservation. In recent years all five nations have served on the World Heritage Committee and during that time have expressed an overt public dissatisfaction with the recommendations of the Advisory Bodies.[29] Brazil, China, and South Africa served on the 2011 World Heritage Committee and Russia, India, and South Africa served in 2012 and 2013.

If we examine the number of years served on the World Heritage Committee between 2003 and 2013, the number of nominations to the list, and the number of delegates participating at sessions, then India, China, Russia, and South Africa are in the top echelon.[30] Considering verbal interventions during that same decade as a proxy for international profile and influence in decision-making, these three BRICS nations have repeatedly, and successfully, challenged the recommendations of ICOMOS and the IUCN. Significantly, India was the most outspoken member of the World Heritage Committee during its last tenure, between 2011 and 2015.[31] In theory, only the twenty-one members of the Committee are empowered to speak during the sessions, whereas all the rest are considered observer states. Members of the Committee are, first and foremost, state representatives who are free to pursue their own national interests, maximize power, push their economic self-interest, and minimize their transaction costs. National imperatives and economic necessities now prove more binding than any ethical norms related to the international and intergovernmental responsibility over the protection of World Heritage as defined in the World Heritage Convention.[32]

India has been extremely influential and persuasive. It has secured many new sites on the list and protected the status of those already inscribed, even in the face of mounting criticism over their preservation. One such example is the Group of Monuments at Hampi, the capital of the last great Hindu kingdom, Vijayanagara. Abandoned in the sixteenth century, this remarkable archaeological landscape was inscribed on the World Heritage List in 1986 and then on the List of World Heritage in Danger between 1999 and 2006 after the construction of two suspension bridges. This checkered conservation past came to a head again in 2010 when the Archaeological Survey of India took control of the Virupaksha Temple and Hampi Bazaar and declared its residents to be squatters and stripped them of any legal rights. The stalls, shops, restaurants, and dwellings around the main temple were deemed illegal encroachments despite having their own living histories. Then in July 2011 bulldozers leveled shops, stalls, and hotels, damaging the original medieval fabric of the bazaar in their wake. More demolition and destruction happened during the next summer.

Neither the Integrated Management Plan for Hampi nor UNESCO itself had recommended the removal of the local population from the bazaar.[33] Indeed, commercial activity in Hampi Bazaar was in accordance with the site's medieval tradition, according to archaeologists, and part of its living heritage. Despite protests, however, the problem remains that these traditions are seen as modern and intrusive, detracting from ancient monumentalities rather than giving life to them, unmistakably reflected in their static "group of monuments" designation. Instead of viewing Hampi as a cultural landscape with ancient and living components, the vast site has been conceived as some sixteen hundred monuments within a sanitized zone. With such an architectural and monumental conservation focus, the community is effectively sidelined, and many villagers blame both the archaeologists and UNESCO for their plight.[34] When I spoke to former Hampi residents in 2016 about the relocation and the ensuing destruction of their houses and shops, they complained that there was that no community consultation and that the evictions occurred without adequate warning or preparation. Moreover, various other intrusive structures across the site remained intact, revealing the contradictions, inconsistencies, and corruption, all of which combine to create a sense of embittered alienation. An example of what Michael Herzfeld calls "spatial cleansing": the Indian government's deployment of a "conservation" program against its own citizens, transforming long-term residents into inauthentic intruders.[35]

Given the graphic images of the bulldozed bazaar, together with a collapsed bridge that killed eight workers—the same bridge that incurred the danger listing and on which construction had been halted nine years earlier—ICOMOS presented a dire report to the World Heritage Committee in 2013.[36] Given the seriousness of the situation, ICOMOS recommended sending a reactive monitoring mission to India.[37] There were various difficulties the Indian authorities had to resolve. They had to clear the debris from the collapsed bridge, relocate a new bridge outside of the property, submit the final integrated management plan, and, "in

FIGURE 4.3 Virupaksha Temple, Hampi, India, courtesy of Shutterstock

close cooperation with the local community, [develop] a strategy and action plan for the bazaar."[38] Furthermore, "the World Heritage Centre and the Advisory Bodies consider[ed] that the living function of the Virupaksha temple needs to be recognized as supporting the Outstanding Universal Value of the property. They are of the view that the relationship between modern use and protection of the fabric and setting of the Virupaksha temple needs to be managed with the utmost sensitivity."[39] People had to be part of the picture, and India with its great tradition of living heritage would need to find a balance between the religious ruins of the past and religious practices of the present.

India swiftly mobilized its BRICS allies and blocked the World Heritage Committee from requesting that the State Party host a monitoring mission. In a carefully scripted statement, the Russian ambassador imme-diately countered that Hampi was an exceptional archaeological site and there was no need to send an independent mission to assess the State of Conservation. Instead she suggested that the local UNESCO office in India simply liaise with the State Party. South Africa, another BRICS partner, concurred. Conversely, Senegal insisted that an independent mission was needed for proper assessment, and Switzerland agreed. But Russia and South Africa proved too powerful; joined by Malaysia, Qatar, Iraq, Ethiopia, Algeria, and the United Arab Emirates, they managed to quash the matter of the mission. India would continue to go on as it had started, without impartial and international conservation oversight, evading cen-sure and scrutiny, resulting in future incursions for Hampi residents and risks to their heritage. During the overlapping tenure of BRICS members on the Committee they have successfully defended each other's infra-structural, extractive, and exploitative projects while retaining the coveted World Heritage brand for their sites. Similarly, they strategized effectively to protect their international interests abroad, ensuring the conservation label for powerful partners such as Panama, despite the destruction and dereliction that were unfolding.

The Unsightliness of History

The Historic District of Panama was the first European settlement on the Pacific coast of the Americas, founded in 1519 CE. The original city was destroyed by pirates in 1671 and officially moved to a new fortified site in 1673. It was inscribed as World Heritage in 1997 for its unique blending of Spanish, French, and early American architecture and later extended in

2003 to include the archaeological site of Panama Viejo.[40] Panama's strategic position enabled colonial Spain to expand its rule throughout the New World. Today that same strategic access has allowed the Panamanian government to hold hostage historic sites and impoverished residents. World Heritage now jostles between the recognition of empires: one looking back to the sixteenth century and the other poised toward the future, both capitalist projects, both committed to controlling an oceangoing trade.

The threat to the Historic District of Panama from the construction of the Cinta Costera maritime highway was debated in 2013, as it had been for eight years at that point, consuming countless hours of Committee time. Yet more time was spent discussing the property, and lobbying, away from the official venues. The Cinta Costera included reclamation of around thirty hectares of land in Panama Bay to accommodate a four-lane highway costing US$189 million. The Brazilian company Norberto Odebrecht constructed the seven-kilometer-long road, which includes a breakwater and two elevated viaducts that encircle and endanger the World Heritage site.[41] All three project phases cost some US$800 million, and Odebrecht had previously garnered government contracts worth nearly US$3.5 billion.[42] During the 2012 World Heritage Committee meetings in St. Petersburg, Panama denied the existence of the viaduct, even after a series of damning photographs of the construction were repeatedly projected onto the screen, revealing vast pylons sunk into the sea around the historic settlement. When questioned, the State Party denied that the photos were evidence of a viaduct and affirmed that the Cinta Costera project had not begun.[43]

Defined by the limits of diplomacy, representatives from the World Heritage Centre were unable to challenge or contradict the State Party and could only politely gesture to the photographic evidence in response. In some surrealist sense of "this is not a construction," those attending the World Heritage Committee sessions, including international delegations, official observers, academics, journalists, and NGOs, were being asked to suspend disbelief. Later that year a video was leaked that revealed plans for Nuevo Amador, a two-hundred-hectare high-rise district resembling Dubai, at the entrance to the Panama Canal. This further fueled suspicions that the raison d'être for the viaduct was less about traffic, as conveyed to the Panamanian people, and more about unregulated development and economic ambition. While the government first denied the scheme, video footage showing the Panamanian president, Ricardo Martinelli, holding plans soon led to a retraction.

FIGURE 4.4 Panama City, Panama, courtesy of Shutterstock

With a country like Panama, so strategically positioned and with powerful allies, heritage protection can be effectively elided, destruction tolerated, and integrity imperiled. Retaining the UNESCO trademark, however, was vitally important despite the undermining of site preservation. The World Heritage brand was part of the overall economic strategy, since many investors had poured money into the Historic District expecting that the designation would elevate property values. For the state and the developer alike, the project was designed to encourage coastal development and add value. What remains of the Historic District today is the town layout, a complex grid with streets and blocks of different widths and sizes and fortifications that was considered to be, at the time of inscription, an exceptional example of seventeenth-century colonial town planning in the Americas.

Circumventing the Historic District with a highway has not enhanced its position; rather, it has choked off the region's views, created unwanted noise and pollution, and essentially quarantined the area and surrounded it with new development and highways. In 2012, the Via Cincuentenario cut through the archaeological complex of Panama Viejo, damaging the archaeology and destroying parts of standing monuments including La

Merced, San Francisco, Casas Sur, and La Alhóndiga. The near invisibility of Panama Viejo in broader discussions of threats and dangers is clear: the archaeological site has no economic value, cannot be further developed, and is thus of little relevance to the government.

The Brazilian company Norberto Odebrecht has since been charged with bribery and corruption in several countries.[44] Odebrecht enjoyed a long and profitable history with the Panamanian government, blurring the boundaries between culture and commerce on many occasions. Executives from Norberto Odebrecht sat with the national delegation representing Panama at the UNESCO sessions in Cambodia in 2013, and two of them were listed as heritage officials with the National Institute of Culture (INAC).[45] On three different occasions Panama has extended paid invitations to all twenty-one delegations to the World Heritage Committee to visit Panama, and many accepted.[46] Members of UNESCO's Secretariat were also invited, but declined and offered to meet in Paris instead.[47] World Heritage sites, by definition, have always operated within a global economy of prestige, but we are currently witnessing a scaling up of operations. Excessive and expensive lobbying is de rigueur, especially if countries and their corporate partners are going to convince Committee members that they can both conserve and capitalize culture simultaneously. Sophia Labadi has similarly documented how branding and title accumulation in Liverpool, the World Heritage–listed Maritime-Mercantile City, has both encouraged renovation and led to a large-scale development program that now threatens the property.[48] Instead of salvaging sites or shoring up ancient buildings, the Convention is being used to prop up state projects, gentrification, mining, logging, and construction—indeed, to prop up state ambitions.

During the July 2013 UNESCO meetings in Cambodia many hours of live-streamed Committee sessions were consumed by Panama. BRICS representatives dismissed more photographs confirming the existence of the viaduct; the extents of buffer zones, exclusion zones, and impacts to visual integrity were refuted, so much so that the UNESCO Secretariat and legal advisors were called upon.[49] South African ambassador Dolana Msimang gestured to photographs of the sixteenth-century buildings, saying, "There are already unsightly village[s] or whatever around the site itself, and for me I think it does improve, the viaduct, the viaduct improves the view and it sort of cordons off the unsightliness and packages the site much better than what it was." Irrespective of the substitution of an unfinished Brazilian viaduct for Spanish colonial heritage, she persisted and, in agreement with India and Qatar, asserted that "from the bridge itself you now have a better viewing point of the site which you didn't have before . . . this actually does enhance the heritage site rather than hinders it." India argued that the viaduct "added" to the property, much like the Golden Gate Bridge or the Sydney Harbor Bridge. For BRICS partners the viaduct does not detract from the value of the historic site; instead it adds value. It cordons off the unsightliness of history. In this astonishing turn of events, the highway *becomes* the World Heritage site and improves it as a modern installation, in contrast to the poorly maintained historic district.[50] This inversion undermines the credibility of the Committee and the Convention, effectively jettisoning conservation from their remit.

Two days and three meetings later a decision was presented to the Committee *not* to inscribe Panama Viejo on the List of World Heritage in Danger. Instead there would be several more years of extensions, delaying tactics, and other obfuscations. Furthermore, since the construction work by Odebrecht has been completed, UNESCO is powerless to safeguard the site. Today it can only lament the demolition and severe deterioration of historic buildings that has transpired in tandem with further urban development. Panama has still not addressed the substantive problems with legislation and management. There is still no conservation plan and the historic structures are not being maintained.[51] The World Heritage Centre also noted unresolved conflicts of interest and displacement of local residents, much as in Hampi. The example of the Historic District of Panama reminds us that it is typically the local communities living in and around sites that have the most to lose with the capitalization of culture.

BRICS members serving on the Committee might easily dismiss the World Heritage property as a collection of "unsightly villages" in comparison with the Panama Canal, which has global politico-economic consequence.[52] Patrimony and progress are thus inseparable. In this highly inventive scenario the Cinta Costera was transformed into global patrimony at the expense of the Spanish colonial settlement. Indeed, everything looks better from the bridge, as the South African ambassador opined. After the 2013 decision, Panama publicly expressed its gratitude to "other peer persons specially to Mr. Oberoi, Ambassador Oberoi [India], Madame Mitrofanova from Russia, and our dear friend the delegate from Brazil that is always around us, helping on those issues and giving us the best advice."[53] This further reinforces BRICS pacting and influence, the idea that international economic interests trump local sociopolitical concerns, and the belief that World Heritage, while not significant enough to conserve, is so closely sutured to national pride and global competition that its brand cannot willingly be jettisoned.

The 1972 Convention Concerning the Protection of the World Cultural and Natural Heritage is not so much about protection anymore, but instead about branding, marketing, and promoting ever more inscriptions in an increasingly acquisitive heritage economy. The original intent of the Convention, the duties and obligations of states bound together by a legal instrument, has been increasingly relegated to history. It has become a matter of keeping while giving, to use Annette Weiner's famous phrase.[54] This entails keeping the World Heritage label at all cost as an inalienable right while at the same time sacrificing site preservation, and often the living communities that have the most to lose as long-term stewards of the past. In this regard the regional grouping of Europe and North America is statistically the worst offender, but the trend has increasingly become a global issue.[55] Conserving the past is no longer focused on *developing strategies* for material remains; quite the reverse—it is about *strategic development*. For the states parties to the Convention, conservation might be understood as a normative set of measures, virtues, and expectations that are further entangled in a widening web of reciprocities and relationships. Global conservation efforts serve a broad array of purposes, from the Cold War political and developmental agendas with Abu Simbel to today's vast transnational cultural and economic empire of the Silk Road. Internationalism is being reinvigorated through the circulating "global goods" of cultural preservation to fulfill the needs of nation-states, by pragmatic and sometimes pernicious means.

Restoring Internationalism

Conserving the past is a recognized global good that nation-states can promote as a sign of their modernity, progress, and international citizenship. Not only is the preservation effort a mark of recognition, but the process by which conservation is negotiated and manufactured with foreign partners and participation is also an indicator of international standing. Choosing the right timing and the right partners is key. As a striking recent example, Myanmar had its first inscription to UNESCO's World Heritage List in 2014. The Pyu Ancient Cities refers to the three archaeological sites of Halin, Beikthano, and Sri Ksetra, walled and moated cities that flourished between 200 BCE and 900 CE.[56] The nomination received strong support from Myanmar's Asian neighbors serving on the Committee: Malaysia, the Philippines, India, Japan, and Vietnam. Myanmar had exhaustively lobbied ICOMOS and the states parties in the lead-up to, and throughout, the meetings in Doha. Yet the problems of preservation and protection remained, according to the experts. The archaeological sites suffered from serious neglect and adverse effects that ICOMOS outlined in some detail. Under British rule, for example, roads and railways negatively impacted these ancient sites. Then the Burmese had made injudicious repairs, according to ICOMOS, using modern materials such as concrete and brick over the top of the ancient structures.[57] A more contextual perspective might consider that in some cases such acts could be considered merit-making in Buddhist thought, where the restoration of ruins is a spiritual endeavor and an act of worship.[58] Rather than attending to various conservation problems and impending infrastructural threats prior to the nomination of Pyu, the Burmese authorities chose to push the dossier forward. Conservation was a tool of cultural diplomacy and a mark of good global citizenship, and Myanmar had gambled that promoting conservation would redound to its benefit.

Myanmar's new civilian government took charge in March 2011, and in 2015 the EU lifted sanctions it had imposed on the country as a response to human rights violations and a crackdown by the military. This enabled international activities to shift from an emergency basis to long-term approaches that promoted development. Italy offered assistance for cultural heritage, in yet another example of how expertise is leveraged as an instrument of foreign policy, as described previously. Even before the sanctions were lifted, in 2002 the Italian Ministry of Foreign Affairs and the Lerici Foundation began working with Myanmar's Ministry of Culture, providing scientific and technical training for archaeologists. A decade later the Italians were working with local conservators, and then they developed the idea of nominating Pyu Ancient Cities. The Italian government sponsored a project called Capacity Building to Safeguard Cultural Heritage in Myanmar, broadening the network to include the Lerici Foundation and UNESCO's Rome-based partner agency ICCROM. Together they offered technical expertise in mural and monument conservation, archaeological assessment, site management, and GIS, and assisted in working with communities.[59] With such an august group of experts and backers, Myanmar capitalized upon a transnational network of supporters and advocates. It is therefore not surprising that they refuted the negative ICOMOS decision and expected World Heritage inscription.[60] From another angle, given the one-way flow of European expertise over the years, it is remarkable that the Pyu sites had such extensive problems with site integrity and management.

Timing is everything. During the Doha meetings there was a palpable sense of urgency and excitement in welcoming Myanmar to the international club. Committee members chose to focus not on the site's significance or conservation issues but rather on Myanmar's participation in world government, its nascent democracy and development, and the particular timing of this international imprimatur. Inscribing the Pyu Ancient Cities was critical because it was Myanmar's first World Heritage nomination, many said, not because of its archaeological importance or conservation status. Other consequences would follow from World Heritage recognition. The network of international governments assisting Myanmar with conservation was extended to include Norway, Switzerland, and Japan.[61] The Italian Lerici Foundation continued its contributions to site management and conservation laboratories. In doing so, international experts found further advisory roles for themselves as they embarked on preparations for a new dossier nominating Bagan, Myanmar's second potential World Heritage site.[62] Bagan is a spectacular ancient city dating to the ninth through thirteenth centuries CE that today has more than two thousand Buddhist temples, pagodas, and monasteries. Beyond networks of transnational advocacy, these collaborative strategies also bolster the networks of experts, consultants, universities, NGOs, and governments that ensure reciprocal access, contracts, projects, and partnerships that proliferate when a country such as Myanmar emerges from isolation.

The trajectory of Myanmar's Pyu Ancient Cities offers another example of the entanglements binding World Heritage, conservation regimes, transnational politics, and international recognition. Myanmar had been snubbed before and as a result had retreated from UNESCO's global heritage arena, leaving ancient sites to be restored and developed in ways that were widely criticized. A suspicion had since developed toward UNESCO that was expressed during my meetings in Myanmar and in UNESCO's regional offices across Asia. Myanmar ratified the World Heritage Convention in 1994 and submitted its first properties to the Tentative List in 1996. That same year the Bagan Archaeological Area and Monuments was proposed as the first nomination despite serious concerns over Bagan's legal protection. There were further problems with its site boundaries and buffer zones, a road cut through the property, and there was also a golf course, all of which negatively impacted the site.[63] Adding to the rejection, proper preservation of the site was linked to widespread criticisms

FIGURE 4.5 Bagan Archaeological Park, Myanmar, courtesy of the author

of Myanmar's military regime.[64] In response the generals decided to take charge of the restoration, rebuilding and gilding stupas for their own personal merit-making and constructing a luxury hotel within the property, thus associating their regime with Bagan's ancient glory. When I discussed Bagan with Myanmar's ambassador to UNESCO in 2015 following the Pyu Ancient Cities inscription, he affirmed that any national ill will or suspicion had evaporated. Ambassador Han Thu resorted to UNESCO's own discourse of legitimation, explaining that today the site "belonged not just to Myanmar but to humanity, to every country in the world." Furthermore, the internationalism that accompanies World Heritage accreditation would "bring development." Now that Bagan's thousands of temples are back on the agenda, Myanmar is once more harnessing UNESCO's conservation mission and the international community's willingness to cooperate to fulfill myriad political ends, domestic and foreign.

Myanmar's strategy of using cultural heritage protection as the opening gambit for a renewed internationalism is not an isolated case.[65] In the late 1980s UNESCO fell under the spell of Angkor, the ancient capital of the Khmer Empire, when the promise of World Heritage was a reward for a war-ravaged Cambodia. Timing was key here too, intersecting with the economic and political imperatives of the international community. Restoration of the nation's material heritage, which evinced an ethos of care and respect, served as a useful exemplar and tool for further civilizational recovery.[66] Director-General Federico Mayor proclaimed that it was "in Angkor, a magnificent symbol of creation, that the Khmer people see the possibility of rising from their depressed and humiliated state."[67] Angkor Wat had been a national icon par excellence throughout each historical epoch: "during the struggle for independence and decolonization, under the Vietnamese occupation and the genocidal Khmer Rouge regime, and finally as a global icon of contemporary heritage schemes" facilitated by UN and UNESCO intervention. Monumental restoration would be used to further shift the spectacle of a genocidal revolution toward a civilizing vision of humanitarian care and universal responsibility for heritage.[68] Anton Prohaska, the Austrian delegate to UNESCO, wrote to the Director-General as early as 1982 that UNESCO's intervention "could be similar to that of the Red Cross in the area of humanitarian intervention."[69] A political past in ruins was thus elided by hopes for a technocratic future founded on international conservation principles, multilateral aid and cooperation, and other genuflections to modernity.

A striking example of what has been termed "stone-temple nationalism," Angkor was incorporated into the Khmer Rouge's revolutionary and genocidal megalomania.[70] On April 17, 1975, they began a staged three-day victory celebration within the precincts of Angkor Wat temple, sparing the French conservation team from the bloodshed of the subsequent evacuation.[71] But between 1979 and 1989 Cambodia came under Vietnamese occupation and the Khmer Rouge was driven into exile.[72] Remarkably, the United Nations recognized their legal authority under the name of Democratic Kampuchea. Back in Paris, representatives of the scientific and technical commission of Democratic Kampuchea skillfully drew UNESCO into discussions over Angkor. Safeguarding the site could only be achieved in a neutralized zone, a declared "zone of peace"—in other words, liberation from the Vietnamese. Concerns were raised that during the conflict Angkor had suffered from neglect and decay and an illicit international trade in antiquities had taken hold: all such accusations could be deployed by the exiles against the Vietnamese regime. Director-General Amadou M'Bow insisted that UNESCO be shielded from all political interpretation of its efforts in Cambodia, as he considered theirs "a purely scientific and technical undertaking" and any assistance would be a humanitarian effort, thus exempt from the UN resolutions.[73] The 1989 peace negotiations in Jakarta enabled UNESCO to send an official fact-finding mission. That same year Hun Sen, the prime minister of the People's

FIGURE 4.6 Angkor Archaeological Park, Cambodia, courtesy of the author

Republic of Kampuchea, based in Phnom Penh, also requested assistance from UNESCO for international cooperation at Angkor.[74]

But it was the exiled King Norodom Sihanouk, the leading figure in the Khmer Rouge–Republican–Royalist coalition government, who, employing UNESCO's rhetoric of a common humanity and supported by the organization, appealed for an international campaign to safeguard Angkor.[75] UNESCO's new Director-General, Federico Mayor, reinforced Sihanouk's appeal after his first official visit to the site in 1991. Recognizing Angkor as World Heritage, according to Michael Falser, was an idea essentially devised by the exiled Khmer Rouge in Paris to bolster their territorial claims. It is reminiscent of Mazower's description of the UN and its ideological diversity, where delegates rub shoulders with dictators and despots.[76] After the UN-supervised elections in Cambodia, Angkor was inscribed in 1992 on the World Heritage List and, simultaneously, the List of World Heritage in Danger. The World Heritage Committee, noting the exceptional situation in Cambodia and the need to take urgent action for the protection of the site, decided to waive its concerns about management and conservation.[77] In such an extreme case, the dream of peace outweighed technical matters.

After decades of brutal conflict and isolation, saving Angkor brought Cambodia back within the international fold, and the site's ongoing conservation and management similarly contributed to the country's political and economic reconstruction. Director-General Mayor referred to these combined processes as "rehabilitation."[78] Conservation would thus serve as a driver for socioeconomic and spiritual uplift, and a kind of "stone-temple internationalism" was set in motion. Today UNESCO claims Angkor as one of its most successful conservation projects of all time. Both UNESCO and Angkor's International Coordination Committee for the Safeguarding of the Historic Site of Angkor (ICC) have further proclaimed their success as a model of international cooperation generally. That success, however, has been recently marred by evidence of the negligible inclusion of local communities.[79] As a technocratic committee dominated by France and Japan, the International Coordination Committee is largely concerned with overseeing the consistency of any proposed foreign projects, which numbered about one hundred in the first decade, and their technical and financial aspects.

Angkor developed into one of the largest archaeological sites in the world, albeit without UNESCO coordination. Since 1995 there has also been a national administrative partner, the Authority for the Protection and Management of Angkor and the Region of Siem Reap (APSARA). Philippe Peycam's long-term research has demonstrated the intricate geopolitical networks and strategies amongst all the different national and intergovernmental groups involved with the Angkor site, premised as they are on religious, political, economic, and colonial connections. He documents how the French management plan was too technocratic and non-inclusive and thus failed. Access to the site was then privatized, and corporate collusion effectively robbed the state of much-needed funds. Japanese involvement, while more cooperative and successful though no more inclusive, served the utilitarian goals of providing consultancies and contracts for Japanese companies while also materializing Japanese benevolence against its history of military actions across Southeast Asia.[80]

Keiko Miura has further recorded what "managing the remarkable" entails in and around Angkor Archaeological Park: the restrictions placed upon local people by the Cambodian state. Along with forcible relocation there are regulations on the construction of new houses, land clearance, cultivation, hunting, management of animals, and harvesting of forest products. World Heritage designation translated into a harsh new regime where customary practices and even religious ones were forbidden and basic human rights impinged upon.[81] Miura documents how APSARA's own armed police force engaged in the demolition of houses, thefts, intimidation, and violence. In 2003 ICCROM proposed "living heritage" as a lens through which the Cambodian authorities might alternatively reconsider local communities as stakeholders and guardians of ancient heritage. However, terms for national patrimony in Khmer are officially used to supplant more personal definitions that pertain to individuals and generational inheritance. Cambodian elites have since used "tradition" to suit their own purposes, their ultimate aim being to project the image of a managed and modern World Heritage destination to both UNESCO and the international tourism market.

In considering these international ambitions, it is worth noting that achieving membership in UNESCO is not as arduous as gaining admission to the United Nations. There is no recourse to members of the Security Council with their potential right of veto, and only a two-thirds majority is required. States desiring international recognition, such as Cambodia and Myanmar, can thus marshal their cultural treasures, their commitment to conservation, and other badges of modernity and civility to gain entry to UNESCO. Unlike the earlier salvage campaigns, the World Heritage Convention and its World Heritage List provide the perfect mechanism of accession. In the case of Cambodia the appeals to save Angkor were strategically timed and placed, coming from Khmer Rouge exiles in Paris, the heartland of UNESCO and Cambodia's former colonial regime. Concern for the monumental past goes hand in hand with other forms of good governance, aid and development programs, and acceptance of foreign expertise and long-term intervention. Recognition through restoration is one important exercise in good global citizenship, appealing to and reaffirming UNESCO's fundamental dream to create a lasting peace in the "minds of men."

Conclusions

It is hard to imagine what a world without World Heritage conservation might look like today. Almost certainly we would be witnessing even greater degrees of development and exploitation than are currently being challenged by multilateral agencies, NGOs, and civil society. From this perspective, UNESCO has proved extremely successful in mobilizing external commitment and intellectual resources for its projects, World Heritage perhaps being the ultimate example. Indeed, it is hard to critique UNESCO's nobility of purpose or desire to forge intellectual ties around the globe. However, its norms still remain expert-driven, while its treaties lack incentives for compliance and implementation amongst its Member States.[82]

In terms of saving the world's most emblematic sites, the ways in which UNESCO's Member States have hijacked its conservation program, and for what ends, are often troubling. They underline just how far we have diverged from the ideals promulgated with the founding of UNESCO, guided by leading intellectuals and statesmen who are simply absent from today's World Heritage arena. With the dominance of states and their political representatives at UNESCO, conservation priorities have devolved into political webs of reciprocities and relationships that increasingly relegate conservation to the wings, rather than placing it at center stage. The triumphalism and achievements of Nubia and other early salvage campaigns, while not unproblematic, might in retrospect look preferable to the situation today, where the ambition of many States Parties is to capitalize sites rather than conserve them. As outlined above, the most notable culprits have been European and North American nations: instead of developing strategies for preservation, they have been promoting strategic development that enables the capitalization of culture while keeping UNESCO's global imprimatur. Sir Mortimer Wheeler acknowledged that the rot had set in when he called Venice the "aging bride of the Adriatic, an illusion if you like, an illusion of fairyland."[83] Yet perhaps Lord Byron deserves the last word, since his "Ode on Venice" is more pertinent today than at its time of writing two hundred years ago in light of the dangerous mix of unrestricted development, environmental degradation, climate change, and commercialization:

O Venice! Venice! when thy marble walls
Are level with the waters, there shall be
A cry of nations o'er thy sunken halls
A loud lament along the sweeping sea!

Conferring World Heritage status and maintaining it are now the primary tasks of the Committee and have become, literally and figuratively, business as usual. Currently an increasing number of sites worldwide, including Venice and Panama, are jeopardized through the unhindered interventions of tourism, infrastructure development, and extractive industries. Governments and their UNESCO representatives for the most part can stay removed from or, at worst, unconcerned with preservation if they have enough political leverage to stave off international censure. It is only with faced with the threat of having their sites placed on the List of World Heritage in Danger or adverse international publicity that they need mobilize and lobby. As we have seen, the mechanisms for holding states accountable are remarkably weak, since the Convention was designed to entreat participation rather than dole out punishment. So as the rush for World Heritage inscription increases, the long-term conservation of sites already listed wanes and economic and geopolitical alliances between nations intensify. The machinations of the BRICS nations—Brazil, Russia, India, China, and South Africa—exemplify this trend in the recent World Heritage meetings. Unfortunately, Rajiv Gandhi's speech delivered at UNESCO in 1985, in which he asserted that the "instinct of conservation is the best antidote to the exploitative tendency," has gone unheeded.

But there is also the matter of the enduring Eurocentrism within the World Heritage Committee and its List that has spanned some four decades. European exceptionalism has a long pedigree at UNESCO, as exemplified in René Maheu's speeches about saving Venice in the 1960s through to those delivered at World Heritage Committee meetings in recent years. Looking over the history of decisions taken and the composition of the List itself, emerging nations are understandably dissatisfied by the double standards according to which powerful nations occupy prized positions and can thus escape censure, while less influential nations cannot. The latter have followed the former's lead and developed alliances and strategies to evade criticism. Such lobbying and pacting are now commonplace and often called "cultural diplomacy" to add a veneer of respectability. It is in fact another tool in the arsenal of soft power—the idea of using cultural or economic influence, rather than coercion, in international relations—where international recognition in conservation is equated with good governance, transparency, civility, and modernity. It is no wonder that the stakes for keeping World Heritage status are so high and the possibility of international interference and oversight in sovereign matters so unwelcomed. This polarity between national ambition and international interest underscores a central tension within World Heritage, in which national patrimony is claimed for humanity as a whole and for the future.

There are also fundamentally different cultural notions of conservation. While Eurocentrism has been the order of the day there too, from the ideas of the League of Nations to the Venice Charter and the 1972 Convention, there are other ways of living with the past. Most normative instruments fail to adequately embrace diverse cultural and historic modes of preservation and restoration, as we saw in Myanmar, but the same is true across much of Asia and Africa for traditional practices and methods. There are further issues of site use and access rather than the cordon sanitaire that typically remains in force: Hampi is a pertinent example of the potential shortfalls. Not only do we risk fundamental misunderstandings of ancient places by taking purely monument-centered, fabric-based approaches, but we also risk attenuating the living histories and the communities whose knowledge and skill created them and the associated traditions that persist. The dynamism of heritage is too often lost in attempts to ossify the past at some arbitrary moment that an expert deems valuable.

Finally, and perhaps most important, we must probe more deeply to discover who are the beneficiaries of international conservation efforts and who are the victims; the removals of residents at Hampi and Angkor are prime examples of the latter. There are problems of violence and serious infractions of human rights, often perpetrated by governments, that threaten the lives of residents in and around World Heritage sites as witnessed in Old Panama and Angkor. These matters are increasingly being addressed within the ambit of ICOMOS and the World Heritage Centre; however, given the hegemony of its Member States, UNESCO has little power to direct or determine the actions of nations. Quotidian acts of social injustice need to be traced and confronted more readily in intergovernmental spheres, rather than solely setting our sights on the fate of monuments. Conservation and conflict have been present throughout human history, yet it is the human dimension of both that surely matters. Julian Huxley knew from the outset the daunting task set for the organization when he referred to the "impossibility of UNESCO producing the rabbit of political peace out of a cultural and scientific hat."[84]

5

Inscription

Everything begins in mysticism and ends in politics.
—CHARLES PÉGUY, 1909

ON JULY 7, 2008, Preah Vihear, a Hindu temple perched along an escarpment in the Dângrêk Mountains, was added to the World Heritage List. A gem of Khmer architecture, the temple dates to the first half of the eleventh century CE and features a series of sanctuaries linked by a system of pavements and staircases over an eight-hundred-meter-long axis. Preah Vihear Temple is considered a masterpiece in terms of its plan, decoration, and relationship to the spectacular landscape setting. Nominated by Cambodia and announced at the World Heritage Committee meetings in Quebec City, the inscription immediately provoked border clashes with neighboring Thailand. Not restricted to Preah Vihear, the conflict rippled along the border as Thai soldiers occupied the Ta Moan Temple complex some 150 kilometers to the west. Cambodia retaliated by taking Ta Krabei Temple, thirteen kilometers east of Ta Moan. Contrary to the aspirations set forth in UNESCO's constitution, recognition by the organization had not so much engendered peace in the "minds of men" as inflamed a long-standing history of violence. Preah Vihear and its environs were at the center of a long historical territorial dispute between Cambodia and Thailand, and the International Court of Justice had ruled in favor of Cambodia, first in 1962, then again after inscription to settle the hostilities in 2011 and once more in 2013.[1] The World Heritage Centre was also drawn into the transnational struggle, readily apparent during the very public nomination process and precipitated by listing.[2] Less visible was how "stone temple nationalism" was in fact intricately tied to broader issues of foreign policy and investment, much of it engineered behind the scenes by the United States.

In Thailand and Cambodia I had heard whispers about exchanges for international oil contracts and American involvement in other dealings. On the surface, however, the official World Heritage nomination process involved only negotiations between the sovereign states of Cambodia and Thailand, brokered to some degree by UNESCO's own brand of intergovernmental diplomacy. Moreover, the escalation of this intensely regional conflict seemed disconnected from the United States, which neither shared a border with either country nor had any immediate interest in the dispute. The United States, however, had been a member of the World Heritage Committee over the crucial period from 2005 to 2009. What asset value could a temple dedicated to Shiva in such a remote location possibly have? Sources in Paris and Bangkok encouraged me to dig deeper. To discover how and why American support was instrumental to Preah Vihear's inscription, I needed look no further than WikiLeaks.[3]

Preah Vihear features in some 150 diplomatic cables containing almost 100,000 words from May 19, 2005, to February 12, 2010. Significantly, these dates cover the lead-up to the temple's nomination in 2007, its inscription in 2008, the fallout with Thailand, and the violence that ensued. What the leaked diplomatic cables reveal are the linkages between seemingly unrelated spheres and events, underscoring the intricate hyperconnectivity of heritage at a global scale. Prior to the World Heritage meetings in 2008,

FIGURE 5.1 Preah Vihear Temple, Cambodia, courtesy of Dara Mang

one cable entitled "Cambodia: Investment, Temple Controversy, Debt and Overlapping Claims Headline Business Delegation Meeting" shows just how seemingly separate issues were conjoined.[4] Joseph Mussomeli, the American ambassador to Cambodia, had cabled the US Department of Commerce, the Secretary of State, and his colleagues in Paris about what he called "a wave of increased US investor interest in Cambodia." He mentioned "the pending inscription of the Preah Vihear temple on the UNESCO World Heritage List and Cambodia's bilateral debt with the US. Delegation members and the embassy believe that successful resolution of the Preah Vihear issue could open the door to a resolution of the overlapping claims area in the Gulf of Thailand." The claims he referred to critically affected the ability of the United States and its corporate partners to secure contracts to drill for natural gas in the gulf. The ambassador went on to say that "inscribing Preah Vihear on the UNESCO World Heritage List, if handled correctly, actually could open opportunities for the two countries to work more closely both on cultural issues and the more lucrative issue of the overlapping claims in the Gulf of Thailand." A series of exchanges was set in motion underscoring the transactional potentials of World Heritage inscription in an intensely interconnected global arena. Those exchanges reveal that national patrimony is underwritten by, and constituted through, increasingly international arrangements.

If the Preah Vihear dispute could be resolved, it might potentially resolve the overlapping maritime claims in the Gulf of Thailand. For the United States this would mean access to vast natural gas reserves to be exploited by US companies such as Chevron, which have since been granted extended concessions.[5] Linking territorial disputes from the temple to the sea, one Cambodian representative explained that there was "no overlapping claim" with Preah Vihear, as there was with the Gulf of Thailand. Both commodities and flows were inextricably linked for the main players and their American brokers. An equation began to emerge: if Cambodia retained its temple, Thailand might enhance its underwater assets, and the United States might negotiate for extended contracts. Furthermore, during the period covered by the leaked diplomatic cables there was an upsurge in US investor interest in Cambodia from major corporations including Boeing, Nike, McDonald's, Pizza Hut, and Marlboro, and this interest was discussed in the cables.[6] Indeed, the cables disclose how governments privilege the economic interests of large corporations and not simply national interests abroad. The political, the economic, and the cultural became inseparable, and this connection was made not only in the leaked diplomatic cables but also in the Thai media, which accused their government of exchanging Preah Vihear and its border territories for access to natural gas rights in Cambodia's Koh Kong province.[7] And all of this was being leveraged, in the name of conservation, around the inscription of one site on the UNESCO World Heritage List.

While the national appeared front and center with Preah Vihear, negotiations around its World Heritage recognition involved a broader range of entities, including the work of national legislatures and judiciaries, intergovernmental agencies, the international operations of national companies and markets, political projects of nonstate actors, and changes in the relationship between citizens and the state. For example, the United States has maintained a significant military stake in the region since the Second World War, with bases in Thailand such as Utapao offering air and sea capability. Another cable purports that "the relationship has evolved into a partnership that provides the US with unique benefits. As one of five US treaty allies in Asia and straddling a major force projection air/sea corridor, Thailand remains crucial to American interests in the Asia-Pacific region and beyond."[8] Thus, being seen to support Thailand in an international dispute, whether over territory or temples, had implications.

The cables reveal the eagerness of the United States to strengthen its presence in Southeast Asia, especially in light of the region's growing ties to China. The State Party of China, like the United States, is a member of the International Coordinating Committee for Preah Vihear and thus instrumental in the site's future. During 2008 China had invested heavily around Preah Vihear in mining and industry and by funding a bridge and a major road to the temple. That same year the Chinese government gave US$290 million for a new road linking the temple to Cambodia's other World Heritage site, Angkor. The China Railway Group also built the north-south railway connecting the Chinese-owned Cambodia Iron and Steel Mining Industry Group's factory in Preah Vihear province to a new port in Koh Kong province. According to some delegations in Paris, it was the broader issue of Chinese insertion into Cambodia that was the real stimulus behind American intervention in Preah Vihear's inscription.[9] Resolving the temple and its border war was bound up in, and inseparable from, larger international bartering that the United States saw as advantageous. The cables convey that the desired outcome was a peaceful resolution incorporating a role for Thailand. American diplomats noted that the "US remains the country of first choice for arms procurement" for Thailand, with sales worth US$2 billion then in process.[10] Recalling his

experience of US involvement in the inscription, one experienced diplomat put it bluntly: "They think their business is the world."

The listing of Preah Vihear was imbricated with national political
intrigues, international border wars, bilateral negotiations surrounding
gas and steel contracts, and regional military alignments. The very fact that
so much politicking occurred around this one site, which was largely invisible in international heritage circles until its controversial World Heritage
inscription and the resultant border war, is telling. Globalization and
world-making projects such as UNESCO's 1972 Convention have changed
the stakes for inscription of particular places. Through processes that have
led to greater interdependence and connectivity, sites are transformed
into transactional commodities with exchange values that transcend their
materialities, wresting them from those contexts to serve other international interests. The transactions supporting and surrounding site inscription can thus be traced from the level of international networks to national
negotiations, right down to the level of the site and its embedded potentials
for social, political, and economic production. Here too the modalities of
recovery are privileged over discovery.

World Heritage Transactions

The 1972 World Heritage Convention stipulates that all properties like
Preah Vihear are nominated by the sovereign state on whose territory
they are located.[11] World Heritage sites should thus embody some of the
most inalienable of all objects. Yet the process of listing Preah Vihear
was caught up in an assemblage of distinct elements that have been
denationalized through political, economic, and military interventions.
Inscribing the temple might constitute what Saskia Sassen calls a "tipping
point," shifting from an era marked by the ascendance of the nation-state
and its capture of all major aspects of social, economic, political, and subjective life to one marked by a proliferation of orders.[12] WikiLeaks reveals
such proliferation: the scalar transformation of global connectivity across
political, military, institutional, corporate, and cultural lines enabling new
capabilities and logics. Yet such machinations are typically hidden from
view, particularly given the confidentiality and diplomacy employed to
shield nomination dossiers.[13] As Ambassador Mussomeli warned, "The
US's overarching interest in maintaining regional stability does not allow
us the luxury of indefinitely standing on the sidelines of this dispute."[14]
The timing of the temple dispute was also crucial for larger security

concerns and jockeying for power on other high-profile UN committees. Cambodia was seeking support for its UN Security Council bid on a platform celebrating its modern stewardship of ancient heritage, specifically the restoration of Angkor.[15] Cambodia also wanted US backing to join Asia-Pacific Economic Cooperation (APEC), thereby overturning that forum's embargo on new members. Across international organizations, divergent interests create implicit or explicit markets for trading political support. Known as logrolling, this form of vote trading has become increasingly commonplace at UNESCO and across the UN.[16] World Heritage offers an incredibly pliant mechanism for soft power and UNESCO itself a promising antechamber to the UN.

Even prior to inscription, potential World Heritage sites offer a transactional stimulus in a network of political and economic imperatives. Not simply a reflection of regional dominance or political blocs, World Heritage inscription is also a matter of financial capacity, relentless lobbying, and fluid international alignments. This tentacular reach is exemplified in one stalled Indian government initiative known as Project Mausam, potentially bridging archaeological and historic sites across many nations all linked by the effects of the monsoon across the Indian Ocean.[17] An ambitious venture stretching from Singapore to Somalia, in its early incarnation the project promised to join countries with shared maritime histories and living traditions, inscribing much of the Indian Ocean as a single World Heritage entity. Spearheaded by India but relying on the cooperation of other Asian, Middle Eastern, and possibly African partners, Project Mausam was very publicly launched during the 2014 Doha World Heritage Committee meetings.

Director-General Irina Bokova was in attendance at the side event and was skillfully called upon to endorse the nascent nomination. Lavish gift bags containing an array of Indian spices, prepared by the Tourism Department of the State Government of Kerala in acknowledgement of Kerala's historical role in the spice trade, were distributed to participants. There was an air of unrestrained enthusiasm as delegates from many nations clamored to join the venture. Yet the ambitious transnational project derailed in 2015 due to the uneasy relationship between governmental directives and academic scholarship, an overweening national bureaucracy, redirected commercialism, and shifting international alliances. Indian government ministers saw the nomination as an opportunity to forge ties with powerful allies across the region that mapped onto neither historical relationships nor relevant cultural sites that academic advisors had identified for inclusion. Moreover, the dossier had vast political implications, as India's government under Prime Minister Narendra Modi uses the same term, Project Mausam, for a policy that extends Indian influence in the region and fends off Chinese counterclaims for maritime military and trade supremacy, particularly in the Indian Ocean.[18] The key to Mausam's fate was right there in the gift bag: a monsoonal maritime landscape was supplanted by the commercial surety of India's Spice Route, and the tourist powerhouse of Kerala assumed priority in terms of cultural commodification and tourism revenues.[19] Ancient and modern trade routes were thus jostling for visibility amidst the scramble for national capacity, UNESCO recognition, and the limits of international traffic.

World Heritage properties, and the very process of inscribing and subsequently managing and conserving them, produce a dynamic market place for international trade and exchange. Sites are tokens that leverage ancillary goods and exchanges in ever-widening circuits of economic and political power.[20] The formal process of inscription may take many years, millions of dollars, and much unofficial negotiation and lobbying. In 2015 Jamaica spent US$13 million on its first inscription, while Japan's government under Prime Minister Shinzo Abe sent envoys to fifteen countries to push for, and ensure, its controversial nomination of the Sites of Japan's Meiji Industrial Revolution: Iron and Steel, Shipbuilding and Coal Mining.[21] For a State Party, the first official requirement is that the potential property must be inventoried on the national Tentative List. Even this step can prove controversial, as territorial incursions and disputations are made manifest. An exhaustive nomination dossier of maps and supporting documents is compiled by the country and submitted to the World Heritage Centre for review. Once a nomination file is determined complete, the Centre forwards it to the appropriate Advisory Body for evaluation.[22] The International Council on Monuments and Sites (ICOMOS) evaluates cultural sites and landscapes, whereas the World Conservation Union (IUCN) examines natural properties; both are involved if the site is proposed as mixed.[23] ICOMOS is said to practice a kind of scientific realism, producing reports based on the belief in both observable and unobservable aspects of the world. Field missions are mobilized to assess site authenticity, integrity, and protection, which further constitute this "scenography of empiricism."[24]

While the Advisory Bodies make recommendations, it is ultimately the World Heritage Committee that makes the final decision during its annual meetings. Every stage of the process is subject to contestation, whether between the States Parties and the Secretariat or between the Advisory Bodies and the World Heritage Committee. To be included on the List, sites are supposed to possess "Outstanding Universal Value" (OUV), as set out in Chapter 3, and meet at least one of the ten selection criteria. While the understanding of what constitutes OUV has changed throughout the history of the Convention, this rather mystical quality lacks precise definition. However, there is a faint echo of President Nixon's "Special Message to Congress Proposing the 1971 Environmental Program," in which he put forth the idea that "there are certain areas of such unique worldwide value that they should be treated as part of the heritage of all mankind and accorded special recognition as part of a World Heritage Trust."[25]

During the Committee sessions, the few days that are devoted to site inscription are the most critical for the States Parties. One Indian ambassador impressed upon me that attaining the brand is more important than conservation or even a danger listing. She considered development, both economic and social, more compelling to "the man in the street." The pressure around listing is so intense and debate so vociferous that one senior official described it to me as a "spectator sport." Advisory Body evaluators have limited categories of recommendations that they can make: inscription, referral, deferral, and non-inscription. Inscription is straightforward and has rarely been challenged by the Committee throughout the Convention's history.[26] A referral entails a request for some minor additional information from the country to supplement the original dossier. Deferral requires more significant additional information from the country, or actions that the country must take, and a new evaluation mission must be sent to the property. The decision not to inscribe means that the dossier is, in theory, closed and cannot be presented again to the Committee.

Members of the Advisory Bodies describe their recommendations as "helpful tools" whereby states are empowered to work in conjunction with the World Heritage Centre toward greater preparedness for site nomination and potential inscription, whereas the States Parties perceive any decision that is not an inscription as a "poisoned gift"—a term that delegates regularly use with some disdain.[27] The delaying of inscription for further revision is regarded as a highly subjective and spurious criticism directed at countries that have already expended vast resources and mobilized their political capital in preparing dossiers. These two distinctly different views of the process constitute the greatest source of contention and dissatisfaction between the states parties, the Advisory Bodies, and the Secretariat, and such conflicts have become increasingly intractable.

The role of the Advisory Bodies was formulated partly to neutralize the selection process, depoliticizing it through the application of criteria by independent experts and external oversight of the process.[28] Yet as legal scholar Ana Vrdoljak notes, all such experts can be subject to scrutiny in terms of accountability and transparency, notwithstanding the composition of the organization itself. From the mid-1990s onward there have been controversies over the lack of coordination, the restricted expert pool, conflicts of interest, evaluation methods, and, in the case of ICOMOS, the entire classification system or lack thereof.[29] The States Parties have been the most vigorous critics and in defiance have systematically ignored and overturned Advisory Body recommendations. Expressing his frustration at regulations regarding site protection, Vinay Sheel Oberoi, the Indian ambassador, charged that the "pyramids would never have been built if ICOMOS and the World Heritage Committee had been there."[30] ICOMOS, he implied, did not stand for heritage and was guilty of constantly overstepping the mark.

During the past decade the Committee has pushed its recommendations toward inscription: from referral to inscription, from deferral to referral or even inscription, and so on. Thus there is major disagreement between the expert evaluations of properties and the decisions made by the World Heritage Committee. This polarization is often due to the site selection process, which now reflects national rather than global interests.[31] In 2013 Brazil and India argued that the Convention's Operational Guidelines should be changed to allow countries to solicit their own independent evaluators, to reduce the role of the Advisory Bodies, and to inscribe a larger quota of sites per country. Other delegations would prefer that the World Heritage process be enabling and collaborative rather than competitive and rule-bound.[32] A former director of the World Heritage Centre, Kishore Rao, also agreed that the vast expenditures of time, effort, and money would be better channeled into a system of cooperation and mentoring.[33] As a result of growing dissatisfaction, many states parties have taken matters into their own hands, bypassing official channels and directly petitioning Committee members and other States Parties for their support. This type of "planetary bargaining" has become a feature of multilateral life, whether one examines the workings of World Heritage or the World Bank.[34]

UNESCO claims that the impact of the 1972 Convention has expanded to inspire greater involvement by governments, communities and individuals, universities, foundations, and the private sector. This is certainly true, but how that impact now manifests itself is progressively more political. Inscription has become a political tool for nations to bolster their sovereign interests, using global patrimony as a pawn. Applying excessive pressure, sometimes accompanied by intimidation and unwelcome advances, on members of the Secretariat, the Advisory Bodies, and other Member States has become more commonplace. Some countries are more aggressive than others and feel they have more to win or lose in the scramble for recognition. A major turning point was the 2010 World Heritage Committee session held in Brasilia, when the *Economist* reported that "the UN agency [was] bending its own rules under pressure from Member States."[35] Conversely, the Brazilian delegation was proud of its transparency and negotiation skills during that meeting, and its members explained to me how they helped resolve tensions between Cambodia and Thailand over Preah Vihear. However, that same year a Norwegian study reported that decisions were made behind the scenes in Brasilia rather than through public debate.[36] It claimed China had put pressure on other members to secure its own nominated sites for inscription and several countries had expressed concern. Then an explosive French documentary revealed the full extent of the lobbying and pressure exerted on Committee members during the 2013 meetings in Cambodia. The result surprised many diplomats in Paris, who had naively been interviewed and filmed "doing business." The special investigation captured, among others, the Russian ambassador's relentless pressuring of other delegations to support the nomination of the medieval Bolgar Historical and Archaeological Complex in Tatarstan.[37]

The politics of inscription enables sites to be wrested from their particular context and mobilized instead as transactional devices that both mask and enable a multifarious network of political and economic values. "Transaction" here not only refers to the process of "doing business" and the exchange of commodities and services in the World Heritage arena but also encompasses the reciprocal influences and communicative activities between parties. Successful nominations are linked to the support not just of one or two neighbors but also of a wide array of countries spanning the globe. Moreover, these interdependencies are no longer confined to a single group of countries (e.g., the West, or industrialized democracies) but have expanded to encompass a diverse range of economic regime types, religions, and cultures.[38] Indeed, support for inscription is more closely tied to former colonial relationships and trade partnerships than to regional, religious, or linguistic affiliations.[39]

In response to the rising pressures and international censure, Director-General Bokova addressed the World Heritage Committee in St. Petersburg, saying, "The credibility of the inscription process must be absolute at all stages of the proceedings." In light of this "growing criticism," she warned, the Committee was now "at the crossroads" and could either "continue to gather, year after year, as accountants of the World Heritage label, adding more sites to the list, adhering less and less strictly to its criteria. Or we can choose another path. We can decide to act and think as visionaries, to rejuvenate the World Heritage Convention and confront the challenges of the 21st century. World Heritage is not a beauty contest."[40] Yet inscription is just that: an international competition. Some, such as the Cuban ambassador, have since likened it to FIFA, world soccer's governing body; others compare it to the Olympics or, worse, the Eurovision song contest.

Why has World Heritage listing become so important? The notion that World Heritage properties are commodities that mobilize national and international flows is not surprising. The use of the word "property" in official UNESCO discourse makes that evident from the outset, and it anchors sites firmly within the nation-state.[41] World Heritage recognition offers

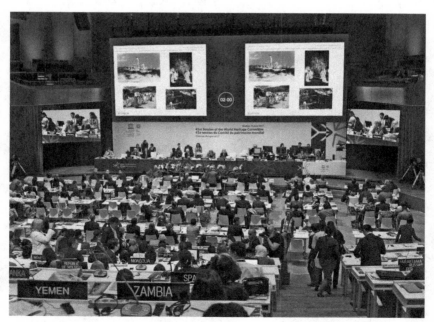

FIGURE 5.2 World Heritage Committee meetings, Krakow, Poland, courtesy of the author

the possibility of direct tourist and other economic revenues for national governments as well as the private sector, though a consideration of the situation in many developing nations shows that this occurs unevenly. The Convention's original mandate to protect and conserve the world's most important cultural and natural heritage places has been largely replaced by an international desire for securing and mobilizing the brand.

UNESCO branding has been studied from various disciplinary perspectives, most often through tourism, site management, and international politics.[42] Venice, Angkor, and Pompeii are all good examples, but there are also less dramatic cases, such as the Causses and the Cévennes, a property in southern France inscribed in 2011 after five years of concerted state effort.[43] Proposed on the basis of "the relationship between agro-pastoral systems and their biophysical environment" and the continued tradition of summer transhumance, the property is primarily a picturesque landscape. The sheep may sometimes be hard to spot, but an impressive consortium of regional and local tourist development agencies is ubiquitous, alongside nature conservancies and local businesses with the *appellation d'origine controlée* label that have commercialized and capitalized on the UNESCO designation. Similar to the English Cotswolds and beautiful like much of southern France, the Causses and the Cévennes is a bijou tourist destination offering accommodation in chateaux, hiking and rafting, local crafts, and organic produce to a wealthy clientele. France is adept at inscribing and marketing its World Heritage sites, aided considerably by UNESCO's Parisian headquarters, the numerous French bureaucrats employed there, and the France-UNESCO cooperation agreement. The Champagne Hillsides, Houses, and Cellars and the Climats, Terroirs of Burgundy, are two other recent inscriptions.

Beyond such immediate returns, the mechanism of World Heritage decision-making has transformed heritage places into emblematic and reflective values that mobilize supplementary tangible benefits in other domains. Transactional heritage is thus transformative, leveraging and consolidating relationships, strategic partnerships, and worldviews that are determined by economic, ethnic, religious or geographical imperatives. Increasingly, it is the *process* of inscription itself—particularly the political alliances and, by extension, forms of gifting from one party to another—that reveals how the World Heritage process is entangled in an ecology of exchange. Cultural, commercial, and diplomatic reciprocities may occur between nations and their representatives or between members of UNESCO's Advisory Bodies and their cohort of evaluators, as well as between individuals and consultants who traverse these different networks. As a prime example of elite capture, several thousand people attend the World Heritage meetings to do business, whether for their government, international agency, consultancy firm, university, or themselves. While the Committee sessions proper feature scripted performances of protocol, with raised nameplates, timed interventions, and points of order, quite the reverse is true of the coffee breaks, buffet lunches, and receptions, where the exchange of business cards, brochures, books, tokens, and gifts is constant. There are nation-to-nation transactions, with ambassadors and diplomats as intermediaries for their respective countries and sovereign concerns. Government ministers and sheiks can be seen lobbying for their heritage sites one minute, then leveraging support for other orders of business the next. Through receptions, informal meetings, and royal audiences, individuals use World Heritage as cultural diplomacy's softest option in order to initiate discussions about more substantive political matters.

Asset Management

The foregoing examines the global stakes for inscription for sites like Preah Vihear and the benefits of asset branding for the Causses and the Cévennes; both are instances of the transactional nature of listing and its supplemental effects in wider world. These exchanges operate beyond the Convention, extending the process and products of inscription out from the World Heritage arena via circuits of power and influence. Site bargaining happens relentlessly, sometimes over many years, in the Paris offices of national delegations and, most visibly, at the annual meetings. How states navigate Committee meetings, steering their particular interests and managing their assets, reveals another sphere of enterprise. While the former could be described as international, the latter would be intergovernmental. In conjunction with various actors' demands for greater transparency, securing observer status at UNESCO has enabled me to examine more closely how nations with a seat on the Committee operate within the Convention in the observable and calculable metrics of World Heritage participation.

The Convention's rules stipulate equitable representation on the Committee from different regions and cultures of the world. Because only the delegates of states parties that are members of the Committee are empowered to speak and make decisions, election to the Committee is fiercely coveted. Yet in 2013 the politics of representation was laid bare as six African nations proposed their candidature to the World Heritage Committee but none were selected. This left an entire continent unrepresented. UNESCO had also publicly pledged to prioritize Africa between 2014 and 2021.[44] In the wake of this scandal Brazil proposed a system based on UNESCO's own electoral groups in order to reinstate what they argued were the principles of justice, equity, and credibility.[45]

A seat on the Committee carries with it the enhanced possibilities of formal and informal influence in heritage matters and beyond. Tracing the metrics of the Committee through time, my colleagues Enrico Bertacchini, Claudia Liuzza, Donatella Saccone, and I have shown that Western nations have long maintained a dominant position in terms of attaining seats and the length of Committee mandate.[46] Western nations such as France, Germany, and Italy have in the past served several consecutive terms. And there is a positive and statistically significant correlation between States Parties that are Committee members, their nomination activity, and the likelihood of obtaining an inscription.[47] Membership bestows the political power to vigorously promote site nomination. Most States Parties anticipate their membership some years ahead, lobby for support beforehand, and accordingly prepare their nomination dossiers well in advance.[48]

Cultural properties are assets for States Parties, and the best way to promote their inscription is to nominate them while serving on the twenty-one-member World Heritage Committee. European countries such as France and Germany have aggressively pursued this option, despite concerted efforts by other nations to prohibit serving Committee members from nominating sites in their own country. Imposing a new regulation requires approval, and it is perhaps not surprising that Committee members swiftly vetoed the recommendation. This obvious conflict of interest is raised each year by a small number of nations such as Finland, Switzerland, and Estonia that advocate abstention during membership, whereas many more nations, including Turkey, Russia, India, China, and Japan, to name a few, take the opposite position.

One example that reveals some adept maneuvering by a Committee member was the German nomination in 2012 of Schwetzingen: A Prince Selector's Summer Residence.[49] ICOMOS recommended to defer the decision as to whether the palatial property be inscribed on the List. Its evaluators considered the site representative but not remarkable, since it lacked that elusive quality, "Outstanding Universal Value." During her forceful rebuttal to ICOMOS, the German ambassador, Martina Nibbeling-Wriessnig, adeptly reconfigured the nomination to focus on one particular aspect of the property—an eighteenth-century "decorative mosque." Given that the Committee included the Arab states of Qatar, Iraq, Algeria, and the United Arab Emirates plus countries with majority Muslim populations such as Senegal, Mali, and Malaysia, this repackaging was a calculated strategy. In a previous and unsuccessful iteration of the dossier Germany had associated the site with Freemasonry, not Islam.[50] Now Germany invoked the site's Islamic connection and purported multiculturalism, declaring that Schwetzingen possessed the earliest mosque in Europe. The mayor of the city took the microphone to claim Schwetzingen was a site of tolerance. Some Arab states were supportive; others were curious to hear more from Germany about this early Orientalism. But France and Switzerland stood firm, arguing that the "decorative mosque" should not obscure the problems raised by ICOMOS. "We are nominating a palace . . . not a mosque," Switzerland affirmed. Somewhat exasperatedly, Senegal made the obvious point that "it is not a mosque, it's a decorative element." In the end, after ninety minutes of heated debate, Germany conceded, "You don't want more baroque residences, we can accept that."[51]

Being on the Committee affords the opportunity not only to speak in support of one's own properties but also to forge critical alliances by supporting inscription of sites proposed by other countries. From an analysis of 340 nominations submitted between 2003 and 2013 my colleagues and I found that taking the floor during debates served different political aims.[52] Committee members are typically given two minutes to speak. These brief speeches may enable one country to introduce additional information about a property or directly influence the final decision by making concrete statements of support. Committee members often address the Advisory Bodies too, either to challenge or ask for further explanation of certain technicalities. This strategy can be employed to support inscription or alternatively to underscore problems with the dossier. Given that many delegates privately confess to not reading the documents fully—this would entail reading many thousands of pages, after all—these interventions are typically prompted, and scripted, by the nominating countries.

During the Istanbul meetings in 2016 the United States prepared a typed script advocating its nomination of Frank Lloyd Wright buildings, and in the midst of heated debate on the property, one long-serving US delegate left his seat, approached an African Committee member, and handed over a script to read.[53] A young delegate from Ethiopia put it candidly some years ago when he said, "Sometimes the document on the table is the

Convention, but the document in action is politics." A vulnerable nation with a seat on the Committee may find itself regularly pressured by powerful and predatory states. Such performances are finely "calibrated to the needs of certain institutional structures," becoming instruments of power and even tyranny that can be deployed quite variably by differently situated actors.[54] By being vocal and authoritative a State Party can attain legitimation in the Committee, and this status enables it to reinforce even stronger diplomatic ties with other nations. This has certainly been the case for India, with its tradition of very vocal and critical ambassadors. Ironically, it was one outspoken Indian diplomat who likened the Committee of twenty-one representatives to "gods on Olympus" and then privately confided to me that the situation must change.

Being able to take the microphone is itself a valuable asset. Indeed, decisions are made by consensus through discussion at the World Heritage meetings, not normally by a formal vote, making persuasive speech more important and instrumental. My colleagues and I found that the frequency of speeches is therefore a proxy for a Committee member's profile in the decision-making process: there is a positive correlation between the frequency of statements a country makes and the level of political influence that country exerts in the final decision whether or not to inscribe a site.[55] For instance, we found that Egypt, India, China, Russia, South Africa, Thailand, and Japan exercised the greatest formal and informal influence. Often this entailed speaking against the Advisory Bodies when their recommendation did not support site inscription. These states further maintained their high profile by the number of years they served on the World Heritage Committee, the number of nominations they submitted, and the number of delegates they sent to participate and lobby at the sessions.[56] We also found that countries in a second group, including Switzerland, Estonia, and the United Kingdom, were very vocal as well, but they supported the evaluations of the Advisory Bodies and challenged their colleagues when they attempted to upgrade a recommendation. The ability to speak has become so critical that the issue cannot be left to the Convention or UNESCO's rules of procedure; instead it is an asset best managed by the States Parties themselves.[57]

A minor revolution over the right to speak and the resultant "conflict of interest," prompted by the Indian ambassador in 2013, is a case in point. During the 2013 Phnom Penh meetings some delegates proposed suspending the Convention's regulations and thus allowing States Parties to speak in support of their own nominations—not simply when invited to do so by a Committee member, as was the rule, but as a matter of course. Ambassador Vinay Sheel Oberoi led the charge to suspend the rule, in the spirit of "transparency and openness," claiming that the official process had permitted "a degree of hypocrisy we could do without."[58] This, he maintained, "would eliminate lobbying and hypocrisy." Oberoi invoked technocratic best practice, arguing that this was a way of getting "direct information" from the nominating country. Russia, South Africa, Iraq, Senegal, Algeria, Qatar, Colombia, and Japan all concurred with India. Switzerland, Germany, France, and Estonia, however, were not convinced. Estonia regarded it as a blatant conflict of interest, saying, "I do know what advocacy is and I have heard it enough in the Committee. I have listened to embarrassing self commandments." A State Party seeking inscription, Estonia stated, "cannot be the 22nd member of a Committee."[59] Oberoi's indictment also served another purpose. As part of his sustained attack on the credibility of ICOMOS, the ambassador argued that the nominating state should be given the opportunity to speak *after* the Advisory Body's evaluation, allowing the State Party to effectively overturn any negative recommendation and ostensibly have the last word, thus formalizing the self-interest. South Africa put it more bluntly: "States Parties pay their contributions and keep this show on the road." In such an acquisitive heritage economy, speaking, advocating, lobbying, and intimidation form a sliding scale of possible modalities to guarantee inscription on the World Heritage List.

An Archaeology of Inscription

The processes of nomination and inscription have capillary effects across various levels, from the global and intergovernmental through to the national and local. Telescoping down to the level of the site underscores the micropolitics of representation, evaluation, and the consequences of inscription. Here I briefly focus on the World Heritage site of Çatalhöyük, a nine-thousand-year-old Neolithic settlement in Central Anatolia where I have worked as an archaeologist since 2004.[60] Having Çatalhöyük listed was vital for the Turkish government to reestablish its engagement with World Heritage after a hiatus. Between 1998 and 2011 Turkey had not put forward a single site for listing. Çatalhöyük was inventoried on the Tentative List in 2009, and the three-hundred-page dossier was swiftly submitted for inscription in 2011.[61] Having such uncommon access to one cultural site enables me to trace the lead-up to inscription, the site evaluation, stakeholder dynamics, national politics, and the subsequent fallout for neighboring communities. While inclusion on the World Heritage List is intended to bestow public goods, locally and globally, the effects on the ground are tightly scripted and controlled by the State Party, being the ultimate arbiter for any future in ruins.

The Çatalhöyük evaluation mission took place over two days in late September 2011 and included an ICOMOS representative and one external expert, trained as an archaeologist and now a heritage consultant. The Turkish authorities managed this rather like a royal visit. On the first day the mission was met by a welcome committee, which included children bearing flowers. In fact, the dusty archaeological site was strewn with flower boxes, the road had been graded, and the whole area looked as if it had been swept clean. I had seen similar state rituals when Britain's Prince Charles visited Çatalhöyük some years previously. Lunch at the excavation house was another formal, almost exclusively male affair, with tables bedecked in flowers sprouting from modern ceramic vases resembling Neolithic effigies. The heritage consultant was also taken aback; her focus was European prehistory, not Middle Eastern archaeology, and she specialized in sites thousands of miles from Turkey and thousands of years later in time. Her eagerness to undertake the mission was not because of any possible financial benefit, she explained, but rather because it would further her own research and experience. Çatalhöyük is a well-known archaeological site, made more famous to some degree because of its long-term archaeological excavation and research. The nomination process was, in her view, a catalyst for change, a mechanism for developing heritage and archaeological sites that would not receive such attention otherwise.

FIGURE 5.3 Çatalhöyük archaeological site, Turkey, courtesy of the Çatalhöyük Research Project and Jason Quinlan

She described this process as an inward-moving spiral that gathers momentum, and at its core were priorities such as conservation, management, museums, communities, narratives, and interpretations. Because she was a heritage consultant, her technocratic focus quickly homed in on the site's management plan (which was outdated), the state's provisions for long-term funding, and integration of the various actors, public and private.

On the second day a meeting was convened at the regional museum in the nearby city of Konya. It included representatives from a long list of government offices: the General Directorate of Cultural Heritage and Museums, the Provincial Directorate of Culture and Tourism, the Regional Conservation Council for Conservation of Cultural and Natural Assets, the Archaeological Museum, the Directorate of Surveying and Monuments, and the local municipality. Also present were several members of the excavation team. Rather than simply listening to presentations or asking questions, the evaluator preferred to establish a dialogue with her Turkish interlocutors, offering advice and guidance for the future management of Çatalhöyük. The afternoon meeting had a different purpose, however, and was orchestrated to showcase the various stakeholders and local buy-in: NGOs and the local village mayor as well as community and school representatives were solicited for their views. The state's primary strategy here was to display *evidence* of participation, rather than to actually incorporate local communities into site management or interpretation.[62] In compliance with UNESCO's regulations, Turkish bureaucrats and politicians were setting the scenography of participation to conform to World Heritage requirements, but were at the same time shoring up their own authority as representatives of the state and Recep Tayyip Erdoğan's autocratic government.

Turkey's highly centralized bureaucracy had previously clashed with UNESCO's shifting standards for site management, obstructing Turkey's full participation in the World Heritage arena. Then in 2004, in response to increasing EU and UNESCO pressure for greater participation by local communities, Turkey introduced new conservation legislation designed to give the semblance of democratization and consultation. This resulted in a conflation of UNESCO's concept of community participation with UNESCO's notion of a management mechanism.[63] Archaeologist Helen Human documents how the "full and active involvement of local communities is reinterpreted as formal stakeholder consultation in a narrow site management planning process, controlled by either the central state or local government." Under the normative guise of "best practice" these processes actually bolster the state. The international requirements for World Heritage inscription were simply transliterated into the Erdoğan government's discourse of decentralization, thus reinforcing existing hierarchies and extending the reach of Turkey's deep state.

After the perceived success of the evaluation mission to Çatalhöyük, ICOMOS wrote to request a timetable for the revisions of the outdated site management plan. Turkish officials from the Ministry of Culture and Tourism began compiling evidence that they had formally implemented the participatory site management process. But this is where local involvement ended. NGO and community representatives were not consulted again, and their presence in the process, as well as the promises made to them in front of international assessors, all but evaporated. There would be no local museum, no development for tourism or village inclusion in the site's future, though such assurances had been strategically deployed at a critical juncture. Given the primacy of the nation-state within the 1972 Convention, there is no mechanism to hold states accountable for such actions. This has been a long-standing critique of World Heritage listing, especially as it pertains to indigenous custodians and other vested communities.[64] It is one source of tension and conflict on the rise globally, whether the World Heritage properties being examined are in Australia or Afghanistan. Ironically, Turkey was rewarded for its legalistic approach to community inclusion.[65] The World Heritage Centre endorsed Turkey's limited understanding of site management simply because the legal amendments made were "seen as an important step in giving greater local ownership of cultural heritage."[66]

In the lead-up to the Committee's discussion of the dossier during its St. Petersburg meeting, a senior Turkish government official, on learning that I was an archaeologist working at Çatalhöyük, took the opportunity to express his frustration. He was angry about UNESCO's interference in what he considered exclusively national matters; he also wanted all foreign archaeologists out of Turkey. ICOMOS had questioned the ongoing commitment of the Turkish authorities to funding the site's preservation. He stated categorically that his government could provide the millions of dollars required annually for excavation and conservation of the site that were currently being raised by the Çatalhöyük Research Project. From his perspective, there was no need for the international team, many of whom were in fact Turkish. Like the local community, archaeologists were expedient participants when showcasing the site and research contributions needed to justify its "Outstanding Universal Value" but could, after inscription, be jettisoned.

Despite a positive evaluation from the field mission, the final ICOMOS recommendation was for site referral. Concerns were raised over long-term oversight and funding, the role of local authorities, and the fate of Çatalhöyük after 2018, when the twenty-five-year excavation project would end. Irrespective of requests for further information and guarantees from Turkey, it took only twenty-five minutes for Çatalhöyük to be inscribed on the World Heritage List. On July 1, 2012, the ICOMOS recommendation for referral was transformed into inscription, eradicating any concerns over the sustainability of site funding or management. The Indian ambassador, who had urged the Committee to move immediately to inscription, described it as one of the "more joyful moments in this meeting... this is momentous, you actually have a site that is probably the first of its kind... the World Heritage List *must* have this site, it's the other way around, without this you're incomplete."[67] He and other members congratulated Turkey's efforts, noting that "the main management issues at Çatalhöyük had been defined based on, in part, information derived from a stakeholder consultation."[68]

There have been several consequences of World Heritage listing at Çatalhöyük. Most visibly, more than twenty new official signs brandishing UNESCO's logo now line the road covering the short distance from the city of Konya to the excavation site of Çatalhöyük. This marketing is geared to the phenomenon of World Heritage tourism, catering primarily to Asian visitors. After inscription, visitor numbers to the site rose significantly. Less publicly visible was the government directive in 2015 that archaeologists could no longer conduct public outreach or work in the nearby village, thus inhibiting a long-term partnership. This aspect of the archaeological project, along with its long-term education initiatives, had been included in the original UNESCO dossier. The Çatalhöyük Research Project had developed in tandem with a commitment to local collaboration and inclusion spanning more than twenty years; these relationships were now forbidden under the archaeological site permit, just as the state's promises for local development had been promptly withdrawn.[69] These partnerships had served their purpose and were not simply abandoned by the state—they were prohibited.

Archaeology, as practiced globally, has developed along a more participatory, community-oriented, and rights-based trajectory since the 1980s, well before such priorities were acknowledged within the World

Heritage sphere. The facility for including other voices, dialogue and dissent, and alternative pasts and futures forms an integral dimension of archaeology today, yet that threatens Turkey's government, which increasingly suppresses its minorities and indeed any opposition.[70] With Turkey's increasing Islamicization, the site of Çatalhöyük has become more difficult to embrace within the national imaginary than it was when the site was first inventoried on the Tentative List, because the site represents the problem of prehistory, the problem of foreign presence in the form of archaeologists, and the problem of closer international scrutiny and multilateral assessment from UNESCO. Konya constitutes the heartland of Erdoğan's Justice and Development Party, the Adalet ve Kalkınma Partisi (AKP). However, the rural population living around Çatalhöyük remains largely inconsequential in the modalities of state power. Before becoming president, Recep Tayyip Erdoğan was mayor of Istanbul, and his vision for Turkey remains intensely urban-centered and pro-business. This realization, coupled with a failed coup in 2016, sustained terror attacks, and the discovery of ISIS cells in Konya, has only fueled local exclusion, disillusionment, and alienation following the 2012 inscription.[71] Unfortunately, expressions of disaffection and violence have become more common around heritage sites, whether one examines post-collapse Greece or religious tensions in Indonesia. In this escalation the particular visibility and status of UNESCO World Heritage has often been transformed from international icon to international target.

Conclusions

Since the end of the Second World War UNESCO has dedicated itself to saving the monuments of the past for its particular vision of the future. One major development in that mission was the invention of the World Heritage List more than forty years ago. Today the business of inscribing World Heritage properties has reached new heights, enticing almost all the nations of the world to ratify the 1972 Convention and have their national patrimony internationally recognized. Yet precisely how national aspirations for listing become manifest and the lengths to which States Parties are willing to go to achieve their goals vary considerably. Moreover, under these diverse political conditions, determining whether UNESCO recognition ensures the long-term sustainability of remarkable places is a more uncertain prospect.

Today there are complex levels of interconnectivity at every stage of the inscriptional process, as the WikiLeaks cables effectively reveal. Indeed, this extends back to the selection and nomination process before the business of inscription itself takes place in World Heritage Committee sessions. On one hand, these negotiations are characterized by expanding international circuits, but on the other, the listing of sites is infused with the most intense national aspirations of territoriality, identity claims, and economic ambition. The example of inscribing the Preah Vihear Temple encapsulates the dense web of connectivity between national and international interests. Heritage recognition is thus a vehicle to make manifest broad and powerful claims on history and territory. Yet World Heritage inscription is no longer sutured to the specificities of the material past, and World Heritage Committee attention to historical narratives and veracity is minimal. Rather, listing is tantamount to investing in the potentialities of political, military, monetary, and cultural transactions and gains. Committee deliberations over specific properties, their inscription on the World Heritage List, and their protection or even destruction have become largely irrelevant in substance, yet highly valuable in state-to-state negotiations and exchanges of social capital.

World Heritage designation is also considered by the states parties as an investment in the future. Examples in this chapter from France, Germany, and India evince how capitalizing culture now offers a suite of new modalities garnered through multiple transactions. These developments have not gone unnoticed, and NGOs such as the World Wildlife Fund have been eager to develop metrics for measuring "good" or "poor" conservation performance by individual states parties. This is one external attempt by a conservation agency to keep states in line through naming and shaming, something that UNESCO, as an intergovernmental organization, cannot undertake. The business of heritage thus acts as a proxy for other global benchmarks such as good governance, transparency, sustainability, and modernity, as the conservation and management of Angkor demonstrated for Cambodia. It is not only a presencing of the nation's past in the present but also an instantiation of sovereign commitments for the future.

In view of the strategies nations employ and the money expended on compiling nomination dossiers and pursuing inscription, there is a growing dissatisfaction with the official process and serious attempts have been made to change the rules. As the Lebanese delegate Jad Tabet warns, World Heritage is now considered "too serious" a matter to be left to mere experts, despite such shifts being in contradiction with the

1972 Convention. State Party dissatisfaction with the status quo has been exacerbated by the fact that some states use their election to the Committee to submit a maximum of nominated properties, others apply for membership repeatedly, and most countries employ still other modes of influence to fulfill their ambitions. However, it not simply the issue of states parties bending the rules: the Advisory Bodies are increasingly under closer scrutiny for their professional practices, capacity, and potential conflicts of interest. "ICOMOS seems to behave as if it were a thesis committee where the student is judged on the level and quality of its services!" Tabet once chided. Other prominent ambassadors have been quick to suggest that the annual meetings should be restructured and that precious time could be saved if documents were sent out ahead of presentations instead of having to follow them. From their perspective, this would leave time for the important issues, which means site inscriptions first and foremost.

Why is having a national site on an international register seen as so important today? Nation-states see UNESCO recognition as an effective means to accrue tourism revenues, branding and development, national acknowledgment and justification, and, increasingly, a path toward greater self-determination in the face of competition and conflict. Yet these intensely national agendas are best acknowledged and bolstered by the international community, and UNESCO's soft power instruments are a prime medium to see those sovereign ambitions met. UNESCO offers the perfect forum to satisfy domestic desires through international accords. Comparatively speaking, UNESCO might seem to be a low-profile agency within the United Nations, largely serving the cultural sector. However, securing a seat on the twenty-one-member World Heritage Committee is seen by many states parties as one way to effectively raise their profiles across the UN more generally. Influence in matters of global patrimony offers a soft option in the realm of international influence underpinned by the workings of cultural diplomacy. In an expansive ecology of exchange, these cross-sectoral alliances and arrangements have been observed across the UN, the World Bank, and the International Monetary Fund. Vote-swapping across these agencies, including UNESCO and support for Committee membership or site inscription, has become a familiar and well-attested practice.[72]

In all of this politicking, the conservation of the world's heritage may be the loser. Jad Tabet concludes that today the World Heritage List is not a list of properties of "Outstanding Universal Value" in the sense originally defined in the Convention, but a list of properties that are representative of different cultures and regions. What ultimately matters is to find ways to ensure the long-term conservation of these properties.[73] But there are other consequences too for the communities who are historically, culturally, or spiritually connected to these significant places. As documented through the process of inscribing Çatalhöyük, there are real consequences before and after listing that are keenly felt by connected communities: they can become the victims or beneficiaries of World Heritage inscription depending entirely on the role of the state and relations with its citizens. Here UNESCO and the World Heritage Centre possess little traction to monitor, much less hold states to account.

The challenge today of protecting the world's heritage, of managing the remarkable, is one salient issue. The role of UNESCO and its List in that process is another. Whatever scrutiny is applied, we must recognize that, as an organization with a global reach, for the past seventy years UNESCO been deeply influential in making that protection possible. But at the supranational level of multilateral organizations, the most significant issue remains, in my view, the inability to reconcile fundamentally different worldviews. This was brought home to me after lively discussions with one Scandinavian and one Latin American delegation, both of which had served on the World Heritage Committee. The Scandinavian State Party was committed to gender equality and education and regularly offers financial support across Africa and for human rights development. They are aware of being ridiculed for their naivety in political matters, but still maintain that the "conduct of conduct" in the Committee has gone awry. Considering these developments pragmatically, they still maintain that UNESCO provides a noncombative forum to air grievances and differences. Their outlook remains optimistic. The Latin American State Party did not agree that the Committee has become more politicized. In fact, they argued for greater and far-reaching changes to serve the needs of the States Parties, thus overturning the authority of the Advisory Bodies or the Secretariat. They caricatured rule-following Committee members such as Estonia and Switzerland, who upheld the recommendations of these bodies. One official put his hands to his head, making the sign of the devil, and laughed as he told me, "We call them the axis of evil."

6

Conflict

*The hottest places in Hell are reserved for those who in time
of moral crisis preserve their neutrality.*
—JOHN F. KENNEDY (MISQUOTING DANTE), 1963

TURKEY HOSTED THE World Heritage Committee meetings in Istanbul in July 2016 amidst a taut atmosphere of high-profile attacks perpetrated by ISIS and the Kurdistan Workers Party (PKK). Ten days before the meetings commenced on July 10, gunmen had killed scores of people and injured hundreds more at Atatürk International Airport in Istanbul. In light of the instability, some national delegations, such as Australia, withdrew from the meetings; many international observers did the same. The World Heritage Committee meetings were held in the Istanbul Congress Center, close to Taksim Square, known for its anti-government demonstrations, like those protesting the urban development of nearby Gezi Park. We were flanked on one side by a police station and on the other by the Harbiye Military House, making us a potential target for ISIS and PKK insurgents. With such intense armed military and police presence surrounding us, nerves were frayed. Delegates entered the Congress Center daily through police barricades and body scanners, with heightened security checks and screening. Then midway through the meetings, on the evening of July 15, a military coup was staged in Istanbul and Ankara. Military aircraft fired on targets in both cities, tanks rolled through the streets, civilians joined in the fighting. More than three hundred people were killed during the night and many thousands were detained in the immediate aftermath. A further 160,000 have been purged since the coup: military officials, police officers, judges, governors, university deans, professors, teachers, journalists, and civil servants. Torture, detention, and social unrest ensued, leading many to speculate without evidence that the coup was staged and orchestrated by President Erdoğan himself in order to justify a brutal crackdown and extend his already significant personal powers.

In the midst of this suspension of democracy and human rights, UNESCO was put in an awkward position: accede to the UN security directive and return to Paris or bow to Turkey's pressure to resume the Committee meetings as if nothing had happened. Given the constraints of diplomacy, the UNESCO webpage for the live-streamed sessions on July 16 simply said "suspended until further notice." UNESCO's staff and some national delegations, including those serving on the Committee, were staying in the adjacent Hilton Hotel—its construction, backed by the US Marshall Plan, is a monument to midcentury Cold War tensions.[1] Those participants had ample security, briefings, and travel assistance, whereas other delegations and observers were left to fend for themselves. Some woke up to find shattered glass and blood on the pavement; others actually slept through the bombardment and turned up the next day expecting a regular session. Many participants complained that neither assistance nor information had been offered, and since international flights had been cancelled, they felt left to the mercy of others. Moreover, their continued presence in Istanbul was being used domestically for political purposes.

A compromise was reached whereby the Committee would resume its work for one more day and then postpone the rest of the agenda till they could meet again in November at UNESCO's Paris headquarters. Significantly, since the meetings had been interrupted in the midst of the all-important nominations to the World Heritage List, the impetus to continue was strong, not just for Turkey but for other States Parties to get what they had come for. During his speech on July 17, the Turkish minister for culture and tourism, Nabi Avcı, disagreed with the decision to postpone, stating that Turkey "would have liked for the 40th Committee [to continue], right through to the 20th, and the highest possible security measures were taken. So despite the re-assurance that security was ensured, the UN security division and UNESCO [decided] the final day of work would be today."[2] The Turkish Committee chair, Lale Ülker, repeated this same statement several months later in Paris. Turkey saw the UN decision as a lack of recognition of its resolve and control of the situation. Turkish authorities had guaranteed the safety of participants, since the Congress Center would be heavily secured. But in reality the place was deserted in the wake of the coup; with so many arrests and the detentions, the armored water cannon and police vehicles at the entrance were unmanned. Another lasting image was the Turkish ambassador corralling

Committee members in a corridor, interviewing them about their experience in Turkey, all of which was recorded on a shaky iPhone video, echoing Erdoğan's now famous FaceTime call to arms during the coup only two days earlier.

After the night of the coup and the resumption of the session on July 17, States Parties that took the floor first expressed their sympathy and solidarity with Turkey. Each scripted performance was captured in a live stream and archived on UNESCO's website. This was also a moment when UNESCO and its Secretariat could have been co-opted. Previously Turkish representatives had distributed Turkish flags to the members of the Secretariat on the podium, perhaps hoping that they would be inclined to wave them in a global show of support for the government; they did not. All around Taksim Square vast flags were draped over buildings, and lines of flags hung up and down all the streets in an orchestrated show of defiance. This had been a momentous meeting for Turkey, demonstrating not only its resilience and resolve against insurrection but also its resources for, and commitment to, World Heritage. Both had come together on July 15, 2016.

The day had started with a political victory, with Turkey's controversial nomination of the archaeological site of Ani.[3] This historic landscape had been considered part of Armenian territory in the Treaty of Sèvres, signed in 1920 at the Paris Peace Conference, only to be awarded to Turkey under the Treaty of Lausanne in 1923. At present Turkey and Armenia have no diplomatic relationship, only a bitter hostility in large part fueled by Turkey's denial of the Armenian genocide (1915–1922).[4] Starting at 4:40 p.m., the live transmission of the Committee session was blocked and did not resume till Turkish ambassador Huseyin Botsalı took the floor, after all discussion of Ani had concluded and the site was inscribed.[5] Turkey had banned the UNESCO broadcast, as the government does for all events that it finds problematic. Later that evening coverage of the coup would also be blocked in Turkey, and updates were only available through foreign news agencies.

Ani is an archaeological landscape, with the remains of churches, mosques, temples, ramparts, palaces, and rock-carved dwellings. But most celebrated are the Armenian churches from the tenth through thirteenth centuries CE. Known as the "City of 1,001 Churches," Ani was the capital of the medieval Armenian Bagratid Kingdom.[6] ICOMOS had commissioned an extraordinary number of site evaluators for Ani, knowing the transnational significance and potential volatility: its recommendation had been for deferral.[7] Turkey's proposed cultural landscape concept was not developed, the management plan was not coordinated, the comparative analysis was lacking, and there were only nods to multiculturalism. In their view, another expert mission to Ani would be required after their numerous recommendations had been implemented. Enormous pressure was placed on ICOMOS representatives during the nomination process and in the lead-up to the meetings. For some of the less-experienced evaluators this was both shocking and frightening. Turkish officials had previously met with ICOMOS in Paris and dismissed their findings, responding that no matter what the report said, Turkey would have Ani inscribed. They were holding the meetings in Istanbul and it would go through. While Turkey had lobbied hard amongst the Committee members, Korea resolutely called upon Turkey to actively work with others to present the full and complex history of the site. When the paragraph pertaining to this issue was "accidentally" cut from the final decision, Korea again spoke up to have it reinstated. This was an important recognition for Armenia.

Paradoxically, given the specter of the Armenian genocide, Ambassador Botsalı claimed that "Anatolia is not a cemetery of cultures and civilizations, Anatolia is a museum of cultures and civilizations." Using every opportunity to recast the insidious politics underlying the inscription, he purported

FIGURE 6.1 Archaeological landscape of Ani, Turkey, courtesy of Sarah Murray

to be "happy to see that our neighbors Iran, Georgia and Armenia also are present during the deliberations of this important resolution. I was also happy to see my counterpart from Armenia came to congratulate us." Given the overt politics and history of violence, including Turkey's official denial of the genocide, the State Party of Armenia then took the floor, saying, "If it is a jewel it belongs to humanity not to just one nation." Drawing upon their diplomatic reserves, Armenia acknowledged that theirs was a nation "70% of whose cultural heritage is situated outside its administrative borders," with many neighboring states responsible for the protection and preservation of its patrimony. No mention was made of the Turkish overrestoration in the 1990s that erased Ani's Christian symbols, its fictional reconstructions, and its excessive use of cement, much less the genocide.[8]

Resurrecting the Past

Ani is a potent example of a recent trend in World Heritage inscriptions where sites are explicitly selected because they both signify and materialize nodal points in historical conflicts and territorial disputes. UNESCO is increasingly drawn into these global disputes, yet its conventions do not make adequate provision for the adjudication or resolution of such conflicts. Moreover, when a State Party is shown to be in direct violation of a convention, there is no effective mechanism to hold it accountable, much less impose a penalty or reverse the conflict. It is noteworthy that in some cases involving historical conflicts it is the aggressors that nominate contested sites and then celebrate anew those hostilities. For Turkey, the "new truth regime" of the AKP, as it has been termed, hides behind the rhetoric of multiculturalism and rapprochement that agencies such as UNESCO hope to promulgate. Thus heritage recognition can be mobilized to "open new domains for manipulation, injury, and re-victimization."[9] Sites such as Ani constitute the cultural battleground for hearts and minds, for recognition and social justice, as well as being physically embroiled in struggles over national sovereignty.

Like Preah Vihear in Cambodia, Ani is strategically situated along a sensitive international border; the boundary once divided NATO from the Soviet Union. The border between the Republics of Armenia and Turkey has been closed since 1993.[10] The nomination of Ani could well have been a transboundary effort between Turkey and Armenia, just as Preah Vihear's nomination could have included Thailand. If, as Ambassador

Botsalı stressed, inscribing Ani reflected a new era of "dialogue, compromise and reconciliation above all other considerations," then why not collaborate with Armenia in the nomination? After all, Turkey claimed the inscription was "a gift, a vision, a vision of hope for future generations, generations across the border not only in Turkey but in the neighboring states." Botsalı's rhetoric, summed up by the phrase "a moment of hope, a time to heal," was merely a performance for the international community. Yet on the ground, the Armenian presence in Anatolia and even use of the term "Armenian" in Turkey today remain negatively inflected. Given the AKP's antipathy toward free speech and the harsh penal code against insulting the Turkish nation, public intellectuals have been prosecuted for even engaging in debate over the Armenian genocide perpetrated during the final years of Ottoman rule.[11] A century ago Henry Morgenthau, the US ambassador to the Ottoman Empire, published his chilling encounter with Turkish officials and in doing so revealed that the atrocities were not religiously motivated but "a cold-blooded, calculating state policy." Morganthau considered that Turkey had brokered new "methods of massacre" and, moreover, "that the whole history of the human race contains no such horrible episode as this."[12]

What motivates a country like Turkey to nominate a conflictual landscape like Ani? Conservation of its historic remains had not been a priority in the past. In fact, as architectural historian Heghnar Watenpaugh documents, Ani was in the international spotlight precisely because its future was endangered under Turkey's management. The integrity of its monuments has been threatened by natural disasters over the course of the last hundred years, and by the human ravages of war, neglect, looting, and intentional damage. Given its precarious position, Ani regularly featured on the World Monuments Fund's high-profile watch list of monuments in danger.[13] Another conservation NGO, the Global Heritage Fund, recently designated Ani as one of twelve cultural heritage sites on the verge of vanishing altogether. Given the negative report from ICOMOS, it is safe to conclude that the conservation of Ani remains a low priority for Turkey and will likely continue to be so. The real gains here are international: recognizing Turkey's sovereignty and regional dominance, crafting an image of Turkey's modernity and civility in multicultural matters, and rewriting history to systematically erase an Armenian past. Redrawing the lines involves a rewriting of history in the UNESCO dossier, recasting Ani as the entry point of Turkic peoples into Anatolia, followed by the widespread adoption and dominance of "Turkish culture."[14] World Heritage inscription thus provides an internationally sanctioned instrument for manufacturing the past, dispensing with historical justice and reconciliation, and potentially reviving old hostilities anew.

In previous decades only a small number of properties received World Heritage recognition on the basis of their intensely negative heritage. Yet such sites have been included from the beginning of the Convention.[15] The Island of Gorée, in Senegal, was inscribed in 1978 as a reminder of human exploitation during the international slave trade; Auschwitz Birkenau German Nazi Concentration and Extermination Camp, inscribed in 1979, reveals the conditions within which the Nazi genocide took place and remains a potent symbol of humanity's cruelty; and the Hiroshima Peace Memorial, listed in 1996, was the only structure left standing in the area where the first atomic bomb exploded on August 6, 1945.[16] A negative historical value conveyed a lesson for the future, from this perspective, and served a "dreadful warning against any recurrence of the events which took place there." Importantly, all of these sites were listed on the basis of World Heritage criterion (vi), being directly or tangibly associated with events or living traditions, with ideas, with beliefs, or with artistic and literary works of outstanding universal significance. However, it has been the preference of the World Heritage Secretariat and Committee that this criterion not be used alone, but rather be taken in conjunction with other criteria.[17] There has also been a general unwillingness to inscribe more sites of violence on the List. And yet Rwanda would like to list sites associated with the 1994 genocide, while South Africa is eager to enshrine its liberation struggle and has two such nominations on the Tentative List. Moreover, Thailand has expressed dissatisfaction with being deterred from nominating conflict sites such as the Death Railway, the Burma-Siam Railway built by Japan using forced labor and prisoners of war. Thailand has developed its portion of the railway as a major tourist attraction, and inscription and UNESCO branding would further boost these initiatives.[18] Irrespective of UNESCO's position, the Thai Fine Arts Department wants this dossier to move forward. When asked about the potential for igniting conflicts with other countries, one Ministry of Culture representative in Bangkok explained to me that he did not consider this to be the pertinent issue. Instead he asked why European sites from the Second World War should be inscribed as World Heritage but not Asian ones. This was surely just another example of European exceptionalism.

Eclipsed by the dystopic destruction of heritage sites in the Middle East, we have perhaps overlooked the more routinized and symbolic violence that has started to seep into the World Heritage system. UNESCO was, after all, born of war and established in the wake of conflict with the dream of overcoming future conflict. From that perspective, European properties such as the Historic Centre of Warsaw and Auschwitz Birkenau are deeply symbolic sites that not only demonstrate human resilience to overcome the brutality of war but also enshrine something of UNESCO's own story.[19] It was, after all, the devastation and cultural destruction in Europe, rather than Asia per se, that guided many of UNESCO's early efforts, recommendations, and indeed conventions. It should come as no surprise, then, that other regions of the world, particularly in that other arena of war, Asia, consider it only fair and balanced to propose their own historical sites for recognition. However, in several recent cases resurrecting the past has only exacerbated simmering tensions, historical denials, and unresolved territorial struggles. Japan's recent inscription of the Meiji sites, for example, signals the Abe government's hard-line stance on nationalism, militarism, and historical memory. Abe's refusal to apologize for atrocities committed during the Second World War, coupled with the inscription of sites where the forcible exploitation of foreign women took place, has deeply offended both China and Korea.[20] While the industrial ruins of Hashima, also known as Battleship Island, served as a dystopian backdrop in the James Bond film *Skyfall*, its twentieth-century history reveals a more pernicious real-life conflict.

The Sites of Japan's Meiji Industrial Revolution: Iron and Steel, Shipbuilding and Coal Mining has some twenty-three components dating from the mid-nineteenth century to the early twentieth century and was inscribed in 2015 on the basis of criteria (ii) and (iv).[21] The Meiji sites purportedly show how feudal Japan sought the first technology transfer from the West, industrializing the nation according to its own social traditions. What has not been highlighted are the forced labor and sexual slavery of thousands of Chinese and Koreans in that process of industrialization. Strategically, Japan chose British and Australian experts in industrial heritage to help compile the dossier so as to impress ICOMOS and guarantee a positive recommendation. Given the sensitivities involved, this was always going to be a fraught case, resisting containment and laden with the potential to further inflame hostilities. During the Bonn meetings, the German chair rigidly controlled the proceedings by disallowing any Committee discussion and by reading aloud a prepared text. All the negotiations had been dealt with "offstage." Only Germany would be permitted to take the floor for one amendment, adding a footnote requiring "an understanding

FIGURE 6.2 Gunkanjima or Battleship Island, Nagasaki, Japan one of the Meiji industrial sites, courtesy of Shutterstock

of the full history of each site" in the new interpretive strategy. Whether Germany took this role as host nation or because of its shared role as historic aggressor in the same conflict was never stated.

After inscription, Japan first took the floor, reading a text directly prepared by the government. They were willing "to take measures that allow an understanding that there were a large number of Koreans and others who were brought against their will and forced to work under harsh conditions at some sites in 1940s, and that during World War Two the government of Japan also implemented its policy of requisition." The victims would be remembered in an information center. Korea responded by repeating the Japanese admission that their citizens "were forced to work." But they had joined the Committee consensus to inscribe the site, trusting that the Committee would continue to follow up on all measures promised by Japan. Korea concluded by "remembering the pain and suffering of the victims, healing the painful wounds of history and reaffirming that the historical truth of the unfortunate past should also be reflected in an objective manner." China was also outraged about the inscription and circulated a letter of protest but was not called upon to speak, since it was not a Committee member.[22] The next day the Japanese foreign minister confirmed in the press that his government's position remained unchanged. Revealing the pretense of diplomacy that was performed in Bonn, Fumio

Kishida countered that being "forced to work" is not the same as "forced labor."[23]

Back in Paris one Japanese representative confirmed to me that the impetus for inscribing the Meiji sites had come straight from Abe's office. He and the deputy prime minister had nominated sites from both their prefectures. The dossier was part of a concerted new strategy, departing from Japan's former passivity and acquiescence: the Meiji sites highlighted that Japan was a great power, having a long history of technological sophistication. Asked whether the listing was a direct provocation, he looked down and declined to respond directly, saying, "Culture is political." Japan received significant pressure in the lead-up to inscription from China and Korea to withdraw the nomination, but the country felt that it had to remain forceful and not back down. Japan suffers from a kind of "apology fatigue," and while many of its citizens accept their country's responsibility for its role in the conflict, they also cynically regard China's increasing demands as a diplomatic offensive to gain advantage.[24] Japan uses UNESCO very effectively for its own program of cultural nationalism, whereby international recognition of public and politicized culture, based on authenticity, bolsters national identity and autonomy.[25] Japan is not frightened of UNESCO, one diplomat announced to me over a lavish lunch, not like smaller Asian nations or small states on the World Heritage Committee. He noted that Japan was now the largest donor to UNESCO after the US financial withdrawal and so would not be put off from nominating other controversial sites. Put simply, Japan was fully prepared for the Meiji sites to spark conflict leading to a protracted negotiation.

Korea, on the other hand, had hoped that Japan would back down during the long process of diplomatic negotiation. One delegate, clearly frustrated that there was no mechanism to incorporate Korea's viewpoint, described how Committee members simply retreated from the conflict, using the pretense of "politicization," when they wished to avoid any involvement. Several States Parties on the Committee explained to him that "we must be immune, insulated from politics." This feigned neutrality struck him as a "false position" given the history and constitution of UNESCO. For Korea this was neither a peaceful process nor one in the spirit of the 1972 Convention. Despite the scripted speeches in Bonn, they remained very unhappy. The live-streaming of the event also added to the pain, since there were still survivors and this history was felt very much at home. The scale of this conflict and its connectivity at the highest levels were reflected in the simultaneous replacement of both the Japanese and Korean ambassadors for UNESCO relations after serving only two years. The dossier, I was told repeatedly, was so contentious that new faces were needed, with less history and political baggage. Among international diplomats this irregular diplomatic shuffle signaled power plays from the very top. Japan's unwillingness to relinquish the Meiji nomination, despite resurrecting old conflicts and inciting new ones, reveals all the hallmarks of the "internationalization of nationalism."

The doctrine of national self-determination is entrenched as a basic principle in the United Nations Charter and in various treaties, including the World Heritage Convention, and invoked repeatedly in the theater of conflict.[26] More than simply deploying nationalistic fervor through affirming territorial jurisdiction and political sovereignty, nation-states must demonstrate a measure of cultural unity and solidarity, as well as cultural uniqueness in terms of language, religion, customs, and cultural history. This is yet another reason World Heritage recognition, with all its systemic entanglements, has become so charged in an international arena. Rather than diminishing the influence of nationalism or dissolving the fabric of nations in aspirations of universalism, world-making processes such as World Heritage inventorying instead "encourage nations to become more participant and distinctive."[27] The instrumentalization of culture and heritage in arenas of conflict, both to resurrect historic struggles and to ignite new hostilities, is being played out on a global scale at UNESCO, and there is little within the framework of its "soft" international treaties to take powerful states to task.

Bombs and Mines

Describing the lead-up to the 2008 World Heritage Committee meetings, the director of the World Heritage Centre at the time, Francesco Bandarin, shared with the US delegation "certain issues that are already sure to spark intense debate, which he called the 'bombs.'" In the leaked diplomatic cable, American diplomats further divulged that the director's "concern is trying to identify the unseen 'mines' which have not yet been anticipated."[28] In Quebec that same year the Preah Vihear Temple was inscribed and immediately sparked a cross-border conflict with Thailand, as described in Chapter 5. UNESCO responded to the crisis by sending a Reinforced Monitoring mission in 2009, the objective being to assess "the State of Conservation of the World Heritage property . . . without attempting to determine the dynamics of events or the responsibilities of the parties involved."[29] Military standoffs continued to flare up almost to the brink of full-scale war, not only damaging bilateral talks but also threatening the unity of ASEAN.[30] In February and April 2011 tense border clashes resumed, with many casualties and the displacement of thousands of civilians. That conflict lasted several years, resulting in loss of life and livelihoods and destruction to property, including to the Shiva temple itself. To document the disaster, Cambodia had prepared a booklet of photographs for the 2011 World Heritage Committee meetings in Paris showing the evidence of real bombs and mines around the site.

Leading up to the World Heritage meetings in Paris, UNESCO Director-General Irina Bokova convened a dialogue between Thailand and Cambodia, hoping to "foster common understanding of the issues affecting the World Heritage site, and to reach agreement on enhancing its State of Conservation following recent threats to the property."[31] In an example of failed diplomacy, the latent cross-border struggle was revived through the processes of nomination and inscription and the subsequent deliberations.[32] Given that UNESCO listing sparked the most recent spate of violence and that other measures might have been taken beforehand, the organization was in a weaker position than usual to forge a peaceful outcome.[33] Legal scholars have written extensively on the need for an explicit mechanism within World Heritage to consider political disputes under the general principles of international law, some calling for an arbitrational body to be established to deal with cases like Preah Vihear. Unlike other fields of international law, such as foreign investment or human rights, "international cultural heritage law does not have an ad hoc mechanism of norms enforcement and dispute settlement."[34] Increasingly, the World Heritage Committee must navigate incendiary conflicts, such as those between Thailand and Cambodia, Turkey and Armenia, and Russia and Ukraine, that entail border disputes and long-standing tensions. And of course there are slow-burning conflicts involving Kosovo and Jerusalem that have extended over many years, in plain sight, but tend to be muted in Committee deliberations. What typically happens in these cases is suspension of all Committee debate, with the agenda item postponed till the following year, stanching overt hostility by papering over the crisis indefinitely. World Heritage with its mantle of shared humanity, cultural Esperanto, and presumed neutrality has clearly been progressively drawn into international conflicts, not simply as reflective fallout of past violence but rather as constitutive of contemporary conflict.

In recent years UNESCO has witnessed a predictable war of nominations and recriminations, often traversing different international treaties, whether the 1972 World Heritage Convention or the Memory of the World Register. Japan and China's conflicts have been played out in both arenas, with China confronting Japan with controversies such as those of the "comfort women" and the Nanjing massacre, and Japan retaliating by listing the Meiji industrial sites.[35] Tokyo has challenged UNESCO's neutrality and has threatened to suspend its funding to UNESCO, following the strategy employed by the United States.[36] Undeterred by the Meiji conflict, in 2016 Japan entered another controversial property onto its Tentative List, Amami-Oshima Island, Tokunoshima Island, the northern part of Okinawa Island, and Iriomote Island.[37] These four islands lie at the heart of a bitter territorial dispute in the East China Sea, where China claims that neither it nor Japan has "carried out maritime delimitation. Therefore the waters beyond territorial water of the islands are overlapping area of the two countries' maritime claims. The unilateral move of Japan will cause prejudice to China's maritime interests."[38] Japan, sidestepping the issue of overlapping claims, purports that the islands offer "outstanding examples of speciation and phylogenetic diversification of terrestrial organisms at various stages through varying extents of geographic isolation." The international maneuvers by Japan and China reveal a tit-for-tat trading of insults and injuries by way of different cultural conventions. Moreover, they demonstrate how the materiality of heritage is deployed to further leverage territorial advantage, a strategy that appears to be escalating.

These escalations run counter to UNESCO's central tenet of advancing dialogue and inclusiveness between nations or "learning to live together." According to their Medium Term Strategy covering 2014–21, "UNESCO will promote the role of shared or cross-border cultural heritage and initiatives to build bridges among nations and communities. Efforts will be undertaken to offer new perspectives on disseminating and teaching knowledge of history."[39] But instead, the ramping up of conflictual heritage, whereby contentious sites are knowingly proposed and pushed, suggests that World Heritage is being mobilized as a proxy for international conflict. Given culture's soft power potential, UNESCO recognition can easily mask the hostile political intent of states through the pretense of gesturing toward monumental, artistic, and conservation concerns. This public performance in support of global heritage belies the dense network of transactions, exchanges, and consequences that occur offstage. In the case of the Meiji sites, many other Asian States Parties were pressured, lobbied, and placed in the impossible position of offending either China and Korea, on one hand, or Japan, on the other. The stakes are not insignificant for Asian nations such as Vietnam and the Philippines, which at the time were serving on the World Heritage Committee. Backstage transactions and diplomatic exchanges do not necessarily result in the mutually beneficial economic arrangements that the case of Preah Vihear reveals, but rather may involve webs of coercion, threats, and retaliation.

Like other fictions of neutrality at UNESCO, contentious nominations and listings are typically handled like mines rather than bombs: as threats that have not yet emerged into the open, and which can be defused through diplomatic protocol. In this way the "political" is masked as the "technical" during World Heritage deliberations. Through these restrained performances, difficult issues and conflicts between nations can be aired, and possibly even resolved, without taking sides or apportioning blame. Chairing a difficult meeting on revisions to the Convention's Operation Guidelines, Jad Tabet remarked, "This is not a technical issue. It is a question of sovereignty." Tabet was attempting to ease the friction between Japan and China over putting forward the four islands in the East China Sea on Japan's Tentative List. This was all being done under the guise of revising one paragraph of the Operational Guidelines pertaining to the Tentative Lists that States Parties compile. Everyone in the room was aware of the underlying tensions; however, no delegate would explicitly name the property or the disputing states, so the debate was transmuted into the technicalities of documentation, including how data might be uploaded, verified, and presented on UNESCO's website. Frustrated by the unwillingness of delegates to address the underlying problem of sovereignty, Tabet declared, "We are talking about one State Party nominating a site that another feels it is in their property. Right now any State Party can claim any site on the Tentative List. A few years ago there was a kind of decency that states didn't nominate sites in conflict, but that decency has disappeared and sites are nominated in contested situations." The performance of neutrality, obfuscation, and maintenance of the status quo are all hallmarks of multilateral organizations and, in a sense, allow them to function amidst the conflicts of their Member States.

The World Heritage Committee is not compelled to consider potential conflict or existing hostilities when making its decisions. However, the Convention and guidelines are not entirely silent on the subject of potential disputes.[40] Article 11.3 of the World Heritage Convention indicates that State Party consent is required for inclusion on the World Heritage

List and that "inclusion of a property situated in a territory, sovereignty or jurisdiction over which is claimed by more than one State shall in no way prejudice the rights of the parties to the dispute."[41] Yet as mentioned above, the 1972 Convention fails to provide a road map for how disputes might be resolved or even considered in the context of site inscription. Furthermore, as legal scholar Allan Galis notes, the provision is silent as to cases where State Parties do not willingly cooperate, such as Thailand and Cambodia, particularly when nominated sites are located on disputed borders. Because the Convention indicates that disputed sovereignty over a property will not prejudice the rights of the disagreeing parties to later seek inscription under their respective names, there is no incentive for states to resolve the conflict themselves before initiating the nomination process.[42] To remedy such a situation, Galis proposes the establishment of an independent body "composed entirely of neutral state representatives" to enable mediation and arbitration and allow interested state representatives to petition that body.

The proposed body would conduct hearings and consolidate the interested parties' motions, and could be responsive in ruling on cases on a rolling basis, rather than delaying until the annual World Heritage Committee meeting.[43] Such a major undertaking would necessitate changes to the Operational Guidelines and support from the World Heritage Committee, which may not accede to yet another authority and level of interference in what most states parties regard as sovereign matters. States are generally reluctant to commit to any compulsory jurisdiction and prefer to engage in direct negotiation, since this affords them greater control.[44] Yet even if such a body was established, how might such decisions be implemented, especially in light of fundamental disagreement and conflict over such incendiary issues as identity, history, territory, and sovereignty? Given the World Heritage Committee's and the World Heritage Centre's reticence to publicly debate and mediate conflicts, and their preferred recourse to behind-the-scenes diplomacy, imposing any additional structural and legal frameworks upon an already fraught system would prove exceedingly difficult.

A case in point was the Russian Federation's annexation of Crimea in late March 2014 and the implications for sites on Ukraine's World Heritage List and Tentative List. With Crimea, Russian president Vladimir Putin purported to be embracing international law, but was in effect "exploit[ing] the tension between a fundamental principle that prohibits the acquisition of territory through the use of force and an equally fundamental right of self-determination to take Crimea as its own."[45] Putin's legal argument rests on the right of intervention to protect ethnic Russians, appealing to the right of self-determination and subsequently independence. However, in response to Putin's military adventurism the UN General Assembly adopted a resolution affirming the sovereignty, political independence, unity, and territorial integrity of Ukraine within its internationally recognized borders. Following that resolution, and at the request of Ukraine, UNESCO drafted a statement after the 194th session of the Executive Board.[46] It outlined the ever-growing presence of Russian military forces and the resulting negative impact on Crimean cultural heritage. The Ancient City of Tauric Chersonese and its Chora was a specific concern: dating back to the ancient Greek colonization of the area in the fifth century BCE, this World Heritage site is in close proximity to Sevastopol, where the Russian Black Sea fleet is deployed.[47] Significantly, President Putin appropriated the World Heritage site as explicitly Russian heritage in his speeches, going so far as to use its history to justify the annexation.[48] The fight for Crimea, Putin lectured a group of young historians, is the fight for Chersonesus; the site has a sacred significance, considered the initial font of Russia's baptism. Crimea, he concluded, "is an essential part of our cultural life, our cultural code."[49]

Apart from the ancient city of Chersonesus, four other cultural sites on Ukraine's Tentative List have halted all activities with regard to their inclusion on the UNESCO World Heritage List. Concerns were also raised by Ukraine over the massive transfer of cultural objects from Crimean museums to the Russian capital, recalling Russia's obligations under international law related to cultural property. In rapid response to the criticism, Russian ambassador Eleonora Mitrofanova claimed that the text "presented by Ukraine is extremely politicized and does not reflect the actual situation in the peninsula. This document not only does not envisage any real assistance to the improvement of the situation in Crimea, but on the contrary, disorients UNESCO Member States and is therefore unacceptable."[50] However, in a 2016 State of Conservation report, Chersonesus was found to be in poor condition, with some structures being close to collapse.[51] Given the regional instability, neither ICOMOS nor UNESCO can send in evaluators or retrieve reliable information, and so they face another impasse.

In a reflection of the practical difficulties of independent World Heritage arbitration and mediation in the violation of international law, the Russian Ministry of Foreign Affairs has been adamant that any action taken by UNESCO in Crimea would first require the consent of the Russian Federation.[52] Ukraine, on the other hand, continues to report Russia's direct violations of UNESCO's 1972 World Heritage Convention, coupled with its 1954 Hague Convention, the 1970 Convention on the Means of Prohibiting and Preventing the Illicit Import, Export and Transfer of Ownership of Cultural Property, and the 1995 UNIDROIT Convention on Stolen or Illegally Exported Cultural Objects.[53] Other reports of gross violations have been widely circulated at UNESCO from partner agencies including the United Nations Office of the High Commissioner for Human Rights, the Council of Europe's Commissioner for Human Rights, and Amnesty International. It is one of those cases where the accumulation of paperwork documenting the problem both stands in for and masks the capacity to address issues directly. In some ways the Crimean situation is quite clear-cut, and a UN resolution was summarily passed; UNESCO has, however, been hamstrung in doing more than documenting the conflict, and has not been publicly outspoken in condemning it. The organization, perhaps understandably, takes refuge in its "fields of competence" stance, an assertion that the agency must primarily concern itself with culture rather than conflict.[54] Yet what is unfolding in Ukraine speaks precisely to UNESCO's fields of competence: cultural heritage, site conservation, protection for journalists, freedom of expression, religious and human rights, and so on.

Russia is patently in violation of the UNESCO cultural heritage conventions it has ratified. The reluctance to discuss this case more fully in World Heritage meetings undoubtedly pivots on the exceedingly powerful position of the State Party of Russia in terms of political and economic capital at UNESCO, on one hand, and its aggressive lobbying and intimidation of other Member States, on the other. As spokesperson for Russia's official position on UNESCO, Ambassador Mitrofanova asserted that "today we are witnessing a struggle for shaping a new world order. There are attempts to impose a pyramidal arrangement on the world, with the US and its allies on top as leaders and the rest doing their bidding and following their rules." Such an arrangement, she argued, ignores the opinion of the majority of Member States, and these "dead-end approaches" further "escalate tensions and instability in the world. Most countries in the world do not agree with them. And it is international organizations that shape common attitudes and formulate future agendas."[55] The language of a "new world order" ominously harks back to Woodrow Wilson's call for a League of Nations after the devastation of the First World War and, perhaps also in this context, to the end of the Cold War. Both embody significant meanings for the Russian Federation.

When the Secretariat, States Parties, and Committee have to contend with the "bombs" or "mines" of nomination, inscription, or conservation, each has a limited repertoire of legal mechanisms to assist with its resolution. On one hand, they must face the escalation of conflict through controversial site listing; on the other, they are charged with the conservation and management of those properties during and after episodes of conflict or destruction. The Convention was envisaged as an international treaty for conservation, and its drafters likely never predicted the entanglements of invasion, intentional destruction, and cultural cleansing that have sadly become more commonplace. With UNESCO lacking the legal provisions to check or censure, much less sanction, states are ostensibly free to incite second-order conflicts, this time within the diplomatic sphere, that further contravene the Convention's raison d'être and challenge the Committee and Secretariat's capacity. This is intergovernmental UNESCO at work rather than global UNESCO, and it does not always square with the original aims of the organization, its wartime founding, or its aspirations for world peace.

Amongst the national delegations stationed at the Rue Miollis annex of UNESCO's Paris headquarters there is general agreement about the current moment reflecting a heightened period of tension. One Scandinavian delegation opined that the World Heritage Committee operates like many other UN arenas in that nation-states use the cultural platform as a proxy for other political negotiations, typically around territory, rights, and the rehearsing of historical conflicts. Acting more like a stop valve, such international meetings offer a softer setting for Member States to air grievances instead of engaging in open hostilities. This accords with Jan Turtinen's observation that UNESCO affords, in many cases, a nonconfrontational intergovernmental platform for states to engage with each other.[56] From this perspective, UNESCO fulfills different needs in the current global milieu than it did when it was founded, and thus heritage friction in the diplomatic sphere is not inherently negative. As one experienced Scandinavian diplomat described it, the UN process operates on several levels: the first is the apparent substance of debate, in this case World Heritage sites; the second level is the realpolitik at work, whereby the UN is a "stage" for economic, political, and geographical interests to be enacted; and on the third level the UN functions as a "normative policy arena" for dialogue around sensitive issues and normative concepts.

While this formulation effectively captures the tiered operations of today's multilateral organizations, many national delegations also agree that World Heritage machinations are in fact more volatile than those being rehearsed in other UN sectors, in the field of human rights or world health, simply because cultural heritage is so symbolic and emotive. This is most dramatically illustrated with Jerusalem, a site of such countervailing forces of religion, politics, and identity that it could only produce a *"cocktail explosif,"* one Middle Eastern ambassador explained in the days after the controversial 2016 Jerusalem Resolution was passed in Paris.

Impasse Management

One hundred years ago the British Empire embarked upon its crusade against the Ottoman Empire in the Middle East in what was called the "Jerusalem Operations." In October 1917 the British were plotting how to secure mandatory power in Palestine, entailing the same effects as colonization but without the political baggage and international censure. Winston Churchill later wrote that there would be no annexation; rather, the mandates would simply be granted to the principal powers. The French had no such qualms about annexation or the quasi-colonizing overtones of the mandate system and saw it as their right as part of the civilizing mission: their crushing of the Syrian Revolt (1925–27) would prove a stark reminder.

On December 11, 1917, General Edmund Allenby made his famous entry on foot through the Jaffa Gate into the Old City of Jerusalem, following plans carefully devised by Colonel Sir Tatton Benvenuto Mark Sykes, one of the architects of the secret Sykes-Picot agreement between Great Britain and France to carve up the Middle East.[57] The Ottoman governor had written to the British two days earlier, informing them, "Due to the severity of the siege of the city and the suffering that this peaceful country has endured from your heavy guns; and for fear that these deadly bombs will hit the holy places, we are forced to hand over to you the city through Hussein al-Husseini, the mayor of Jerusalem, hoping that you will protect Jerusalem the way we have protected it for more than five hundred years."[58] General Allenby reportedly claimed that "the wars of the crusades are now complete."[59] Back in London, the British prime minister, David Lloyd George, awaited the capture of Jerusalem as no less than "a Christmas present for the British people."[60] Allenby was advised to take the city before the holidays.

The Christian occupation of Jerusalem sealed the fate of the ancient city, with dramatic consequences for all faiths represented therein, their respective heritages, and the safeguarding of historic places. World Heritage has not been immune. Jerusalem has been prominent in UNESCO's programs since the agency's foundation in 1945, from its refugee efforts for Palestinians to education in the West Bank or tracing the impacts of Israel's archaeological excavations in East Jerusalem.[61] No other historic site embodies such conflict as the Holy City—a situation not entirely of its own making, but born of international struggles for territory and religious control, Ottoman and British colonial domination and redrawing of national lines, the war of 1948, the 1967 annexation, and the occupation of East Jerusalem.[62]

UNESCO has continually found itself in an impossible situation over Jerusalem, and on the occasions when it has taken measures, such as the controversial resolutions of 1974 and 2016, there have been dire consequences for the organization.[63] Indeed, as we have seen above, official mechanisms to defuse contentious conservation issues such as those facing Jerusalem for much of the twentieth century are nowhere outlined in UNESCO's World Heritage Convention.[64] International pressure to preserve the ancient city has devolved into a kind of "impasse management" whereby the conflict continues unabated, little progress is made, and the most difficult issues are routinely avoided. At its highest levels, UNESCO once again demurs, citing its "spheres of competence" argument, despite the fact that the issues are exactly those of heritage and conservation. Impasse management means suspending major issues for fear of igniting greater conflict, though this does not solve the underlying dispute or antagonism, but rather leaves it "in suspense." And as UN official George Sherry quipped after his many years trying to quell crises around the world, "few things are more permanent than temporary arrangements."[65]

Jerusalem presents such a vast and complex case that one can capture only a snapshot of the broader conflict and try to tease apart the different positions held by the Member States as opposed to the organization and, to some degree, its chosen experts. Two salient moments in the site's fraught timeline indicate the agency's attempts to deal with heritage conflict by producing two important sets of resolutions: in 1974 before the site was declared World Heritage, and most recently in 2016. During these episodes it was UNESCO's committees that voiced their concerns, took a position on difficult heritage issues, and attempted to hold states accountable. In the 1970s UNESCO as an organization and its Directors-General were deeply engaged with the issues: they ordered inquiries and reports and considered seriously any breaches of the international conventions, whereas forty years later, Irina Bokova sought to distance herself from the World Heritage Committee's decision on Jerusalem.[66] But as the drawn-out decades of heritage conflict in Jerusalem have shown, even specific moments of action by different actors would produce little in the way of enforceable change or progress. The World Heritage Centre's correspondence files on Jerusalem are officially "off-limits" due to their patent sensitivity, and I was duly informed that there was no exception. However, it is possible to partially circumvent the embargo. The many documents and State of Conservation reports published online provide some background, as do the correspondence files in the "Dossiers par Matière Directeur de Cabinet" in UNESCO's Paris archives.[67]

The background to the first set of resolutions began just after the 1967 War. UNESCO Assistant Director-General Richard Hoggart believed then that the "Israel resolutions" constituted the biggest challenge in the agency's history. The substance of these resolutions claimed that Israel had damaged the cultural heritage of Jerusalem, especially through its state-sponsored archaeological excavations.[68] UNESCO's response might then be considered a logical outcome of a series of earlier grievances about cultural heritage dating from the late 1960s onward that were lodged on technical and political grounds. For example, during the fifteenth session of the General Conference in 1968, UNESCO was already urgently calling upon "Israel to desist from any archaeological excavations in the City of Jerusalem and from any alteration of its features or its cultural and historical character, particularly with regard to Christian and Islamic religious sites."[69] It considered that Israel was "taking advantage of its military occupation of the territory" to "unilaterally and in defiance of all accepted laws . . . alter the configuration and status of the City of Jerusalem."[70] In 1969 UNESCO's consultant for Jerusalem, Guglielmo De Angelis d'Ossat, wrote that "a condemnation or censorship of Israel's action appears to be inevitable if the exact consequences of the existing premises are taken into account."[71] Then in 1971 UN Security Council Resolution 298 censured Israel for "expropriation of land and properties, transfer of populations, and legislation aimed at the incorporation of the occupied section," all of which impinged upon the possibilities of "a just and lasting peace."[72] The 1974 resolutions that followed raised the issue of to which regional grouping Israel should belong: Israel had requested membership in the European region, but the UNESCO General Conference rejected the request.[73] Finally, UNESCO was urged to maintain a permanent presence in Jerusalem so as to monitor the situation on the ground.

The material specificities have remained constant over many decades: claims of unwarranted excavation and modification of sites in tandem with the refashioning of the city "from an oriental to occidental" one, as one Palestinian diplomat described it.[74] For more than forty years, UNESCO Directors-General have been caught up in conflicts over the management and protection of Jerusalem, as well as the resolutions that have been generated. Political scientist Simone Ricca, analyzing UNESCO's responses to restoration and excavation in the city, details how the organization has maintained a clear position on such actions since 1969. Though its statements are diplomatically couched, UNESCO has consistently rejected Israeli plans for the city. In 1971 the Belgian art and architectural historian Raymond Lemaire was asked by Director-General Maheu to report on the conservation status of cultural heritage in Jerusalem. His personal view was that the climate in Israel was not favorable to interventions by major international organizations, and he feared that such actions would only aggravate the conflict. Lemaire suggested that adopting an expert, or technocratic, approach was preferable.[75] Then in 1973 the post of special representative for the city was formed to report on the evolution of Jerusalem's urban fabric: Raymond Lemaire was appointed and held that position for the next twenty-six years. There, by the permission of Israel, Lemaire walked a political tightrope, and his reports reflect a "generally positive attitude to the ongoing transformations."[76] At the same time he was in "no doubt that, both in conception and as regards certain restoration techniques, the work is often below what one might have hoped." However, closer scrutiny of the substance of his reports, many archived in UNESCO's Paris headquarters, reveals a grittier materiality.

While not trained as an archaeologist, a salient point given the issue of archaeological excavation and UNESCO's understanding of it, Lemaire nevertheless acknowledged "the damage the 1967 and 1969 demolitions caused." He further noted that the digging of a tunnel by Israeli military forces "has nothing to do with any archaeological research programme and did not follow scientific excavation methods."[77] Furthermore, he indirectly called attention to political and nationalist agendas by openly admitting that "no legal justification may be invoked for excavations undertaken solely in pursuit of archaeological research such as those conducted by Professor B. Mazar."[78] Lemaire concluded that the "state of Jerusalem's Islamic Heritage is bordering on disaster," so much so that "the safeguarding and restoration of the Islamic monuments is a long-term undertaking calling for considerable financial resources that are far beyond the means of the authorities who are the owners or are responsible for their management."[79] Given his observations, Lemaire ultimately agreed with the Director-General to launch an appeal for an international Safeguarding Campaign. Once more it was archaeology, this time in the service of the state, that would capture the international spotlight. Unlike UNESCO's efforts in Nubia or Venice, however, there would be no celebrations for spectacular salvage, monumental findings, or feats of engineering in Jerusalem; what was highlighted instead was archaeology's destructive capabilities, the potential of its practitioners to magnify certain pasts while erasing others, choosing which histories to preserve and which to jettison.[80]

Some forty years later, Decision 40 COM 7A.13 concerning the Old City of Jerusalem and its Walls was adopted by the World Heritage Committee in Paris on October 26, 2016.[81] The text was submitted by Algeria, Egypt, Lebanon, Morocco, Oman, Qatar, and Sudan and addressed the status of Jerusalem on the List of World Heritage in Danger, documenting the ongoing infractions of UNESCO and Geneva conventions. Of the twenty-six

FIGURE 6.3 Excavations in the Old City of Jerusalem, photo by Lefkos Kyriacou and courtesy of Conflict in Cities/Centre for Urban Conflicts Research

points raised in the text, each relates to issues of archaeology and excavation, heritage restoration, or future conservation in the light of proposed infrastructural development: in other words, the familiar threats outlined in the majority of endangered World Heritage properties. For instance, mention is made of "illegal archaeological excavations" and the "continuous, intrusive archaeological demolitions and excavations in and around the Mughrabi Gate Ascent." The text notes that "damage caused by the Israeli security forces . . . to the historic Gates and windows of the Qibli Mosque inside Al-Aqsa Mosque" occurred in 2014. Efforts since to conserve these structures had been blocked by the Israeli authorities. Episodes of violence at Al-Aqsa have continued, more recently fueled by a heightened military presence. Israeli settlers have stormed the mosque, worship has been banned, and restrictions were even placed on children playing in Al-Aqsa's courtyard, leading to an outcry over the violation of international conventions. Further alarm was raised over the "damaging effect of the Jerusalem Light rail (tram line) [a] few meters from the Walls of the Old City of Jerusalem" and, in addition, future "plans to build a two-line cable car system in East Jerusalem." In sum, the document raised concerns for "safeguarding of the authenticity, integrity and cultural heritage" of the site. Lastly, the text urged Israel "to accept and facilitate the implementation" of a UNESCO Reactive Monitoring mission in the Old City.[82] Since 2003 the frequency of UNESCO's own external State of Conservation reporting has risen exponentially, citing diverse factors negatively impacting Jerusalem, including archaeological excavations, the deterioration of monuments, alteration of the urban and social fabric of the site, lack of planning, governance and management processes, concerns with the urban environment and visual integrity, and problems with transportation infrastructure, traffic, and access.[83]

Deliberations over Jerusalem, like those regarding Kosovo and other sites of extreme conflict, are typically postponed year after year in World Heritage Committee sessions as an exercise in impasse management, primarily to avoid igniting further conflict.[84] Yet when destruction is dressed up as reconstruction, as Jordan had implied in 2014, it was "time to put diplomatic courtesy aside." In 2016 matters came to a head and Committee members were forced to consider what was happening to heritage on the ground and indeed to formally vote, by secret ballot, on the draft decision. In the final moments before voting there was an intervention from Tanzania, seconded by Croatia, to vote not on the consensus that had been agreed upon earlier but rather on the text of the decision: a technical sleight of hand that had political implications for some nations. One experienced ambassador on the Committee confided to me afterward that he had seen "money changing hands." Tempers were frayed, delegates were frustrated, the legal advisor was called upon several times, and finally a five-minute suspension was called so that the Committee could make sense of Tanzania's irregular proposal.

Irrespective of Tanzania's intervention, a majority vote saw the decision adopted. Committee members including Kazakhstan, Cuba, Lebanon, Indonesia, Tunisia, and Kuwait took the floor to affirm that they would not be "held hostage to politics" but would "uphold the spirit of the Convention" in regard to the long-term preservation of Jerusalem. Predictably, the vote immediately sparked a set of hostile responses and gestures, all of which were live-streamed to the world. "This is yet another absurd resolution against the State of Israel, the Jewish people and historical truth," Israel's envoy, Carmel Shama-Hacohen, said following the vote. UNESCO's resolution on Jerusalem, he said, belonged in the "garbage bin of history." Reflecting back on the day in 1975 when Israel's Chaim Herzog physically tore another such resolution to shreds at the United Nations, he said, "I have no intention of doing this today—not because of your dignity, or the dignity of this organization, but because it is not even worthy of the energy needed for tearing it apart." And with that he lifted up a black trash can for all to see, with the word "History" attached to it, and dropped the text inside.

If these two episodes teach us anything, it is that impasse management is a short-term strategy and not a solution for conflicts that need to be addressed in the international arena, just as UNESCO, as a multilateral organization, has effectively taken on issues like apartheid, racism, and gender equity throughout its history. Neutrality, or the unwillingness to face conflict for fear of repercussion, is no defense, especially when it comes to supporting resolutions and decisions adopted across other UN bodies. Some have explained the silencing of issues around Jerusalem by saying that it is a regional conflict, unlike the cases involving two disputing nations, such as those of Preah Vihear, Ani, or even the Meiji sites. Yet one might conclude that each of these cases has both regional and sovereign territorial implications, albeit less volatile than the Israeli-Palestinian conflict. In my interviews, several influential European delegations conflated any discussion of excavation, conservation, or development issues in Jerusalem with the Israeli-Palestinian conflict, retreating into the impossibility of solving the Middle East crisis and rendering any decisions over the fate of World Heritage impossible. Delegates from other regions often expressed different concerns and felt strongly that, given the substance of the debate, the Committee could not retreat from adjudicating on heritage conservation issues, which patently fall within UNESCO's sphere of competence. Jerusalem could not continue in its state of exception.

Conclusions

UNESCO was born of war with an explicit mission to end global conflict and help the world rebuild materially and morally, yet its history is increasingly entwined with that of international politics and violence. Tied to the constitution of the United Nations, it was the self-interest of those states, rather than their respect for global goods, that internationalist Gilbert Murray called the "flaw in the machinery" of world government.[85] In 1939 Murray had argued that "the appeal should be to supreme international authority, as far removed as possible from political passions" and instead committed to a judicial and disinterested atmosphere. The "clue to our tragedy" was that the "safety of civilization depends on the great world issues being settled in accordance with the interests of the world: yet, under the system of national states, any statesman who attempted to settle them would be facing great danger. For it is not the votes of other nations by which he stands or falls, but only the votes of his own people."[86] The intellectual mission was gradually but deftly surpassed by the political—evidenced in conflicting positions today over matters as diverse as global heritage, human rights, and climate change. The paradox, for insiders like Richard Hoggart, was how UNESCO might retain both the support of Member States and at the same time "the respect of the world's best intellectuals and scientists when they are making free, professional judgments on its performance."[87] Referring to the crisis over excavations in Jerusalem since the late 1960s, he was not to know how UNESCO's own reputation would be embroiled in the international debacles that would unfold.

Right from the start the organization would be faced with entrenched issues such as the status of colonial powers and their colonies, as well as the emergence of new conflicts around the globe and the impossibility of holding states accountable. Back in 1947, just two years after the foundation of the United Nations, the case of Palestine and colonial rule already suggested that while the organization "could shine a bright light of publicity on colonial rule" when the "superpowers chose to act—the United States was the first to recognize Israeli independence de facto, the USSR de jure—there was little the rest of the UN could do."[88] Today in an age of American, and increasingly Russian, exceptionalism, the major powers have little to fear from international organizations and their legal instruments, whether UNESCO conventions or prosecutions in the International Criminal Court. As we will see in the final chapters, it is the world's weakest nations that have the most to fear.[89]

In the case of powerful Member States such as Russia, direct confrontation over annexation or other World Heritage infractions is studiously avoided in official forums because of Russia's influence and financial support of the organization. This reticence underlines the hypocrisy of the organization in not addressing Russia's annexation of Crimea, or for that matter its bombardment of Syria. Increasingly UNESCO retreats into its "fields of competence" position in order to recuse itself from political bombshells such as Crimea, the long-standing occupation of East Jerusalem, and the plight of Palestine. Heritage then becomes a proxy for more expansive hostilities and dangers, no less volatile although with seemingly softer contours. Consequently, influential states can deploy the past with impunity. Impasse management as a strategy, however, only masks the danger in the short term, whereas historically we can trace how such conflicts only escalate rather than subside over time. As we have seen, there is little in UNESCO's operational remit that can be mobilized, and any further attempt to remedy these shortfalls by legal intervention would likely be vetoed by vested Member States, as has happened with UN Security Council resolutions.

As the World Heritage Committee meetings in Istanbul recently revealed, UNESCO's creation of World Heritage is now explicitly caught in the crossfire, literally and metaphorically. In our archaeological work at the World Heritage site of Çatalhöyük in central Turkey, just prior to the UNESCO meetings, my colleagues and I were forced to consider all manner of attacks on the archaeological site, whether from an ISIS cell operating in the nearby city of Konya or from other insurgents. Being inscribed on the World Heritage List invited a new suite of clear and present dangers. Steel gates and barriers were erected at our dig house, a security consultant from Control Risk (UK) lectured us on evasive maneuvers during a terrorist attack, and the team was confronted with safety drills, alarms, pepper sprays, and smoke canisters. Research into the past was eclipsed by paranoia and insecurity as a direct result of events in Palmyra and our visible UNESCO status. The project had ostensibly become what our security consultant called a "soft target."[90] Thus we can see that there is now a broader range of conflicts in which material heritage is not merely another passive casualty of war but rather a monumental target in the conflict. The examples of destruction in Mali, Syria, and Iraq are salutary. Given their prized status, World Heritage sites are also held for ransom by factions that are alienated from and hostile to the international community, as we have seen with the Bamiyan Buddhas in Afghanistan.

Territorial conflicts are now waged, and incursions marked, by cultural properties being nominated, inscribed, claimed, and counterclaimed through UNESCO's instruments. So "while global mobilization may in some respects be an attempt to supersede nationalism," as Michael Herzfeld suggests, "it can also foment it."[91] The Turkish nomination of Ani was destined to inflame an already dangerous history, just as the nomination of Preah Vihear some years earlier signaled the disasters that follow from years of failed diplomacy and institutional mismanagement. Many nation-states' desires in the heritage arena are less about conservation of properties than about redrawing the lines, in terms of both territorial sovereignty and historical narratives. While Preah Vihear exemplifies border conflicts over competing claims to a singular monumentality and ownership, the case of Ani concerns appropriation and an extraterritorial silencing of history. Like Japan's Meiji sites, with their attendant charges of celebrating forced labor and victimhood, inscription on the World Heritage List further serves to sanction the past for powerful nations. Through international recognition one version of history is not only recognized but enshrined, rendering UNESCO complicit in incorporating episodes of illegal occupation, atrocities, war crimes, and even genocide, while the victims are left to relive the trauma. This is the dark side of heritage branding.

Increasingly it is more difficult for UNESCO to fulfill its dream of "justice and liberty and peace [that] are indispensable to the dignity of man and constitute a sacred duty which all these nations must fulfill in a spirit of mutual assistance and concern," as its constitution stated so profoundly in 1945. As the example of Jerusalem demonstrates, UNESCO has spent the last fifty years endeavoring to monitor and protect the ancient city, while both matters of conflict and conservation have been nearly impossible to influence, much less regulate. UNESCO's committees and functionaries, in attempting to conduct their business in harrowing times, thus resort to an illusory neutrality, facilitated by retreating into technocracy or performing fictive solidarity, much like the Russian orchestra that played on in the ruins of Palmyra. However, cycles of conflict and occupation that stretch back to the colonial carving up of the Middle East by competing British and French forces have only been followed by further episodes of violence and alienation. UNESCO's attempts at impasse management have proven to be the most temporary of arrangements. The specter of history repeating itself across the Middle East seems to have been foreshadowed in Nicholas Michell's nineteenth-century verse entitled *Ruins of Many Lands*, published in the twilight of the Ottoman Empire.[92] He wrote:

> Glory to proud Palmyra sighed adieu,
> And o'er her shrines Destruction's angel flew.

7

Danger

The United Nations was not created in order to bring us to heaven, but in order to save us from hell.

—DAG HAMMARSKJÖLD, 1954

OCTOBER WITNESSED THE worst aerial bombardment of Damascus, after which a wave of violence and bloodshed overtook the historic city. Aleppo, Hama, and Homs were also under attack. At 5:00 p.m. on Sunday, October 18, without warning, the bombardment started from the citadel and from the hills north of Damascus; it continued for two days. Tanks rolled through the streets, machine guns were turned upon unarmed civilians, and homes were looted. Insurgents and their supporters were summarily executed and their bodies were desecrated. Proper burial was disallowed and corpses were paraded through the streets to send a chilling message to any survivors. A Christian inhabitant of the city was the first to report that poison gas was being used in an attempt to exterminate an entire people: he quite rightly called it a crime against humanity. Fires blazed through six or eight square blocks in the center of the city occupied by historic bazaars and residences. Those between the famous "Street Called Straight" and the Citadel were obliterated, and an untold number of other buildings were damaged across the city, the death toll and the destruction incalculable. Those who managed to escape Damascus describe "days and nights of unforgettable terror," while international commentators consider the bombardment "unparalleled in the history of civilized nations." A wave of horror followed. During November and December the guerilla warfare continued.[1]

Two days of continuous bombardment inflicted unimaginable havoc. Shelling destroyed the famous Souq Hamadieh Bazaar, the magnificent Azem Palace, and the districts of Shaghur and Meidan. Walking through what was once a lively and prosperous historic bazaar now reduced to rubble, reporters were shocked at "the spectacle of destruction and ruin," and even greater damage was apparent the further one ventured. The green and blue tiled Mosque of Sinan Pasha, on the edge of Bab al-Jabiyya, did not escape; shelling had left an enormous hole in its dome and its mosaic windows were destroyed. One eyewitness recounted the irreparable loss at the Palace of Azem, one of the "most beautiful and picturesque buildings in the city," which had housed the Institut d'Art et Archéologie Musulman. The museum was home to "many rare objects, including all recent archaeological discoveries in Syria, and was renowned for its marble fittings and mosaic work. Practically none of these treasures remain."[2] He lamented, "Words fail to describe fittingly the spectacle which the ancient and sacred city now presents." While a swift outcry from the international community was forthcoming, it focused on the destruction of architectural and archaeological treasures, rather than on the human suffering and loss of life.

Given the extensive media coverage of Syria today, revealing the devastation of World Heritage cities such as Damascus and Aleppo and the intentional destruction of archaeological sites like Palmyra at the hands of ISIS, one might be forgiven for thinking that the above description is just another episode in this horrific and drawn-out saga. Yet the account is from 1925 and the perpetrators here were the French, who had bombarded these sites and their civilian populations as part of their quelling of the Great Syrian Revolt, an uprising that sought independence from French colonial forces and the mandate system. Much like the British in Palestine, the French considered that their empire extended through the trustee territories of Syria and Lebanon, accompanied by what men such as Aristide Briand considered their civilizing duty. Their right to ostensibly "occupy" Syria had been formalized under the League of Nations mandate system, with the corollary lines drawn in the sand by the 1916 Sykes-Picot Agreement. In light of the devastation wrought upon Damascus, historian Susan Pederson notes, "Perhaps France's monopoly on 'civilization' was not so secure after all."[3]

Quincy Wright, an American professor of international law at the University of Chicago, traveled to Damascus in November, only a month after the bombardment, to see the damage firsthand. He later published his now-famous reflections on what he termed the French "policy of terrorism" and their flagrant disregard of "provisions with regard to notice, removal of noncombatants and exemption of nonmilitary buildings."[4] Damascus was the center of Arab civilization, he reminded his readers, and the bombardment destroyed many of the finest examples of art and

architecture. French forces in Syria, in his opinion, had violated international law in bombarding Damascus. Wright, along with the Arabs, was
astounded that the League of Nations had not done more. Other European
delegates at the League defended the French, falling back on their "glory
and prestige in the history of civilization." They were simply not capable of
killing, raping, and pillaging in Syria. Here "was the return of civilizational
discourse with a vengeance, with the French, simply by virtue of being
French, judged incapable of brutal acts."[5]

In reply to Wright's article, Captain Elbridge Colby of the US
Army published his own paper, entitled "How to Fight Savage Tribes,"
the following year in the very same journal, the *American Journal of
International Law*. Colby made the distinction that the rules of international law applied only to civilized nations; they did not extend to "savage
or semi-savage" peoples. Uncivilized peoples such as those living in Syria,
Colby concluded, hold that war involves everyone and therefore no distinction exists between combatants and noncombatants. If the entire population of Damascus and Aleppo proved fair game, what respect would there
possibly be for their historic buildings, mosques, museums, houses, and
bazaars? But Colby went further, arguing that such destruction constituted
an effective weapon of war, both materially and psychologically. Through
bombardment on a grand scale, "the inhuman act thus becomes actually
humane, for it shortens the conflict and prevent the shedding of more
excessive quantities of blood."[6] Using this chilling justification, as the
Americans did in Vietnam, destroying villages counted as saving them.
Colby wrote:

> To a Frenchman, a shell striking Rheims Cathedral . . . is a lawless
> act of the enemy which infuriates the temperamental soul and
> arouses wrath and gives a fine incident for overseas propaganda.
> To a fanatical savage, a bomb dropped out of the sky on the sacred
> temple of his omnipotent God is a sign and a symbol that that God
> has withdrawn his favor . . . instead of merely rousing his wrath,
> these acts are much more likely to make him raise his hands in
> surrender. If a few "non-combatants" are killed, the loss of life is
> probably far less than might have been sustained in prolonged op-
> erations of a more polite character.

There are many dangers present here, and they are very much the same
as those we face today: wanton destruction of life and livelihoods, of

history and heritage, continued colonial oppression, violation of human rights and dignity, and suspension of the rule of law. There is also the risk of forgetting our not-so-distant history and the forces whose role has directed us toward the kind of impasse that characterizes Syria or Iraq today. One present reminder of that, itself a historical irony, comes with the French charge that the bombardment of Aleppo by Russian and Syrian forces constitutes war crimes, likening it to the siege of Sarajevo during the Bosnian War and to the carpet-bombing of Guernica during the Spanish Civil War.[7] There are other reverberations here too, circling back to Napoleon's campaigns in Syria and Egypt (1798–1801), the justification of which was establishing scientific enterprise in the Middle East and the familiar protectionism of French trade in fending off competing British interests.[8] Under the French Mandate (1923–1946), the medievalist Paul Deschamps had been charged with acquiring the medieval crusader castle Crac des Chevaliers in the foothills of Jebel Ansariyah.[9] T. E. Lawrence once described it as the "best preserved and most wholly admirable castle in the world."[10] The French widely regarded it as their monument. They spent millions of francs restoring the castle, today an endangered World Heritage site, removing its inhabitants and destroying buildings in their wake. Apart from the obvious aggression, occupation, and violence betrayed in these histories, a lingering danger resides in the appeals and rhetorics of civilization and barbarism, still very much in circulation today, that pose a danger to equality globally and threaten the West's own presumptive "civility."

With the moral outrage fomented in the face of monumental demolition in Syria there has been much less self-reflection as to why global institutions such as UNESCO have failed to secure peace or preserve the past after their seventy year history. Less energy has been expended on contemplating the reasons some groups feel alienated in Mali and Syria, or why they continue to destroy the materiality of the past. After all, it is and has been a practice common among many societies and nations throughout our entire human history, from the ancient Egyptians to modern Europeans. "Every civilization has sacked, crushed, pillaged and burned," UNESCO claimed back in 1954. "Temples, churches and entire cities have been razed."[11] World Heritage and its monumental efforts seem intimately tied to those expressions of intensity on both sides of the equation, whether one desires to preserve or obliterate the cathedrals and temples that Captain Colby described as mere pawns on a vast global chessboard. The French destruction in Syria during 1925 and its apologists remind us too that the past is never dead. It's not even past, as William Faulkner famously said.

Civilizing Business

On May 5, 2016, the ruins of an ancient Roman amphitheater in the World Heritage site of Palmyra played host to the Russian Mariinsky Orchestra. The musicians were there to honor the victims of the recent Syrian war, among other things. President Vladimir Putin was not present, but a live feed from his Black Sea vacation home enabled him to deliver his message about the need for "our civilization to rid itself of this terrible evil." It was Putin's own civilizational message, mixing Soviet-style cultural supremacy with political justification to counter the international criticism meted out over Russia's military intervention, with its massive bombing campaigns and concomitant civilian death toll. Dressed entirely in black, members of the Russian orchestra inadvertently echoed the ghastly images of ISIS executioners in the same theater—all but teenagers, they had executed twenty-five Syrian soldiers there in July 2015. Russian conductor Valery Gergiev described their musical efforts from "war-torn Palmyra" as "our appeal for peace and concord. We protest against barbarians who destroyed wonderful monuments of world's culture."[12] They played music by Johann Sebastian Bach and two Russian composers, Sergei Prokofiev and Rodion Shchedrin.

The theater was lined with Russian soldiers and officials, Syrian soldiers, bused-in envoys of UNESCO wearing bulletproof vests, children in traditional dress holding pictures of President Bashar al-Assad: it was elaborately staged, although not well conceived. This had been the scene of an appalling massacre only months before, and what most images of

FIGURE 7.1 Palmyra Concert, 2016, Syria, courtesy of Lau Svensson, Wikimedia Commons

the killings then failed to capture was the audience of men sitting in the seats watching, the theatricality recalling our images of other ancient martyrs and theaters of war. Fast-forward, and soldiers and international diplomats had succumbed to the hugely symbolic propaganda and soft power peddled by Russia, celebrating a short-lived victory and altogether foreign occupation by Russian forces in Palmyra, replete with their own military bases. For the moment, gunfire had been replaced by the sound of classical music. One reporter for the *Russian Times* described reviving the ancient ruins through music: death and destruction had been replaced by culture, history, and civilization.[13] For historians of Russia, it recalled another orchestral maneuver back in August 1942, during the Nazi siege of Leningrad, when "starving Russian musicians, supplemented by military performers, gave the city's first performance of Dmitri Shostakovich's Symphony No. 7, otherwise known as the Leningrad Symphony."[14] But this was Syria, not Russia, and the victory was not yet at hand.

Russia had taken a similarly controlling position about the status of Syrian heritage sites in the World Heritage Committee meetings in Phnom Penh back in 2013. With their uncompromising support and promotion of the Assad regime, the Russian Federation put up strong resistance to a proposal to inscribe all five Syrian World Heritage sites on the List of World Heritage in Danger: the Ancient City of Damascus, Ancient City of Bosra, Site of Palmyra, Ancient City of Aleppo, Crac des Chevaliers and Qal'at Saalah El-Din, and Ancient Villages of Northern Syria. Russia argued that "there is not active armed conflict across the country, not absolutely everywhere." But other Committee members, including Cambodia, France, Qatar, Iraq, Mali, Estonia, Mexico, and Germany, wanted to move swiftly and inscribe them all. From UNESCO's perspective, additions to the List of World Heritage in Danger are designed to inform the international community of the conditions that threaten site values, typically their physical fabric and setting. This is ostensibly material endangerment with a distinctly monumental set of criteria: deterioration of materials, deterioration of structure and/or ornamental features, deterioration of architectural coherence, significant loss of historical authenticity, and loss of cultural significance are just some of the preconditions.[15] Listing "is not a blackmailing," as the director of the World Heritage Centre concluded; it is intended to encourage corrective action, to raise conservation awareness and funding. Armed conflict and war, natural disasters, pollution, uncontrolled urbanization, and unchecked tourist development all pose major problems worldwide. In the case of Syria, the danger was seemingly incontrovertible.

Russia, however, did not want to include the Ancient City of Damascus on the endangered list. Throughout their interventions over the endangered Syrian sites the Russian delegation laid the blame squarely with "armed groups which are using the castles and citadels as their strongholds and who are destroying them" rather than attaching any blame to the Assad regime. With some caution Ambassador Mitrofanova raised the example of Mali only the year before, where actually "listing these properties in danger led to their bombing and destruction." With the possible exception of BRICS allies India and South Africa, which continually deferred to the Syrian authorities, Russia seemed isolated in its position. Similar to the intense politics of inscription for the World Heritage List described earlier, the political machinations are mobilized in reverse here, to *not* being inscribed on the List of World Heritage in Danger.

Russia further resisted any suggestion made by many other Committee members, especially Mali, which had experienced a similar situation, that Syria should adhere to the Second Protocol to the 1954 Hague Convention for the Protection of Cultural Property in the Event of Armed Conflict.[16] The Indian ambassador called it "mandate creep," while Ambassador Mitrofanova said, "It's a sovereign decision to be taken by the Member State itself, why should UNESCO make recommendations to this effect." There is a considerable historical irony here, for it was the Russian tsar Nicholas II and his foreign minister Mikhail Nikolayevich Muravyov who were instrumental in formulating the first Hague Convention during the Peace Conference of 1899. The treaties focused upon disarmament, protection of people and property, and compulsory arbitration for international disputes.[17] That had been relegated to history.

What followed in Phnom Penh was considerable technocratic wrangling over terms such as "invite" or "encourage" with regard to the 1954 Convention. As outlined in previous chapters, this constituted a technical cover for the political agenda. Further ire was raised when Assistant Director-General for Culture Francesco Bandarin proposed wording in the draft decision about "the creation of a Special Fund to support the conservation of the cultural heritage of Syria." He suggested that many other "heritage organizations could be supported not only the state of Syria." India and Russia reacted angrily: Syria was a member of the Convention and it must be referred to explicitly. The proposed wording, they imputed, minimized the power of the Member States, by which they meant Syria's

Assad government. The fierce debate that ensued took many hours, with BRICS partners at odds with most other Committee members and the World Heritage Secretariat. Despite calls from the Syrian delegation to support the danger listing and their willingness to continue cooperating with UNESCO, Russia continued to prevaricate, signaling its strong political, economic, and military motivations.[18]

At the time of writing Russia remains the strongest supporter of Assad's regime. Previously Russia had vetoed three UN Security Council resolutions in 2011 and 2012 intended to impose sanctions on the Syrian president. Russia and Syria have a historical relationship cemented by massive loans and long-term economic and military deals (arms, natural gas, oil). Palmyra is also adjacent to vast gas fields that supply 45 percent of Syria's gas and electricity resources, so potential earnings and future foreign investment remain critical. The Syrian port of Tartus houses a Soviet-era naval base that can host Russia's nuclear-armed warships, thus strengthening its naval presence in the Mediterranean. There is also a Russian air base out on the edge of Palmyra that ISIS retook late in 2016 in one of the many "Palmyra offensives." Russian defense analyst Ruslan Pukhov explains that "Syria is the only country in the Middle East which follows our advice, this is the country where we can exercise certain tangible influence."[19] From arms to archaeology, World Heritage is not immune from such arrangements and in fact can be used as a diplomatic pawn in a far more lucrative game.

In September 2015, Russia began its military intervention in the Syrian civil war in support of the Assad government, with air strikes against forces opposing his government. From 2000 to 2010, Russia sold around US$1.5 billion worth of arms to Syria.[20] But in 2011 those contracts skyrocketed to well over US$4 billion. Russian involvement in the Syrian crisis had an even more dramatic effect: more than simply the increased sales of arms, the "colossal advertising" that comes when major world powers collide in the Middle East to battle-test and show off the goods in places like Aleppo. This had further boosted Russian's towering status as a military provider. Kremlin insiders hinted that as a result of the Syrian war, sales in 2016 were already up US$7 billion.[21]

Palmyra was retaken by ISIS in December 2016 after what now appears like a premature Russian (and international) show of self-congratulation. It should thus not be surprising that ISIS summarily destroyed part of the same ancient theater where only months before the Russian orchestra had triumphantly played Prokofiev. As UNESCO had previously experienced

in Mali, particularly as a result of the speeches of Director-General Irina
Bokova, the organization's public retaliation over acts decried as "barbarism" can often backfire, antagonizing its adversaries and unleashing further waves of violence.[22]

There are other dangers posed by the civilizational discourses that
UNESCO, at its highest levels, has unwittingly played into. There is the
danger of creating a new list, this time of the haves and have-nots of civilization. Additional dangers result from localizing the problem of illicit
antiquities traffic instead of recognizing the complicity of international
players, and the more serious danger of fetishizing the loss of things over
life itself. From one perspective, the widespread international outcry over
destruction in Syria, especially in the media, must surely be a measure
of UNESCO's success in inculcating their one world perspective. From
another, it has the potential to polarize and alienate groups even further
by creating new discourses of inhumanity. Bokova considers that the
"deliberate destruction of cultural heritage is a war crime, and should
be prosecuted and punished as such."[23] This position has devolved into
another of UNESCO's campaigns, "seeing a new global struggle for the
hearts and minds . . . especially young hearts and minds."[24] Ironically,
by engaging the language of battle, World Heritage sites of "Outstanding
Universal Value" are repositioned as representing and instantiating human
diversity, mutual tolerance, freedom of expression, and global citizenship.

It has been said that UNESCO offers "precisely the antidote to
radicalisation; the antidote to extremism." One captured Syrian combatant
posed the more uncomfortable response, repeatedly recounted in Director-
General Bokova's speeches, when he said that "there is no world heritage,
it doesn't exist." UNESCO, and indeed all of us, should take seriously the
view that the whole notion of one world, and the common heritage of
humanity approach, is underpinned by Western philosophy and values,
promulgated from the safety and vantage of distance. There are further
dangers of global appropriation, a practice with a long colonial pedigree.
Such appeals to universalism may be defensible in theory, but hardly
in practice, especially if one's vantage is not Paris, but Raqqa. Bokova
attempts to navigate this uneasy disjuncture: "We know that Palmyra
belongs to all Syrians, but I would say it belongs to the whole humanity.
And this is why it matters that we bring the international community together."[25] Indeed, understanding the history of international intervention
at the site is important; it has been tied to the familiar entanglements of
colonialism, appropriation, and extraction. In 1915 the British had offered

the French a share of the Roman site as consolation for their own territorial designs from Basra to the Suez Canal.[26] Under the French Mandate
in 1932 the inhabitants of Palmyra were relocated to the nearby village
of Tadmur. What followed was a succession of European-led excavations
by French, German, Swiss, Polish, and Italian archaeologists working
"mid tottering shafts and broken capitals," as the nineteenth-century poet
Nicholas Michell described Palmyra.

   "Mesopotamia, the cradle of human civilization, is being burnt to
ashes," Irina Bokova told an elite group in 2015 at the World Heritage
Committee meetings in Bonn, Germany. The resulting Bonn Declaration
on World Heritage further condemned "barbaric assaults" and "mindless
destructions."[27] Implicit in those texts and speeches is the presumption
that some cultures are "civilized" and their heritage is worth preserving
for posterity. There are extremists committing "acts of barbarism" that
are denounced, their acts characterized as "unknown" in the history of
humanity.[28] Such a position allows Bokova to claim, for example, that
the "Vandals and Visigoths who attacked Rome had no real desire to destroy civilisation—by the 9th century, they gave rise to Charlemagne, who
sought to restore and preserve Rome's heritage."[29] By her comparison,
today instead "we see violent extremists seeking to destroy heritage, to
erase layers of civilization."[30] It is as if some people, at some times, had

FIGURE 7.2 Umayyad Mosque, Aleppo, Syria, 2013, © Molhem Barakat, Reuters

civilization, whereas others simply did not. In more recent history, we might recall the French bombardment of Syria in 1925 and the reaction of the international community to turn a blind eye, considering, however incorrectly, that Frenchmen were incapable of such acts. We might further recall Director-General M'Bow's plea to abandon "the view of history long held by those who, from Ancient Greece and Rome down to the age of modern imperialisms, have always confused civilization with power, reducing to the status of 'barbarians' the subjugated peoples as well as those who rejected their yoke."[31]

The scale of devastation and international traffic in looted artifacts, moreover, forces us to ask: exactly who are the "barbarians" in the conflict? As Bokova notes, "antiquities from Syria and Iraq have been seized in Finland, Jordan, Lebanon, Turkey, France, the United States, as well as the United Kingdom." Speaking at Oxford University, she reminded the audience that customs officials at Heathrow Airport had confiscated 3.4 tons of stolen objects between 2007 and 2009 alone, representing more than 1,500 pieces. The business of civilization is indeed an international one and many nations and individuals have been complicit. In 2017 several of those same "market nations," including France, pledged US$30 million for a fund to protect sites threatened by war, while American philanthropist Thomas Kaplan added another US$1 million.[32] Somewhat ironically, given its well-documented role in the antiquities trade, Switzerland offered administrative and legal support in hosting the new fund in Geneva, effectively bypassing UNESCO. Italy, as is its custom, offered military personnel and conservation experts. Participants in the fund envisage "a network of sites around the world to temporarily store endangered artifacts and to pay for the restoration of sites damaged by war," potentially leading to yet another neocolonial appropriation of other people's pasts.[33] The ability to extract objects from abroad after the cessation of violence and to determine to what sovereign authority they return, as evidenced by other post-conflict cases including Crimea, is likely to only create further cross-border tensions and disagreement.

UNESCO's logic is to combat "extremism" and "cultural cleansing" through various declarations, speeches delivered by the Director-General, and a robust social media campaign. This harks back to the foundation of UNESCO at the end of the Second World War and its belief that culture and education could be instrumentalized together to promote peace. Yet in World Heritage matters UNESCO's technocratic focus and commitments to monumentality continue to garner critique. Today the organization is simultaneously attempting to rebrand itself in view of criticism that it has placed a greater importance on saving monuments rather than lives, on technical preservation rather than wellbeing. A recent media campaign developed by UNESCO, "People Protecting Places," still quips, "We're not asking you to save the world. Just its greatest places."[34] Thus there remains a clear directive about the materiality of the past and the specific sites that the West has deemed valuable and whose loss it has subsequently bemoaned. Like many before her, Irina Bokova has proposed establishing islands of conservation in war-torn settings such as Syria, appealing for the creation of "protected cultural zones" that would start by efforts to "safeguard at least *one* highly iconic site."[35] The danger here is intervening in the rescue of a purely material heritage, often a Classical antiquity for which Western nations consider themselves to be the legitimate inheritors, while not fully addressing those living and dying through the ongoing conflict or the resultant refugee crisis. Western cultural elites have spent more time lamenting damage to a single site, the Classical ruins of Palmyra, than the destruction inflicted on hundreds of Islamic mosques and shrines across Iraq and Syria combined.

Running parallel to such campaigns are concerted attempts to recast UNESCO as an agency driven by "much more than saving stones and buildings."[36] Thus heritage violations are now sutured to human rights infractions and the wider humanitarian crisis, not simply to monumentality of destruction, but the human costs. "*UNESCO is out of touch—people are dying and they only care about stones.* . . . This has changed," Bokova told a London audience in 2015. "Violent extremists don't choose between attacks against culture and people—they are attacking both. We must defend both together."[37] Speaking at Yale University in 2016, she admitted, "It has not been easy for us—for UNESCO to shine light on this destruction—while children, women and men are being killed, or are suffering."[38] After seventy years, the lingering tensions over whether UNESCO's fundamental mission would be technical assistance or world peace remain. Reflecting precisely on that history, the Director-General told listeners at London's Ismaili Centre, "I believe the 'soft power' of UNESCO has never been so relevant."[39] Choosing what to deploy from the arsenal of soft power, however, requires considerable diplomacy and cultural sensitivity.

"As soon as they destroy something," one member of the Secretariat proudly informed me, "we will rebuild it." He was lecturing me during the World Heritage Committee session in Bonn, and referring to ISIS, after I had questioned the substance and tone of the messages broadcast at the opening ceremony. A fervent adherence to technocratic solutions by UNESCO staff is reflected in the belief that monumental reconstruction or replacement is another "antidote for extremism." Exhibits such as *Eternal Sites* in the Grand Palais in Paris have further buoyed this optimism. Under UNESCO's patronage the exhibit explicitly promotes 3-D recording, representation, and reconstitution of monuments.[40] The self-congratulation surrounding this new technology is also largely felt in the West, and is epitomized by media coverage of a computerized stone-cutter drilling a replica of Palmyra's Arch of Triumph in Tuscany, close to the spot where Michelangelo selected his marble for *David*. The fact that we *can* does not always mean that we *should*. Striking here too is the fact that the replica arch, proclaimed a "visual representation of a civilization," should be showcased first in Trafalgar Square, London, and then in New York.[41] Archaeologist Karen Holmberg attended the Manhattan unveiling in late 2016 and described the "uncomfortable line" that was being treaded by fetishizing objects "when the living people are a more important priority." Moreover, with such replicas "the data and the context" are "completely lost. And it's the warfare itself and the violence itself that is the core issue."[42]

The Syrian Director-General of antiquities and museums, Maamoun Abdelkarim, would likely agree. "We will never rebuild new buildings in the ancient city. We are archaeologists, we do traditional work," he said in London.[43] Later in Paris he reaffirmed that Palmyra is "not going to be a Disneyland. We don't have the money for such things and there is so much to do for the Syrian people."[44] While some European experts at the World Heritage Centre adopt a combative stance when it comes to deploying new digital technologies as another kind of antidote to extremism, some from Middle Eastern backgrounds are more cautious and sensitive to both local and labor issues, to the possibilities of developing heritage skills, capacity building, and empowering youth in war-ravaged countries such as Syria and Iraq. Importing digital technologies, and their attendant experts, from England, France, and Italy may just exacerbate the existing attitudes that fueled the destruction in the first place, a situation that UNESCO has previously confronted in Mali, as we will see in Chapter 8.

Saving the World

Modernity suffers from an overburden of the past, Nietzsche thought; others describe it as "the illness of historicism."[45] Today there is almost an obsession with saving everything and a penchant to date everything because, as Bruno Latour posits, this affirms our definitive break with the past and all that it has come to represent. As an archaeologist, I can only agree that the past remains with us, and even returns, as the time-line of events in Syria demonstrates. Latour suggests that as we have accumulated more and more revolutions throughout our history, so too we have accumulated the past through the combined processes of looting, salvaging, displaying, musealizing, and capitalizing upon various forms of restitution. From Napoleon to Putin, we might say that a "maniacal destruction is counterbalanced by an equally maniacal conservation."[46]

There is an uncanny element of history repeating itself in UNESCO's battle to "snatch something from death," the oft-quoted phrase André Malraux used for the Nubian Campaign. With the massive destruction wrought by the Second World War, UNESCO defined part of its raison d'être as identifying sites and monuments that were in danger across European cities such as London, Caen, and Warsaw, and those that were completely destroyed, like Coventry Cathedral. Haunting photographs of bombed buildings appeared in publications like the *UNESCO Courier* over many decades. One lasting image UNESCO used to great advantage in its quest for creating an international public sphere was that of three bedrag-gled children walking through the ruins of Monte Cassino in Italy.[47] The Allies had bombed and destroyed historic and religious buildings there in 1944. Other obvious examples are Dresden, and of course Hiroshima and Nagasaki; Hiroshima was inscribed on the World Heritage List in 1996 for the Genbaku Dome, which withstood the atomic onslaught and now, as the Hiroshima Peace Memorial, still stands as a tragic memorial to in-humanity. Russian and Syrian strikes on Aleppo and Saudi coalition air strikes on Yemen's World Heritage city of Sana'a and two other cultural sites on UNESCO's Tentative List, the historic city of Saada and the eighth-century CE Marib Dam, are more recent cases.[48] The military targeting of Yemeni sites has received much less global coverage and condemnation, especially when compared with Syria. This is primarily because Yemen's material heritage does not recall Classical antiquity and because the bom-bardment is backed by the United States.[49] Like Captain Colby's insidious claim in 1927 that the "inhuman act thus becomes actually humane," Saudi Arabia also purports to be bringing peace and stability.[50] UNESCO has long faced the fact that culture is a victim of war, the perpetrators con-fined neither to one region nor religion of the world.

The #Unite4Heritage Campaign was launched in March 2015 by Director-General Bokova, and in it there are echoes of UNESCO's original postwar educational and publicity machine at work. The current digital media offensive espouses a similar universalist message "conceived in response to the destruction and pillage of cultural heritage in conflict zones, most recently in Iraq." It represents a soft-power retaliation to counter the pervasive global media campaign of ISIS, "propagating this campaign across the world, using all forms of media, especially social media, targeting especially young minds." The web platform "invites people, especially young people from the Arab region, to send photos and write short stories about heritage sites that are important for them."[51] Launched in Baghdad, the campaign initially focused on the Middle East and then gradually, albeit minimally, adopted a more global frame of reference. This is, after all, a worldwide crisis, as the history of UNESCO's properties on the front lines (outlined below) will testify. In one of the many conferences, workshops, and events that the #Unite4Heritage Campaign has generated, it was rightly said that "UNESCO offers a unique forum for debate against destruction and hatred. We must use that space."[52] To date, however, there has been condemnation rather than debate, and very little attempt to understand the reasons behind the strategic violence toward cultural heritage, or to analyze different reactions to the loss. The danger here is in not wanting to ask the uncomfortable questions, in not confronting systemic global inequality or attempting to understand the ideologies of others, at the risk of having history repeat itself again in another place and time.

What we are confronted with today cannot easily be dismissed as "random moments of barbarity, mass media spectacle and/or historical re-enactments motivated by a simplistic return to primitive attitudes."[53] For ISIS, these attacks are guided by very real theological and political principles, as Benjamin Isakhan and José Antonio González Zarandona have convincingly shown. Both sets of principles are carefully articulated and deliberately designed. From this perspective the term "iconoclasm" cannot fully capture the reasoning behind their coherent theological framework and broader geopolitical agenda to forge a new Islamic state, however much the West finds it abhorrent. ISIS has gone to great lengths in numerous publications and media "to explain the religious doctrine and the historical precedent to their destruction, situating their attacks within key Islamist principles and alongside some of the key figures of Abrahamic monotheism, Islamic history and prominent Salafi-Wahhabi iconoclasts."[54] Heritage sites are reconfigured as material impediments and transformed into proxies for their ideological adversaries, whether Shia authorities, Western imperialism, nationalist pride, or international organizations such as UNESCO. More uncomfortably, the destruction of pre-monotheistic sites such as Hatra, Nimrud, and Palmyra represents more than retaliation for polytheism or idolatry. It signifies a brutal material corrective to Western colonial occupations and their extractive archaeologies and those who employed those material symbols to construct modern nation-states, thereby manipulating the region's past for a future in ruins.[55]

Back in 1948 at the Beirut Conference UNESCO was already grappling with issues of cultural difference and how best to incorporate the modern Middle East into their one world model. One member of the Secretariat spelled out its position in a polarized world: "Although the Arabs are heirs to one of the world's great cultural possessions, handed down to them over centuries of eventful history, they find themselves today striving vigorously for a cultural rebirth which twentieth-century conditions generally, and their aloofness and isolation from the rest of the world, render more difficult."[56] While many would find such a stance today both orientalist and unacceptable, such views seep imperceptibly into the organization in its most Eurocentric moments, when the focus on places not people prevails, and when not too distant histories of colonialism, occupation, and invasion by Western powers are elided. In Beirut Julian Huxley was optimistic that he could find "a gleam on the dark and disturbed waters of the world today" after the horrors of a world at war. He had hoped that with "good leadership and some luck, it may yet achieve—a stilling of the waters to a peace in which they might reflect the glory of the mind's inheritance for generations yet to come."[57] Seventy years on, the challenge remains the same.

UNESCO has always encountered difficulties in its efforts to save the world. Examining the fate of World Heritage sites on the front lines of war since the establishment of the 1972 World Heritage Convention, albeit part of a much longer history, is instructive. The first major episode revealing extensive damage to UNESCO's inscribed cultural properties took place during the Iran-Iraq War (1980–88). This occurred irrespective of Iran's historical monuments being registered under the 1954 Hague Convention and the country having three sites inscribed on the World Heritage List in 1979: Tchogha Zanbil, Persepolis, and Meidan Emam in Isfahan. The ancient site of Susa was also under artillery fire and aerial attack.[58] Other historic cities including Dezful, Burujerd, Abadan, and Tehran were severely damaged and endangered in what has been seen as a calculated and targeted assault. Given the scale of devastation in Iran at the hands of Saddam Hussein, backed by both the Americans and Soviets, it is remarkable that the longest war of the twentieth century remains largely forgotten by the rest of the world.

No longer collateral damage, heritage properties came to reside at the heart of struggles for self-determination and defiance. On January 21, 1985, a major attack by Indonesian Islamists occurred at Borobudur Temple in Central Java, Indonesia. Nine bombs exploded at the Buddhist temple that UNESCO and the international community had helped restore in their well-known salvage campaign.[59] While there was no loss of life, nine stupas on the temple's upper terraces were badly damaged in the blast. What followed, however, received less international attention. The Indonesian authorities carried out interrogations and even torture of local people in their attempts to identify the culprits. Tensions with the community have been further exacerbated by their restricted access to the temple, the banning of ritual activities, and the general lack of local involvement in site management leading to further alienation.[60]

Turning to Europe, the intentional destruction of cultural property that characterized the Balkan crisis in the 1990s would confront the newly established World Heritage Centre in Paris. As fallout from the violent breakup of Yugoslavia, cultural heritage was damaged and destroyed by all parties in the conflict.[61] The bombardment of Dubrovnik in 1991 included the shelling of its Old Town that had been inscribed on the World Heritage List in 1979. After surviving a major earthquake in 1667, the city had managed to preserve its Gothic, Renaissance, and Baroque churches, monasteries, palaces, and fountains, but with the hostilities it was placed on the List of World Heritage in Danger in 1991. Intentional destruction wrought by the Yugoslav People's Army provoked strong international condemnation, followed by diplomatic and economic isolation for Serbia and Montenegro and support for an independent Croatia. Dubrovnik's Old Town became an icon of the targeting of heritage in wartime and overt cultural violations that began to be described as a crime against humanity.

The war in Bosnia (1992–95) has been called the most devastating conflict in Europe since the end of the Second World War. Once again emblematic monuments and sites were transmuted into vulnerable targets on the frontline.[62] A newly independent Bosnia and Herzegovina was swift to petition for UNESCO membership, achieving it on June 2, 1993. As a State Party, it immediately requested protection for the Old Bridge in Mostar and for UNESCO to send an urgent mission. Over the next few weeks Bosnia promptly acceded to the 1972 Convention and the 1954 Hague Convention, among others, in an effort to secure protection for its historic sites in the escalating conflict. Between June 1993 and April 1994 Croatian forces had besieged the historic town of Mostar. Civilians were killed, humanitarian aid was blocked, much of the historic town with its many mosques was destroyed, and despite the appeal to UNESCO the Mostar Bridge was shelled till collapse in November 1993, only four months after Bosnia's plea to the international community.[63]

In view of the organization's perceived failure during the war, the bridge was completely reconstructed in 2004 under UNESCO's auspices and parts of the Old Town were restored or rebuilt with the contribution of an international scientific committee.[64] The organization turned the destruction and its own incapacity around and now hails it as one of its great successes. As a didactic testament to those efforts, the Old Bridge Area of the Old City of Mostar was inscribed on the World Heritage List in 2005. UNESCO declared that with the "renaissance" of the Old Bridge and its surroundings, the symbolic power and meaning of the city of Mostar— as an exceptional and universal symbol of coexistence of communities from diverse cultural, ethnic and religious backgrounds—has been reinforced and strengthened, underlining the unlimited efforts of human solidarity for peace and powerful cooperation in the face of overwhelming catastrophes."[65] Despite UNESCO's exuberant claims, researchers on the ground tracking longitudinal developments have documented more subtly how the bridge has been transformed from a site of destruction to one of construction. International staging has, at times, papered over the smoldering religious and ethnic tensions, while some researchers have revealed the inherent danger that reconstruction has not brought reconciliation.[66]

Then the most sacred Buddhist site in Sri Lanka, the Temple of the Tooth Relic of the Buddha, was bombed on January 25, 1998, by Tamil separatists (LTTE) who were fighting for an independent state. The temple was a key feature of the seventeenth-and-eighteenth-century complex of Kandy, Sri Lanka's last precolonial capital, inscribed as a World Heritage site in 1988.[67] As Gamini Wijesuriya notes, there had been an earlier attack on worshippers at the sacred bodhi tree in the ancient city of Anuradhapura, another World Heritage property.[68] Significantly, 1998 marked the fiftieth anniversary of independence from British rule and elaborate arrangements had been planned for the celebration. Alongside the human death toll there was extensive damage to the temple: the wooden roof collapsed, walls cracked, and painted murals were damaged, although the relic shrine had been protected from the blast. The attack was designed to strike at the heart of Sinhala Buddhist identity and pride.[69]

One site that captured the world's attention, historically tied to UNESCO's conservation program over many decades, was the Bamiyan Buddhas in Afghanistan.[70] Under the Taliban regime the two colossal Buddhas were intentionally demolished over several weeks in early March 2001. Declared idols by Mullah Mohammad Omar, they were dynamited in deliberate defiance of appeals made by the UN and other international bodies. The timing of the edict was key, issued as it was during a high-profile UNESCO conference on the fate of cultural heritage in Central Asia. The Taliban leader claimed his decision was spurred by foreign concern and funding for the Buddhas at a time when the Afghan people were starving. Adding to this tension, the Metropolitan Museum of Art in New York had previously offered to buy the statues. Japan offered to move them. Envoys were sent to intercede with unofficial UNESCO assistance, including a group of religious leaders. The Organization of the Islamic Conference called upon the Taliban to spare the statues and UNESCO sent letters of protest. All these efforts failed.

The destruction was a strategic international play to draw attention to Afghanistan's plight and to counter specific forms of Western intervention and its perceived priorities. In retrospect there were other complex, collateral factors involving military operations, internal politics, sectarian tensions, and international relationships that explain why heritage was held hostage.[71] UNESCO and the international community had successfully staved off one threat of demolition in 1997. However, given the UN's failure to recognize the Taliban, they indirectly made it impossible to place Bamiyan on the World Heritage List, arousing further animosity.[72] The loss of the Buddhas is a poignant "example in this history of cultural infamy," according to legal scholars, that exhibits "new features in the pathology of State behaviour toward cultural heritage."[73] It diverged from previous attacks on heritage properties in that the "demolition was carefully planned, painstakingly announced to the media all over the world, and cynically documented in all its phases of preparation, bombing and ultimate destruction."[74] In many ways Bamiyan was a dramatic precursor to the sustained attacks perpetrated by ISIS in Syria and Iraq in the decade to follow.

The Iraq War in 2003 saw untold destruction and looting of sites and museums. During the conflict archaeological and historic sites were intentionally vandalized, often by the so-called liberators of the Iraqi people. The failure and indifference of the US-led occupation to protect the Iraq National Museum after the fall of the Baathist regime is well documented. Yet it eclipsed coverage of the coalition forces that deployed and damaged major heritage sites to build military bases, including the archaeological site of Babylon with its famous ziggurat and Ishtar Gate.[75] Inscribed on UNESCO's Tentative List in 2003, the third-millennium-BC site was renamed Camp Alpha. In 2005 coalition forces used part of the ninth-century Great Mosque of Samarra to construct military barracks and a training camp for 1,500 Iraqi National Police.[76] Looting and damage by British and American forces were similarly neglected, along with the deliberate destruction of many important sites of Islamic heritage.[77] Looting began on the day war broke out, and it has subsequently intensified, at the World Heritage sites of Hatra and Ashur, as well as those on the Tentative List, Nimrud and Nineveh.[78] As Benjamin Isakhan argues, the widespread destruction of "cultural heritage has enabled various entities to propagate their divisive rhetoric in the absence of a cohesive national identity," resulting in an upsurge of violence.[79] ISIS in a destructive rampage has further capitalized on the negative legacy of the Iraq invasion.

As outlined in earlier chapters, Thailand and Cambodia were thrust into a border conflict precipitated by the inscription of Preah Vihear Temple on the World Heritage List in 2008. Though never inscribed on the List of World Heritage in Danger, there was loss of life and destruction to property and the Shiva Temple was damaged by artillery fire as the dispute raged on until 2011. The following year the World Heritage Committee was again confronted with two more sites in imminent danger: Timbuktu and the Tomb of Askia in Mali.[80] Both were placed on the List of World Heritage in Danger in 2012 due to the armed conflict and targeting of mausoleums led by the militant group Ansar Dine. As described previously, during the Committee meetings in St. Petersburg Director-General Bokova publicly appealed for a halt to the destruction. Yet she may have unwittingly exacerbated those tensions by claiming that "when a World Heritage site is destroyed, because of stupidity and violence, the whole of humanity feels it has been deprived of part of itself; that it has been injured."[81] Such a stance effectively jettisons Ansar Dine from an "assumed common feeling of humanity."[82] The public spectacle of UNESCO's international meetings seemed to only escalate the tensions and subsequent violations.

The spokesman for the Ansar Dine insurgents responded directly: "God is unique," he told reporters. "All of this is *haram* (or forbidden in Islam). We are all Muslims. Unesco is what?"[83] As anthropologist Charlotte Joy explains, the danger here was that UNESCO was "not only participating in conversations about what it means to be Muslim in Mali today through drawing attention to buildings and sites, but through its very presence, which comes to be associated with the buildings it seeks to protect and its global humanitarian project."[84]

Most recently heritage has been once again under attack in Iraq and Syria, the latter discussed above. For Iraq, the sites of Ashur, Hatra, and Samarra have all been placed on the List of World Heritage in Danger. All three are archaeological sites that ISIS has occupied in recent years and where it subsequently implemented a program of cultural cleansing, according to the Iraqi authorities.[85] The famous ancient Assyrian cities near Mosul, Nimrud and Nineveh, were severely damaged by ISIS. The violent demolition of ancient buildings and statuary was broadcast to the world in graphic detail. Iraq has officially conveyed to the World Heritage Centre, quite rightly, that the warring parties have neither understood nor respected UNESCO's international conventions. Moreover, coalition troops and air-craft "bombing Islamic State sites" have also inflicted considerable damage to historic monuments that now involves "the United States, Canada, Australia, France, UAE, Jordan and other States."[86] The disentangling of perpetrators and causalities in such conflicts has become increasingly diffi-cult, not to mention the impacts of so-called collateral damage.

This trend of increasing heritage destruction uncomfortably suggests that there is something specific about the World Heritage stamp that has rendered sites valuable targets. Their imputed protected legal status under international treaties, the resources channeled to them, their visi-bility and symbolic value as the purported "heritage of humanity," and the outrage of the international community at their targeting have attracted new modalities of danger. Ultimately, the conflation of heritage with other types of resources and international interests may be the very con-nectivity that intensifies the violence in the first instance. World Heritage sites that draw greater international intervention, coverage, and concern might be the very ones where we will see continued violence, as we have in Afghanistan, Mali, Syria, and Iraq, but also post–Arab Spring in Libya and Tunisia.[87] Their internationalism may be at the heart of their destruction.

World Heritage sites have been embroiled in war and conflict from the outset of the 1972 Convention. Indeed, the enhanced protection of monuments was a primary concern for the founders of UNESCO back in 1945. Yet it is the 1954 Hague Convention that is the main legal instrument for addressing culture in the context of war.[88] As of 2018 some 131 states are parties to that convention; 108 have ratified its First Protocol but only 75 the Second Protocol. While in 1954 the First Protocol was a response to the systematic pillage of cultural property in occupied territories during the Second World War, the Second Protocol in 1999 created a new category of enhanced protection for cultural property. In late 2016 I had the opportunity to attend the committee sessions for the Hague Convention in Paris. Given the severity of heritage crises unfolding in Crimea, Syria, Iraq, and Yemen, I imagined many hundreds of national delegates, NGOs, and observers would attend, ensconced in days of impassioned speech. Instead there was scant representation from the Member States, the small auditorium was always half empty, discussions were compressed into a mere two days, and the convention's budget was minuscule. The wealthiest and most powerful nations were not in attendance, nor were those responsible for the devastating airstrikes on Yemen and Syria.

Goethe once said that "many wonders of the world have been lost in war and strife; he who protects and preserves has the happiest lot." While the first claim is self-evident, the second is questionable. At UNESCO the particular work of saving the world has been severely curbed by sovereign ambitions or alternatively national disinterest coupled with the current fiscal crisis. For instance, the committee's ability to assist nations such as Mali was restricted to providing paltry sums of US$35,000. The Hague Convention was yet another victim of the agency-wide cuts following the US withholding of dues. Other matters in the committee ranged from the possibilities and politics of creating "safe havens" for artifacts in danger during wartime and the difficulties of conferring "enhanced protection" for World Heritage sites. The Member States Cambodia, Mali, Bosnia and Herzegovina, Nigeria, Georgia, Libya, and Mali all requested assistance. At that 2016 meeting Mali was granted "enhanced protection" for the Tomb of Askia.[89] In the Istanbul meetings a Malian site manager attempted to warn his audience that the newly restored sites were not yet safe. He claimed there was a degree of hostility amongst the community about the resources that had been visibly funneled into material heritage rather than the people themselves—and that the material heritage was still very much in danger.[90] While there had been jubilation at UNESCO about the success of its sponsored rebuilding efforts, as discussed in Chapter 8, the feeling on the ground was rather less sanguine.

Living Dangerously

It was a watershed moment for UNESCO when Palestine was admitted as a Member State in 2011. The UN and UNESCO have long supported Palestine, from the 1949 establishment of the United Nations Relief and Works Agency for Palestine Refugees in the Near East (UNRWA) to granting observer status to the Palestine Liberation Organization in the 1970s and attempts in the early 1990s to admit Palestine as a full member of UNESCO.[91] Since the early 2000s, UNESCO has been very active in the West Bank in an effort to save heritage in danger, largely because Gaza and Jerusalem have posed other extreme dangers.[92] For Palestine, World Heritage designation and the promise of protection for their many archaeological and historic sites are vital. International recognition like that of UNESCO offers what Chiara de Cesari calls "anticipatory representation" in global governance. The World Heritage platform, like others across the organization, might then serve to shine a light on ongoing tensions over endangered heritage both living and material, incursions into territory, and the future potentials of sovereignty—in essence issues that stem from the twentieth-century colonization and carving up of the region between the colonial powers.

Palestinian admission to UNESCO culminated in their first nomination, the Birthplace of Jesus: Church of the Nativity and the Pilgrimage Route, Bethlehem, in 2012 to the World Heritage List and simultaneously, on an emergency basis, to the List of World Heritage in Danger.[93] Bethlehem is revered by many religions, though primarily regarded as a Christian rather than Muslim site. While the church was first completed in 339 CE, the Palestinians made clear that the property also included Latin, Greek Orthodox, Franciscan, and Armenian features, and a pilgrimage route. It was also a site steeped in a long and dangerous history. Over a tense month in 2002 Israeli Defense Force snipers targeted the church and tanks were deployed near Manger Square in what has been called the Siege of the Church of the Nativity in Bethlehem. An ICOMOS report following the cessation of hostilities claimed that the destruction wrought totaled $US1.4 million in damages.[94]

An ICOMOS evaluation of Bethlehem almost a decade later confirmed other threats, including development pressures, tourism and environmental pressures, and the need for conservation and structural repair. Yet they stopped short of acknowledging the emergency situation. Palestine argued that restoration works had been hindered because of the political situation since 1967. Indeed, Bethlehem 2000, UNESCO's own ambitious program for the rehabilitation of the historic city and its religious complex, had not succeeded in any major restoration of the Church of the Nativity.[95] The World Heritage Committee in St. Petersburg decided, after a tense vote, that the site should be inscribed on both lists. While hundreds of delegates cheered at the announcement and Palestine celebrated "a people's right to self-determination," the decision highlighted the sweeping financial and structural repercussions for the organization.

With the admission of Palestine to UNESCO the United States announced its intention to withdraw financial support. Similarly, Israel withheld its financial contribution and further announced the construction of two thousand additional housing units across the West Bank and East Jerusalem. Moreover, Israel stopped the transfer of the tax revenues collected from the control of its external borders on behalf of the Palestinian Authority.[96] Undeterred, Palestine submitted its second nomination on an emergency basis in 2012, the Jerusalem Southern Terraces Landscape, also known as the cultural landscape of Battir. Situated in the Central Highlands between Nablus and Hebron, the West Bank village of Battir is surrounded by an irrigated farming system dating back to the Roman period. Battir had received the Melina Mercouri International Prize for the Safeguarding and Management of Cultural Landscapes in 2011.[97] Yet it was, as landscape expert Peter Fowler warned, "a landscape produced by centuries of hard work; it could be destroyed in days by ill-considered actions."[98]

The residents of Battir understood this only too well. The core of their residential neighborhood had been destroyed by the Israeli military in the 1980s.[99] The Palestinian nomination dossier claimed that Israeli authorities had also confiscated some of their terraces, but the main dangers lay in the occupation itself, the ongoing expansion of colonial settlement, and the construction of the so-called Separation Barrier.[100] The wall "runs for the most part deep into the West Bank, and has thus been the object of worldwide criticism as, among other things, a disguised form of territorial annexation." The proposed construction would not only "cause grave damage to the heritage of Battir," according to De Cesari, but also entail "the loss of large tracts of land for the Palestinian villagers, who appealed to the Israeli High Court of Justice to stop its construction."[101] During the 2014 World Heritage Committee discussions in Doha the German ambassador questioned the process that Palestine had followed, pursing an emergency procedure rather than what he described as the "normal manner."

ICOMOS took the floor and clarified that it did not consider the case of Battir "an emergency." In its evaluation report ICOMOS had repeatedly referred to the separation wall as a "fence."[102] In swift response, the chair of the World Heritage Committee, Sheikha Al-Mayassa bint Hamad bin Khalifa Al-Thani, addressed the ICOMOS representative directly: "So are you saying that the state of Palestine is not an emergency?" In this unusual state of affairs and suspension of presumptive neutrality, the Qatari chair shared her own sentiments: "Palestine is a state of emergency, so I'm just throwing this out for my information."[103] The Committee concurred, and Lebanon, Turkey, Senegal, Algeria, Kazakhstan, Peru, Qatar, Malaysia, Jamaica, and India all supported Battir's inscription.

Germany requested a secret ballot. However, its attempt to scupper the nomination was quashed by a final vote of eleven to three, and the renamed Palestine: Land of Olives and Vines—Cultural Landscape of Southern Jerusalem, Battir, was inscribed on the List of World Heritage and the List of World Heritage in Danger.[104] Following Palestine's acceptance speech, Israel described the decision as a "negative landmark" and a "brutal abuse and complete neglect of procedures and guidelines." Following the UNESCO decision and after years of debate, the Israeli High Court of Justice then rejected the Israeli military's request to continue the construction of the Separation Barrier. The court considered that the proposed route, cutting through the terraced landscape of Battir, would irreversibly destroy the canal irrigation system that had existed since Roman times.[105] In 2017 Hebron was also nominated on an emergency basis and successfully inscribed in similarly tense negotiations. Palestine had documented escalating threat conditions and a number of violations: there were acts of vandalism, site damage, and other attacks on the property. Danger listing, they argued in a letter to the Secretariat, would ensure adequate safeguarding and bring international standards of conservation to the site.[106]

While some Member States are critical of this continual recourse to danger listing, most recognize that Palestine is operating under siege conditions and its heritage has also been on the front lines of conflict. The case of Palestine underscores that there are multiple levels of danger: heritage in danger, the perils of living in occupied territories, the precariousness of conservation efforts, and even the future of UNESCO itself. Palestine's admission to UNESCO sparked the third suspension of funding by the United States, resulting in financial and administrative cuts the agency can ill afford. In 2011 the Director-General warned the United States that withholding "dues and other financial contributions . . . will weaken UNESCO's effectiveness and undermine its ability to build free and open societies."[107] Bokova's message was that the decision would severely hamper American ambitions abroad, particularly in the Middle East.

The US Congress passed legislation in 1990 and 1994 intended to block the normalization of Palestinian relations and activities among the international community.[108] Two Americans working at UNESCO during the 1950s—Walter Laves, a former Deputy Director of the organization, and Charles Thomson—claimed then that the American government never fully understood what could be done by cooperative action through UNESCO to achieve the goals of the United Nations as well as US foreign policy. Moreover, the United States failed to understand the prestige garnered from supporting UNESCO's cultural and intellectual values or the advantages of participating in multilateral technical assistance.[109] Since 2011, the financial withdrawal has signaled a broader swath of dangers, including nonparticipation in a range of international bodies and noncompliance with international agreements, which further American isolation and severely restrict UNESCO's ability to carry out its functions. Moreover, the financial ruin that has ensued has serious implications for conservation and communities worldwide.

UNESCO and the United States have had a contentious history, often mired in conspiracy, politics, and isolation. Between 1953 and 1954 Senator Joseph McCarthy claimed that the American delegation and State Department officials who dealt with UNESCO were part of a communist conspiracy.[110] Secret investigations by the CIA into UNESCO began in 1947, only one year after the agency's establishment. As noted earlier, America has suspended financial support to UNESCO twice before—once in 1977, when Israel's petition to be considered part of Europe was denied, and again in 1984, over national interest and Cold War conspiracy—costing UNESCO some US$43 million in lost revenues.[111] Another point of contention was UNESCO's resolutions over Israel's illegal excavation in Jerusalem.[112]

Since the Ronald Reagan administration, the United States has routinely accused UNESCO of politicization, financial mismanagement, and an unworkable bureaucracy. In the 1980s some decried sacrificing UNESCO as a concession to the New Right, and some likened the attack to the US invasion of Grenada, targeting the weakest UN organization. Reinforcing the wider political implications, Director-General M'Bow criticized the decision "to break off relations with the countries of the South" and forcing "them to adopt policies and measures which will impoverish many of their inhabitants and sooner or later create situations of tension and serious internal crises."[113] The US decision in 1984 underscored a general cynicism toward multilateralism and confirmed that it was better to end rather than mend the relationship.[114] It further signaled the death knell of an internationalist ethos in mainstream US political life, and the political idealism epitomized during the Nubian Campaign was supplanted by contempt and derision.[115]

If saving Abu Simbel represents the first foray into international heritage diplomacy, leading ultimately to the crafting of the 1972 Convention, then with the listing of Bethlehem we see its potential undoing in the divisiveness and impolitic practices of a few powerful yet isolated nations. Assisting Egypt in the 1960s fulfilled strategic ambitions in the Cold War era, whereas supporting Palestine today presents a problem for Western European nations such as France and Germany as well as the United States. Political wrangling is now systemic throughout the Convention; however, withholding contributions, as the United States has routinely done, or even threatening to, is a path now being pursued by other nations such as Japan when their political aims are in danger of being thwarted. Threats over funding are increasingly used to inflame existing conflicts, rather than to promote the early cooperation demonstrated in Egypt, Pakistan, and Indonesia all those decades ago. Peace appears to be off the agenda and danger may be the new normal.

Conclusions

There are many dangers not only to heritage but also to the people whose lives are entwined with historic sites and ancient landscapes, many of whose territories have been exploited, exchanged, or fought over by successive occupying regimes. Like its predecessor the League of Nations, UNESCO's planetary utopia elevated monumental heritage to a universal issue the world might rally around when it could not effectively do so around human life. Today "uniting for heritage" has become a slogan that similarly attempts to save sites while human survival in those selfsame places is parlous and conditions are inhuman. Focusing on the fabric of the past, as something that outlives the average human lifespan, survives generations, and might be preserved for the future, would seem then to override and displace the political, religious, and cultural differences that persist and divide. When antiquity is imperiled many of us have been conditioned to recognize that both the past and the future are in danger. But there are other accompanying dangers in the hostilities occurring around, and directed toward, ancient sites, such as the creation of an index of civilized cultures and practices as opposed to barbaric ones. The reemergence of civilizational discourse itself poses a danger and threatens to provoke further alienation and division. Recalling the bombardment of Syrian cities and their civilians by French colonial forces in 1925, and most recently by Russia, reveals the ways in which European civility has conversely been endangered. At the founding of the United Nations, General Jan Smuts, a veteran of many military campaigns, warned that now the "world will be alive with danger . . . Do not ask me who is the enemy. I do not know. It may be ourselves."[116]

Russian intervention in Syria is also a civilizing business, creating expansive new markets for military technologies while cementing strategic political partnerships for the future. It reminds us of the hyperconnectivity of heritage, so prevalent around the inscription of Preah Vihear, and that UNESCO's cultural recognition, protection, or even danger listing provides an opportunity for lucrative and calculated economic adventures for an ever-widening set of vested nations and corporations. This now extends well beyond regional interests and alliances to global interconnections. Superpowers such as Russia, China, and the United States impose their influence, stretching well beyond the frontiers of cultural diplomacy and revealing the hypocrisies of the multilateral system, so acutely perceived by smaller nations. For decades the United States has been an outspoken critic of politicization at UNESCO, and in recent years, while it withholds funding, it continues to manipulate the system to its advantage. In October 2017 President Donald Trump affirmed that the United States would be withdrawing its membership. On the wrong side of history, from its conspiracy claims during the Cold War to its most recent financial withdrawal, decisions and positions adopted by the United States have posed a significant danger to UNESCO's fulfilling of its mission.

Regardless of UNESCO's aspirational mandate, the lingering problems of global inequality, religious intolerance, illegal occupation, and self-determination have not been easily incorporated into UNESCO's legal and operational remit. Even high-profile Security Council resolutions and partnerships with INTERPOL and other agencies still leave UNESCO focusing on the physical reconstruction of sites post-conflict, training conservators, virtual reality, and social media. Paradoxically, the fixation on rebuilding monuments, as witnessed in Mali and on the drawing board for Iraq and Syria, challenges the stated principles of authenticity and integrity that World Heritage experts have always deemed the criteria for inscription. Alternatively, it may reflect an easing of the restrictive criteria that European experts have long promulgated. Whichever scenario dominates, it further reinforces how technocratic solutions continue to be privileged in the face of waning competence to confront the social and political context of conflict. Then there is the situation in Palestine, which evinces more quotidian and ingrained episodes of heritage destruction. While historically UNESCO has attempted to intervene, some efforts have been thwarted or restricted by the actions of unsupportive or hostile states under the guise of neutrality, expertise, or jurisdiction. Calls for conservation and peace have thus been framed diametrically by some States Parties, silencing any proposal for either and further entrenching the impasse. Ultimately, this brings us full circle to the tensions that have surrounded UNESCO from its inception: science versus religion, preservation versus politics, peace-building versus technocracy.

Taken together, the dramatic developments that have recently emerged in the Middle East necessitate critical reflection upon the shortcomings and failures of UNESCO's philosophies and practice over the past seventy years. How has an organization rising from the ashes of conflict found itself again embroiled in a war of cultural difference and misunderstanding—a specifically material violence surrounding the vestiges of the past and its particular valuation in the present? This situation too represents a type of danger, in addition to the ruination in Aleppo, Nimrud, Sana'a, or Timbuktu. At one of many seventieth-anniversary events at UNESCO headquarters in Paris, one member of the Secretariat posed a question to a panel of historians: if UNESCO's employees were not constrained by confidentiality clauses, could they speak about institutional failures and even learn from them? It recalled a reflection from the Nubian Monuments Campaign made by archaeologist William Y. Adams in his plea for demythification: "We can only benefit, in hindsight, from real mistakes and from real successes; not imagined ones."[117] Citing the constraining organizational structure, another audience member asked how the world would fare without UNESCO. What did the future hold for the "laboratory of the world"? Typically, such questions are not formally aired, and there was some good-humored chiding afterward in the corridors. But the message was clear: subscribing to the mission is everything.

Historians on the panel responded that at the very beginning, enshrined in the preamble to its constitution, UNESCO set its sights on the future with the highest aspirations. And while the organization has not always been successful, the immense creativity that was generated and its programmatic vision must today be acknowledged. Amongst UNESCO's achievements they counted holistic approaches to basic education, freedom of expression as a fundamental right, preservation of the diversity of cultural expressions, the concept of a culture of peace, sustainable development and culture for development, and an understanding of heritage as shared by humanity as a whole. These are indeed watershed contributions that have made planetary advances, albeit driven by particular regions of the world and their philosophies rather than being evenly distributed. Yet any universal framing of "heritage without any regard for its historical emergence from a culturally and historically specific context in Europe," Herzfeld predicts, is bound to run into local resistance. Such unevenness is flattened and concealed under the banner of "heritage." Yet the terms themselves, including *patrimoine* in French and *patrimonio* in Italian, reveal the linkage between a patrilineal conception of inheritance, property ownership, and individualism. A product of early modern Europe, it has never extended to the world's heritage as a whole.[118]

Global interventions such as the creation of World Heritage also have a history, entailing winners and losers, and having implications for power, authority, and legitimation that invite closer scrutiny. The collision of worldviews, particularly those with perspectives and practices that have not been incorporated into the one-world model, has potential consequences for both communities and conservation. One consequence is that increasingly dystopian scenarios are playing out that intentionally target UNESCO's listed sites. As Orwell predicted in *1984*, the past "had not merely been altered, it had been actually destroyed. For how could you establish even the most obvious fact when there existed no record outside your own memory?"

8

Dystopia

*So if you open this door it has been said that it would lead
to the end of the world.*

—AHMED AL FAQI AL MAHDI, 2016

ON AUGUST 22, 2016, a Tuareg man from Timbuktu named Ahmed Al
Faqi Al Mahdi appeared in The Hague's International Criminal Court (ICC)
and made history. He was the first person to plead guilty to a war crime
at the ICC under Article 8 of the Rome Statute. It was also the first time
that the charge of deliberate destruction of cultural property had been the
primary indictment before the court. Al Mahdi was accused with crimes
committed over a ten-day period from June to July 2012 in his hometown
of Timbuktu, Mali. He had been captured in Niger in late September 2015.
There he admitted to authorities the role he played, as a religious specialist
and head of the Hesbah or morality police for the Islamist group Ansar
Dine, in the destruction of the nine mausoleums of venerated Islamic
saints and the door of the Sidi Yahia mosque in Timbuktu. Under Article
8 he was convicted of "extensive destruction and appropriation of property,
not justified by military necessity and carried out unlawfully and wan-
tonly." That destruction was equated with other war crimes such as willful
killing, torture, inhuman treatment, hostage-taking, and deportation.[1]

Al Mahdi's prosecution and the public spectacle that ensued were met
with a kind of jubilation from UNESCO and the world media. Yet watching
the trial and delving into the transcripts, one is left with a more troubling
view that ultimately "you are judging one man," as Jean-Louis Gilissen, a
lawyer for the defense, noted. No other prosecutions have been brought
against Islamic militants for the atrocities perpetrated against civilians
in Mali: murder, execution, rape, amputation, robbery, violence, intimidation, and use of child soldiers. Malian security forces responded to the
uprising with their own unlawful detention and torture, targeting civilians

and ethnic groups.[2] War crimes have been well documented on both sides of the conflict. Yet the perpetrators of these abuses will not appear before the ICC. Given these disparities, we have succeeded in making cultural heritage the scapegoat for the instrumental failures to hold individuals accountable for much graver crimes. Significantly, Al Mahdi himself was not involved in any violence toward the people of Timbuktu and, in his own words, he wanted to be looked upon as "a son who has lost his way." As Gilissen asked, "What is more serious, to pull down walls or to destroy lives? Blow up buildings or shoot down people?" He reminded the court that "there is the dark side of retribution of course. And by adding to the evil already done, when one does harm to the accused, is this going to lead to a better outcome? Yes, this is a symbolic debate."

That debate, and indeed the entire Al Mahdi case, has brought many unsettling contradictions to the fore. Events in Mali impel us to consider different interpretations of the relationship between religious doctrine and material heritage and the implications that follow. Rather than resorting to a presumptive universality, we might also question the nature and extent of local injury versus international grievance. Is the harm done to the people of Timbuktu more direct and consequential than that done to humanity as a whole, or some sectors of the international community? While some of these issues were raised briefly during the trial, they have not been expounded upon in the corridors of UNESCO. Yet this might be precisely the moment to reflect upon the ways in which World Heritage has been instrumentalized, whether by Ansar Dine, ISIS, or UNESCO, to promote their particular yet divergent worldviews. Why does such radical difference persist after all the efforts and programs geared toward internationalism over the past century and why have World Heritage sites become so enmeshed in the resulting conflicts?[3] More uncomfortably, these questions inevitably lead us back to the stark inequities that still exist between different nations, many of which are derivative of colonial occupation, exploitation, and decision-making, particularly in a country like Mali, but also in Syria and Iraq. ISIS literally bulldozed part of the border between Iraq and Syria, imposed almost a century ago by British and French bureaucrats after the collapse of the Ottoman Empire.[4] Advancing British interests while fending off French counterclaims, Sir Mark Sykes had drawn a line in the sand that could be traced on a map of the Middle East from the *e* in Acre to the last *k* in Kirkuk.[5] These colonial histories recall the particular European genealogy of international organizations from the League of Nations to UNESCO and their limitations to inculcate a culture of peace and to reconcile fundamentally different worldviews. Finally, what transpired in The Hague was not simply that monumental acts were being prosecuted, but rather that the very status of heritage was on trial.

Just as the name of Timbuktu has become synonymous with a distant place or the end of the world, so too has the dystopia that pervaded the Malian conflict.[6] Amnesty International warned that although attacks on religious and historical monuments can destroy the culture and identity of a population, we should not "lose sight of the fact that hundreds of civilians were murdered, tortured and raped during the 2012 conflict in Mali. The ICC should therefore continue to investigate crimes committed by all sides to the conflict."[7] That monumental destruction now constitutes a war crime underlines that while UNESCO hoped to manufacture the universal concept of a one-world heritage through treaties and conventions, it failed to sufficiently develop the principle so as to embrace a world of difference and thus contribute to a lasting peace. Hostile acts toward internationally listed monuments have now been elevated to the category of cultural cleansing, especially in the eyes of UNESCO.[8]

Established in the fifth century CE, Timbuktu is located at the point where the Niger River flows northward into the southern edge of the Sahara Desert. This geographical position made Timbuktu a veritable crossroads between peoples, including the Songhai, Wangara, Fulani, Arabs, and Tuareg, as well as a trading center for gold, salt, books, and other commodities. In 1354 the medieval explorer Muhammad Ibn Batuta famously described the wealth and gold of Timbuktu, giving rise to the myth of an African El Dorado. In the fifteenth and sixteenth centuries the town developed into an intellectual and spiritual capital and a center for Islam throughout Africa: scholars, engineers, and architects all assembled there. Along with the University of Sankore, there were 180 Quranic schools and 25,000 students, accounting for one-quarter of the estimated population. It is often called the City of 333 Saints, and the many mudbrick structures, mosques, tombs, and shrines throughout Timbuktu were the product of African and Arab architectural traditions. For these reasons it was nominated for UNESCO's World Heritage List in 1987.

Regardless of the many historic buildings in the city of Timbuktu, ICOMOS only supported the inscription of the three major mosques (Djingareyber, Sankore, and Sidi Yahia) and sixteen mausoleums, as outlined in their brief six-page document.[9] In 1980 the World Heritage Committee deferred Mali's proposal to inscribe the entire city of Timbuktu, suggesting instead a restrictive dossier of religious monuments. ICOMOS noted then that this "fragile group of buildings [was] threatened by dangers as diverse as sand drifts and urban development."[10] At the time of inscription in 1988 UNESCO recognized that "although continuously restored, these monuments are today under threat."[11] In 1994 further risks were flagged, including those from the annual replastering maintenance activities. Evaluators discovered that serious alterations to both the mud construction materials and the structures themselves jeopardized the site's long-term integrity and conservation.[12] Timbuktu was placed on the List of World Heritage in Danger, where it remained until 2005. With the armed conflict of 2012 the World Heritage Committee placed Mali's Timbuktu and the Tomb of Askia in Gao on the List of World Heritage in Danger.[13] A State of Conservation report described the "degradation of the Timbuktu tombs" and "threats to the conservation of the Outstanding Universal Value."[14]

Grave Crimes

Timbuktu has often been called "the pearl of the desert." Prosecutors in the Al Mahdi trial often referred to it as such, stressing the site's centrality for the heritage of Africa. This is in part because comparatively few major cultural sites in Africa, particularly those of an urban character, have been recognized, much less inscribed on the World Heritage List. On one hand, this is a product of the long-standing Eurocentrism that has dominated the process of listing sites, as discussed in earlier chapters. On the other, the seemingly unique position of Timbuktu is a result of the widespread destruction of other major African centers by the British, French, and other colonial forces in what has been called the "scramble for Africa."[15] That "scramble" refers to a period of new imperialism between 1881 and 1914 when European powers invaded, occupied, divided, colonized, and annexed most of the African continent. These incursions had devastating consequences for both people and places: the British destroyed the urban center of Benin in their punitive expedition of 1897, as they had done with the Asante capital, Kumasi, in 1874.[16] Timbuktu, then, stands for all that has been not only lost but also intentionally destroyed by successive groups in a violent quest to impose their own ideologies.

When colonial rule finally ended in 1960 the French reneged on their promise to the Tuareg to create a separate Saharan territory, a fatal decision that has been further exacerbated by the neglect of the region by subsequent Malian governments.[17] The Tuareg are a semi-nomadic group of largely Berber descent and Muslim faith that for centuries have controlled the trans-Saharan trade routes from Libya to Burkina Faso. In recent decades the Tuareg have suffered considerable hardship, from drought to food shortages, spurring uprisings against state authorities in Bamako and new alliances with Islamist groups in the hopes of independence. This latest conflict had its roots in a military coup staged in March 2012, provoked by anger over corrupt Malian political elites and their handling of international donor funds. The resulting political instability prompted the Tuareg rebels, also known as the National Movement for the Liberation of Azawad (MNLA), to join forces with other militants. Between April 2012 and January 2013 the Islamist groups Ansar Dine and Al Qaeda in the Islamic Maghreb (AQIM) occupied Timbuktu, and Ahmed Al Mahdi worked with their leaders.

Nine mausoleums were attacked in what ICC chief prosecutor Fatou Bensouda called "a callous assault" on Timbuktu's "irreplaceable historic monuments."[18] Al Mahdi identified the sites, stipulated the order of destruction, provided the means, and, in some cases, also participated in the demolition: this was photographed and filmed, and the images were circulated in the global media. He delivered a sermon dedicated to the destruction of the mausoleums and gave public speeches while the attacks took place.[19] In Bensouda's opening statement she described how the "the heritage of mankind was ransacked" over those ten days in a "destructive rage" that constituted a "deep attack upon the identity of a population, their memory and their very future" as well as the "universal values that we must protect."[20] She described how the people of Timbuktu were powerless to intervene while "all of this was reduced to dust."

To take one example, the Sheikh Sidi El Mokhtar Ben Sidi Mouhammad Al Kabir Al Kounti Mausoleum, located in the Sidi El Mokhtar Cemetery, was a popular site of pilgrimage for the people of Mali. On June 30, 2012, Al Mahdi supervised the destruction and gave instructions, along with tools, to the attackers. At the site, he told journalists that "if a tomb is higher than the others, it must be leveled . . . we are going to rid the landscape of anything that is out of place."[21] This resonates with anthropologist Mary Douglas's aphorism that dirt is simply "matter out of place."[22] Douglas argued that within any given social context there is a set of ordered relations, and any contravention of that order will likely lead to the rejection of inappropriate elements. Considered a taboo in Ansar Dine's understanding of shari'a law, the construction of tomb superstructures above a certain height, coupled with their attendant veneration by the community, sparked a violent "reaction which condemns any object or idea likely to confuse or contradict cherished classifications." From that perspective, specific structures should be leveled so as to put matters right; the graves themselves were not desecrated. As events in Timbuktu demonstrate, "cultural categories are public matters," to quote Douglas. One "cannot neglect the challenge of aberrant forms."[23] Ridding the landscape of all "matter out of place" was thus deemed an appropriate response for one group of people to the religious prohibition against ostentatious grave markers.[24]

Douglas wrote that such strict impositions of purity either impose great discomfort or lead to considerable contradictions, especially when there are "uncomfortable facts which refuse to be fitted in."[25] At one level the destruction of mausoleums demonstrates a fundamental religious difference in the limits of spatial and social life that is currently being played out in many countries between the ultraconservative strictures of Wahhabism and other forms of Islamic doctrine and practice amongst mainstream Sunni and Shia Muslims.[26] Video footage presented at his trial shows Al Mahdi justifying an attack on the Sidi Yahia Mosque, the ornate wooden door of which was broken down using an axe: "So if you open this door it has been said that it would lead to the end of the world. We are in charge of fighting superstition and that is why we have decided to pull down this door." This specific interpretation of Islam and its classificatory and juridical system was on trial along with Al Mahdi at the ICC. With Wahhabism's long history of iconoclasm, the majority of Muslims purportedly challenge the movement and its interpretation and adjudication of Quranic doctrine. It is the sect most often blamed for the rise of global terror, though this obscures the divergent historical and regional factors that have given rise to militant groups such as the Taliban, Al Qaeda, Ansar Dine, and ISIS.

Al Mahdi stated in the trial that the heritage of Timbuktu would not be changed or lost, despite his actions. Asked by Judge Antoine Kesia-Mbe Mindua whether he had changed his religious convictions, Al Mahdi testified he was not convinced that demolishing the structures was the right course of action. "I told them, quote, 'At this stage I don't recommend you do it because it might . . . hurt people's feelings.' "[27] But it was a legal decision, he explained, resting upon "a theory according to which one cannot build anything on tombs, and a tomb, according to the religious beliefs, should not be over 1 inch above the ground, and those mausoleums are far higher than that. So is this something agreed upon or not? Those who believe that they can do it consider that it's okay that others believe that those buildings should be destroyed. And I acted because I believed that one is not allowed to build upon tombs." But from a legal and political viewpoint, he continued, "one should not undertake actions that will cause damage that is higher or more severe than the usefulness of the action."[28] Despite believing that the mausoleums were "not as harmful as the contradiction they represent," he was asked to carry out the attacks by the leaders of Ansar Dine, and he complied. Islamic law stipulates that some things are allowed while others are not, Al Mahdi explained to the court at length. Here we enter the realm of jurisprudence, whether one follows Romano-Germanic law, also known as civil law, that has been adopted in continental Europe and in the ICC, or shari'a law. In fact, the court is obliged under the Rome Statute to apply general principles of law that are derived from other legal systems worldwide, including the "national laws of states that would normally exercise jurisdiction over the crime." To date, some legal scholars argue, the court has relied purely upon Western inspiration and neglected Islamic law, further belying its claims to universality. [29]

There is also the matter of whether the Timbuktu shrines are viewed as primarily religious structures, heritage sites, or both, and for which groups. Sanda Ould Boumama, a spokesperson for Ansar Dine, took a hard line following the destruction of the Alpha Moya mausoleum. He stated, "We must go and destroy all the mausoleums and that is exactly what we are doing." When a Radio France International interviewer responded by asking, "But these mausoleums are part of the UNESCO heritage?" his answer was categorical: "That is not our business. We have said that we are here for the Shari'a, the Shari'a and nothing else. We will have our meeting and do whatever has been recommended and leave nothing undone."[30] Provocatively, he asked, "UNESCO is what?"[31] However as we shall see, UNESCO played an exceedingly prominent role throughout the proceedings and, as one judge made evident, since the majority of monuments were recognized by UNESCO, "their attack appears to be of a particular gravity" aimed at the international community.[32]

Turning first to the local community, it is critical to consider the responses of the residents of Timbuktu, their relationships to the monuments, and the scale of damage done. One Malian witness testified that the "mausoleums also are a reflection of life in Timbuktu because they are a reflection of the people's commitment to Islam. The communities of Timbuktu consider the mausoleums as places of prayer and they provide psychological safety nets for the people, to the extent that the people perceive them as protection." He regarded them as both places of religious observance and heritage creation. They formed "part of the socialization of the people. So for each of the items of a people's cultural heritage you can always find a relation, a relationship to the community, a link to ethics with a link to cultural identity as it emerges from within a people." But assigning the structures the category of heritage raised certain anxieties: "Because the classification in national heritage, and on the UNESCO List of World Heritage sites as well, means that the building is kept in its entirety, in its whole state, and when part is destroyed this whole entirety is destroyed and this takes away the universal exceptional value of it. The reason why the building figured on the UNESCO List on the first place." The international system had changed things on the ground and had implications for local understandings of risk, integrity, and loss.

Every crime has a victim, and these destructive acts were repeatedly described in the chamber as "breaking the soul of a people." Prosecution lawyer Mayombo Kassongo represented eight anonymous victims. "It is not possible to defend spirits," Kassongo remarked; "rather the spirits protect and defend living people." He recounted the animistic beliefs still held by the residents of Timbuktu, with ancestor worship existing in tandem with the shari'a law that had been imposed on local customs through the processes of Islamicization. The victims, he claimed, experienced shame, suffering, and financial losses from the decline in the already meager tourism that Timbuktu generates. Judge Mindua asked, under Romano-Germanic law, exactly what harm had been done and what compensation would cover their losses. What had been lost? Avoiding the "Western idea" of income, Kassongo explained that these people had lived their lives by the monuments. Tourists would come and locals might earn "a few cents here and there." Since the insurgency Mali had been considered unsafe and tourism was negligible, so that "material harm" must be "adjusted to take into account local realities." Local realities were something I had witnessed firsthand during May 2008. I visited Timbuktu along with other historic sites in Mali as part of a team examining heritage development strategies. Invited by a group of Malian elites keen to shake off any remaining colonial vestiges of French occupation, the issues we confronted could not be relegated to the past. They concerned more pressing needs for water, sanitation, health care, employment, and infrastructure. Local realities in Timbuktu, I discovered, were indeed stark.

UNESCO had marshaled every effort to rebuild all the mausoleums in 2016 and had gone so far as to arrange a "consecration ceremony." It was touted as a victory for the organization, which was much in need of a positive image to dispel the dystopia that was then unfolding across Syria and Iraq. Others considered it a material failure. Kassongo argued that UNESCO-sponsored reconstruction of the mausoleums did not reunite the Timbuktu community with the saints. It did not repair the spirit of the people during what he called "the reconstruction exercise." Nevertheless, the Director-General in her visits saluted the work of the masons. "These mausoleums are now once again standing," she said, which provides "irrefutable proof that unity is possible and peace is even stronger than before. We did it and we can do it again."[33] Yet contradictory messages emerged from different quarters. Some affirmed the positive process and outcome of rebuilding the mudbrick mausoleums and repairing the mosque door by employing local people and expertise.[34] However, in the chamber of the ICC we heard that the "restoration of cultural heritage never brings back its inherent value." What remains are the "broken links" and irreparable prejudice.

At the World Heritage Committee meetings in Istanbul in 2016 another picture emerged. Despite the high-profile rebuilding efforts, Mali was still not in a position to produce a State of Conservation report for Timbuktu. The fragility of the security situation had further prevented an evaluation mission.[35] As mentioned in Chapter 7, the site manager for Timbuktu expressed his concerns about ongoing security issues. Rather than celebrating the reconstruction, he cautioned that any vandal could still gain access to mausoleums, the monuments were scattered around the city, and all this work could again be destroyed in a short time. "We have been reproached by our lack of reports, the main concern is to make the sites safe, they are at the mercy of armed Islamist groups who are in the site of Timbuktu—with French armed forces in the region we need to make these sites safe otherwise we will be back where we were in 2012."[36] He forewarned that there might be hostile reactions to the restoration. Previously, UNESCO's restoration programs, for the Bamiyan Buddhas in Afghanistan and for sites in other conflict zones, had proven controversial: funding was being channeled into preserving monuments at the very moment when living people needed the greatest support.

Flanked by court guards, Ahmed Al Mahdi confessed that "we have to be true to ourselves even if that truthfulness would burn our hands. It is with deep regret, with great pain that I had to enter a guilty plea and all the charges brought against me are accurate and correct. I am really sorry, I am really remorseful."[37] He implored Muslims across the world not to get involved in such deeds. Moreover, he wanted to contribute to the post-conflict future of Timbuktu, not only because his family still lived there, but for all the city's inhabitants. The defense had argued that "he wanted in some way to help us reach the truth and national reconciliation in Mali." One UNESCO official I spoke with saw Al Mahdi's remorse as marking a potentially important step that could be employed to educate young people, to create a dialogue, and to take positive steps toward peace. This was reminiscent of UNESCO's early mission to rehabilitate materially and spiritually after the war: a program that included the defeated aggressors. From the official's perspective, Mali was a lost opportunity if the organization only focused on the victory and historic conviction, rather than the underlying problems and future directions it might take. However, her carefully considered position, coupled with her regional expertise, rendered her the exception not the rule.

Crimes Against UNESCO

"What is at stake here is not just walls and stones," the chief prosecutor reminded the ICC. The mausoleums were deemed important for history, religion, and identity. Indeed, she repeatedly called them "irreplaceable historic monuments." The lawyer for the eight victims, Mayombo Kassongo, reiterated this distinction: these were not "piles of stones" but rather had been listed as World Heritage in 1988. They were "not a mass of stones and tombs," they represented the "grandeur of African civilization." Kassongo reminded the court that Timbuktu was one of the first African sites on the World Heritage List, likening it to the Eiffel Tower, which is synonymous with the French nation and attracts many tourists. Timbuktu was important for Islam, important for trade, and important for the international community. The last was reinforced by UNESCO Director-General Bokova's speeches, which appealed on no less than ten occasions for protection of Malian sites. Kassongo recounted how UNESCO had sent letters to the African Union, the Economic Community of West African States (ECOWAS), the Islamic Educational, Scientific, and Cultural Organization (ISESCO), the EU, the UN Secretary-General, the ICC, and neighboring countries. Indeed, the entire history of World Heritage and procedures for listing were explained in great detail, much more so than the local meanings attributed by the community. It appeared as if the crime was directed at UNESCO and its instruments, rather than religious targets.

Discussions at the ICC reveal how World Heritage sites are mobilized in international systems and how UNESCO's vision for a "common heritage of humanity" has taken root. The status of Timbuktu on the World Heritage

List was key in the proceedings. Moreover, since Mali is a State Party to the Rome Statute, whereas many nations are not, events in Timbuktu became emblematic of a wider swath of site destructions. Following UNESCO's lead, the court heard how the 2012 Malian attacks were the worst since the Taliban's obliteration of the Bamiyan Buddhas in 2001. Even more indicative of a spatiotemporal slippage, Bensouda projected forward from the Malian crisis to the attacks wrought by ISIS since 2015 in Aleppo and Palmyra. The symbolic dimension of the Al Mahdi conviction could not be overstated.

The prosecution invoked heritage destruction during the Balkan wars in the early 1990s: this was one of the indictments against Slobodan Milošević.[38] They also invoked the 1994 genocide in Rwanda. Both of these conflicts, in different ways, attempted to destroy a people. Yet Al Mahdi's actions were aimed neither at the living nor at ethnic cleansing.[39] They were predicated upon a fundamental difference of religious interpretation, and that had devastating implications for materiality and monumentality. The similarity with the former Yugoslavia, however, lay in Ansar Dine's intent to prohibit a way of life or curtail living traditions, namely the visitation and veneration of shrines. Citing Raphael Lemkin, the lawyer who coined the term "genocide," Kassongo argued that Al Mahdi had committed the most serious of international war crimes, those related to the soul or *genos* of a people. The implication was that such acts constituted cultural genocide.[40] Citing the international community's enduring failures to protect (or prosecute) in Afghanistan, Syria, and Iraq, the prosecution characterized Al Mahdi's actions as a "historic crime." His conviction would be equally "historical," and the prosecution asked that his punishment be appropriately severe, "both for the past and the future." Irreparable harm had been done, Kassongo argued, not just to a city of stone, but to all of humanity.

It fell to Judge Mindua to pursue the exact nature of "damage that may be felt or experienced, so to speak, by humanity in general." There were two parts to his question: "The monuments and buildings are protected, or should I say listed by UNESCO. What, to your mind, is the damage suffered by UNESCO and what would be the damage suffered by humanity itself when it comes to the Bamiyan Buddhas and to the case of Palmyra? Can you assess that there is damage or prejudice suffered at one level or at two levels?"[41] The key witness for UNESCO, Francesco Bandarin, provided an illuminating answer. He responded that the destruction of heritage "concerns both UNESCO and those who believe in the international system for protection of heritage . . . When this site was destroyed, of course we are suffering because we show that our system has limits."[42] This institutional suffering is surely a conceptual state of affairs: UNESCO is "damaged because we show the limits of the international system of protection." Regarding the archaeological site of Palmyra, Bandarin emphasized the "huge reactions from the public opinion, from institutions, cultural institutions around the world, the big museums and so on." Those who believe that "heritage is a fundamental component of cultural, modern cultural life" are suffering.[43] Responding to a reparations order, in August 2017 the ICC ordered Al Mahdi to pay one symbolic euro to the Malian state and one to UNESCO. His total assessed liability for reparations was set at €2.7 million.[44]

UNESCO's loss is symbolic and abstract, an indirect intellectual loss. The damage and loss for the people of Timbuktu are more likely to be palpable, having direct negative effects upon individuals, many of who have suffered repressive regimes and social disintegration, in other words dystopian political conditions.[45] Some legal scholars argue that in cases like this we should depart from the prevailing universalist reasoning and instead utilize a relativist approach in determining the gravity of the destruction.[46] Others suggest that the doctrine of responsibility to protect (R2P), which permits international intervention in cases of gross human rights abuses, should be extended beyond its remit of protecting lives to protecting cultural property.[47] This ramping up of protection for things seeks to place them on an equal footing with people, and while this view has gained traction in Western settings like the ICC and UNESCO, it is by no means subscribed to universally.

According to Charlotte Joy, who has studied Malian World Heritage sites on the ground, UNESCO's humanist vision is undermined when confronted with too much difference, like the monumental destruction in Timbuktu.[48] At the same time the agency seeks to protect cultural particularities from the impacts of globalization, finding itself caught in a number of intractable contradictions. As described at the start of this book, UNESCO's foundational humanism, which aspired to achieve global peace through intercultural dialogue and understanding, has routinely been undercut by state agendas that have no place for ethnic, religious, indigenous, or other minorities. The Tuareg and their aspirations for self-determination provide a powerful example of the consequences of this history of exclusion, ultimately leading to the disaffection and destruction witnessed in Timbuktu. Those voices are not reflected when the State

Party of Mali takes the floor at UNESCO or the ICC to speak for the nation and its patrimony.

As one of 123 States Parties to the Rome Statute, Mali is empowered to bring such charges before the ICC. While frequently invoked throughout the trial, the States Parties of Syria and Iraq are not signatories to the treaty, and neither is Bosnia and Herzegovina, where the Mostar Bridge was bombed and rebuilt.[49] Recently the ICC has been criticized for being simply another tool of Western imperialism, seeking to punish leaders from small, weak states while ignoring those crimes committed by richer and more powerful ones. For example, Russia withdrew from the treaty the day after release of an ICC report classifying the annexation of Crimea as "occupation." Not wanting to be held accountable, the United States has never ratified the Rome Statute, nor have India, China, and Saudi Arabia. As a result, the ICC has been perceived as focusing too narrowly upon the violations of individuals from Africa rather than addressing unsanctioned invasions like that of Iraq, illegal occupations like that of Crimea, or the cluster bombing of Yemen by Saudi Arabia with support from the United States and the United Kingdom, to name just a few. However, if the relevant State Party fails to petition the ICC, as has been the case with Syria, the United Nations (as a representative of states outside the affected territory) can do so. Unfortunately, the UN Security Council has failed to react to the Syrian crisis in a unified and concrete manner, despite producing a number of new resolutions.[50] Given Russia's right of veto on the Council and its support of the current regime, future prosecutions are unlikely.[51]

In 1998, the same year that Timbuktu was inscribed on the World Heritage List, the Saudi Arabian government bulldozed and burned the tomb of Aminah, the mother of Mohammed. The wholesale destruction of Islamic heritage in Saudi Arabia has been met with scant coverage or criticism.[52] A vast number of historic mosques, mausoleums, and monuments have been razed in recent years to make way for skyscrapers and shopping malls.[53] Even the holy site of Mecca has not been spared, as the Ottoman and Abbasid marble columns around the Kaaba were demolished in 2014. The Saudis may have escaped censure from agencies such as UNESCO because Mecca is not a World Heritage site and their actions do not contravene the 1972 Convention. Although the clandestine demolitions often occur at night, they are not considered casualties of war or conflict. However, signatory nations to the World Heritage Convention agree to protect national heritage, cultural and natural, within their borders.[54] This is yet another example of the exception made for powerful nations including Saudi Arabia and why the case against Al Mahdi needs to be placed in its broader international perspective.

Heritage destruction, it is currently held, is often the precursor to the worst outrages committed against a population. Destruction and its aftermath have thus become an increasingly familiar component of the global humanitarian crisis. Described as a weapon of war, such devastation targets and seeks to erase traces of peoples, communities, traditions, and histories as though they never existed. Moreover, in Syria and Iraq the widespread looting and illicit trafficking of antiquities has funded and fueled international terrorism and armed conflict.[55] Following liberation of the Iraqi site of Hatra in April 2017, the Director-General reiterated, "UNESCO will do everything in its power to ensure these crimes do not go unpunished."[56] In the global outcry that has understandably arisen, greater attention has been focused on a narrow prosecution of crimes rather than on examination of the different logics and justifications that spawn them.[57] The latter requires questioning the different histories, motivations, and complicities that gave rise, at various times, to Ansar Dine in Mali and to ISIS in Syria.[58] It entails paying closer attention to the devastation of heritage and the humanitarian crisis in Yemen, not solely at the hands of insurgents but instead from Saudi airstrikes and blockades backed by a coalition that includes America and Britain. UNESCO has conflated all these Middle Eastern conflicts in the dystopia of destruction, whether in the Bonn Declaration of 2015 or the Director-General's speeches, rather than identifying the powerful Member States guilty of transgressing international law.[59] Taken together, this confirms the need for a greater reflection on the new challenges posed to the World Heritage regime and the residual problems that have not been reconciled effectively over the organization's history.

Since the wartime years of devastation the world has faced recurrent threats to civilian populations and their heritage, including among others international conflicts in Korea, Vietnam, the Balkans, and Iraq, right down to what has been called the "forgotten war" being waged in Yemen. Today, more often than not, UNESCO's Secretariat finds itself in the invidious position of avoiding confrontation with its Member States, as opposed to condemning terrorist groups and nonstate actors. While one can champion the adoption of a united stance that denounces militants, it is another matter for States Parties to confront each other, particularly when those states are pernicious. While considered theoretically equal across the United Nations, some states clearly carry greater weight and corollary attention. Post–Arab Spring destruction in Tunisia and Libya, for instance, received scant attention from the World Heritage Centre and Committee. Comparing the World Heritage Committee response to the targeting of cultural heritage in Yemen, as opposed to Syria and Iraq, is another case in point.

In June 2015, some ten days before the World Heritage Committee met in Bonn, the UNESCO-listed Old City of Sana'a was bombarded by Saudi airstrikes. Listed on the basis of its religious heritage and unique traditional architecture, Sana'a has been continuously inhabited for more than 2,500 years.[60] The strikes were part of a pattern of targeted and systemic destruction of cultural heritage sites by Saudi Arabia, according to archaeologist Lamya Khalidi. In 2016 Yemen's General Organization for Antiquities, Museums, and Manuscripts listed some fifty sites either damaged or destroyed, museums and archaeological encampments among them. Yemen is a signatory to the 1972 World Heritage Convention and the 1954 Hague Convention and both its protocols. At the beginning of the war UNESCO's office in Doha had even furnished the Saudi-led coalition with a list of sites and their coordinates to avoid in the airstrikes.[61]

FIGURE 8.1 Sana'a, Yemen, © Mohamed al-Sayaghi, Reuters

Back in Bonn the Yemeni delegation described its dire predicament: airstrikes, loss of life, malaria and famine, and one million left homeless. ICOMOS reported that there was no conservation or donor support, while Nabil Munassar from the Ministry of Culture appealed for both financial and technical assistance. Norway had funded Munassar's attendance at the meeting, without which Yemen would have had no representation. He reminded Yemen's neighbors that they had an obligation to stop the traffic in stolen artifacts. But nothing could be claimed about the culprits; they were sheltered by the fiction of international cooperation and diplomacy. Yemen's plight was grave, yet the members of the World Heritage Committee remained largely silent, a stark comparison with their robust responses and many hours of debate about Syria. Along with Yemen's unique indigenous heritage, the foundational principle of a common humanity was also in danger.

Since Wars Begin in the Minds of Men . . .

The wholesale bombing, looting, and destruction of Europe's rich heritage during the Second World War, on both sides of the conflict, was formative in the establishment and ideals of UNESCO. According to the Norwegian politician Trygve Lie, the first UN Secretary-General, the new agency was faced with the "task of repairing material disaster, to build up the ruins . . . to re-establish favourable conditions for the spiritual life of the world."[62] UNESCO may not have been able to guarantee world peace, it was realized back then, but it could contribute to the dream of peace. One of the first steps was to rehabilitate and reconstruct war-ravaged nations. Cultural heritage was high on the agenda, but changing the "minds of men" would prove more intractable. Lie was correct when he called his "the most impossible job on this earth."[63]

UNESCO saw that job as no less than reconstructing humanity. This idea was taken up by leaders like Julian Huxley and, whether under the rubrics of scientific humanism or universal heritage, all other institutional commitments flowed from that utopian aspiration.[64] The ideals that presided over the creation of UNESCO included combating nihilism, skepticism, and doctrines injurious to human dignity.[65] Its constitution set forth that "ignorance of each other's ways and lives" coupled with "suspicion and mistrust between the peoples of the word" were the common cause of conflict. Combating this to secure a lasting peace and security was best accomplished by "promoting collaboration among the nations through education, science and culture."[66] Exactly how it would be achieved in practice remains highly contentious, as we have seen throughout the book: the directionality of cooperation, which cultures would be reified or vilified, and how a balance might be struck between "preserving the independence, integrity and fruitful diversity of the cultures."

Today those issues remain as pertinent as they did in Huxley's imaginings of one world. Yet the natures of those challenges have themselves diversified and been reconfigured in a globalized world. Whose "humanity" and "civilization" would be embraced, preserved, and deployed, as opposed to jettisoned, has attracted sustained critique with regard to human rights, cultural diversity, freedom of expression, intangible culture, and global heritage. Such questioning leads us in directions beyond any single, bounded view of monumentality and preservation and toward the more expansive immaterial dimensions of heritage for people today, including site access, use, participation, rights, obligations, and benefits. These commitments are familiar to scholars working in archaeology, anthropology, and heritage fields, made central over the past few decades by ethical engagement and collaborative efforts. However, they represent relatively new challenges for the organization that necessitate change at UNESCO, amongst its Member States, and most notably for those participating in decision-making committees such as World Heritage.

Changing the "minds of men" is no easy mission. Part of UNESCO's current task is to craft a "universal respect for justice, for the rule of law and for . . . human rights."[67] While such a goal is laudable, with respect to World Heritage processes Amund Sinding-Larsen argues that rights-based approaches are yet to be incorporated into either the nomination or management of sites. One key impediment is the lack of State Party support for such initiatives, ensuring that minorities within nations have restricted agency, authority, and visibility in the UNESCO process. Bypassing the constraints exerted by Member States on the World Heritage Centre and the Committee, agencies such as ICOMOS, particularly their Australian and Scandinavian chapters, are independently pursuing and promoting close consultations with indigenous and connected communities.[68] This entails a change not only in procedures but also in organizational mindset. In recent years ICOMOS representatives have held side meetings at the annual World Heritage Committee sessions in an attempt to instill human rights principles in all stages of the World Heritage process.[69] Though sparsely attended by national delegates, these events should be recognized as part of a much-needed redress for the histories of appropriation and marginalization in the World Heritage arena.

Just as UNESCO's formulation of culture and human rights has been debated for decades, so too its heritage policies would be better served by recognizing that this is a field of contestation, which ideally embraces dialogue and consent, sometimes dissent, and, importantly, the right of veto. Increasingly the two spheres are brought together in discussions about heritage rights and responsibilities. Indigenous participation and expertise in World Heritage matters, within a broader framing of human rights, has presented considerable difficulties for UNESCO. Ana Vrdoljak clearly shows how and why indigenous representatives remain dissatisfied with the workings of the 1972 Convention and the World Heritage Committee. They have repeatedly emphasized that the UN agency must fulfill its human rights mandate, particularly during the formal processes for nomination of World Heritage properties.[70] She further highlights UNESCO's shortfall in regard to indigenous rights, despite the "decades-long campaign for effective participation in decision-making concerning the protection of their cultural heritage (and related human rights) at the international level and its transformational impact on international law and international institutions." The lack of harmonization between the World Heritage Convention and other UN treaties such as the Declaration on the Rights of Indigenous Peoples remains puzzling.[71]

In 2015 UN special rapporteur James Anaya wrote to the director of the World Heritage Centre. Expressing his dissatisfaction, he called for greater transparency in the World Heritage nomination and implementation process, for benefit-sharing and enhanced safeguarding of land, resource rights, and cultures, as well as redress for violations of indigenous peoples' rights.[72] In 2011 he urged UNESCO to meet international standards. Anaya flagged a lack of adequate consultation with indigenous peoples, leading to "profound expressions of discontent, mistrust and even anger." No audit has been conducted to determine exactly how many World Heritage sites impact indigenous communities. States Parties are not obliged to provide such information; neither are they compelled to make nomination materials available to indigenous communities. As late as 2015 the World Heritage Committee had actively blocked attempts to broaden participation in decision-making.[73] This is yet further evidence of what Vrdoljak calls the "implementation gap."[74]

It was only in 2016 that the 1972 Convention's Operational Guidelines were changed to include any reference to free, prior, and informed

consent, specifically in regard to indigenous peoples. This is exceedingly slow, and the World Heritage Committee had previously declined
to establish panels of indigenous experts to advise on World Heritage
issues.[75] Again, powerful Member States fearing losses to identity and
sovereignty, such as France and the United States, had vetoed this important recognition of indigenous expertise. Yet even in this revised text,
gaining consent is encouraged rather than required: "States Parties are
encouraged to prepare nominations with the widest possible participation
of stakeholders and to demonstrate, as appropriate, that the free, prior and
informed consent of indigenous peoples has been obtained, through, inter
alia making the nominations publicly available in appropriate languages
and public consultations and hearings."[76] Further headway was made in
2017 Committee meetings in Krakow when Angola introduced an amendment establishing an International Indigenous Peoples Forum on World
Heritage to enhance their involvement. However, attending to a document,
as we have seen in previous chapters, does not guarantee action or implementation within the World Heritage system. Without active and equal
inclusion, consultation, and collaboration it is likely that the tensions and
conflicts over state-led regulation and preservation regimes will continue
to intensify, as can be traced from India to Italy.

The challenges outlined above are tied to the recognition of the spiritual, immaterial, and lived dimensions of World Heritage. Instead of
developing an entirely new treaty to recognize the immaterial aspects of
heritage places and practice, as was done with the 2003 Convention for the
Safeguarding of Intangible Cultural Heritage, a broader understanding
of the material past and its roles in the present still needs to be established.[77] Delegates from many States Parties, particularly those in Africa,
Asia, and Latin America, have expressed to me their desire to have these
elements incorporated into the 1972 Convention, since it remains their top
priority for cultural recognition in the multilateral arena. As legal scholar
Francesco Francioni explains, intangible heritage conventions, such as the
2005 convention on cultural diversity, result from a growing concern for
the preservation of cultural pluralism.[78] Other ways of living with the past
need to be acknowledged and incorporated into UNESCO's programmatic
vision.

Intangible heritage, in Francioni's view, reflects a confluence of international cultural heritage law with human rights law, the protection of
minorities, and the emerging law on the protection of the rights of indigenous peoples.[79] A more expansive view of protection could then be

developed, extending to people, traditions, practices, and rights.[80] The responsibility to protect (R2P) is now being considered by UNESCO's experts to extend UN mandate to the context of cultural heritage.[81] However, these developments cannot simply focus on fabric. Cultural heritage understandings today, Alessandro Chechi argues, now extend protection beyond the material to encompass their intangible and human dimensions. This incorporates the multiple meanings that heritage supplies for individuals and peoples with regard to identity and experience, the lives of their ancestors, and their societies.[82] Those meanings are culturally situated, rather than universally prescribed, recalling the frictions described throughout the book between local, national, and international heritage regimes. The ways in which international bodies, national governments, local authorities, communities, and individuals value, understand, use, and want access to sites are greatly at variance. As we have seen, the stakes are significantly raised when those places are deemed World Heritage sites. Some examples of those tensions over access, use, and quality of life can been seen in the mounting tensions in Venice, Panama City, Angkor, Hampi, Battir, and Jerusalem.

Differences in religious practice remain a major factor since so many inscriptions of monumental sites on the List pertain to religious buildings, whether cathedrals, temples, shrines, mausoleums, or landscapes. This presents another challenge to the monumental approach, although UNESCO's concept of "cultural landscapes" might be employed more broadly.[83] Focusing on architectural wonders rather than the broader understanding of sacred landscapes, ritual practice, veneration, and pilgrimage will always curtail the peopled and lived dimensions of heritage. Ironically, it is often the tacit power of this human connection that propels site nominations in the first place, whether in Mali or Myanmar. Yet following inscription those connections are often severed or proscribed. Given the sovereign nature of World Heritage management, steps taken to prohibit access are enacted by state governments, as we have seen in Turkey or India, and not by UNESCO, as commonly assumed. And while governments are keen to reap the rewards of global tourism, a major rationale for acquiring the World Heritage label, many are less accepting toward the presence of local communities and others who claim rights to the past.

World Heritage sites, such as Ayutthaya in Thailand, that allow ritual activities reveal a richness of culture and tradition that endow sites with meaning and salience in people's lives. Too often sites have been stripped of their inhabitants through forced removals, often justified in the name of conservation but engendering alienation and hostility, as seen in famous sites including Petra, Angkor, Hampi, or Bodhgaya.[84] Conservation has created refugees in the global movement to save cultural and natural places.[85] The Nubian Monuments Campaign provides another example where local populations and their heritages were rendered largely invisible in the international effort and were not salvaged in the same ways as the monuments. Some of these displacement strategies reveal sustained colonial histories yet have contemporary consequences whether in Egypt, Afghanistan, Syria, or Palestine. We forget these histories at our peril, many of which represent twentieth-century war crimes including occupation, destruction, bombardment, and the use of chemical weapons on civilian populations: the French in Syria, the British in Egypt and Palestine. The carving up of other people's countries, whether in the Middle East or West Africa, as in the case of Mali and the Tuareg, constitutes a negative heritage that is still felt today.

Incorporating a world of difference, whether cultural, religious, economic, or ideological, remains the broader challenge for UNESCO. Appealing to the international community during the Nubian Monuments Campaign, Director-General Vittorino Veronese declared that "when a thing of beauty, whose loveliness increases rather than diminishes by being shared, is lost, then all men alike are the losers."[86] That utopian ideal found its full expression in the World Heritage Convention. Yet the tension between universalism and difference was similarly enshrined, straddling as the Convention does the divide between the realities of national patrimony and sovereignty on the ground and the conceptual spirit of internationalism and global governance. Striking a balance, furthermore, between international obligations to shoulder the burden of preserving heritage and national agendas to capitalize it remains intractable. Some sixty years after Veronese, another senior official would testify during the Al Mahdi case that UNESCO was formative in the "creation of a very important idea that heritage that belongs to one society can also belong to the world."[87] Yet as we have seen, that notion of "belonging" can serve as a gloss for appropriation, often without necessary recourse to rights or responsibilities.[88] Indigenous and minority groups and other rights-holders continue to confront those historical injustices, while similarly appealing for corrective measures for the future of World Heritage: inclusion, human rights, benefits, and the right of veto all require structural changes. As the Swedish feminist Alva Myrdal, head of social science at UNESCO, recognized back in the 1940s, the challenge for peace and security did not pivot on a lack of cultural understanding between nations.[89] Instead it was premised upon inequalities between European and colonized nations, what we would today describe as the fundamental divide between those who *have* and those who *want*.

Conclusions

UNESCO's appeals to one-worldism and universality were ambitious and legible in the aftermath of a world war. For better or worse, the commitment that UNESCO embodies has been accompanied by an unshakeable confidence in the possibility of human improvement and an optimistic adherence to its mission. Still clinging to premises of universality, it remains essentially a midcentury, modernist organization that has robustly resisted external critique.[90] Marc Askew suggests today's heritage arena, both "channeled and appropriated by UNESCO[,] reflects a long history of internationalism, with its origins in late-eighteenth-century romanticism, enlightenment universalism, and a missionary zeal among intellectuals aiming for human betterment by cooperating across national boundaries."[91] Given this genealogy and purpose, those working within the organization and their supporters are offended or perplexed when programs like World Heritage are critiqued. To resist such universalizing as a strategy of simplification typically casts outsiders and academics as troublemakers. What they trouble is the smooth surface of prefabricated knowledge.[92]

UNESCO is a quintessential product of its time. Created in response to a particular set of challenges that beset Europe in the wake of international conflict, it has since had to adapt to a changing world, however imperfectly. Internationalist Gilbert Murray astutely predicted that it was always destined to be "a confused mixture of success and failure."[93] As I have argued throughout the book, structurally its mission to change the "minds of men" has been hampered by the agendas of its primary constituents, the Member States. UNESCO's direct recourse to the nation-state continues to be problematic in a globalized world, particularly its ability to implement overarching legal instruments that were originally intended not to maintain a world of difference but rather to realign it within a universalizing vision.

Whereas UNESCO's founders envisaged an assembly of great statesmen, it rapidly devolved into an organization of powerful states. From the early safeguarding campaigns to the workings of World Heritage, nation-state interest would prove overweening in conservation matters. Predatory states would have their agendas supported through various channels, whether lobbying, coercion, or financial incentives. States would also use the mechanism of conservation citizenship and World Heritage listing to pursue the furtherance of other ambitions in economic, political, territorial, or even military domains, as witnessed in the Puy Cities, Preah Vihear, and Old Panama. Increasingly, the adherence to conservation principles might be jettisoned after inscription, whether for developmental, infrastructural, or financial motives, as Venice reveals. There is little that can be done to hold states accountable. Moreover, the sovereign nature of inscription means that self-determination and appeals to distinctive nationalisms have flourished, as with Ani and the Meiji sites, in tandem with aggressive claims to territory and attempts to rewrite history. Legally there is no mechanism within the Convention to mediate such disputes. Attaining World Heritage status has come to matter a great deal, not simply for the recognition of past glory and resilient identities but for future rewards as well. Bagan, Bethlehem, and Battir remind us that the politics of the past might be rectified and redressed by the international community. Politics infuses every stage of the World Heritage process.

The proliferation of political meanings and potentials has brought with it the greater threat of heritage conflict. While having a sustained history of violence from Iraq to Indonesia, World Heritage sites have undergone a transformation such that they are now commonly targeted as a means to outrage both local and international communities, as witnessed in the Balkans, Bamiyan, Aleppo, and Palmyra. Both ISIS and Saudi Arabia have flaunted the legal protection of sites and civilians. Neither is likely to be prosecuted under international law. In Timbuktu militants further questioned the status of UNESCO itself, confronting the organization's ability to incorporate religious difference. A swift justice descended on one perpetrator of the attacks on Timbuktu's mausoleums, Ahmed Al Mahdi, in The Hague's International Criminal Court. This was a crime with a victim, the prosecution argued. However, the victim was more often configured as the "universal values that we must protect." Convicting Al Mahdi thus "sen[t] an important and positive message to the entire world."[94] One message was that cultural destruction constitutes a war crime and that damage to the material past does irreparable harm to generations. Thus the materiality of the past cannot be relegated to history, or a list, but instead must be interwoven with living, connected communities. Another message was that some states have more to fear from international censure than others. It reinforced the hypocrisy that Russia, Saudi Arabia, and the United States are exempt from prosecution since they are not signatories to the Rome Statute. There is also a faint echo of the French bombardment of Syria in 1925, when members of the League of Nations considered the French too civilized to have committed such atrocities. Here lies the danger in the prevailing civilizational discourse developing around the tragic events in Mali, Syria, and Iraq, which reverberates with some of the worst offenses of the twentieth century.

Back in UNESCO's own prehistory, Julian Huxley had planned to include archaeology in his creation of a one-world civilization, past and future. In those early days and following on from the League's attempts to regulate world archaeology, it seemed as though the intellectual vision for field collaboration endowed the discipline with great promise for internationalism. But it was heritage, rather than archaeology, that would become the hallmark of civilization and could bear the burden of the future. Monumental heritage and its preservation offered a symbol, both for the nation and for the international community, free from the encumbrances of archaeological research projects with their vast teams, collaborations, scientific and humanistic allegiances, and spiraling costs. The uncertainty of archaeology's research programs and the long timeframes involved stood in stark contrast to the fixity and promise of great sites that brought with them certain developmental and tourist potentials.[95] Both the discipline and the institution lost out in this formulation.

Despite coming at the end of empire, UNESCO offered archaeology an intellectual platform for engagement in real-world issues, whether politics, education, or development. Its inclusion in the UN agency could have extended archaeology's academic reach and standing rather than simply its technical contributions, as UNESCO did for history, philosophy, and even anthropology throughout the agency's history. For UNESCO, the demise of archaeology signaled the loss of an integral discipline that straddled its science and culture sectors and could have benefitted both, as Huxley instinctively realized. UNESCO further lost out on the wider contributions to our understandings and modes of researching the past, as archaeology gradually developed to embrace long-term international collaborations, academic networks, indigenous partnerships, reflexivity, multivocality, ethics, and rights-based approaches. Though archaeology is an imperfect discipline and by no means offers solutions to the manifold problems confronting World Heritage today, considering how it has changed may prove instructive when thinking about how UNESCO's conventions, understandings, programs, and interactions could have been differently conceived and undertaken.

Despite their initial good intentions, many international organizations are struggling or have failed to implement their vision to improve the lot of great swathes of the world. Whether in the fields of environment and climate change, economic development, global health, or human rights, the impediments to international organizations are most often their Member States. Perhaps it should not be surprising then that World Heritage has become so contentious. Culture and heritage are supposed to constitute a benign forum for soft power negotiations, but in fact they are intimately sutured to identity, sovereignty, territory, and history-making, with ever more fraught and fatal consequences. As UNESCO's highly visible flagship program, the stamp of World Heritage may prove to be both the source and the solution to that dilemma.

As the adage goes, if UNESCO did not exist we would have to invent it. Without its contributions in the fields of education, science, and culture it is all too easy to imagine a world in ruins. In November 1945 Ellen Wilkinson embodied those fears and "hopes for the future of mankind." As minister for education under Prime Ministers Winston Churchill and Clement Atlee and a prominent figure in UNESCO's founding, Wilkinson called upon "those who teach, those who discover, those who write, those who express their inspiration in music and art" to accept a great responsibility in forging the new world. Today that vision has many detractors, from the academy and national delegations to local communities worldwide, that fundamentally disagree with UNESCO's abiding premises and philosophies. The enduring acrimony between the United States and UNESCO is one salient example that has had dire consequences. Scholars of heritage have also critiqued the organization, oftentimes in superficial and uninformed ways, I have argued, without fully recognizing that the major decision-makers are its Member States. Ethical critique is best directed toward the major power brokers, their circuits of influence, and the geopolitical intrigues that have ultimately produced winners and losers in the business of heritage.

When *global* UNESCO was replaced by its *intergovernmental* incarnation, what remained was a mere shadow of its former ambition for peace and mutual understanding between peoples.[96] Politicians and the designs of predatory states hijacked that vision, and so the overreach of governments now permeates all levels of World Heritage, from its committees to its consultants, from technical assistance to site inscription.

Certainly there are systemic issues and, as this book outlines, we can no longer simply privilege the technical, but we need to revisit UNESCO's early commitments to creating a better world. As UN Secretary-General Antonio Guterres said, to fulfill its purpose, the United Nations must also change and focus on delivery, not process; on people, not bureaucracy.[97] In the World Heritage arena that may entail not inscribing sites on a list at all, but rather allowing communities to determine their own paths. Institutional alternatives to UNESCO are, however, thin on the ground, and since many nation-states still marginalize and persecute their minorities, simply appealing to sovereign entities offers no solution. The measure of international oversight that World Heritage affords is valuable. The past practices of working closely with nongovernmental agencies, universities, and other institutions might be further reinvigorated, although those organizations lack UNESCO's reach and capacity to embrace the world and have their own agendas. In such a time of reduced circumstances, expanding networks and collaborations may prove expedient.

Perhaps the real and unstated problem is that we imagine international organizations to be more powerful than they really are and expect them to deliver on impossible promises. Like good utopians, we hope that such august bodies might offer up the "genie of global amity and co-operation."[98] Collectively we expect that they can be better than us as individuals. The utopian dream of UNESCO, while not fatally flawed, was nonetheless tainted by the same human history and politics that it sought to overcome. Emerging from dystopia, the organization would advance its mission over the next seventy years in the best of times and the worst of times. Founded in London on November 16, 1945, UNESCO has remained "poised between the impossible expectations of its charter and the abysmal realities it had to confront daily, an elusive hope bouncing in the wake of bipolar and multilateral conflict and confrontation, where poverty, hunger, disease, ignorance, and underdevelopment had first claims on the minds of men in most parts of the world."[99]

Notes

PREFACE

1. P. Betts, "Humanity's New Heritage: Unesco and the Rewriting of World History," *Past and Present* 228, no. 1 (2015): 252–53.

2. Welcoming Address by the British Prime Minister the Rt. Hon. C. R. Attlee (Prime Minister of Great Britain and Northern Ireland), Conference for the Establishment of the United Nations Educational, Scientific and Cultural Organisation, held at the Institute of Civil Engineers, London, November 1–16, 1945, http://unesdoc. unesco.org/images/0011/001176/117626e.pdf (accessed February 17, 2017).

3. W. H. C. Laves and C. A. Thomson, *UNESCO: Purpose, Progress, Prospects* (Bloomington: University of Indianna Press, 1957), 6.

4. V. Pavone, *From the Labyrinth of the World to the Paradise of the Heart: Science and Humanism in UNESCO's Approach to Globalization* (New York: Lexington, 2008), 1.

5. Opening Address by the President of the Conference, the Rt. Hon. Ellen Wilkinson, M.P. (Minister of Education), Conference for the Establishment of the United Nations Educational, Scientific and Cultural Organisation, held at the Institute of Civil Engineers, London, November 1–16, 1945, http://unesdoc. unesco.org/images/0011/001176/117626e.pdf (accessed February 17, 2017).

6. Pavone, *From the Labyrinth of the World*, 70.

7. Laves and Thomson, *UNESCO*, 345. UNESCO is an autonomous intergovernmental agency of the United Nations with its own membership, legislative and executive bodies, secretariats, and budgets. It is one of fourteen such specialized agencies, including the World Bank, International Monetary Fund, International Labor Organization, and World Health Organization.

8. V. Pavone, "From Intergovernmental to Global: UNESCO's Response to Globalization," *Review of International Organizations* 2, no. 1 (2007): 82.

9. P. Duedahl, ed., *A History of UNESCO: Global Actions and Impacts* (New York: Palgrave Macmillan, 2016).

10. Belgium, Czechoslovakia, Greece, Holland, Luxembourg, Norway, Poland, Yugoslavia, and the French National Committee of Liberation.
11. Laves and Thomson, *UNESCO*, 11–13. See also A. Iriye, *Global Community: The Role of International Organizations in the Making of the Contemporary World* (Berkeley: University of California Press, 2002).
12. P. Betts, "The Warden of World Heritage: UNESCO and the Rescue of the Nubian Monuments," *Past and Present* 226, suppl. 10 (2015): 107.
13. R.-P. Droit, *Humanity in the Making: Overview of the Intellectual History of UNESCO 1945–2005* (Paris: UNESCO, 2005), 24.
14. Ibid.; Duedahl, *History*; S. Dutt, *The Politicization of the United Nations Specialized Agencies: A Case Study of UNESCO* (Lewiston, ME: Edwin Mellen Press, 1995); R. Hoggart, *An Idea and Its Servants: UNESCO from Within* (Piscataway, NJ: Transaction, 2011); J. Huxley, *UNESCO: Its Purpose and Its Philosophy* (Washington, DC: Public Affairs Press, 1947); Laves and Thomson, *UNESCO*; C. Maurel, *Histoire de l'UNESCO* (Paris: L'Harmattan, 2010); F. Mayor, *The New Page* (Paris: UNESCO, 1999); J. P. Sewell, *UNESCO and World Politics* (Princeton, NJ: Princeton University Press, 1975); J. P. Singh, *United Nations Educational, Scientific and Cultural Organization (UNESCO): Creating Norms for a Complex World* (London: Routledge, 2011); F. Valderrama, *A History of UNESCO* (Paris: UNESCO, 1995).
15. Evaluation of UNESCO's Standard-Setting Work of the Culture Sector Part III—1972 Convention Concerning the Protection of the World Cultural and Natural Heritage, Draft Report 10 March 2014 by F. Francioni, IOS/EVS/PI/132, http://unesdoc.unesco.org/images/0022/002269/226922e.pdf (accessed January 21, 2017).
16. I. Anatole-Gabriel, *La fabrique du patrimoine de l'humanité, L'UNESCO et la protection patrimoniale (1945–1992)* (Paris: FMSH, 2016); M. Batisse and G. Bolla, *The Invention of "World Heritage"* (Paris: Association of Former UNESCO Staff Members, 2005); H. Cleere, "The 1972 UNESCO World Heritage Convention," *Heritage and Society* 4, no. 2 (2011): 173–86; A. E. Gfeller and J. Eisenberg, "UNESCO and the Shaping of Global Heritage," in *A History of UNESCO*, ed. P. Duedahl (New York: Springer, 2016), 279–99; Y. R. Isar, "UNESCO and Heritage: Global Doctrine and Global Practice," in *Cultures and Globalization: Heritage, Memory and Identity*, ed. H. K. Anheier and Y. R. Isar (London: Sage, 2011), 39–52; S. Labadi, *UNESCO, Cultural Heritage and Outstanding Universal Value* (Walnut Creek, CA: AltaMira Press, 2013); S. Labadi and F. Bandarin, *World Heritage: Challenges for the Millennium* (Paris: UNESCO, 2007); L. Pressouyre, *The World Heritage Convention, Twenty Years Later* (Paris: UNESCO Publishing, 1996); C. Brumann, "Shifting Tides of World-Making in the UNESCO World Heritage Convention: Cosmopolitanisms Colliding," *Ethnic and Racial Studies* 37, no. 12 (2014): 2176–92; S. Ekern et al., *World Heritage Management and Human Rights* (Abingdon: Routledge, 2015);

F. Francioni and F. Lenzerini, *The 1972 World Heritage Convention: A Commentary* (Oxford: Oxford University Press, 2008); B. S. Frey and L. Steiner, "World Heritage List: Does It Make Sense?," *International Journal of Cultural Policy* 17, no. 5 (2011): 555–73; S. Labadi, "The Upstream Process: The Way Forward for the World Heritage Convention?," *Heritage and Society* 7, no. 1 (2014): 57–58; L. M. Meskell, "UNESCO's World Heritage Convention at 40: Challenging the Economic and Political Order of International Heritage Conservation," *Current Anthropology* 54, no. 4 (2013): 483–94; J. Musitelli, "World Heritage, Between Universalism and Globalization," *International Journal of Cultural Property* 11, no. 2 (2002): 323–36; K. Rao, "A New Paradigm for the Identification, Nomination and Inscription of Properties on the World Heritage List," *International Journal of Heritage Studies* 16, no. 3 (2010): 161–72; M. Rössler, "Challenges of World Heritage Interpretation: World Heritage and Associative Values," in *International Conference on World Heritage Interpretation (November 2, 2016)* (Seoul, 2016); P. Strasser, "'Putting Reform into Action'—Thirty Years of the World Heritage Convention: How to Reform a Convention Without Changing Its Regulations," *International Journal of Cultural Property* 11 (2002): 215–66; B. Van der Aa, "Preserving the Heritage of Humanity? Obtaining World Heritage Status and the Impacts of Listing," Ph.D. dissertation, Netherlands Organisation for Scientific Research, 2005; B. von Droste, "The Concept of Outstanding Universal Value and Its Application: 'From the Seven Wonders of the Ancient World to the 1,000 World Heritage Places Today,'" *Journal of Cultural Heritage Management and Sustainable Development* 1, no. 1 (2011): 26–41; D. Zacharias, "The UNESCO Regime for the Protection of World Heritage as Prototype of an Autonomy-Gaining International Institution," in *The Exercise of Public Authority by International Institutions*, ed. A. von Bogdandy (Berlin: Springer-Verlag, 2010), 301–36; C. Cameron and M. Rössler, *Many Voices, One Vision: The Early Years of the World Heritage Convention* (Surrey: Ashgate, 2013); J. Jokilehto and C. Cameron, *The World Heritage List: What Is OUV?: Defining the Outstanding Universal Value of Cultural World Heritage Properties* (Berlin: Bässler Verlag, 2008).

17. "Convention Concerning the Protection of the World Cultural and Natural Heritage," 1972, http://whc.unesco.org/en/conventiontext (accessed April 15, 2017).

18. On the globalizing strategies of World Heritage: J. Turtinen, *Globalising Heritage: On UNESCO and the Transnational Construction of a World Heritage* (Stockholm: Stockholm Center for Organizational Research, 2000); S. Labadi, "Representations of the Nation and Cultural Diversity in Discourses on World Heritage," *Journal of Social Archaeology* 7, no. 2 (2007): 147–70; D. Berliner and C. Bortolotto, "Introduction. Le monde selon l'Unesco," *Gradhiva* 2 (2013): 4–21; Brumann, "Shifting Tides of World-Making." On issues of governance, diplomacy, and bureaucracy: C. Brumann, "Heritage Agnosticism: A Third Path for the Study of Cultural Heritage," *Social Anthropology* 22, no. 2

(2014): 173–88; T. M. Schmitt, "Global Cultural Governance: Decision-Making Concerning World Heritage Between Politics and Science," *Erdkunde* 63, no. 2 (2009): 103–21; T. M. Schmitt, *Cultural Governance: Zur Kulturgeographie Des UNESCO-Welterberegimes* (Wiesbaden: Franz Steiner Verlag, 2012); L. M. Meskell and C. Brumann, "UNESCO and New World Orders," in *Global Heritage: A Reader*, ed. L. Meskell (Oxford: Wiley Blackwell, 2015), 22–42; M. M. Kersel and C. Luke, "A Crack in the Diplomatic Armor: The United States and the Palestinian Authority's Bid for UNESCO Recognition," *Journal of Field Archaeology* 37, no. 2 (2012): 143–44; M. M. Kersel and C. Luke, "Diplomacy and Neo-Imperialism," in *Global Heritage: A Reader*, ed. L. Meskell (Oxford: Wiley Blackwell, 2015), 70–93; C. Luke and M. M. Kersel, *US Cultural Diplomacy and Archaeology: Soft Power, Hard Heritage* (London: Routledge, 2013). On the political economy of culture and rights: D. Berliner, "Multiple Nostalgias: The Fabric of Heritage in Luang Prabang (Lao PDR)," *Journal of the Royal Anthropological Institute* 18, no. 4 (2012): 769–86; W. Logan, "Closing Pandora's Box: Human Rights Conudrums in Cultural Heritage Protection," in *Cultural Heritage and Human Rights*, ed. H. Silverman and D. Fairchild Ruggles (New York: Springer, 2008), 33–52; W. Logan, "Cultural Diversity, Cultural Heritage and Human Rights: Towards Heritage Management as Human Rights-Based Cultural Practice," *International Journal of Heritage Studies* 18, no. 3 (2012): 231–44; A. Sinding-Larsen, "Lhasa Community, World Heritage and Human Rights," *International Journal of Heritage Studies* 18, no. 3 (2012): 297–306; L. M. Meskell, "From Paris to Pontdrift: UNESCO Meetings, Mapungubwe and Mining," *South African Archaeological Bulletin* 66, no. 194 (2011): 149–56; L. M. Meskell, "UNESCO and the Fate of the World Heritage Indigenous Peoples Council of Experts (WHIPCOE)," *International Journal of Cultural Property* 20, no. 2 (2013): 155–74; C. De Cesari, "World Heritage and the Nation-State," in *Transnational Memory: Circulation, Articulation, Scales*, ed. C. De Cesari and A. Rigney (Berlin: de Gruyter, 2014), 247–70.

19. Schmitt, "Global Cultural Governance"; Schmitt, *Cultural Governance*.

20. Observers must apply for authorization to the World Heritage Center and are admitted under Rule 8.3 of the Committee's Rules of Procedure. They typically include representatives of international governmental organizations, international nongovernmental organizations, nongovernmental organizations, permanent observer missions to UNESCO, and nonprofit institutions.

21. Here I am extremely grateful to Enrico Bertacchini, Donatella Saccone, and especially Claudia Liuzza in this collaboration; see E. Bertacchini, C. Liuzza, and L. Meskell, "Shifting the Balance of Power in the UNESCO World Heritage Committee: An Empirical Assessment," *International Journal of Cultural Policy* (2015): 1–21; E. Bertacchini et al., "The Politicization of UNESCO World Heritage Decision Making," *Public Choice* 167, nos. 1–2 (2016): 1–35; L. M. Meskell et al., "Multilateralism and UNESCO World Heritage: Decision-Making,

States Parties and Political Processes," *International Journal of Heritage Studies* 21, no. 5 (2015): 423–40.

22. Berliner and Bortolotto, "Introduction."

23. R. Bendix, "The Power of Perseverance: Exploring the Negotiation Dynamics at the World Intellectual Property Organization," in *The Gloss of Harmony: The Politics of Policy-Making in Multilateral Organisations*, ed. B. Müller (London: Pluto Press, 2013), 23–45; C. Shore, "European Integration in Anthropological Perspective: Studying the 'Culture' of the EU Civil Service," in *Observing Government Elites: Up Close and Personal*, ed. R. A. W. Rhodes, P. 't Hart, and M. Noordegraaf (New York: Palgrave Macmillan, 2007), 180–205; B. Müller, "Lifting the Veil of Harmony: Anthropologists Approach International Organizations," in *The Gloss of Harmony: The Politics of Policy-Making in Multilateral Organisations*, ed. B. Müller (London: Pluto Press, 2013), 1–20; B. Nielsen, "UNESCO and the 'Right' Kind of Culture: Bureaucratic Production and Articulation," *Critique of Anthropology* 31, no. 4 (2011): 273–92; L. M. Meskell, "Transacting UNESCO World Heritage: Gifts and Exchanges on a Global Stage," *Social Anthropology/Anthropologie Sociale* 23, no. 1 (2015): 3–21.

CHAPTER 1

1. J. Huxley, *From an Antique Land: Ancient and Modern in the Middle East* (Boston: Beacon Press, 1966), 80. The book first appeared in 1954 and was updated in 1966.

2. Notebooks now in Rice University Manuscript collection, Julian S. Huxley Papers, Travel Materials, Box 103, Folders 4 and 7. I am grateful to Brett Bennett for making copies available.

3. Huxley, *From an Antique Land*, 14.

4. Letter from Julian Huxley to Professor J. B. S. Haldane concerning V. Childe, October 20, 1941, Wellcome Library Archives, Haldane/4/22/1/3, reference b19921950.

5. Telegram no. 1798, March 19, 1945, from Gladwyn Jebb to the Earl of Halifax, marked "This telegram is of particular secrecy cypher," in the National Archives (United Kingdom) (henceforth TNA), BT11/2540, item 11, page 3. See also E. Rothschild, "The Archives of Universal History," *Journal of World History* 19, no. 3 (2008): 375–401. The original US contribution was cut from $7.5 million to $6.5 million. J. Toye and R. Toye, "One World, Two Cultures? Alfred Zimmern, Julian Huxley and the Ideological Origins of UNESCO," *History* 95, no. 319 (2010): 308–31, at 330.

6. Quoted in a confidential letter from Dr. Grace Morley, Museums Section, to Director-General Julian Huxley, June 11, 1948. The subject of the letter is "Protection of Monuments in Palestine, Transjordan, Egypt, etc. Document Reference 069.707.8 (559:4) MUS." In the letter Marshall begrudgingly states

that "one must throw a sop to the artists" and that he expected to be appointed
to the budget committee, putting "very great pressure" on Morley. UNESCO
Archives, file reference 069: 7A 218 (569.4) "48".

7. Huxley, *From an Antique Land*, 131, 202.

8. Ibid., 15.

9. Ibid., 56.

10. UNESCO, *Report of the Director-General on the Activities of the Organization in 1948* (UNESCO: Paris, 1948).

11. R. S. Deese, "Twilight of Utopias: Julian and Aldous Huxley in the Twentieth Century," *Journal for the Study of Religion, Nature and Culture* 5, no. 2 (2011): 210–40. For Huxley, the utopian calling involved identifying a problem of global magnitude to be solved, namely world peace, through a kind of inventive ingenuity where a number of solutions were proposed and tested. F. Jameson, *Archaeologies of the Future: The Desire Called Utopia and Other Science Fictions* (New York: Verso, 2005).

12. J. Huxley, *UNESCO: Its Purpose and Its Philosophy* (Washington, DC: Public Affairs Press, 1947).

13. See Article 1 of the 1972 Convention. The emerging dominance of architects in the World Heritage Centre and at ICOMOS has resulted in a narrow vision of heritage as constituted by major structures, their settings, fabrics, and conservation. For a full critique, see G. Wijesuriya, "Conservation in Context," in *Conservation and Preservation Interactions Between Theory and Practice: In Memoriam Alois Riegl (1858–1905). Proceedings of the International Conference of the ICOMOS International Scientific Committee for the Theory and the Philosophy of Conservation and Restoration*, ed. M. Falser, W. Lipp, and A. Tomaszewski (Florence: Edizioni Polistampa, 2010), 233–47. In a 2013 UNESCO resource manual, *Managing World Heritage*, there is an attempt to broaden the definition of heritage as "evidence of past societies [that] can provide a sense of belonging and security to modern societies and be an anchor in a rapidly changing world. In many societies, too, heritage can be an important definer of identity. Understanding the past can also be of great help for managing the problems of the present and the future" (http://whc.unesco.org/en/managing-cultural-world-heritage, accessed February 5, 2017). In academic circles, cultural heritage is understood to be a more interdisciplinary study, often bridging archaeology, anthropology, sociology, economics, history, and so on; see, for examples, contributions in L. M. Meskell, ed., *Global Heritage: A Reader* (Oxford: Wiley Blackwell, 2015).

14. See the opening statement in UNESCO, *Protection of Mankind's Cultural Heritage: Sites and Monuments* (Paris: UNESCO, 1970), 9: "Historic monuments are the adornments with which Man has decked the earth; they're the common heritage of mankind and remind us that civilization is made up of contributions from all peoples, and that technique has ever gone hand in hand with the cult of the beautiful, and the taste for the new with the search for the imperishable."

15. C. Luke, "The 40th World Heritage Session in Istanbul, Turkey: A Reflection on the Legacies of Heritage Policy and Missed Mega-Heritage," *Journal of Field Archaeology* 41, no. 6 (2016): 641–44; A. F. Vrdoljak, "Self-Determination and Cultural Rights," in *Cultural Human Rights*, ed. F. Francioni and M. Scheinin (Leiden: Brill, 2008), 41–78.

16. M. A. Elliott and V. Schmutz, "World Heritage: Constructing a Universal Cultural Order," *Poetics* 40, no. 3 (2012): 256–77, at 264.

17. G. Sluga, *Internationalism in the Age of Nationalism* (Philadelphia: University of Pennsylvania Press, 2013), 63.

18. Blanck explains that the Instituto di Corrispondenza Archeologica, like later institutions, focused not on excavation per se but on collecting and publishing notes and documents of new archaeological discoveries and known monuments that had undergone a new interpretation. It also collated information of artworks, ancient architecture, topography, epigraphy, and numismatics. See H. Blanck, "The Instituto di Corrispondenza Archeologica," *Fragmenta* 2 (2008): 63–78; A. Schnapp, "Archéologie et tradition académique en Europe aux XVIIIe et XIXe siècles," *Annales. Histoire, Sciences Sociales* 37, nos. 5/6 (1982): 760–77; A. Guidi, "Nationalism Without a Nation: The Italian Case," in *Nationalism and Archaeology in Europe*, ed. M. Díaz-Andreu and T. Champion (London: Routledge, 1996), 108–18; C. Weickert, "Zur Geschichte des Deutschen Archäologischen Institute," *Archäologischer Anzeiger* LXX (1955): 127–56. I am grateful to Alain Schnapp for directing me to the Instituto.

19. "Report of the Committee on the Work of Its Nineteenth Plenary Session," ICIC, League of Nations, Geneva, August 9, 1937, UNESCO Archives, file reference C. 327 M. 220.1937. XII.

20. Notes on excavation by Sir Arthur Evans. UNESCO Archives, file reference OIM XII 6.

21. Letter from Flinders Petrie in response to enquiry on systems of excavation, August 24, 1937, UNESCO Archives, file reference OIM XII 6.

22. International Museums Office, ed., *Manual on the Technique of Archaeological Excavations* (Paris: International Institute of Intellectual Cooperation, 1940).

23. "Report of the Committee on the Work of Its Nineteenth Plenary Session," 85.

24. International Museums Office, *Manual*, 9.

25. A. F. Vrdoljak, "International Exchange and Trade in Cultural Objects," in *Culture and International Economic Law*, ed. V. Vadi and B. de Witte (London: Routledge, 2015), 124–42.

26. Original letter sent out to raise the question of convening the conference "Archaeology After the War," 1943, UNESCO Archives, file reference OIM XII 6.

27. Quoted in M. Mazower, *Governing the World: The History of an Idea* (London: Penguin, 2012), 128.

28. Porphyrios Dikaios, the Cypriot archaeologist, and Roland de Vaux, who worked on the Dead Sea Scrolls, called many of the ideas utopian.

29. F. Mayor, *The New Page* (Paris: UNESCO, 1999), 9.
30. L. S. Woolf, *International Government* (Westminster: Fabian Society, 1916), p. 97.
31. T. More, *Utopia* (1516), http://history-world.org/Utopia_T.pdf, 76, 81, 116.
32. See M. Mazower, *No Enchanted Palace: The End of Empire and the Ideological Origins of the United Nations* (Princeton: Princeton University Press, 2009); Mazower, *Governing the World: The History of an Idea.*
33. Rothschild, "The Archives of Universal History" 392.
34. R. S. Deese, *We Are Amphibians: Julian and Aldous Huxley on the Future of Our Species* (Berkeley: University of California Press, 2014).
35. See also V. Pavone, "From Intergovernmental to Global: UNESCO's Response to Globalization," *Review of International Organizations* 2, no. 1 (2007): 77–95.
36. P. Duedahl, "Selling Mankind: UNESCO and the Invention of Global History, 1945–1976," *Journal of World History* 22, no. 1 (2011): 106–7.
37. http://www.unesco.org/archives/multimedia/?s=films_details&pg=33&id=4049, accessed December 16, 2016.
38. Duedahl, "Selling Mankind," 132.
39. J. Hawkes and L. Woolley, *Prehistory and the Beginnings of Civilization*, vol. 1 (New York: Harper & Row, 1963). The project was led by Huxley and included his friend Joseph Needham and Lucian Febvre as its other supporters. Huxley was concerned about the name of the series, noting that Grahame Clark was about to publish a book entitled *World Prehistory* (letter to Paulo E. de Berrêdo Carneiro, March 22, 1961, UNESCO Archives, AG 8 Secretariat Records, file reference SCHM 17, Series 2 Implementation of scheme 2.623.3–2.625.1).
40. Letter from Jacquetta Hawkes to Guy Métraux, August 22, 1954, UNESCO Archives, file reference SCHM/28 C003: H1.
41. Letter from Julian Huxley to Guy Métraux, February 7, 1956, UNESCO Archives, AG 8 Secretariat Records, file reference SCHM 17, Series 2 Implementation of scheme 2.623.3–2.625.1. There is a letter from the Russian historian I. M. Diakanoff to Sir Leonard Woolley dated June 28, 1956, stating, "If I adhere to the Marxist view on the origin and development of what you would call the city civilization, it is because I consider it a most adequate interpretation of the existing objective fact." UNESCO Archives, file reference SCHM 19 2.83(3). Huxley had previously thought the series should be taken away from UNESCO's direct control, commenting that it would be unwise to leave it in the hands of administrators who would be subject to the wishes of governments. UNESCO Archives, file reference SCHM/28 C003/H/1.
42. Letter from Julian Huxley to Paulo E. de Berrêdo Carneiro, April 17, 1961, UNESCO Archives, AG 8 Secretariat Records, file reference SCHM 17, Series 2 Implementation of scheme 2.623.3–2.625.1. For a full discussion, see P. Betts, "Humanity's New Heritage: Unesco and the Rewriting of World History," *Past and Present* 228, no. 1 (2015): 249–85.

43. UNESCO meeting of experts on the teaching of history held at UNESCO House, December 12–16, 1949, Summary Record, see UNESCO/ED/Conf/SR. Paris, January 12, 1950.

44. S. Amrith and G. Sluga, "New Histories of the United Nations," *Journal of World History* 19, no. 3 (2008): 270. See also Betts, "Humanity's New Heritage."

45. Amrith and Sluga, "New Histories of the United Nations," 271.

46. Mazower, *No Enchanted Palace*. For a discussion on this issue with the League of Nations, see S. Pedersen, "Empires, States and the League of Nations," in *Internationalisms: A Twentieth-Century History*, ed. G. Sluga and P. Clavin (Cambridge: Cambridge University Press, 2017), 113–38.

47. Deese, "Twilight of Utopias," 216.

48. G. Sluga, "Imagining Internationalism," *Arts: The Journal of the Sydney University Arts Association* 32 (2012): 60.

49. J. M. Hodge, *Triumph of the Expert: Agrarian Doctrines of Development and the Legacies of British Colonialism* (Athens: Ohio University Press, 2007), 257.

50. Huxley, *UNESCO*, 17.

51. Hodge, *Triumph of the Expert*, 11.

52. Huxley, *UNESCO*. Although the book first appeared under the imprint of the Preparatory Commission, UNESCO later represented this pamphlet as a private publication and disclaimers were added to the 1946 printings. Its preface sets out that "although this paper was prepared by Mr. Huxley in connection with his responsibilities as Executive Secretary of the Preparatory Commission of the United Nations Educational, Scientific, and Cultural Organization, the views presented herein do not necessarily reflect the official policies of the Commission or the Organization."

53. UNESCO, *General Conference, First Session, Held at UNESCO House, Paris, from 20 November to 10 December 1946* (Paris: UNESCO, 1947), 20, 42 (unesdoc. unesco.org/images/0011/001145/114580e.pdf, accessed December 15, 2016).

54. UNESCO Archives, General Conference, Third Session, Programme and Budget Commission, Access to Archaeological Sites, 2C/3 Resolution 4.5. Beirut November 8, 1948. 3C/PRG/ 0.4, p. 166.

55. UNESCO, *Records of the General Conference, Second Session, Mexico 1947* (Paris: UNESCO, 1949).

56. Sluga, *Internationalism in the Age of Nationalism*, 75. She recalls how in 1951, Stephen Spender stated that after World War I, there were great expectations of the League of Nations, but few people were "prepared to abandon national sovereignty." By comparison, at the end of World War II, "a great many everywhere are prepared to sacrifice a great deal of nationhood and possessions which they formerly clung to, but they do not believe in the United Nations. The most important condition of change—a widespread realism—has been achieved."

57. The International Council of Museums (ICOM) was created in 1946. It is a global organization of museums and museum professionals committed to the promotion and protection of natural and cultural heritage.

58. UNESCO Archives, General Conference, Third Session, Programme and Budget Commission, Access to Archaeological Sites, 2C/3 Resolution 4.5. Beirut November 8, 1948. 3C/PRG/0.4.

59. Motion submitted by the delegations of Brazil and Egypt (Document 3C/53), UNESCO Archives, Records of the General Conference of UNESCO, Third Session, Beirut, 1948, Volume I, Proceedings, 267.

60. UNESCO, *Report of the Director-General of the Activities of the Organization from October 1949 to March 1950* (Paris: UNESCO, 1950), 52. See also http:// unesdoc.unesco.org/images/0014/001482/148239eb.pdf, accessed December 15, 2016. The issue of cultural property in the event of armed conflict would culminate in UNESCO's 1954 Hague Convention. Letters of invitation were sent to China, Egypt, France, India, Mexico, the Netherlands, Peru, Poland, Sweden, the United Kingdom, and the United States. This was a narrow group of nations representing eleven delegations. In the April 5, 1954, expert meeting, only thirteen delegates or experts were expected plus five observers, according to internal documents. For the 1953 meeting of the International Committee on Monuments, Artistic and Historical Sites and Archaeological Excavations only eight delegates attended: two from France and one each from Austria, India, Iran, Lebanon, the United Kingdom, and the United States. UNESCO Archives, file references 069.707.806.231.063 "54" and 069.707.806.231.063 "53.09".

61. Foundoukidis was former Secretary-General of ICOM. The quote appears in UNESCO Meeting of Experts on Sites and Monuments of Art and History, UNESCO Archives, UNESCO/MUS/Conf. 1/SR. 1 (prov) PARIS, October 17, 1949. Provisional Summary Record of the First Meeting held at UNESCO House. See http://unesdoc.unesco.org/images/0014/001482/148240eb.pdf, accessed December 15, 2016.

62. Pavone, "From Intergovernmental to Global"; T. V. Sathyamurthy, *The Politics of International Cooperation: Contrasting Conceptions of Unesco* (Geneva: Librairie Droz, 1964). See also R. Niebuhr, "The Theory and Practice of UNESCO," *International Organization* 4, no. 1 (1950): 3–11; J. P. Sewell, *UNESCO and World Politics* (Princeton, NJ: Princeton University Press, 1975).

63. See *Cuzco: Reconstruction of the Town and Restoration of its Monuments*, Museums and Monuments III (Paris: UNESCO, 1952). The three-man team claimed to have "entered literally every building in the city in their programme of preparing a detailed record of each item of historical, artistic or archaeological interest." This mission was largely a survey and draft plan for the future of a zoned city of four districts: an archaeological and historical zone to be conserved and restored; a residential district susceptible of modification; districts in which total rebuilding was permissible; and districts for future urban growth.

64. Under the authority of Programme Resolution 4.22, to organize a technical mission to assist a requesting Member State on the conservation and restoration of monuments and sites (Assistance to Member States $10,000). UNESCO, *General Conference, 5th Sessions, Florence 1950 for Proposed Programme and Budget for 1951* (UNESCO, Paris, 1950), 187. The same amount was allocated for the next year, 1952.

65. The governor of the colonial "trust territory" of Tanganyika requested support for the study of rock art. However, given the colonial order of the day and possible difficulties with the Trusteeship Council in New York, the request was not granted. The matter was dealt with through confidential correspondence between the National Commission for the United Kingdom and UNESCO, and expeditiously dismissed "owing to a lack of funds." See letter dated February 11, 1954, from J. L. Nevinson, National Commission for the United Kingdom, to J. K. van der Haagen, UNESCO Archives, file reference 069.707.8 (678) 078.31.

66. Pavone, "From Intergovernmental to Global," 80–81. See also W. R. Pendergast, "UNESCO and French Cultural Relations 1945–1970," *International Organization* 30, no. 3 (1976): 453–83.

67. In some accounts the documentation center was a French proposal led by Christiane Desroches-Noblecourt, an Egyptologist from the Department of Egyptian Antiquities at the Louvre. The French retained a high profile, as did the center, during UNESCO's Nubian salvage campaign, though it was originally focused on the Theban tombs. In other documents the government of Egypt requested assistance to set up the center in 1954. See also P. Betts, "The Warden of World Heritage: UNESCO and the Rescue of the Nubian Monuments," *Past and Present* 226, suppl. 10 (2015): 100–125. During the Eighth Session of UNESCO's General Conference, held in Montevideo in 1954, it became clear that the center should focus on photographic and photogrammetric documentation in Nubia; see F. A. Hassan, "The Aswan High Dam and the International Rescue Nubia Campaign," *African Archaeological Review* 24, nos. 3–4 (2007): 73–94. There was also an issue of *Museum*, volume 3, issue 1, 1950, entitled "Monuments and Sites of History and Art and Archaeological Excavations: Problems of Today." The focus throughout is primarily architectural heritage, much of which was based in Europe and needed restoration after the war.

68. The eight-week mission to Lebanon was undertaken by three experts, headed by Swiss archaeologist Paul Collart and accompanied by Italian architect Armando Dillon. The result was *Suggestions for the Plan of Tripoli and for the surroundings of the Baalbek Acropolis*, Museums and Monuments VI (Paris: UNESCO, 1954). The ten-week Syrian mission was carried out by Collart and Dillon; UNESCO tended to fall back on the same experts again and again for field missions, a critique that still remains pertinent today. It resulted in *Syria: Problems of Preservation and Presentation of Sites and Monuments*, Museums and Monuments VII (Paris: UNESCO, 1954).

69. UNESCO International Principles Governing Archaeological Excavations, Preliminary Report compiled in accordance with the Provisions of Article 10.1 of the Rules of Procedure concerning Recommendations to Member States and International Conventions covered by the Terms of Article IV, paragraph 4 of the Constitution, UNESCO/CUA/68 Paris, August 9, 1955. In a letter from J. K. van der Haagen, Head of the Museum and Monuments division at UNESCO, to J. O. Brew in 1954, he expressed his concern over a State Department letter requesting to "suppress every mention of internal legislation, as we are afraid that in so doing, our whole little building will fall into ruins." He goes on to say that they are in agreement that the instrument should be a recommendation, not a convention, but does not "understand why the limitation asked for by the US Government should be necessary." UNESCO Archives, file reference 069:72 A02/06 IV–069:930.26 (436) AHS.

70. It consists of some four pages: http://unesdoc.unesco.org/images/0011/001145/114585e.pdf#page=40, accessed November 19, 2016.

71. UNESCO, *Report of the Director-General of the Activities of the Organization in 1956* (Paris: UNESCO, 1958), 123–24.

72. Address delivered by the Director-General at the meeting of the International Committee on Monuments, Artistic and Historical Sites and Archaeological Excavations, UNESCO House, May 21, 1951, UNESCO Archives, UNESCO/DG/128, file reference 069: A074 (94) 53.

73. It was principles concerning the protection of cultural property during armed conflict, as established in the Conventions of The Hague of 1899 and of 1907 and in the Washington Pact of April 15, 1935. S. Labadi and F. Bandarin, *World Heritage: Challenges for the Millennium* (Paris: UNESCO, 2007), 27.

74. UNESCO, Convention for the Protection of Cultural Property in the Event of Armed Conflict, http://www.unesco.org/new/en/culture/themes/armed-conflict-and-heritage/convention-and-protocols/1954-hague-convention/text/#c284179, accessed February 18, 2017. See also A. F. Vrdoljak, *International Law, Museums, and the Return of Cultural Objects* (Cambridge: Cambridge University Press, 2006); A. F. Vrdoljak, "Challenges for International Cultural Hertiage Law," in *Blackwell Companion to the New Heritage Studies*, ed. W. Logan, M. Nic Craith, and U. Kockel (New York: Wiley Blackwell, 2016).

75. J. Hawkes, *Adventures in Archaeology: The Biography of Sir Mortimer Wheeler* (New York: St. Martin's Press, 1982), 259, 262. Wheeler soon learned that there had already been a scramble for UNESCO jobs and none were available.

76. Ibid., 6.

77. D. L. Brenneis, "Sand, Stability and Stakeholders," in *Heritage Regimes and the State*, ed. R. Bendix, A. Eggert, and A. Peselmann (Göttingen: Universitätsverlag Göttingen, 2013), 370.

78. See M. Falser, "Cultural Heritage as Civilizing Mission: Methodological Considerations," in *Cultural Heritage as Civilizing Mission*, ed. M. Falser (New York: Springer, 2015), 1–32.

79. Mazower, *No Enchanted Palace.* See also G. Sluga, "UNESCO and the (One) World of Julian Huxley," *Journal of World History* 21, no. 3 (2010): 393–418. Huxley attended the United Nations meeting in San Francisco in 1945. Despite any official role, Huxley argued for "an international colonial convention, a colonial charter, and an International Colonial Office that would oversee bringing backward colonies to the same educational level as the more modern states" (408).

80. Huxley, *From an Antique Land,* 42.

81. Ibid., 131.

82. Ibid., 202.

83. Arjun Appadurai has been involved in discussions at UNESCO headquarters on cultural diversity, cultural rights, sustainable development, and globalization; see R.-P. Droit, *Humanity in the Making: Overview of the Intellectual History of UNESCO 1945–2005* (Paris: UNESCO, 2005), 13. Homi Bhabha has lectured recently on humanism. Previously, American anthropologists including Margaret Mead, Ruth Benedict, Charles Wagley, Marvin Harris, and Robert Redfield were involved with the organization.

84. T. H. Eriksen, "Between Universalism and Relativism: A Critique of the UNESCO Concept of Culture," in *Human Rights: An Anthropological Reader,* ed. M. Goodale (Malden, MA: Wiley-Blackwell, 2009), 356–71; D. Berliner and C. Bortolotto, "Introduction. Le monde selon l'Unesco," *Gradhiva* 2 (2013): 4–21; M. Herzfeld, *Anthropology: Theoretical Practice in Culture and Society* (Paris: UNESCO, 2000); A. Métraux, "UNESCO and Anthropology," *American Anthropologist* 53, no. 2 (1951): 294–300; L. Arizpe, "The Intellectual History of Culture and Development Institutions," in *Culture, Diversity and Heritage: Major Studies,* ed. L. Arizpe (New York: Springer, 2015), 58–81; C. Joy, "'UNESCO Is What?' World Heritage, Militant Islam and the Search for a Common Humanity in Mali," in *World Heritage on the Ground: Ethnographic Perspectives,* ed. C. Brumann and D. Berliner (Oxford: Berghahn, 2016), 60–77. Eriksen describes the role of Lévi-Strauss and the controversial books commissioned by UNESCO, one on race and culture and the other race and history.

85. For a full discussion, see Eriksen, "Between Universalism and Relativism." Also see UNESCO, *Our Creative Diversity. Report of the World Commission on Culture and Development* (Paris: UNESCO, 1995).

86. For a discussion on the place of theory in French archaeology, see S. Cleuziou et al., "The Use of Theory in French Archaeology," in *Archaeological Theory in Europe: The Last Three Decades,* ed. I. Hodder (London: Routledge, 1991), 91–128; F. Audouze and A. Leroi-Gourhan, "France: A Continental Insularity," *World Archaeology* 13, no. 2 (1981): 170–89.

87. Pendergast, "UNESCO and French Cultural Relations 1945–1970."

88. W. Carruthers, "Multilateral Possibilities: Decolonization, Preservation and the Case of Egypt," *Future Anterior: Journal of Historic Preservation History Theory and Criticism* 13, no. 1 (2016): 36–48.

89. UNESCO, *Report of the Director-General of the Activities of the Organization in 1956* (Paris: UNESCO, 1958), 122.

90. Sluga, "UNESCO and the (One) World of Julian Huxley," 417.

91. Pavone, "From Intergovernmental to Global."

92. Mazower, *Governing the World.*

93. Elliott and Schmutz, "World Heritage."

94. K. Marx and J. O'Malley, *Critique of Hegel's "Philosophy of Right"* (Cambridge: Cambridge University Press, 1977).

95. Mazower, *Governing the World.* In international relations functionalism is a theory that arose during the interwar period principally from the strong concern about the obsolescence of the state as a form of social organization. Rather than the self-interest of nation-states that realists see as a motivating factor, functionalists focus on common interests and needs shared by states and non-state actors in a process of global integration triggered by the erosion of state sovereignty and the increasing weight of knowledge, and hence of scientists and experts, in the process of policy-making. B. Rosamond, *Theories of European Integration* (New York: Pagrave Macmillan, 2000).

96. Quote from David Mitrany, the main proponent of functionalism, in D. Mitrany, *A Working Peace System* (Chicago: Quadrangle Books, 1966), 28.

97. See http://portal.unesco.org/en/ev.php-URL_ID=15244&URL_DO=DO_TOPIC & URL_SECTION=201.html, accessed December 15, 2016, and S. Dutt, "Striving to Promote Shared Values: UNESCO in the Troubled World of the Twenty-First Century," *India Quarterly: A Journal of International Affairs* 65, no. 1 (2009): 83–95.

98. Letter from Julian Huxley to Vittorio Veronese, February 2, 1960, UNESCO Archives, file reference 069 (62) Nubia/PC. Huxley was knighted in 1958.

CHAPTER 2

1. R. McNamara, *Britain, Nasser and the Balance of Power in the Middle East, 1952–1977: From the Egyptian Revolution to the Six Day War* (London: Routledge, 2004); R. J. McAlexander, "Couscous Mussolini: US Perceptions of Gamal Abdel Nasser, the 1958 Intervention in Lebanon and the Origins of the US–Israeli Special Relationship," *Cold War History* 11, no. 3 (2011): 363–85; L. Richardson, "Avoiding and Incurring Losses: Decision-Making in the Suez Crisis," *International Journal* 47, no. 2 (1992): 370–401; M. Shemesh and S. I. Troen, eds., *The Suez-Sinai Crisis: A Retrospective and Reappraisal* (London: Routledge, 2005).

2. For further discussion of the politics and impacts of the first Aswan dam, also in terms of archaeology, see F. A. Hassan, "The Aswan High Dam and the International Rescue Nubia Campaign," *African Archaeological Review* 24, nos. 3–4 (2007): 73–94; P. Betts, "The Warden of World Heritage: UNESCO and the Rescue of the Nubian Monuments," *Past and Present* 226, suppl. 10

(2015): 100–125. Betts argues that there was a dominance of technocrats over preservationists. He also provides a more detailed account of the lead-up to the Suez crisis and the aftermath, setting it in the wider Cold War context. T. Mitchell, *Rule of Experts* (Berkeley: University of California Press, 2002), 45, argues that the Aswan High Dam became the centerpiece of postwar nation-making in Egypt despite the problems of "salinization, waterlogging, declining soil fertility, the displacement of the people of Nubia, the loss of an archaeological heritage, increased disease, coastal erosion, the destruction of a large fishing industry, the loss of water due to evaporation and seepage, and other problems already evident from the first dam."

3. A. Shokr, "Hydropolitics, Economy, and the Aswan High Dam in Mid-Century Egypt," *Arab Studies Journal* 17, no. 1 (2009): 9–31.

4. The United States blocked Britain from obtaining any loans from the United States or the International Monetary Fund and refused to provide oil shipments to Britain and France. D. B. Kunz, "When Money Counts and Doesn't: Economic Power and Diplomatic Objectives," *Diplomatic History* 18, no. 4 (1994): 451–62.

5. See also P. B. Heller, *The United Nations Under Dag Hammarskjold, 1953–1961* (Lanham, MD: Scarecrow Press, 2001).

6. G. Sluga, "UNESCO and the (One) World of Julian Huxley," *Journal of World History* 21, no. 3 (2010): 418.

7. T. Scudder, "Aswan High Dam Resettlement of Egyptian Nubians," in *Aswan High Dam Resettlement of Egyptian Nubians* (Singapore: Springer, 2016), 1–52.

8. Quoted in J. P. Sewell, *UNESCO and World Politics* (Princeton, NJ: Princeton University Press, 1975), 266.

9. L. Allais, "The Design of the Nubian Desert: Monuments, Mobility, and the Space of Global Culture," in *Governing by Design: Architecture, Economy, and Politics in the Twentieth Century*, ed. Aggregate (Pittsburgh: University of Pittsburgh Press, 2012), 179–215; L. Allais, "Integrities: The Salvage of Abu Simbel," *Grey Room* 50 (2013): 6–45; Betts, "The Warden of World Heritage"; Hassan, "The Aswan High Dam"; C. Maurel, "Le sauvetage des monuments de Nubie par l'Unesco (1955–1968)," *Égypte/Monde Arabe* 10 (2013); W. Carruthers, "Multilateral Possibilities: Decolonization, Preservation and the Case of Egypt," *Future Anterior: Journal of Historic Preservation History Theory and Criticism* 13, no. 1 (2016): 36–48.

10. See J. Toye and R. Toye, "One World, Two Cultures? Alfred Zimmern, Julian Huxley and the Ideological Origins of UNESCO," *History* 95, no. 319 (2010): 308–31. C. P. Snow famously claimed that Britain had two cultures, a culture of the literary intellectuals and a culture of the scientists, separated by barriers of mutual incomprehension. See also E. H. Carr, *The Twenty Years' Crisis, 1919–1939: An Introduction to the Study of International Relations* (London: Macmillan, 1946).

11. Quoted in M. Mazower, "The End of Eurocentrism," *Critical Inquiry* 40, no. 4 (2014): 298.

12. Toye and Toye, "One World, Two Cultures," 324.

13. G. Sluga, "Imagining Internationalism," *Arts: The Journal of the Sydney University Arts Association* 32 (2012): 55–68.

14. In May 1959 Egypt put in a request, while Sudan did later in October. According to Säve-Söderbergh, "the reason why the Sudan delayed its demand was presumably that the Sudanese government expected the costs for rescuing the antiquities of the inundation area to be included in the indemnities to be paid by Egypt to the Sudan for its losses in connection with the execution of the High Dam project." T. Säve-Söderbergh, "International Salvage Archaeology: Some Organizational and Technical Aspects of the Nubian Campaign," *Annals of the Royal Science Academy* 15–16 (1972): 120.

15. Excavation ended in Egypt in 1965 and in Sudan in 1973. Work on the Aswan Dam was inaugurated in 1960 and completed in 1969. The relocation of Abu Simbel was completed by 1968, at which point the campaign to save Philae Temple took over.

16. March 8 appeal by Vittorino Veronese, Director-General of Unesco, *UNESCO Courier*, May 1960, 7, cited in Betts, "The Warden of World Heritage," 117.

17. Maheu in *UNESCO Courier*, December 1964.

18. See "Abu Simbel—Now or Never," *UNESCO Courier*, October 1961, 4.

19. Allais, "Integrities."

20. See the cover of *UNESCO Courier*, October 1961. See also Italconsult, "Planning for Saving the Abu Simbel Temple," http://www.italconsult.com/en/projects/ projects-delivering-cutting-edge-projects-around-world-projects-planning-saving-abu-simbel-temple, accessed December 10, 2016.

21. Allais, "Integrities," 19. See statements by US representative Max McCullough in the Executive Committee of the International Campaign to Save the Monuments of Nubia, Meeting of the Bureau, The Hague, June 15, 1963, UNESCO/NUBIA/ CE/BUR/1.

22. Allais, "Integrities," 20 n. 41.

23. Report of the 11th Session of the Board of Consultants for the Abu Simbel Projects, June 27, 1966, UNESCO Archives, file reference 069 (62) N/Abu Simbel/A 02.

24. R. Calder, "Jacking Up a Mountain of Stone," in *UNESCO Courier*, October 1961, 14.

25. Ibid., 10. See also T. Säve-Söderbergh, *Temples and Tombs of Ancient Nubia: The International Rescue Campaign at Abu Simbel, Philae and Other Sites* (London: Thames and Hudson, 1987), 92.

26. See, for example, several short films by UNESCO: *Opération Nubie* (1966), http:// www.unesco.org/archives/multimedia/?s=films_details&pg=33&id=3841; *The World Saves Abu Simbel* (1967), http://www.unesco.org/archives/multimedia/ ?s=films_details&pg=33&id=67; and *Victory in Nubia* (1982), http://www.unesco.

org/archives/multimedia/?s=films_details&pg=33&id=63, accessed December 10, 2016.

27. Säve-Söderbergh, *Temples and Tombs*, 104.

28. Allais, "Integrities," 22.

29. Statement by John A. Wilson, Professor of Egyptology, University of Chicago, to the US Senate, Mutual Security Act of 1960, https://catalog.hathitrust.org/Record/101706169, accessed December 10, 2016.

30. See the objectives listed in document UNESCO/SN/IAC/2, International Campaign to Save the Monuments of Nubia, Meeting of the International Action Committee Paris, May 16–17 1960. "The experts recommended that excavations should be carried out by missions of archaeologists and experts on prehistory at the sites which will be submerged. Governments and competent institutions will doubtless wish to organize at their own expense expeditions which will be of great scientific interest. Unesco will not collect funds for the financing of such expeditions, but will act merely as intermediary between their organizers and the Government of the United Arab Republic."

31. Säve-Söderbergh, *Temples and Tombs*, 64. The University of Alexandria undertook work, as did the Egyptian Department of Antiquities.

32. Confidential letter from Ali Vrioni to Louis Christophe, January 30, 1963, UNESCO Archives, file reference 069 (62) N/Abu-Simbel Part IV from I/IV/62. Nasser's quote appears in Calder, "Jacking Up a Mountain of Stone," 6.

33. Starting from the First Cataract and going up the Nile to the Second Cataract, the sites were allotted for excavation by specific nations: Debod (Poland), Dehmit (Italy), Khor, Dehmit, Kalabsha (USA and Switzerland), Taffeh (Czechoslovakia), Kalabsha, Gerf Hussein (Czechoslovakia), Sabagura (Italy), Dakka and Wadi Allaql (USSR), Maharraqah, Ikhmindi (Italy), Sayala (Austria), Medik (France), Sheikh Da'ud (Spain), Afya (Netherlands), Aniba (Egypt), Ibrim (UK) spelling, Ermenneh-Tockhe (USA), Tamit (Italy), Abu Simbel, East Bank (Italy), Jebel Adda necropolis (West Germany), Jebel Adda fortress (Egypt, USA), Ballana and Qustul (USA), Ermenneh and Sudanese border (USA), Faras West (Poland), Aksha (France, Argentina), Serra East (USA), Argin (Spain), sites between the Egyptian border and Gemai (joint mission of the Scandinavian countries), and Buhen (UK). In Egypt there were archaeologists from West Germany, Argentina, Canada, Spain, Denmark, Finland, France, India, Italy, Japan, Norway, Poland, Egypt, Sweden, Switzerland, Czechoslovakia, the USSR, the United Kingdom, and the United States. In Sudan archaeologists came from West Germany, Belgium, Spain, Ghana, Netherlands, Poland, Sudan, Sweden, Yugoslavia, the United Kingdom, and the United States.

34. Säve-Söderbergh, *Temples and Tombs*, 89.

35. B. B. Lal, "Expeditions Outside India," *Indian Archaeology* 1961–2 (1964): 64–70. Lal was trained by Mortimer Wheeler and later played various roles for UNESCO.

36. S. Zuringa, "The Spanish Nubian Salvage Campaign Through the Media and Official Archives," in *The Kushite World: Proceeedings of the 11th International Conference for Meroitic Studies*, ed. M. H. Zach (Vienna: Verein der Förderer der Sudanforschung, 2008), 613–22; X. Ayán Vila and A. González-Ruibal, "Spanish Archaeology Abroad," in *European Archaeology Abroad: Global Settings, Comparative Perspectives*, ed. S. van de Linde et al. (Leiden: Sidestone Press, 2012), 85–104.

37. J. A. Wilson, "The Nubian Campaign: An Exercise in International Archaeology," *Proceedings of the American Philosophical Society* 111, no. 5 (1967): 268–71. Wilson claimed that "the appeal to foreign institutions to come into Nubia reversed the distrustful nationalism of the Near Eastern countries, so *l'esprit de la Nubie* has eroded the isolated arrogance of the archaeologists. The cooperative effort not only achieved its goal of rescuing monuments and antiquities; it also brought working scholars into harmonious relations. Channels of communication have been opened up, and mutual distrusts and diffidences have been abated" (271).

38. W. Y. Adams, "The Nubian Archaeological Campaigns of 1959–1969: Myths and Realities, Successes and Failures," in *Études Nubiennes, Conférence de Genève. Actes du VIIe Congrès International d'Études Nubiennes*, ed. C. Bonnet (Geneva: Sociéte d'Études Nubiennes, 1992), 3.

39. Säve-Söderbergh, *Temples and Tombs*, 201.

40. W. Y. Adams, "Organizational Problems in International Salvage Archaeology," *Anthropological Quarterly* 41, no. 3 (1968): 110–21.

41. He notes that administrative responsibility for the Nubian operation was lodged in the Museums and Monuments Division of the Department of Cultural Activities because there was no envisioned role for archaeology.

42. Adams, "The Nubian Archaeological Campaigns," 3.

43. Adams, "Organizational Problems." Adams wrote, "Many archaeologists complained of this allocation of priorities, arguing that well-known and fully studied temples were of less importance than unknown and unexcavated sites. They ignored the essential fact that Unesco's participation in the Nubian campaign from the start was founded on the principle of conservation of cultural treasures and not on the advancement of knowledge" (113). Part of the problem was methodological, and Adams claims that "different approaches to the problem emerged in the two countries. In Egypt, the entire threatened area was divided into territorial segments of about equal size; participating expeditions were invited to select one or more segments and to investigate all of the important antiquities of every period and type within them. Those expeditions concerned with prehistoric remains were allowed to range over much larger areas and to exercise a selection of sites consistent with their normal operating strategy. In the Sudan, where the Antiquities Service was itself prepared to take an active part in field work, foreign expeditions were permitted to select individual sites

or groups of sites to suit their special interests, while the Antiquities Service assumed responsibility for the remainder" (114).

44. Adams, "The Nubian Archaeological Campaigns," 4. Adams claims that UNESCO had no financial involvement in the archaeological campaigns.

45. T. Säve-Söderbergh, "The International Nubia Campaign: Two Perspectives," in *Études Nubiennes, Conférence de Genève. Actes du VIIe Congrès International d'Études Nubiennes*, ed. C. Bonnet (Geneva: Sociéte d'Études Nubiennes, 1992).

46. Maurel, "Le sauvetage des monuments de Nubie."

47. Letter from G. Knetch to J. K. van der Haagen, June 18, 1960, UNESCO Archives, file reference 069 (62) Nubia: 93 A 52 (62).

48. Adams, "The Nubian Archaeological Campaigns," 8.

49. See Report of the Committee, International Campaign to Save the Monuments of Nubia, Executive Committee, Fifth Session, Paris, October 7–9, 1963, UNESCO / NUBIA/5, 3.

50. F. Wendorf, *The Prehistory of Nubia* (Dallas, TX: Southern Methodist University Press, 1968). See also Hassan, "The Aswan High Dam," 77.

51. P. L. Shinnie and M. Shinnie, *Debeira West: A Mediaeval Nubian Town* (Warminster: Aris and Phillips, 1978); P. L. Shinnie, *Ancient Nubia* (London: Kegan Paul, 1996).

52. A. J. Mills, "The Reconnaissance Survey from Gemai to Dal: A Preliminary Report for 1963–64," *Kush* 15 (1967–68): 200–210.

53. See L. Suková, "Pictures in Place: A Case Study from Korosko (Lower Nubia)," *Studies in African Archaeology (Poznań Archaeological Museum)* 14 (2015): 119–43.

54. Säve-Söderbergh, "International Salvage Archaeology," 132. This was also the case with Sudan, and UNESCO would launch other salvage campaigns, such as the Merowe Dam. For context and implications, see H. Hafsaas-Tsakos, "Ethical Implications of Salvage Archaeology and Dam Building: The Clash Between Archaeologists and Local People in Dar al-Manasir, Sudan," *Journal of Social Archaeology* 11, no. 1 (2011): 49–76; C. Kleinitz and C. Näser, "The Loss of Innocence: Political and Ethical Dimensions of the Merowe Dam Archaeological Salvage Project at the Fourth Nile Cataract (Sudan)," *Conservation and Management of Archaeological Sites* 13, nos. 2–3 (2011): 253–80; J.-G. Leturcq, "Heritage-Making and Policies of Identity in the 'Post-Conflict Reconstruction' of Sudan," *Égypte/Monde Arabe*, nos. 5–6 (2009): 295–328.

55. Letter from Gerhard Bersu, president of the Union Internationale des Sciences Préhistoriques et Protohistoriques, April 22, 1963, to Ali Vrioni, UNESCO, where he describes the regrettable mix-up by the Americans, UNESCO Archives, file reference 069 (62) Nubia/A 02 Part III. Ralph Solecki (Columbia University) and Fred Wendorf (New Mexico) originally had a permit for Sudan and asked to shift north into Egypt; this also led them to overlap with the Scandinavian concession. Letter from Professor Charles Reed to Louis Christophe states, "Expressing your bewilderment at the conflict of statements in various of his

communications . . . I have talked to both Professors Solecki and Smith by tele-
phone, and we have arrived at an amicable solution of the difficulties of the area
adjacent to Sudan; this solution of ours we are communicating to Dr. Wendorf,
and hope for his approval. We should, thus, be writing to you again in a few days,
with out solution as agreed amongst us, to this difficult problem." UNESCO
Archives, file reference 069 (62) N/ 930.26 (624).

56. F. Wendorf, "The Campaign for Nubian Prehistory," in *Études Nubiennes,
Conférence de Genève. Actes du VIIe Congrès International d'Études Nubiennes*, ed.
C. Bonnet (Geneva: Sociéte d'Études Nubiennes, 1992), 44.

57. Maurel, "Le sauvetage des monuments de Nubie," n. 7: "Ces rivalités, peu
constructives, consternent Louis Christophe, agent de l'Unesco envoyé sur
place: 'la campagne de Nubie n'est pas une foire d'empoigne. Il y a du travail
pour tous les spécialistes. . . . Ne travaillons-nous pas tous dans le même but,
un but scientifique?' " UNESCO Archives, file reference 069 (62) N/Abu Simbel/
A 02. CA 120/29, II: Letter from Louis Christophe to Zbynek Zaba, December
18, 1963.

58. Wilson writes that "it had been hoped that an American of force and distinction might be persuaded to chair the Committee, but the effort to find the right
man failed. The general oversight of the Nubian campaign devolved upon the
Executive Committee of UNESCO, which has shouldered the burden of planning and coordination, but which is not equipped for an international drive for
funds" Wilson, "The Nubian Campaign," 269.

59. Wilson described decisions being taken by consensus rather than vote, but when
a divided vote occurred it "was not so much that Mr. X had voted on the other
side from Mr. Y, but that France had voted against Germany, or the United States
against the Soviet Union" (ibid., 269). He goes on to claim that "most of the
Europeans and all of the Egyptians considered that they were the official representatives of their governments. This was less true of the archaeologist from
Great Britain, and it was not at all true of myself. Not only was I independent of
any American government agency, but I was not even commissioned to speak
for a learned society or my own university. For seven years I have found it impossible to persuade my colleagues on these committees that I speak for myself
alone and not for the United States" (270).

60. See Maurel, "Le sauvetage des monuments de Nubie." Maurel describes a memo
from Louis Christophe from February 16, 1963, where the American archaeologist Ralph Solecki released his research report from Nubia in the journal
Man, vol. 62, November 1962, rather than the agreed UNESCO publications.
Also Anthony Mills, in a letter to Louis Christophe, November 22, 1968, asks
what UNESCO intends "with regard to the post-excavation study of material and
completion of maps and records and eventual scientific publication . . . I hope
the last five years have not been a waste." And in his December 12, 1968, response Christophe reminds Mills that there are no more funds left and that

"because every year after your six-months campaign in Sudanese Nubia, you had time for such a study in Khartoum." UNESCO Archives, file reference 069 (62) N: 930.26 (624).

61. Säve-Söderbergh, "The International Nubia Campaign," 42.

62. See the memo from Louis Christophe to J. K. van der Haagen, March 12, 1962, and confidential letter from Ali Vrioni to Louis Christophe, January 30, 1963, UNESCO Archives, file reference 069 (62) N/Christophe Nubia— Correspondence with M. Christophe Part II. See also letter from Piero Gazzola to Director-General Vittorio Veronese, September 24, 1960, UNESCO Archives, file reference 069 (62) N/ 930.26. For the Scandinavian issue, see the letter from Torgny Säve-Söderbergh to Director-General René Maheu, October 14, 1961, reminding him that the joint Scandinavian project in Nubia was omitted from UNESCO report CUA/109 and that the king of Sweden was playing a key role as patron. He also asks to be given UNESCO or diplomatic status for the leader of the project to help ease practical problems such as vehicle registration.

63. Letter from Walter Emery to J. K. van der Haagen, 1962, about Sudan, UNESCO Archives, file reference 069 (62) Nubia (624) Part I.

64. Letter from J. O. Brew to Director-General René Maheu, August 30, 1961, UNESCO Archives, file reference 069 (62) N/ 930.26.

65. Lassalle, UNESCO Archives, file reference 069 (62) Nubia/A 02/17.

66. See the Nubia Bibliography up to 2000, UNESCO Archives, CLT/CIH/MCO/ 2004/RM/H/1, http://www.unesco.org/ulis/cgi-bin/ulis.pl?catno=150176&set=00 583ED327_ 1_425&gp=1&lin=1&ll=1, accessed November 16, 2016. According to William Adams, "If the results of this endeavour have not in the end quite lived up to the glowing promise which the UNESCO publicists held out, they still add up to an unprecedented record of achievement in both excavation and conservation." W. Y. Adams, *Nubia: Corridor to Africa* (London: Allen Lane, 1977), 81. Adams reports that the Survey of Sudanese Nubia starting in 1960 discovered more than a thousand sites and had excavations in over a third of them (86). The Scandinavians recorded some five hundred, while A. J. Mills listed more than eight hundred sites. See also C. Johansson, "Digital Reconstruction of the Archaeological Landscape in the Concession Area of the Scandinavian Joint Expedition to Sudanese Nubia (1961–1964)," M.A. thesis, Uppsala University, 2014; H.-Å. Nordström, *The West Bank Survey from Faras to Gemai I: Sites of Early Nubian, Middle Nubian and Pharaonic Age* (Oxford: Archaeopress, 2014).

67. Säve-Söderbergh, "International Salvage Archaeology," 119.

68. Betts, "The Warden of World Heritage."

69. Brazil, Ecuador, France, West Germany, India, Italy, Lebanon, Netherlands, Pakistan, Spain, Sudan, Sweden, United Arab Republic, United States of America, and Yugoslavia.

70. Address by M. S. Adiseshiah, Deputy Director-General of UNESCO, Global Meeting of Resident Representatives of the United Nations Development

Programme—UNESCO and UNDP, Turin, June 29, 1966, UNESCO Archives, file reference WS/0766.12.ODG see CAB 1/19, 8. He goes on to say, "The protagonists of intellectual cooperation in Unesco regard the operational aspects, the development assistance function of Unesco, as a useless intrusion—as a diversion, turning the purity of the intellectual storehouse which Unesco represents into a six-and-nine penny store, a magasin de bon marché. I have been accused sometimes of this particular sin over my years in Unesco. The advocates of operational assistance regard intellectual cooperation as airy-fairy, as démodé, forgetting that the fountain of Unesco's development aid springs from the wells of intellectual cooperation and finds its turn validity in the supreme ethical purposes of the Organization. The specialists in the ethical aspect regard all else as distortion and want all efforts to be concentrated on the work for disarmament, the banning of nuclear armaments, the banishing of war, the eradication of all forms of discrimination and a continuing fight against every violation of the Universal Declaration of Human Rights. But Unesco's Member States assembled in the General Conference, have in their wisdom pondered long and hard over these facets of Unesco and have decided on a convergence of all its activities around them. It is this convergence which gives Unesco its personality and its program its unity" (8–9).

71. André Malraux, "TVA of Archaeology," *UNESCO Courier*, May 1960, 8–11. See also Allais, "The Design of the Nubian Desert."

72. J. Huxley, *TVA: Adventure in Planning* (Surrey: Architectural Press, 1943). I am grateful to Christina Luke for this reference.

73. S. Okasha, "Address by H. E. Dr. Sarwat Okasha, Minister of Culture of the United Arab Republic," in *Abu Simbel: Addresses Delivered at the Ceremony to Mark the Completion of the Operations for Saving the Two Temples* (Paris: UNESCO, 1968).

74. Shokr, "Hydropolitics."

75. The quote is taken directly from M. Mazower, *Governing the World: The History of an Idea* (London: Penguin, 2012), 199.

76. Malraux, "TVA of Archaeology."

77. J. O. Brew, "Emergency Archaeology: Salvage in Advance of Technological Progress," *Proceedings of the American Philosophical Society* 105, no. 1 (1961): 1–10.

78. Adams, *Nubia: Corridor to Africa*. Emery and Kirwan investigated some 87 cemeteries and 2,400 individual graves dating from prehistory to the Christian period. They also conducted excavations at the Middle and New Kingdom fortress of Kubban, at Meroitic town sites in Wadi el-Arab and the X-group royal tombs; see 76–77.

79. Säve-Söderbergh, "International Salvage Archaeology," 118.

80. Ibid. See also W. Y. Adams, "A Century of Archaeological Salvage, 1907–2007," *Sudan and Nubia* 11 (2007): 48–56.

81. See Preliminary Report of Archaeological Research of the Yale Prehistoric Expedition to Nubia, Season 1962–1963, UNESCO Archives, file reference 069 (62) Nubia: 93 A 52 (62).

82. Adams also felt Keating's publications "did not bear a close resemblance to what was actually happening in the field." Adams, "The Nubian Archaeological Campaigns," 3.

83. Letter from Rex Keating, Head of Section, to the Director-General, UNESCO, March 27, 1969, Mission to Nubia (12 January–7 February 1969), COM/OPI/4 Memo.470, March, 27, 1969, UNESCO Archives, file reference 069 (62) N: 930.26 (624).

84. For a discussion of these developments in Europe, see J.-P. Demoule, "Rescue Archaeology: A European view," *Annual Review of Anthropology* 41 (2012): 611–26. Of the UNESCO conventions that Demoule cites, he omits the 1968 Recommendation, which is ironically the most relevant to the issue of rescue or preventive archaeology.

85. UNESCO, "Recommendation Concerning the Preservation of Cultural Property Endangered by Public of Private Works," November 19, 1968, http://portal.unesco.org/en/ev.php-URL_ID=13085&URL_DO=DO_TOPIC&URL_SECTION=201.html, accessed December 10, 2016.

86. Adams, "Organizational Problems," 118–19. At the time of writing Adams claimed that during its twenty-one years UNESCO had never employed a professional archaeologist as such at the headquarters level, either in the Nubian Office or in any other operation.

87. G. Sluga, "Editorial—the Transnational History of International Institutions," *Journal of Global History* 6, no. 2 (2011): 219–22.

88. S. Okasha, "Rameses Recrowned: The International Campaign to Preserve the Monuments of Nubia, 1959–68," in *Offerings to the Discerning Eye*, ed. S. H. D'Auria (Leiden: Brill, 2009), 223–44; Hassan, "The Aswan High Dam."

89. Okasha, "Rameses Recrowned," n. 18.

90. Memo entitled Co-operation with USSR, ODG/DDG Memo. 23.695 May 22, 1961, UNESCO Archives, file reference 069 (62) Nubia/A 02 Part III.

91. A. Klimowicz and P. Klimowicz, "The Socio-Political Context of Polish Archaeological Discoveries in Faras, Sudan," in *European Archaeology Abroad: Global Settings, Comparative Perspectives*, ed. S. van de Linde et al. (Leiden: Sidestone Press, 2012), 287. There was also the American-Polish-Egyptian combined prehistoric expedition headed by Fred Wendorf and Romauld Schild.

92. M. Falser, "Cultural Heritage as Civilizing Mission: Methodological Considerations," in *Cultural Heritage as Civilizing Mission*, ed. M. Falser (New York: Springer, 2015), 1–32, 10.

93. Betts, "The Warden of World Heritage," 102.

94. Speech by André Malraux reproduced in *UNESCO Courier*, September 1997, 4–5.

95. Betts, "The Warden of World Heritage." For French cultural diplomacy, see also W. H. C. Laves and C. A. Thomson, *UNESCO: Purpose, Progress, Prospects* (Bloomington: University of Indiana Press, 1957).

96. See W. R. Pendergast, "UNESCO and French Cultural Relations 1945–1970," *International Organization* 30, no. 3 (1976): 453–83; J. Musitelli, "World Heritage, Between Universalism and Globalization," *International Journal of Cultural Property* 11, no. 2 (2002): 323–36.

97. André Malraux, speech delivered at the "Launch of the International Campaign for the Salvage of the Monuments of Nubia, UNESCO House, March 8, 1960," *UNESCO Courier*, May 1960, 8. See also T. Allbeson, "Photographic Diplomacy in the Postwar World: Unesco and the Conception of Photography as a Universal Language, 1946–1956," *Modern Intellectual History* 12, no. 2 (2015): 399–401.

98. The Egyptian minister of culture, Dr. Sarwat Okasha, has written extensively against this position.

99. Betts, "The Warden of World Heritage," 104. See also Maurel, "Le sauvetage des monuments de Nubie," which describes how "à la suite de cette expédition, qui a beaucoup nui aux relations franco-égyptiennes, les fonctionnaires de l'Unesco présents en Égypte ont été assignés à résidence puis évacués en Crète par l'ONU. Les actions de l'Unesco en Égypte sont interrompues. Seule Christiane Desroches-Noblecourt poursuit ses travaux au Caire."

100. D. M. Reid, *Contesting Antiquity in Egypt: Archaeologies, Museums, and the Struggle for Identities from World War I to Nasser* (Cairo: American University in Cairo Press, 2015).

101. J. Barr, *A Line in the Sand: Britain, France and the Struggle That Shaped the Middle East* (New York: Simon and Schuster, 2011).

102. D. M. Reid, "Indigenous Egyptology: The Decolonization of a Profession?," *Journal of the American Oriental Society* 105, no. 2 (1985): 243.

103. Parliamentary Debates (Hansard), House of Commons Official Report, Friday 18th November 1960, Volume 630, No. 14. Adjournment Debate [Col. 718]: Monuments, Nubia (Preservation).

104. Sir Mortimer Wheeler to J. K. van der Haagen, Director of the Service for the Monuments of Nubia, March 12, 1962, UNESCO Archives, file reference 069 (62) N/A 106 Part I.

105. Letter from Shirley Guiton from the UK National Commission to UNESCO and Ministry of Education to Ali Vrioni, Office of the Director-General UNESCO, November 15, 1960, UNESCO Archives, file reference 069 (62) N/ A114 Part III-Part V. Wheeler wrote on October 7, 1960, that the British Academy had raised £20,000 but that was designated to fund its own projects at Buhen, Qasr Ibrim, and the survey of sites in Egyptian Nubia. UNESCO Archives, file reference 069 (62) N/A 114/113 (437).

106. J. Hawkes, *Adventures in Archaeology: The Biography of Sir Mortimer Wheeler* (New York: St. Martin's Press, 1982), 336.

107. UNESCO, *A Common Trust: The Preservation of the Ancient Monuments of Nubia* (Paris: UNESCO 1960).

108. Ziada Arbab, minister of education, Republic of the Sudan, quoted in ibid., 4.

109. See, for example, J. Cuno, *Who Owns Antiquity? Museums and the Battle over Our Ancient Heritage* (Princeton, NJ: Princeton University Press, 2008).

110. Letter from Albert Spaulding at NSF to J. K. van der Haagen, UNESCO, re Clement Meighan, October 10, 1960, UNESCO Archives, file reference 069 (62) N/ 930.26. They were also "clear at the outset that the research divisions of the Foundation have as their primary function the support of programs of basic research which originate in the universities and other institutions."

111. Adams, "The Nubian Archaeological Campaigns," 3.

112. Betts, "The Warden of World Heritage," 108.

113. V. Pavone, "From Intergovernmental to Global: UNESCO's Response to Globalization," *Review of International Organizations* 2, no. 1 (2007): 81.

114. Okasha, "Rameses Recrowned." In November 1958 Okasha recalls a visit from the US ambassador, Raymond A. Hare, and the director of the Metropolitan Museum of Art in New York, James Rorimer. They proposed to buy "one or two temples" threatened with submersion. Okasha admits he was "frankly affronted by this casual offer to purchase our ancestral heritage, rather than a proposal of scientific and technical aid in preserving it for Egypt" (226–27).

115. See Wilson, "The Nubian Campaign," 270: "The American participation, in volume of field work and in financial contribution, has been far greater than that of any other foreign nation. . . . [The officers of] the US National Committee for the Preservation of the Nubian Monuments . . . presented more than two hundred public lectures, and . . . [the United States] claims the credit for the allocation of $16,000,000 to the Nubian campaign. Those monies derived from American credits through the sale of surplus grain to Egypt. We hope that an additional $6,000,000 from the same resource may be made available to rescue the island temples of Philae."

116. Letter to Louis Christophe, February 19, 1963, entitled "Une porte où frapper Les Universités américaines pourraient encore financer le sauvetage d'Abou Simbel," UNESCO Archives, file reference 069 (62) N/Christophe Nubia— Correspondence with M. Christophe Part II.

117. Letter from William Y. Adams to Ralph Solecki, May 3, 1962, UNESCO Archives, file reference 069 (62) N/A 114/ 113 (73), Columbia University. See also Allais, "Integrities," 21, where she states that the United States "held large amounts of Egyptian pounds, derived from the sale to Egypt of agricultural surpluses such as wheat and cotton under the terms of the 'Food for Peace' program established in 1955. The idea that one country gives its excess food to feed the hungry of another might seem simple, almost philanthropic, but this 'gift' was twice mediated by economic transactions: the US government bought wheat from its farmers, then sold that wheat to the Egyptian government, earning local purchasing power. . . . By the time Unesco's fund-raising campaign for Abu Simbel got underway, US-owned Egyptian pounds were accumulating in Cairo, unspent, under threat of devaluation. A cultural project

like the salvage seemed an expedient and, in the words of one cultural attaché, 'non-controversial' way to expend these funds."

118. Senator Hruska, Supplemental Appropriation Bill for 1962, Hearings Before the Committee on Appropriations, United States Senate, 87th Congress, First Session, 642.

119. Mr. Coombs from the State Department, Supplemental Appropriation Bill for 1962, Hearings Before the Committee on Appropriations, United States Senate, 87th Congress, First Session, 647. See also the full text of the earlier Mutual Security Act of 1960 for further explanations of American self-interest: https://catalog.hathitrust.org/Record/101706169, accessed December 12, 2016.

120. Excerpt from House Report, Supplemental Appropriation Bill for 1962, Hearings Before the Committee on Appropriations, United States Senate, 87th Congress, First Session, 549.

121. President John F. Kennedy's letter quoted in the Supplemental Appropriation Bill for 1962, Hearings Before the Committee on the Appropriations, United States Senate, 87th Congress, First Session, 644.

122. Lassalle, born in Mexico, came to the United States in 1935 to attend Columbia University. He became a US citizen and an assistant to Nelson Rockefeller, then a member of the Roosevelt administration, before becoming an American espionage agent in Spain while employed as the European representative of the Walt Disney Company. At the end of the war, he divorced his first wife in order to marry a German princess whose father was an early supporter of Adolf Hitler. Later, he divorced the princess to marry the first of two wealthy American heiresses.

123. Lassalle reiterates the problems with American archaeologists and Egyptologists, who he says are plotting and blackmailing and generally performing a negative service to the project. UNESCO Archives, file reference 069 (62) Nubia/A 02/17.

124. Letter from John A. Wilson to Ali Vrioni, August 8, 1963, UNESCO Archives, file reference 069 (62) N/Abu Simbel/A 02.

125. Letter from Eugene Socho, Acting Assistant Director, US National Commission for UNESCO, to Edmundo de Lassalle, January 23, 1962, UNESCO Archives, file reference 069 (62) Nubia/A 02/17.

126. Confidential memo from Edmundo de Lassalle to Dr. A. Salmamendi, February 1, 1962, UNESCO Archives, file reference 069 (62) Nubia/A 02/17.

127. See document by Dr. J. Vercoutter, Commissioner for Archaeology, Sudan Government, "Antiquities in the Northern Sudan. A Preliminary Report on the Sudanese Monuments and Sites Likely to Be Submerged by the Sudd-el-Ali Scheme," UNESCO Archives, file reference 069 (62) N/ Philae Part IV.

128. Ibid., 4.

129. C. Kleinitz, "Between Valorisation and Devaluation: Making and Unmaking (World) Heritage in Sudan," *Archaeologies* 9, no. 3 (2013): 427–69; Scudder,

"Aswan High Dam Resettlement of Egyptian Nubians"; H. M. Fahim, *Dams, People and Development: The Aswan High Dam Case* (Burlington, VT: Elsevier, 2015); N. S. Hopkins and S. R. Mehanna, *Nubian Encounters: The Story of the Nubian Ethnological Survey 1961–1964* (Oxford: Oxford University Press, 2011).

130. Draft Resolution, Item 15.3, 11/C/DR/7 General Conference, October 18, 1960, UNESCO Archives, file reference 069 (62) N: 398 MUS/NUBIA—Folklore.
131. Säve-Söderbergh, *Temples and Tombs*, 57.
132. Betts, "The Warden of World." See also N. Y. Reynolds, "City of the High Dam: Aswan and the Promise of Postcolonialism in Egypt," *City and Society* 29, no. 1 (2017): 213–35; C. Gilmore, "Speaking Through the Silence," in *Development-Induced Displacement and Resettlement: New Perspectives on Persisting Problems*, ed. I. Satiroglu and N. Choi (Abingdon: Routledge, 2015), 199–211; M. Janmyr, "Human Rights and Nubian Mobilisation in Egypt: Towards Recognition of Indigeneity," *Third World Quarterly* 38, no. 3 (2017): 717–33.
133. Kleinitz, "Between Valorisation and Devaluation," 440–43.
134. Pavone, "From Intergovernmental to Global," 81.
135. Ibid., 82.
136. Adams, "The Nubian Archaeological Campaigns of 1959–1969," 3.
137. See "Preservation and Development of Moenjodaro Archaeological Site, an Updated Master Plan for 1993–2003 by W. Logan," UNDP/PAK/89/031 Assignment Report. The UN declared 1967 as International Tourist Year.
138. W. Preston, E. S. Herman, and H. Schiller, *Hope and Folly: The United States and UNESCO 1945–1985* (Minneapolis: University of Minnesota Press, 1989), 71.
139. Mazower, *Governing the World*, 213.
140. Säve-Söderbergh, *Temples and Tombs*, 93.

CHAPTER 3

1. Wheeler failed to produce a full publication from his excavations at Moenjodaro. He also became embroiled in a bitter exchange with Harvard and Walter Fairservis, leading to the suspension of all foreign excavation permits. See H. P. Ray, *Colonial Archaeology in South Asia: The Legacy of Sir Mortimer Wheeler* (New Delhi: Oxford University Press 2008).
2. NEDECO Engineering Consultants, "Pakistan: Desalinization of the Monuments of Mohenjo Daro," July 1968, UNESCO 654/ BMS.RD/ CLT, http://unesdoc.unesco.org/images/0000/000086/008691eb.pdf, accessed January 24, 2017.
3. Report on Moenjodaro by the UNESCO Mission, October 1968–February 1969, UNESCO Archives, file reference CLT/CH/445, 17.
4. Letter from NEDECO to Gerhard Bolla, Director, Department of Cultural Heritage, UNESCO, March 7, 1973, UNESCO Archives, file reference 069-72 Moenjodaro/4 02.

5. W. Logan, "Preservation and Development of Moenjodaro Archaeological Site, an Updated Master Plan for 1993–2003," UNESCO Archives, file reference UNDP/PAK/89/031.

6. Q. U. Shabab, "Address of Welcome," in *Proceedings of International Symposium on Moenjodaro, 1973*, ed. A. N. Khan (Karachi: National Book Foundation, 1975).

7. René Maheu, "Save Moenjodaro," January 11, 1974, http://unesdoc.unesco.org/images/0000/000095/009534eb.pdf, accessed January 24, 2017. While the appeal was launched in January 1974, it took more than five years to sign the agreement between UNESCO and Pakistan.

8. Ibid. The threat was not simply a natural one; it was exacerbated by construction of the Sukkur Dam and the introduction of irrigation agriculture.

9. Document on Moenjodaro including part of the text by Sir Leonard Woolley headed "How Bronze Age Merchants Built a Civilization by the Indus," UNESCO Archives, file reference 069-72 Moenjodaro/ A II Pt II.

10. Maheu, "Save Moenjodaro." See also memo to Dir/CLT from Chief, CLP/OPS Hiroshi Daifuku, "Possibility of Utilizing Chinese Currency—UNDP—Amount Available Amounts to Approximately US$3.9 million," CLP/02/3/MO/3/99, April 16, 1975, UNESCO Archives, file reference 069-72 Moenjodaro/4 02.

11. Report on Moenjodaro by the UNESCO Mission, October 1968–February 1969, UNESCO Archives, file reference CLT/CH/445, 11–12.

12. The United States made financial contributions in the early 1980s to a new phase of the project. UNESCO felt Moenjodaro was a project that the Chinese could undertake since they had the expertise, the equipment and materials, and the ability to supervise the work. There was also the question of an unspent balance of $5,783,273 in nonconvertible currency in 1977 from the PRC to the UNDP Fund. The Chinese government expected that their funds would be allocated to Chinese teams and subcontractors, thereby paying themselves in their own coin. Aide-Mémoire, "Possibility of a Chinese Contribution for Moenjodaro," UNESCO Archives, file reference 069-72 Moenjodaro/ A II Pt II.

13. Logan, "Preservation and Development of Moenjodaro."

14. Memo from Minya Yang to DIR/WHC (Francesco Bandarin), June 3, 2001, UNESCO Archives, file WHC/741418.1.1.1 Moenjodaro General Correspondence. This is further confirmed in WHC/74/418.8/6 71/PAK dated December 12, 1997, from Bernd von Droste to the Director of Culture, entitled "Pakistan: Follow-up to the Director-General's Meeting with the Head of Pakistani Delegation to the 29th Session of the General Conference." "We were very surprised to learn that one of the recommendations was the establishment of a site management authority. . . . If this is the case, there is need for serious strategic planning before UNESCO brings any additional assistance to the site." UNESCO Archives, file reference 502.7 (549) C Moenjodaro.

15. Logan, "Preservation and Development of Moenjodaro," 83. From 1979 to 1987 an Aachen University Mission to Moenjodaro concentrated on redocumentation

of the previously excavated remains; see FIT/536/PAK/71, Assignment Report by M. Jansen, "Pakistan Moenjodaro—Archaeological Preservation and Documentation," http://unesdoc.unesco.org/images/0009/000955/095523eo.pdf, accessed January 26, 2017.

16. This was between UNESCO's Division for Cultural Heritage and World Heritage Centre; see UNESCO, "Safeguarding Moenjodaro," http://unesco.org.pk/culture/moenjodaro.html, accessed January 24, 2017. In 1972 Raoul Curiel led a team that reviewed the final conservation project of the Government of Pakistan. The first master plan for the site was drafted in 1972, then revised in 1978, and cost almost US$10,000. A new master plan was then commissioned in the 1990s and, like the earlier proposals in the late 1960s, was dominated by engineers.

17. "Archaeological Ruins at Moenjodaro," http://whc.unesco.org/en/list/138/documents and "State of Conservation: Archaeological Ruins at Moenjodaro (Pakistan)," http://whc.unesco.org/en/soc/403, accessed January 24, 2017.

18. "Borobudur Temple Compounds," http://whc.unesco.org/en/list/592, accessed January 24, 2017.

19. V. Pavone, "From Intergovernmental to Global: UNESCO's Response to Globalization," *Review of International Organizations* 2, no. 1 (2007): 77–95. For conservation and politics at Borobudur, see M. Bloembergen and M. Eickhoff, "Decolonizing Borobudur: Moral Engagements and the Fear of Loss," in *Sites, Bodies and Stories: Imagining Indonesian History*, ed. S. Legêne, B. Purwato, and H. Shulte Nordholt (Singapore: NUS Press, 2015), 33–66.

20. J. Musitelli, "World Heritage, Between Universalism and Globalization," *International Journal of Cultural Property* 11, no. 2 (2002): 323–36.

21. This abstract quality, known by its acronym, OUV, and added only at the end of the drafting process, has been a source of debate and controversy amongst States Parties, Advisory Bodies, and academics from the very beginning. S. Labadi, *UNESCO, Cultural Heritage and Outstanding Universal Value* (Walnut Creek, CA: AltaMira Press, 2013); B. von Droste, "The Concept of Outstanding Universal Value and Its Application: 'From the Seven Wonders of the Ancient World to the 1,000 World Heritage Places Today,'" *Journal of Cultural Heritage Management and Sustainable Development* 1, no. 1 (2011): 26–41; H. Cleere, "The 1972 UNESCO World Heritage Convention," *Heritage and Society* 4, no. 2 (2011): 173–86.

22. The UNESCO General Conference adopted the Convention on November 16, 1972 in Paris at its seventeenth session; the text is at http://whc.unesco.org/en/conventiontext, accessed January 9, 2017. Article 1 states that "cultural heritage" consists of "**monuments**: architectural works, works of monumental sculpture and painting, elements or structures of an archaeological nature, inscriptions, cave dwellings and combinations of features, which are of outstanding universal value from the point of view of history, art or science; **groups of buildings**: groups of separate or connected buildings which, because of their architecture, their

homogeneity or their place in the landscape, are of outstanding universal value from the point of view of history, art or science; **sites**: works of man or the combined works of nature and man, and areas including archaeological sites which are of outstanding universal value from the historical, aesthetic, ethnological or anthropological point of view."

23. C. Cameron and M. Rössler, *Many Voices, One Vision: The Early Years of the World Heritage Convention* (Surrey: Ashgate, 2013), 1.

24. For a full account, see A. Kowalski, "When Cultural Capitalization Became Global Practice," in *The Cultural Wealth of Nations*, ed. N. Bandelj and F. F. Wherry (Stanford, CA: Stanford University Press, 2011), 73–89. In 1965 the National Park Service coordinated the meeting "National Resources, Conservation and Development," where the project of a World Heritage Trust "for the identification, establishment and management of the world's most superb natural and scenic areas and historic sites" was proposed and discussed and the term "world heritage" was coined. For a full account, including the role of Joseph L. Fisher, see Cameron and Rössler, *Many Voices*; P. Stott, "The World Heritage Convention and the National Park Service, 1962–1972," *George Wright Forum* 28 (2011): 279–90.

25. von Droste, "The Concept of Outstanding Universal Value." Bernd von Droste, the first World Heritage Centre director, claims that the success of the campaign to save the Nubian temples played a decisive role in shaping the World Heritage Convention and is still regarded as a model. There was also the Hague Convention in 1954 and setting up of ICOMOS in 1965 after development of the Venice Charter in 1964. See also Cameron and Rössler, *Many Voices*.

26. Kowalski, "When Cultural Capitalization Became Global Practice," 81. She states that between April and July 1972 UNESCO's expert group met and amalgamated both cultural and environmental projects. This was presented in Stockholm and given the conference's seal of approval in the summer of 1972. Beyond the substantive point of including nature, the document only minimally accommodated the US requests. Moreover, the "World Heritage Trust" became a fund for heritage in danger. Kowalski argues that both movements found support in distinct sets of organizations: environmental agencies (the US National Park Service and the IUCN) supported by some Western governments, on one hand, and a mobilized international community of cultural experts and academics organized through ICOMOS, supported by an international organization (UNESCO) and by a growing clientele of developing nations, on the other.

27. Taken from M. Weber, *Economy and Society: An Outline of Interpretive Sociology* (Berkeley: University of California Press, 1978), 246. See also D. L. Brenneis, "Sand, Stability and Stakeholders," in *Heritage Regimes and the State*, ed. R. Bendix, A. Eggert, and A. Peselmann (Göttingen: Universitätsverlag Göttingen, 2013), 370, and M. S. Hull, "Documents and Bureaucracy," *Annual Review of Anthropology* 41 (2012): 251–67. Weber argued that bureaucracy constitutes the

most efficient and rational way in which one can organize human activity, and that systematic processes and organized hierarchies were necessary to maintain order, maximize efficiency, and eliminate favoritism.

28. UNESCO, "World Heritage," http://whc.unesco.org/en/about, accessed January 8, 2017. For excellent coverage, see F. Francioni and F. Lenzerini, *The 1972 World Heritage Convention: A Commentary* (Oxford: Oxford University Press, 2008)

29. M. A. Elliott and V. Schmutz, "World Heritage: Constructing a Universal Cultural Order," *Poetics* 40, no. 3 (2012): 261.

30. V. Pavone, *From the Labyrinth of the World to the Paradise of the Heart: Science and Humanism in UNESCO's Approach to Globalization* (New York: Lexington, 2008), 25. Herzfeld makes a similar point about bureaucracy, thus bringing the two together with UNESCO; see M. Herzfeld, *A Place in History: Social and Monumental Time in a Cretan Town* (Princeton, NJ: Princeton University Press, 1991), 20.

31. W. Ndoro and G. Wijesuriya, "Heritage Management and Conservation: From Colonization to Globalization " in *Global Heritage: A Reader*, ed. L. M. Meskell (Oxford: Blackwell, 2015), 131–49. See also G. Wijesuriya, "Conservation in Context," in *Conservation and Preservation: Interactions Between Theory and Practice: In Memoriam Alois Riegl (1858–1905)*, Proceedings of the International Conference of the ICOMOS International Scientific Committee for the Theory and the Philosophy of Conservation and Restoration, ed. M. Falser, W. Lipp, and A. Tomaszewski (Florence: Edizioni Polistampa, 2010), 233–47.

32. "Conserving the Temple of the Tooth Relic, Sri Lanka," *Public Archaeology* 1, no. 2 (2000): 99–108. See also INTACH, "Charter for the Conservation of Unprotected Architectural Heritage and Sites in India," Indian National Trust for Art and Cultural Heritage, New Delhi, 2004.

33. M. Askew, "The Rise of 'Moradok' and the Decline of the 'Yarn': Heritage and Cultural Construction in Urban Thailand," *Sojourn: Journal of Social Issues in Southeast Asia* 11, no. 2 (1996): 183–210; P. Krairiksh, "A Brief History of Heritage Protection in Thailand," in *Protecting Siam's Heritage*, ed. C. J. Baker (Chiang Mai: Siam Society Under Royal Patronage, 2013), 15–40. See also M. Peleggi, *The Politics of Ruins and the Business of Nostalgia* (Bangkok: White Lotus Press, 2002); C. J. Baker, *Protecting Siam's Heritage* (Chiang Mai: Siam Society Under Royal Patronage, 2013).

34. D. C. Harvey, "Heritage Pasts and Heritage Presents: Temporality, Meaning and the Scope of Heritage Studies," *International Journal of Heritage Studies* 7, no. 4 (2001): 319–38.

35. Elliott and Schmutz, "World Heritage"; A. Swenson, *The Rise of Heritage: Preserving the Past in France, Germany and England, 1789–1914* (Cambridge: Cambridge University Press, 2013).

36. P. Betts and C. Ross, "Modern Historical Preservation—Towards a Global Perspective," *Past and Present* 226, suppl. 10 (2015): 10.

37. N. Heinich, *La fabrique du patrimoine: de la cathédrale à la petite cuillère* (Paris: Les Editions de la MSH, 2009).

38. Swenson, *The Rise of Heritage*, 47.

39. For an excellent historical account, see S. Labadi and W. Logan, "Approaches to Urban Heritage, Development and Sustainability," in *Urban Heritage, Development and Sustainability: International Frameworks, National and Local Governance*, ed. S. Labadi and W. Logan (London: Routledge, 2016), 1–20.

40. Elliott and Schmutz, "World Heritage." On heritage internationals, see A. Swenson, "The First Heritage International(s): Rethinking Global Networks Before UNESCO," *Future Anterior: Journal of Historic Preservation History Theory and Criticism* 13, no. 1 (2016): 1–16.

41. Elliott and Schmutz, "World Heritage."

42. I. Anatole-Gabriel, *La fabrique du patrimoine de l'humanité, L'UNESCO et la protection patrimoniale (1945–1992)* (Paris: FMSH Editions, 2016), 53–54.

43. Ibid., 88.

44. Cameron and Rössler, *Many Voices*, 14. See also UNESCO, *Records of the General Conference Fourteenth Session* (Paris: UNESCO, 1967), 61.

45. Cameron and Rössler, *Many Voices*, 15.

46. Ibid.

47. Quoted in F. Lenzerini, "Articles 15–16 World Heritage Fund," in *The 1972 World Heritage Convention: A Commentary*, ed. F. Francioni and F. Lenzerini (Oxford: Oxford University Press, 1972), 274–75. See also Records of the General Conference Seventeenth Session Paris, 17 October to 21 November 1972, Resolutions and Recommendations, http://unesdoc.unesco.org/images/0011/ 001140/114044E.pdf, accessed January 20, 2017.

48. Kowalski, "When Cultural Capitalization Became Global Practice," 84. See also Cameron and Rössler, *Many Voices*, 25. Finally, it was agreed to include an additional article in the Convention that stipulated obligatory contributions were not to be higher than 1 percent of the statutory contribution made by each Member State to UNESCO's regular budget.

49. R. Hoggart, *An Idea and Its Servants: UNESCO from Within* (Piscataway, NJ: Transaction, 2011), 40.

50. The first Operational Guidelines appear in 1977 and the first inscriptions to the World Heritage List in 1978.

51. UNESCO, "Memphis and Its Necropolis: The Pyramid Fields from Giza to Dahshur," http://whc.unesco.org/en/list/86/documents, accessed February 13, 2017.

52. von Droste, "The Concept of Outstanding Universal Value." See also UNESCO, "Intergovernmental Committee for the Protection of the World Cultural and Natural Heritage, Second Session, Final Report," CC-78/CONF.010/10 Rev., October 9, 1978, http://whc.unesco.org/archive/repcom78.htm, accessed January 13, 2017.

53. http://whc.unesco.org/en/conventiontext, accessed January 24, 2017. See especially Article 14.

54. Pavone, "From Intergovernmental to Global," 81.

55. von Droste, "The Concept of Outstanding Universal Value." For a critique of normative understandings of expertise within ICOMOS and UNESCO, see T. Rico, "Technologies, Technocracy, and the Promise of 'Alternative' Heritage Values," in *Heritage in Action*, ed. H. Silverman, E. Waterton, and S. Watson (New York: Springer, 2017), 217–30; "Stakeholder in Practice: 'Us,' 'Them,' and the Problem of Expertise," in *Archaeologies of "Us" and "Them": Debating History, Heritage and Indigeneity*, ed. C. Hillerdal, A. Karlström, and C.-G. Ojala (London: Routledge, 2017); K. Lafrenz Samuels, "Trajectories of Development: International Heritage Management of Archaeology in the Middle East and North Africa," *Archaeologies* 5, no. 1 (2009): 68–91.

56. UNESCO, "Nubian Monuments from Abu Simbel to Philae," http://whc.unesco.org/en/list/88, accessed January 26, 2017.

57. von Droste, "The Concept of Outstanding Universal Value," 31–32. Records show that representatives of Brazil, Bulgaria, Guinea, and Tunisia felt that the Bureau should recommend the Old City of Jerusalem and its ramparts for the List of World Heritage in Danger, whereas the Federal Republic of Germany and Nepal considered that there was not enough information.

58. The full text of the speech appears in W. Preston, E. S. Herman, and H. Schiller, *Hope and Folly: The United States and UNESCO 1945–1985* (Minneapolis: University of Minnesota Press, 1989), Appendix IV.

59. Cable from Makaminan Makiagansar to Director-General M'Bow, September 13, 1982, ADG/CLT, copying notes from Ralph A. Slayter, Chairman of the World Heritage Committee, CLT/CH/01/7.3/027/1084, September 15, 1982, UNESCO Archives, file reference CLT 1982-83 CAB 4/69.

60. F. Valderrama, *A History of UNESCO* (Paris: UNESCO, 1995), 294.

61. Preston, Herman, and Schiller, *Hope and Folly*, 198.

62. Pavone, "From Intergovernmental to Global," 87. The World Heritage Centre acts as the Secretariat and coordinator within UNESCO for all matters related to the Convention. The Centre organizes the annual sessions of the World Heritage Committee and provides advice to states parties in the preparation of site nominations.

63. Pavone, "From Intergovernmental to Global," 87. In 1987 Federico Mayor, the Spanish scientist and poet, was elected UNESCO Director-General and there was a brief return to something resembling Huxley's original vision. Mayor believed intercultural dialogue and the revitalization of cultures might contribute to that very notion of a universal peace. He separated the two into different operational sectors: cultural heritage would remain firmly in the Culture sector, while the Culture of Peace program was a transdisciplinary program.

64. von Droste, "The Concept of Outstanding Universal Value."

65. L. Prott, "From Admonition to Action: UNESCO's Role in the Protection of Cultural Heritage," *Nature and Resources* 28, no. 3 (1992): 4–11.

66. UNESCO, "Global Strategy," http://whc.unesco.org/en/globalstrategy, accessed January 9, 2017. At the time some 410 properties were listed: 304 were cultural sites and only 90 were natural and 16 mixed, the vast majority located in Europe. See also S. Labadi, "Representations of the Nation and Cultural Diversity in Discourses on World Heritage," *Journal of Social Archaeology* 7, no. 2 (2007): 147–70; S. Labadi, "A Review of the Global Strategy for a Balanced, Representative and Credible World Heritage List 1994–2004," *Conservation and Management of Archaeological Sites* 7, no. 2 (2005): 89–102. For results of the 2011 audit of the Global Strategy, see UNESCO, "INF 9.A: Final Report of the Audit of the Global Strategy and the PACT Initiative," May 27, 2011, http://whc.unesco.org/archive/2011/whc11-35com-INF9Ae.pdf, accessed January 11, 2017. Today almost half of the World Heritage List remains in Europe and North America; see L. M. Meskell, C. Liuzza, and N. Brown, "World Heritage Regionalism: UNESCO from Europe to Asia," *International Journal of Cultural Property* (2015). As of February 2018, Europe and North America, the most represented regional group on the World Heritage List, had 506 sites out of the total 1,073.

67. von Droste, "The Concept of Outstanding Universal Value," 33.

68. For a full discussion, see L. M. Meskell, "Negative Heritage and Past Mastering in Archaeology," *Anthropological Quarterly* 75, no. 3 (2002): 557–74.

69. UNESCO, *Protection of Mankind's Cultural Heritage: Sites and Monuments* (Paris: UNESCO, 1970).

70. A. A. Yusuf, "Article 1: Definition of Cultural Heritage," in *The 1972 World Heritage Convention: A Commentary*, ed. F. Francioni and F. Lenzerini (Oxford: Oxford University Press, 2008), 23–50; L. Pressouyre, *The World Heritage Convention, Twenty Years Later* (Paris: UNESCO, 1996).

71. UNESCO, "Status of Contributions to the Regular Budget as at 14 December 2017," http://www.unesco.org/new/fileadmin/MULTIMEDIA/HQ/BFM/MemberStates-Status-of-Contributions.pdf, accessed May 10, 2017

72. See UNESCO, "Key Facts and Figures on the US-UNESCO Cooperation," October 19, 2016, http://www.unesco.org/eri/cp/factsheets/USA_facts_figures.pdf, accessed January 21, 2017. According to Kowalski, the redistributive system of the fund has remained a problematic issue within World Heritage. Its budget initially amounted to a few million dollars reserved for heritage in danger. When compared to the amount raised by Director-General Maheu during the Nubian Monuments Campaign, the impoverishment of the fund is due to the resistance of powerful states to funding projects over which they have no direct control. Kowalski, "When Cultural Capitalization Became Global Practice." See also R. E. Wanner, *UNESCO's Origins, Achievements, Problems and Promises: An Inside/Outside Perspective from the US* (Hong Kong: Comparative Education Research Center, 2015).

73. K. Hüfner, *What Can Save UNESCO?* (Berlin: Frank & Timme, 2015), 69.

74. Ibid., 80. Hüfner states that the Obama administration tried to pay the dues but without success because of opposition from Congress. Reducing the ceiling of the assessment scale from 22 to 10 percent might motivate the US Congress to grant a waiver to the politically outdated legislation from 1990 and 1994.

75. J. P. Sewell, *UNESCO and World Politics* (Princeton, NJ: Princeton University Press, 1975); Hüfner, *What Can Save UNESCO?*

76. L. M. Meskell, "The Rush to Inscribe: Reflections on the 35th Session of the World Heritage Committee, UNESCO Paris, 2011," *Journal of Field Archaeology* 37, no. 2 (2012): 145–51.

77. B. Müller, "Lifting the Veil of Harmony: Anthropologists Approach International Organizations," in *The Gloss of Harmony: The Politics of Policy-Making in Multilateral Organisations*, ed. B. Müller (London: Pluto Press, 2013), 1–20; M. Askew, "The Magic List of Global Status: UNESCO, World Heritage and the Agendas of States," in *Heritage and Globalisation*, ed. S. Labadi and C. Long (London: Routledge, 2010), 19–44.

78. M. Herzfeld, *The Social Production of Indifference* (Chicago: University of Chicago Press, 1993); C. Shore, "European Integration in Anthropological Perspective: Studying the 'Culture' of the EU Civil Service," in *Observing Government Elites: Up Close and Personal*, ed. R. A. W. Rhodes, P. 't Hart, and M. Noordegraaf (New York: Palgrave Macmillan, 2007), 180–205; R. Bendix, "The Power of Perseverance: Exploring the Negotiation Dynamics at the World Intellectual Property Organization," in *The Gloss of Harmony: The Politics of Policy-Making in Multilateral Organisations*, ed. B. Müller (London: Pluto Press, 2013), 23–45; C. Brumann, "Heritage Agnosticism: A Third Path for the Study of Cultural Heritage," *Social Anthropology* 22, no. 2 (2014): 173–88; D. Mosse, "Politics and Ethics: Ethnographies of Expert Knowledge and Professional Identities," in *Policy Worlds: Anthropology and the Analysis of Contemporary Power*, ed. C. Shore, S. Wright, and D. Però (Oxford: Berghan, 2011), 50–67.

79. B. Nielsen, "UNESCO and the 'Right' Kind of Culture: Bureaucratic Production and Articulation," *Critique of Anthropology* 31, no. 4 (2011): 281. See also B. Nielsen, "L'Unesco et le culturellement correct," *Gradhiva* 2 (2013): 74–97.

80. L. M. Meskell, "Transacting UNESCO World Heritage: Gifts and Exchanges on a Global Stage," *Social Anthropology/Anthropologie Sociale* 23, no. 1 (2015): 3–21 Hoggart argued that "UNESCO's executive style was unmistakably French; so much so that one could fancy it had crept up through the floors from the very soil of Paris itself, or along from the nearby Quai d'Orsay. . . . The host country provides virtually all of the servicing personnel—those outside national quotas, the commissionaires, waitresses, security men and the like—and they set the tone at the ground level"; Hoggart, *An Idea and Its Servants*, 19. In 2010 an external audit found that:

French nationals (17 out of 61 positions, or 28%), and more generally individuals from Europe and North America (38 positions, 62% of all staff) are strongly represented among the WHC staff. A marked presence of host-country nationals in General Service posts is probably to be expected. The fact that 17.6% of all professional posts are held by French nationals can be considered high given the universal nature of the Centre's mandate and the composition of the World Heritage List. The General Assembly of States Parties called for "improvements in personnel requirements, taking into account geographical representation."

See External Auditor's Report, Part III, Audit Report on the World Heritage Center, UNESCO Executive Board 184 EX/INF.8. Other overrepresented European countries at UNESCO generally, aside from France, include Italy, Spain, Belgium, and the Netherlands; see https://en.unesco.org/careers/sites/careers/files/Geographical_Distribution.pdf, accessed January 13, 2017.

81. Herzfeld, *A Place in History*, 47.
82. Hoggart, *An Idea and Its Servants*, 57; Preston, Herman, and Schiller, *Hope and Folly*, 11. For a more recent analysis, see the critical 2016 British government report conducted by the Department for International Development (DFID), "Raising the Standard: The Multilateral Development Review 2016," https://www.gov.uk/government/uploads/system/uploads/attachment_data/file/573900/Multilateral-Development-Review-Dec2016.pdf, accessed January 20, 2017.
83. F. Mayor, *The New Page* (Paris: UNESCO, 1999), 80. Contrast this view with that of the United States as seen in the cables released by WikiLeaks: "We know of no other organization that is as self-absorbed as UNESCO and wastes as much time discussing its raison d'être." And later in the cable, "Other troublesome points that emerged over US objections were language that talked of 'sharing' of knowledge rather than 'transmission,' an emphasis on a 'culture of peace,' the highlighting of UNESCO's foresight function, promoting cultural industries and the continued need for the ethics program. (Comment: With no US presence for 19 years, UNESCO has adopted a lot of meaningless buzz words and meaningless programs . . .)." From a cable headed "Medium Term Strategy at UNESCO 175th Executive Board (Fall 2006)," October 26, 2006, https://search.wikileaks.org/plusd/cables/06PARIS7095_a.html, accessed January 20, 2017.
84. Hoggart, *An Idea and Its Servants*, 52.
85. Musitelli, "World Heritage."
86. Meskell, Liuzza, and Brown, "World Heritage Regionalism." For an inside view of funding and national priorities, see WikiLeaks cable from Ambassador David Killion to the Secretary of State entitled "US Opportunities at UNESCO, December 9, 2009." Killion states, "If we want important projects done quickly and according to our wishes, we will in many instances have to help provide UNESCO the manpower to do them. We will thus need to consider concluding an agreement with UNESCO to provide Associate Experts, who can

be compensated out of our extra-budgetary funds. (Italy, UNESCO's largest donor of extra-budgetary funds, for example, makes extensive use of this mechanism to place Italians in positions of strategic importance to Italy.)." Retrieved from https://wikileaks.org/plusd/cables/09UNESCOPARISFR1666_a.html, accessed January 21, 2017.

87. UNESCO, "The World Heritage Committee," http://whc.unesco.org/en/committee, accessed January 21, 2017. See also L. M. Meskell, "UNESCO's World Heritage Convention at 40: Challenging the Economic and Political Order of International Heritage Conservation," *Current Anthropology* 54, no. 4 (2013): 483–94; L. M. Meskell et al., "Multilateralism and UNESCO World Heritage: Decision-Making, States Parties and Political Processes," *International Journal of Heritage Studies* 21, no. 5 (2015): 423–40.

88. The proportion decreased to 16.7% in 2006 and increased to 25% in 2008, increased again to 42.9% in 2010, and dropped to 27% in 2012. Meskell et al., "Multilateralism and UNESCO World Heritage"; Meskell, Liuzza, and Brown, "World Heritage Regionalism"; E. Bertacchini, C. Liuzza, and L. Meskell, "Shifting the Balance of Power in the UNESCO World Heritage Committee: An Empirical Assessment," *International Journal of Cultural Policy* (2015): 1–21; E. Bertacchini et al., "The Politicization of UNESCO World Heritage Decision Making," *Public Choice* 167, nos. 1–2 (2016): 1–35; E. Bertacchini and D. Saccone, "Toward a Political Economy of World Heritage," *Journal of Cultural Economics* 36, no. 4 (2012): 327–52.

89. V. Hafstein, "Intangible Heritage as a List: From Masterpieces to Representation," in *Intangible Heritage*, ed. L.-J. Smith and N. Akagawa (London: Routledge, 2009), 93–111; C. Brumann, "Multilateral Ethnography: Entering the World Heritage Arena," Max Planck Institute for Social Anthropology, Working Paper 136, 2012; L. M. Meskell and C. Brumann, "UNESCO and New World Orders," in *Global Heritage: A Reader* (Oxford: Wiley Blackwell, 2015), 22–42; M. Fresia, "The Making of Global Consensus: Constructing Norms on Refugee Protection at UNHCR," in *The Gloss of Harmony: The Politics of Policy-Making in Multilateral Organisations*, ed. B. Müller (London: Pluto Press, 2013); J. Turtinen, *Globalising Heritage: On UNESCO and the Transnational Construction of a World Heritage* (Stockholm: Stockholm Center for Organizational Research, 2000).

90. M. Foucault, "The Subject and Power," *Critical Inquiry* 8, no. 4 (1982): 777–95.

91. B. Latour, *The Making of Law: An Ethnography of the Conseil d'Etat* (Cambridge, MA: Polity, 2010), 265.

92. Hull, "Documents and Bureaucracy"; A. Riles, "Infinity Within the Brackets," *American Ethnologist* 25, no. 3 (1998): 378–98.

93. Valderrama, *A History of UNESCO*, 16.

94. Hoggart, *An Idea and Its Servants*, 97–98.

95. See "Evaluation of UNESCO's Standard-setting Work of the Culture Sector Part III—1972 Convention Concerning the Protection of the World Cultural and

Natural Heritage Draft Report 10 March 2014," by Francesco Francioni with the assistance of Christine Bakker and Federico Lenzerini, IOS/EVS/PI/132.

96. Quote taken from his preface in Valderrama, *A History of UNESCO*, ix.
97. Hoggart, *An Idea and Its Servants*, 35. Following Preston, Herman, and Schiller, *Hope and Folly*: "UNESCO itself would have to be a jack-of-all trades, initiating, servicing, operating, collecting, preserving, publishing, storing, and analyzing. It would have to be a world educator, librarian, scientist, historian, arts council, archaeologist, social scientist, communicator, diplomat, negotiator, and talent scout" (44).
98. Mayor, *The New Page*, xv.
99. Latour, *The Making of Law*, 226.
100. Labadi, *UNESCO, Cultural Heritage and Outstanding Universal Value*. See also Francioni and Lenzerini, *The 1972 World Heritage Convention: A Commentary*.
101. UNESCO, "Operational Guidelines for the Implementation of the World Heritage Convention," WHC. 12/01, July 2012, http://whc.unesco.org/archive/opguide12-en.pdf, accessed January 11, 2017.
102. UNESCO, "Amami-Oshima Island, Tokunoshima Island, the Northern Part of Okinawa Island and Iriomote Island," http://whc.unesco.org/en/tentativelists/6160, accessed January 26, 2017.
103. The Committee at its 25th Session (Helsinki, 2001) endorsed the recommendation of the 25th session of its Bureau (Paris, June 2001) "to postpone further consideration of this nomination proposal until an agreement on the status of the City of Jerusalem in conformity with International Law is reached, or until the parties concerned submit a joint nomination." It should be noted that the UNESCO General Conference in its Resolutions 32C/39 and 33C/50 affirmed that "nothing in the present decision, which is aimed at the safeguarding of the cultural heritage of the Old City of Jerusalem, shall in any way affect the relevant United Nations resolutions and decisions, in particular the relevant Security Council resolutions on the legal status of Jerusalem." See UNESCO, "Jerusalem," http://whc.unesco.org/en/tentativelists/1483, accessed January 26, 2017.
104. See UNESCO, "Item 9 of the Provisional Agenda: Evaluation of the Global Strategy and the PACT Initiative," WHC-11/35.COM/9A, May 27, 2011, http://whc.unesco.org/archive/2011/whc11-35com-9Ae1.pdf, accessed January 12, 2017. Swiss ambassador Rodolph Imhoof, who led the audit, wrote an open letter in 2011: "J'aimerais ici, comme je l'ai déjà fait à Brasilia, d'abord dénoncer la pratique des feuilles de signatures qui conduit automatiquement à vider la discussion de sa substance au profit du spectacle. La remise en cause presque systématique des mécanismes, des procédures et des avis consultatifs qui s'en suit ne rend pas service à la coopération internationale et à l'UNESCO, encore moins aux gestionnaires de sites et aux communautés locales qui doivent bénéficier de notre appui."
105. Hoggart, *An Idea and Its Servants*, 99.

106. Nielsen, "UNESCO and the 'Right' Kind of Culture," 284. See also Riles, "Infinity Within the Brackets," and Herzfeld, *A Place in History*, 21.

107. Quote taken from his preface in Valderrama, *A History of UNESCO*, ix.

108. P. B. Larsen, "The Politics of Technicality: Guidance Culture in Environmental Governance," in *The Gloss of Harmony: The Politics of Policymaking in Multilateral Organisations*, ed. B. Müller (London: Pluto Press, 2013), 75–100.

109. L. M. Meskell, "Gridlock: UNESCO, Global Conflict and Failed Ambitions," *World Archaeology*, 2015.

110. Letter from Sir Mortimer Wheeler to Dr. F. A. Khan, Director of Archaeology in Pakistan, November 20, 1968 and another letter from Wheeler to Dr. Harold Plenderleith, International Study Center for the Conservation of Cultural Objects, Rome, December 23, 1968, UCL Archives, File Wheeler F/1/2, Mohenjodaro UNESCO Mission 1968–9.

111. Letter from Sir Mortimer Wheeler to Professor J. O. Brew, Harvard University, November 12, 1968, UCL Archives, File Wheeler F/1/2, Mohenjodaro UNESCO Mission 1968–9.

112. Ibid.

113. M. Mazower, *Governing the World: The History of an Idea*. (London: Penguin, 2012), 416.

114. Ibid., 416–17.

115. Turtinen, *Globalising Heritage*.

116. For an excellent discussion see Turtinen, *Globalising Heritage*; Askew, "The Magic List."

117. Larsen, "The Politics of Technicality," 88.

118. http://old.theartnewspaper.com/features/unesco-at-70-fit-for-a-purpose/, accessed January 10, 2018.

119. "Reform for Innovation @ UNESCO," http://en.unesco.org/reform, accessed February 1, 2017. For the UK report, see Department for International Development, "Multilateral Aid Review: UN Education, Scientific and Cultural Organisation (UNESCO)," last updated December 5, 2013, https://www.gov.uk/government/publications/multilateral-aid-review-un-education-scientific-and-cultural-organisation-unesco, and "UNESCO Rejects Findings of the 2016 UK Multilateral Development Review," December 1, 2016, http://en.unesco.org/news/unesco-rejects-findings-2016-uk-multilateral-development-review, accessed February 1, 2017.

120. Address by Federico Mayor, Director-General UNESCO, at the opening of the European Meeting on the Historical and Artistic Heritage and Pollution, Madrid (Spain), November 19, 1992, DG/92/54, http://unesdoc.unesco.org/images/0009/000941/094161e.pdf, accessed February 2, 2017.

121. Hoggart, *An Idea and Its Servants*, 162.

122. For Raqqa, see http://whc.unesco.org/en/tentativelists/1302, accessed May 22, 2017. For the salvage project on the Upper Euphrates in Syria, see M. El-Khatib,

"The Syrian Tabqa Dam: Its Development and Impact," *Geographical Bulletin* 26 (1984): 19; A. Bahnassi, "Le sauvetage des vestiges de la zone de submersion du barrage de tabqa sur l'euphrate," *Monumentum* 17 (1978): 57–70; T. Wilkinson et al., *On the Margin of the Euphrates: Settlement and Land Use at Tell es-Sweyhat and in the Upper Lake Assad Area, Syria* (Chicago: Oriental Institute, 2004).

CHAPTER 4

1. M. Vianello, "The No Grandi Navi Campaign," in *Protest and Resistance in the Tourist City*, ed. C. Colomb and J. Novy (London: Routledge, 2016), 171–90; C. Fletcher and J. Da Mosto, *The Science of Saving Venice* (Turin: Umberto Allenamandi, 2004); P. Gasparoli and F. Trovo, *Fragile Venice* (Venice: Altralinea Edizioni, 2014); S. Settis, *If Venice Dies* (New York: New Vessel Press, 2015).

2. For discussion on the Euro-American civilizational aspects of the campaign and UNESCO's use of moral authority and attempts to raise its own profile, see D. Standish, *Venice in Environmental Peril? Myth and Reality* (Lanham, MD: University Press of America, 2011). Florence was also affected by the floods; see UNESCO, *Protection of Mankind's Cultural Heritage: Sites and Monuments* (Paris: UNESCO, 1970).

3. G. Palewski, "The Struggle to Save Venice," address, October 25, 1972, in the *International Campaign for the Safeguarding of Venice Information Bulletin* 1 (1973), UNESCO Archives, file reference 069.72 Venice Part II.

4. Ibid.

5. Europa Nostra website, http://www.europanostra.org; see also Europa Nostra, "Venice Lagoon, Italy," December 10, 2015, http://7mostendangered.eu/2015/12/10/venice-lagoon-italy, accessed January 27, 2017.

6. UNESCO, "State of Conservation: Venice and Its Lagoon (Italy)," http://whc.unesco.org/en/soc/2830, accessed January 27, 2017.

7. Translated as "nobody is a prophet in his own country." For the full speech, see https://dstandish.com/2016/07/15/unesco-committee-undemocratically-calls-for-blocking-of-projects-backed-by-venices-elected-city-council-and-funded-by-italys-government/, accessed February 5, 2017.

8. UNESCO, "Success Stories," http://whc.unesco.org/en/107, accessed February 6, 2017. It is also greatly influenced by the 1965 Venice Charter; see https://www.icomos.org/charters/venice_e.pdf, accessed February 5, 2017.

9. See particularly Articles 4 and 5 of the 1972 Convention, http://whc.unesco.org/en/conventiontext, accessed January 6, 2017.

10. M. Mauss, *The Gift: The Form and Reason for Exchange in Archaic Societies*, trans. W. D. Halls (New York: W. W. Norton, 1990).

11. On the concept of risk within UNESCO's conservation philosophy, see T. Rico, "The Limits of a 'Heritage at Risk' Framework: The Construction of Post-Disaster Cultural Heritage in Banda Aceh, Indonesia," *Journal of Social Archaeology* 14,

no. 2 (2014): 157–76; T. Rico, "Heritage at Risk: The Authority and Autonomy of a Dominant Preservation Framework," in *Heritage Keywords: Rhetoric and Redescription in Cultural Heritage*, ed. K. Lafrenz Samuels and T. Rico (Boulder, CO: University Press of Colorado, 2015), 147–62. The World Heritage Centre explains that "international campaigns are much broader in their scope, more complex in their technology, and involve millions of US dollars. The Abu Simbel project in Egypt, for example, cost in excess of US$80 million. Over the years, 26 international safeguarding campaigns were organized, costing altogether close to US$1 billion." UNESCO, "Working Together," http://whc.unesco.org/en/107/#international, accessed February 5, 2017.

12. States Parties have an obligation to regularly prepare reports on the State of Conservation (SOC) and the various protection measures put in place at their sites. There is also a system of periodic reporting whereby states parties provide an assessment of the application of the World Heritage Convention. These are prepared on a regional basis and are examined by the World Heritage Committee on a pre-established schedule based on a six-year cycle; see UNESCO, "Reporting and Monitoring," http://whc.unesco.org/en/118, accessed February 5, 2017.

13. https://ifacca.org/en/news/2016/05/16/italy-squanders-150m-eu-grants/, accessed January 27, 2017

14. http://theartnewspaper.com/news/conservation/how-italy-stopped-venice-being-put-on-unesco-s-heritage-in-danger-list, accessed January 28, 2017.

15. Ibid. See also M. N. Topi, "UNESCO, Created in Rome the First 'Blue Helmets of Culture,'" ItalyUN, February 16, 2016, http://www.onuitalia.com/eng/2016/02/16/unesco-created-in-rome-the-first-blue-helmets-of-culture, accessed January 28, 2017.

16. Address by René Maheu, UNESCO Director-General, at the opening of the Third Session of the International Advisory Committee for Venice, Paris, January 25, 1973, DG/73/2, http://unesdoc.unesco.org/images/0000/000030/003063EB.pdf, accessed January 27, 2017, 4–5.

17. Ibid., 6.

18. Ibid.

19. Report by the Director-General on the International Campaign for Venice, Item 4.3.5 of the Provisional Agenda, 83 EX/29 Paris, September 4, 1969, http://unesdoc.unesco.org/images/0000/000010/001041EB.pdf, accessed January 27, 2017.

20. T. Mann, *Death in Venice* (Mineola, NY: Dover Publications, 1995 [1912]), 45.

21. "Flood of 1966," Venipedia, http://www.venipedia.org/wiki/index.php?title=Flood_of_1966, accessed January 28, 2017.

22. Palewski, "The Struggle to Save Venice."

23. For Mary Beard's full account, see https://www.the-tls.co.uk/more-news-from-pompeii; and for a Canadian broadcast describing the fighting between British and German soldiers at Pompeii during the Second World War, see

M. Halton, "Canadians Fight Around the Ruins of Pompeii," CBC, October 5, 1943, http://www.cbc.ca/archives/entry/the-italian-campaign-fighting-around-the-ruins-of-pompeii, accessed March 8, 2017. See also L. García y García, *Danni di guerra a Pompei: una dolorosa vicenda quasi dimenticata: con numerose notizie sul "museo Pompeiano" distrutto nel 1943* (Rome: L'Erma di Bretschneider, 2006).

24. J. Hammer, "The Fall and Rise and Fall of Pompeii," *Smithsonian Magazine,* July 2015; J. Jones, "Pompeii: Is This the Best They Can Do with €105m?," *Guardian,* April 19, 2016. For the position of the new superintendent for Pompeii, Massimo Osanna, in relation to problems with unions, blackmail, and obstruction, amongst other problems, see A. Arachi, "Vi racconto tutti i ricatti di due sindicati: si vendicano di Pompei," *Corriere della Sera,* January 30, 2017.

25. UNESCO, "Report on the Joint WHC/ICOMOS Reactive Monitoring Mission to the Archaeological Areas of Pompei, Herculaneum and Torre Annunziata (Italy), 8-12 November 2014," http://whc.unesco.org/en/documents/135426, accessed January 28, 2017. The conservation issues facing Pompeii are also covered in S. Bentura, *Patrimoine: La face cachée des 1000 merveilles du monde* (Paris: Galaxie, 2014).

26. L. M. Meskell, C. Liuzza, and N. Brown, "World Heritage Regionalism: UNESCO from Europe to Asia," *International Journal of Cultural Property,* 2015; E. Bertacchini, C. Liuzza, and L. Meskell, "Shifting the Balance of Power in the UNESCO World Heritage Committee: An Empirical Assessment," *International Journal of Cultural Policy,* 2015, 1–21.

27. V. Reyes, "The Production of Cultural and Natural Wealth: An Examination of World Heritage Sites," *Poetics* 44 (2014): 42–63. For additional analysis see Meskell, Liuzza, and Brown, "World Heritage Regionalism."

28. Quoted in L. M. Meskell, "Transacting UNESCO World Heritage: Gifts and Exchanges on a Global Stage," *Social Anthropology/Anthropologie Sociale* 23, no. 1 (2015): 8.

29. For a full analysis of BRICS political pacting in World Heritage and across other UN forums, see Bertacchini, Liuzza, and Meskell, "Shifting the Balance of Power"; E. Bertacchini et al., "The Politicization of UNESCO World Heritage Decision Making," *Public Choice* 167, nos. 1–2 (2016): 1–35. See also I. B. Claudi, "The New Kids on the Block: BRICs in the World Heritage Committee," M.A. thesis, Department of Political Science, University of Oslo, Norway, 2011, 53.

30. China has the largest state presence of delegates at World Heritage meetings, with an average of 29 officials per meeting, while South Africa and the Russian Federation have an average of 20 per year. L. M. Meskell et al., "Multilateralism and UNESCO World Heritage: Decision-Making, States Parties and Political Processes," *International Journal of Heritage Studies* 21, no. 5 (2015): 423–40.

31. Ibid., 432.

32. Bertacchini, Liuzza, and Meskell, "Shifting the Balance of Power"; V. Pavone, *From the Labyrinth of the World to the Paradise of the Heart: Science and Humanism in UNESCO's Approach to Globalization* (New York: Lexington, 2008).

33. J. M. Fritz and G. Michell, "Living Heritage at Risk: Searching for a New Approach to Development, Tourism, and Local Needs at the Grand Medieval City of Vijayanagara," *Archaeology* 65, no. 6 (2012): 55–62. The Hampi Integrated Management Plan was drafted for the ASI by Nalini Thakur. She states the constitutional mandate in India for local governance and decentralization provides for a legal, established, and more evolved mode of local community participation. It could be better called "a partnership in the heritage management process."

34. N. Bloch, "Evicting Heritage: Spatial Cleansing and Cultural Legacy at the Hampi UNESCO Site in India," *Critical Asian Studies* 48, no. 4 (2016): 560. Bloch describes a series of boundaries set up to manage the protected area by the various authorities involved in Hampi's heritage management, thus putting villagers within zones that had not previously existed.

35. M. Herzfeld, "Spatial Cleansing: Monumental Vacuity and the Idea of the West," *Journal of Material Culture* 11, nos. 1–2 (2006): 127–49; M. Herzfeld, *Siege of the Spirits: Community and Polity in Bangkok* (Chicago: University of Chicago Press, 2016).

36. UNESCO, "Bridge Collapses at Hampi World Heritage Site (India)," February 13, 2009, http://whc.unesco.org/en/news/487, accessed January 31, 2017.

37. UNESCO defines reactive monitoring as "the reporting by the World Heritage Centre, other sectors of UNESCO and the Advisory Bodies to the World Heritage Committee on the State of Conservation of specific World Heritage properties that are under threat. Reactive monitoring is foreseen in the procedures for the inclusion of properties in the List of World Heritage in Danger and for the removal of properties from the World Heritage List." UNESCO, "Reactive Monitoring Process," http://whc.unesco.org/en/reactive-monitoring, accessed February 3, 2017.

38. UNESCO Decision 37 COM 7 B.61, "Group of Monuments at Hampi (India) (C 241)," http://whc.unesco.org/en/decisions/5073, accessed January 31, 2017.

39. WHC-13/37.COM/7B, "State of Conservation of World Heritage Properties Inscribed on the World Heritage List, World Heritage Committee, Phnom Penh, Cambodia, 2013," http://whc.unesco.org/archive/2013/whc13-37com-7B-en.pdf, 116, accessed January 31, 2017.

40. The Historic District was listed on the basis of cultural criteria (ii), (iv), and (vi); see UNESCO, "Archaeological Site of Panamá Viejo and Historic District of Panamá," http://whc.unesco.org/en/list/790, accessed January 30, 2017. Closely linked to the discovery of the Pacific Ocean, Spanish expansion, and the history of piracy, the Historic District of Panama is a demonstration of interoceanic communication and global interaction. The site should be protected under Executive National Decree No. 51 of April 22, 2004, according to the Procedures

for the Restoration and Rehabilitation of Old Panama City and Law No. 16 of May 22, 2007; UNESCO, "State of Conservation: Archaeological Site of Panamá Viejo and Historic District of Panamá (Panama)," http://whc.unesco.org/en/soc/151, accessed January 31, 2017. The archaeological site of Panama Viejo was inscribed in 2003 on the basis of criteria (ii), (iii), (iv), and (vi); it is considered to have exceptional town planning, building technology and architecture for the period. J. G. Martín and B. Rovira, "The Panamá Viejo Archaeological Project: More than a Decade of Research and Management of Heritage Resources," *Historical Archaeology* 46, no. 3 (2012): 16–26; S. I. Arroyo, "El plan maestro del Conjunto monumental de Panamá Viejo: Diez años después," *Canto Rodado* 5 (2011): 185–212; J. de Arango, "El sitio de Panamá Viejo. Un ejemplo de gestión patrimonial," *Canto Rodado* 1 (2006): 1–15.

41. The State of Conservation report for 2013 states, "The current degree and extent of the adverse impacts on the Outstanding Universal Value of the property derived from the construction of the Maritime Viaduct and the State of Conservation of the built fabric, the World Heritage and the Advisory Bodies note that the World Heritage Committee might wish to inscribe this property on the List of World Heritage in Danger." See WHC-13/37.COM/7B.Add, p. 189.

42. Newsroom Panama, "Concerns Linger over Route of Third Stage of Cinta Costera," 2011.

43. In the 2012 State of Conservation Report, UNESCO found that while Panama "recognizes that it is a problematic project . . . it cannot be deferred as the geography is considered as a constraint to increase the growth of the capital. The new construction to upgrade the Panama Canal, a major infrastructure development foreseen, needs a more accurate communication system with the capitol. The statement of the State Party requesting the assessment of only this proposal does not allow for dialogue about potential solutions." See http://whc.unesco.org/en/soc/151, accessed January 31, 2017.

44. R. Jelmayer, "Odebrecht to Pay $59 Million, Panama Official Says," Wall Street Journal, January 17, 2017. For further recent scandals, see "Odebrecht Group Ready to Return $5 Billion Pipeline Contract to Peru," Reuters, January 20, 2017; A. Rodriguez, "Odebrecht to Pay US$184mn in Dominican Republic Fine," BN Americas, January 23, 2017.

45. Prior to the last few years it would have been highly irregular for a State Party to publicly solicit international support by paying for Committee delegates to fly to the country in question. Moreover, corporate officials would not be considered legitimate members of a State Party delegation, nor attend World Heritage Committee meetings.

46. The State Parties of Serbia, Russian Federation, South Africa, UAE, India, Malaysia, Qatar, Mali, Algeria, Estonia, and Cambodia accepted the Panamanian invitation. Before the 2012 meeting in St. Petersburg, President Martinelli talked personally with the Colombian and Mexican presidents to ask for their support

with the maritime highway. Employees of the Brazilian company Odebrecht also flew to Russia and Cambodia before the World Heritage Committee meetings to lobby for support.

47. On September 12, 2012, Panama made a presentation at the Paris headquarters, "Impact Study of the Cinta Costera III Maritime Viaduct to its Outstanding Universal Value Under the Currently Inscribed Criteria of C790 Property, Archaeological Site of Panama Viejo and Historic District of Panama"; see WHC-13/37.COM/7B.Add, 187.

48. S. Labadi, "The Impacts of Culture and Heritage-Led Development Programmes: The Cases of Liverpool (UK) and Lille (France)," in *Urban Heritage, Development and Sustainability: International Frameworks, National and Local Governance*, ed. S. Labadi and W. Logan (Abingdon: Routledge, 2016), 137–50. See UNESCO, "Liverpool—Maritime Mercantile City," http://whc.unesco.org/en/list/1150, accessed May 28, 2017.

49. Much of the argument turns on the connections between the World Heritage site and its historic links to the sea, ironically one of the original criteria for UNESCO listing put forward by Panama in 1997. In 2002 Panama reinforced the justification of criterion (vi): "[It is] closely linked to the discovery of the Pacific Ocean, Spanish expansion, history of piracy, and to the bullion lifeline to Europe." See K. Osorio Ugarte, "Los atributos del valor universal excepcional de una propiedad considerada Patrimonio Mundial," *Canto Rodado* 7 (2012): 1–27.

50. L. M. Meskell, "States of Conservation: Protection, Politics and Pacting Within UNESCO's World Heritage Committee," *Anthropological Quarterly* 87, no. 1 (2014): 267–92.

51. UNESCO, "State of Conservation: Archaeological Site of Panamá Viejo and Historic District of Panamá (Panama)," http://whc.unesco.org/en/soc/1975, accessed January 30, 2017.

52. A quote from South African ambassador Dolana Msimang.

53. Meskell, "States of Conservation: Protection, Politics and Pacting Within UNESCO's World Heritage Committee."

54. A. Weiner, *Inalienable Possessions: The Paradox of Keeping-While-Giving* (Berkeley: University of California Press, 1992).

55. The reports are available at http://whc.unesco.org/en/soc/?action=list'id_threats=71,8,72,74,73, http://whc.unesco.org/en/soc/?action=list'id_threats=76,79,75,77,78, and http://whc.unesco.org/en/soc/?action=list'id_threats=82,83,81,80,10, accessed February 1, 2017.

56. UNESCO, "Pyu Ancient Cities," http://whc.unesco.org/en/list/1444, accessed February 3, 2017.

57. UNESCO, "Pyu Ancient Cities: Documents," http://whc.unesco.org/en/list/1444/documents, accessed February 1, 2017.

58. On the topic of religion and conservation in Asia, see D. Byrne, "Western Hegemony in Archaeological Heritage Management," *History and Anthropology*

5 (1991): 269–76; D. Byrne, "Buddhist Stupa and Thai Social Practice," *World Archaeology* 27, no. 2 (1995): 266–81; D. Byrne, *Surface Collection: Archaeological Travels in Southeast Asia* (Walnut Creek, CA: AltaMira, 2007); D. Byrne, *Counterheritage: Critical Perspectives on Heritage Conservation in Asia* (London: Routledge, 2014). See also E. H. Moore and W. Maung, "The Social Dynamics of Pagoda Repair in Upper Myanmar," *Journal of Burma Studies* 20, no. 1 (2016): 149–98; P. Pichard, "Today's Pagan: Conservation Under the Generals," in *"Archaeologizing" Heritage?*, ed. M. Falser and M. Juneja (Berlin: Springer, 2013), 235–49.

59. J. Liljeblad, "The Pyu Ancient Cities World Heritage Application: Lessons from Myanmar on Transnational Advocacy Networks," *Journal of Civil Society*, 2016, 1–17.

60. Logan describes the ICOMOS report on the Puy Cities as "bungled." See W. Logan, "Ethnicity, Heritage, Human Rights and Governance in the Union of Myanmar," in *Cultural Contestation: Heritage, Identity and the Role of Government*, ed. J. Rodenberg and P. Wagenaar (New York: Palgrave Macmillan, forthcoming).

61. UNESCO, "Italy's Support Strengthens Safeguarding of Myanmar Heritage," February 4, 2015, http://fr.unesco.org/node/240019, accessed February 1, 2017.

62. Liljeblad, "The Pyu Ancient Cities World Heritage Application."

63. Meskell, Liuzza, and Brown, "World Heritage Regionalism."

64. B. Hudson, "Restoration and Reconstruction of Monuments at Bagan (Pagan), Myanmar (Burma)," *World Archaeology* 40, no. 4 (2008): 553–71; M. Falser, M. Juneja, and P. Pichard, "Today's Pagan: Conservation Under the Generals," in *"Archaeologizing" Heritage?*, ed. M. Falser and M. Juneja (Berlin: Springer, 2013), 235–49; J. Philp, "The Political Appropriation of Burma, Cultural Heritage and Its Implications for Human Rights," in *Cultural Diversity, Heritage, and Human Rights: Intersections in Theory and Practice*, ed. M. Langfield, W. Logan, and M. N. Craith (London: Routledge, 2009), 83–100.

65. W. Logan, "Heritage in Times of Rapid Transformation: A Tale of Two Cities—Yangon and Hanoi," in *Asian Cities: Colonial to Global*, ed. G. Bracken (Amsterdam: Amsterdam University Press, 2015), 279–300; W. Logan, "Cultural Contestation."

66. Falser regards UNESCO's gesture to universalism as a neocolonial salvage paradigm in which cultural heritage now supposedly belongs to all humanity according to imposed and therefore leveling civilizational standards; see M. Falser, "Cultural Heritage as Civilizing Mission: Methodological Considerations," in *Cultural Heritage as Civilizing Mission*, ed. M. Falser (New York: Springer, 2015), 17.

67. Address by Federico Mayor, Director-General of UNESCO, at the opening of the European Meeting on the Historical and Artistic Heritage and Pollution, Madrid (Spain), November 19, 1992. DG/92/54, http://unesdoc.unesco.org/images/0009/000941/094161e.pdf, accessed February 2, 2017.

68. Falser, "Representing Heritage Without Territory: The Khmer Rouge at the UNESCO in Paris During the 1980s and Their Political Strategy for Angkor," in *Cultural Heritage as Civilizing Mission*, ed. M. Falser (New York: Springer, 2015).

69. Letter from Anton Prohaska to Director-General Amadou M'Bow, September 28, 1982, UNESCO Archives, file reference CLT 1982-83, CAB 4/69.

70. H. Locard, "The Myth of Angkor as an Essential Component of the Khmer Rouge Utopia," in *Cultural Heritage as Civilizing Mission*, ed. M. Falser (New York: Springer, 2015), 203.

71. Ibid., 201. Grant Ross provides a brief timeline of Cambodian political regimes: General Lon Nol's takeover in 1970; a military dictatorship, civil war, and extensive American bombing (1970–75); the dismantling of society and genocide under the Khmer Rouge (1975–79); and Vietnamese invasion, international embargo, and continued civil war (1979–99). H. Grant Ross, "The Civilizing Vision of an Enlightened Dictator: Norodom Sihanouk and the Cambodian Post-Independence Experiment (1953–1970)," in *Cultural Heritage as Civilizing Mission*, ed. M. Falser (New York: Springer, 2015), 150.

72. Falser recounts how under the Vietnamese regime India was rewarded for its diplomatic recognition, whereby the Archaeological Survey of India was granted the rights to restore Angkor Wat. This served Indian goals as well, primarily the Indian campaign to unpack an older "Greater India" rhetoric for its restoration project. Falser, "Representing Heritage Without Territory," 225–49. See also M. Falser, "Epilogue: Clearing the Path Towards Civilization: 150 Years of 'Saving Angkor,'" in *Cultural Heritage as Civilizing Mission*, ed. M. Falser (New York: Springer, 2015).

73. Falser, "Representing Heritage Without Territory," 240–42.

74. UNESCO, *Safeguarding and Development of Angkor. Prepared for the Intergovernmental Conference on Angkor, Tokyo, Japan October 12–13, 1993* (Paris: UNESCO, 1993).

75. Falser, "Representing Heritage Without Territory," 26. "The Prince, stating that Angkor was 'not only a heritage of the Khmer people, but of mankind,' agreed to Unesco taking on the responsibility of international co ordination 'outside all political considerations.' He agreed to Unesco organizing a technical round table for Khmer and international experts on the restoration of Angkorian monuments, Unesco involvement in a survey and inventory of the Angkor complex and objects of the National Museum, assistance to the international (i.e. Indian and Polish) conservation teams and the training of Khmers in conservation skills" (246 n. 15).

76. M. Mazower, *No Enchanted Palace: The End of Empire and the Ideological Origins of the United Nations* (Princeton, NJ: Princeton University Press, 2009).

77. UNESCO, World Heritage Committee, Sixteenth Session, Item 10 of the Provisional Agenda, November 18, 1992, http://whc.unesco.org/archive/1992/whc-92-conf002-7reve.pdf, accessed February 2, 2017; K. Miura, "Discourses and

Practices Between Traditions and World Heritage Making in Angkor After 1990," in *Cultural Heritage as Civilizing Mission: From Decay to Recovery*, ed. M. Falser (New York: Springer, 2015), 251–78.

78. P. Peycam, "The International Coordinating Committee for Angkor: A World Heritage Site as an Arena of Competition, Connivance and State(s) Legitimation," *SOJOURN: Journal of Social Issues in Southeast Asia* 31, no. 3 (2016): 744. See the Report by the Director-General on the Conservation of the Monuments of Angkor, Executive Board, 141st Session, 141 EX/33 Paris, March 24, 1993, http://unesdoc.unesco.org/images/0009/000939/093904eo.pdf, accessed February 2, 2017.

79. Miura, "Discourses and Practices"; K. Mirua, "World Heritage Making in Angkor. Global, Regional, National and Local Actors, Interplays and Implications," in *World Heritage Angkor and Beyond: Circumstances and Implications of UNESCO Listings in Cambodia*, ed. B. Hauser-Schäublin (Göttingen: Universitätsverlag Göttingen, 2011), 9–33; Peycam, "The International Coordinating Committee for Angkor."

80. Peycam, "The International Coordinating Committee for Angkor," 760–62.

81. Miura, "Discourses and Practices." See papers in B. Hauser-Schäublin, ed., *World Heritage Angkor and Beyond: Circumstances and Implications of UNESCO Listings in Cambodia* (Göttingen: Universitätsverlag Göttingen, 2011).

82. J. P. Singh, "Global Institutions and Deliberations: Is the World Trade Organization More Participatory than UNESCO?," in *Deliberation and Development: Rethinking the Role of Voice and Collective Action in Unequal Societies*, ed. P. Heller and V. Rao (Washington DC: World Bank Group, 2015), 210.

83. Sir Mortimer Wheeler presenting *Armchair Voyage: Hellenic Cruise Episode 1: Mycenae to Venice*, first aired July 21, 1958. Available at http://www.bbc.co.uk/iplayer/episode/p017horz/armchair-voyage-hellenic-cruise-1-venice-to-mycenae#group=p018818x, accessed April 19, 2017.

84. Quoted in W. H. C. Laves and C. A. Thomson, *UNESCO: Purpose, Progress, Prospects* (Bloomington: University of Indiana Press, 1957), 295.

CHAPTER 5

1. For legal analysis, see S. Chesterman, "The International Court of Justice in Asia: Interpreting the Temple of Preah Vihear Case," *Asian Journal of International Law* 5, no. 1 (2015): 1–6; M. Barnett, "Cambodia v. Thailand: A Case Study on the Use of Provisional Measures to Protect Human Rights in International Border Disputes," *Brooklyn Journal of International Law* 38 (2012): 269; A. F. Vrdoljak, "Challenges for International Cultural Heritage Law," in *Blackwell Companion to the New Heritage Studies*, ed. W. Logan, M. N. Craith, and U. Kockel (New York: Wiley Blackwell, 2016); J. D. Ciorciari, "Request for Interpretation of the Judgment of 15 June 1962 in the Case

Concerning the Temple of Preah Vihear (Cambodia v. Thailand)," *American Journal of International Law* 108, no. 2 (2014): 288–95. For studies of Preah Vihear, see B. Hauser-Schäublin, "Preah Vihear: From Object of Colonial Desire to a Contested World Heritage site," in *World Heritage Angkor and Beyond: Circumstances and Implications of UNESCO Listings in Cambodia*, ed. B. Hauser-Schäublin (Göttingen: Göttingen University Press, 2011), 33–56; B. Hauser-Schäublin and S. Missling, "The Enduring Agency of Borderland Regimes: The Aftermath of Serial Regulations with Different Scopes and Temporal Scales at Preah Vihear, Cambodia," *Journal of Legal Pluralism and Unofficial Law* 46, no. 1 (2014): 79–98; S. K. Lee, "Siam Mismapped: Revisiting the Territorial Dispute over the Preah Vihear Temple," *South East Asia Research* 22, no. 1 (2014): 39–55; U. Yoosuk, "The Preah Vihear Temple: Roots of Thailand-Cambodia Border Dispute," *International Journal of Asian Social Science* 3, no. 4 (2013): 921–29; C. Kasetsiri, P. Sothirak, and P. Chachavalpongpun, *Preah Vihear: A Guide to the Thai-Cambodian Conflict and Its Solutions* (Bangkok: White Lotus Press, 2013); P. Chachavalpongpun, "Temple of Doom: Hysteria About the Preah Vihear Temple in the Thai Nationalist Discourse," in *Legitimacy and Crisis in Thailand*, ed. M. Askew (Chiang Mai: Silkworm Books, 2010), 83–118.

2. Leaked cable entitled "World Heritage Bandarin Debrief" dated April 10, 2008. Here the director of the World Heritage Centre describes "Preah Vihear as a 'total stalemate,' where the Cambodians are 'playing with words and facts.' He said that, while there are many technical problems, in fact, the issue is a political one between Thailand and Cambodia." https://search.wikileaks.org/plusd/cables/08PARIS669_a.html, accessed February 18, 2017.

3. Public Library of US Diplomacy, https://wikileaks.org/plusd, accessed February 8, 2017.

4. Cable dated May 6, 2008, https://search.wikileaks.org/plusd/cables/08PHNOMPENH372_a.html, accessed February 8, 2017.

5. "Chevron Announces First Gas from Platong II Project in Gulf of Thailand," press release, October 24, 2011, http://www.chevron.com/chevron/pressreleases/article/10242011_chevronannouncesfirstgasfromplatongiiprojectingulfofthailand.news, accessed February 8, 2017.

6. "2009 Investment Climate Statement—Cambodia," cable dated January 28, 2009, https://search.wikileaks.org/plusd/cables/09PHNOMPENH71_a.html, accessed February 8, 2017.

7. "Preah Vihear for Koh Kong and Natural Gas/Oil," Thai Political Facts Info, October 16, 2008, https://antithaksin.wordpress.com/2008/10/16/preah-vihear-for-koh-kong-and-natuaral-gasoil; "Preah Vihear Temple: Thais Continue to Support Inscription," cable dated May 15, 2008, https://search.wikileaks.org/plusd/cables/08BANGKOK1486_a.html, accessed February 8, 2017; S. Strate, "A Pile of Stones? Preah Vihear as a Thai Symbol of National Humiliation," *South East Asia Research* 21, no. 1 (2013): 41–68.

8. "2009 Investment Climate Statement—Cambodia." Utapao had previously supported US refueling missions en route to Afghanistan.

9. In several cables the US concern with China is evident: their bilateral investment in Cambodia, infrastructural projects including roads and railways, and the increasing closeness of the two nations. On December 25, 2008, the US ambassador to Cambodia expresses her concern over China, fearing that the current "'Year of China' looks to become its 'Century of China.'" She describes royal banquets, the first-ever visit by a Chinese warship, a growing assistance package, and further trade and investment ties. Cambodia calls this "blank check" diplomacy, and in 2009 China pledged $256 million in assistance; by contrast, the United States was likely only to offer Cambodia $50 million. The Chinese loans are often used to support projects benefitting Chinese companies, whether in oil and mineral exploration or infrastructural projects. See https://search.wikileaks.org/plusd/cables/08PHNOMPENH1027_a.html, accessed February 8, 2017.

10. "Scenesetter for General Casey's Meeting with Thai Army Commander General Anupong," cable dated July 16, 2009, https://search.wikileaks.org/plusd/cables/09BANGKOK1720_a.html, accessed February 8, 2017. A fuller discussion appears in L. M. Meskell, "World Heritage and WikiLeaks: Territory, Trade and Temples on the Thai-Cambodian Border," *Current Anthropology* 57, no. 1 (2016): 72–95.

11. L. Pressouyre, *The World Heritage Convention, Twenty Years Later* (Paris: UNESCO Publishing, 1996).

12. S. Sassen, *Territory, Authority, Rights: From Medieval to Global Assemblages* (Princeton, NJ: Princeton University Press, 2006)

13. Significantly, the World Heritage Centre has a twenty-year moratorium on access to site nomination files and all related correspondence.

14. "Preah Vihear: Tension Unlikely to Dissipate Without Change in Bilateral Dynamic," cable dated July 18, 2008, https://search.wikileaks.org/plusd/cables/08PHNOMPENH581_a.html, accessed February 8, 2017.

15. Thailand had considered running in 2010 but ultimately withdrew. For Cambodia, see Ministry of Foreign Affairs and International Cooperation, "Cambodia: Candidate for the United Nations Security Council, 2013–2014," http://www.cambodianembassy.org.uk/downloads/Cambodia%20UN%20Brochure%20BLUE.pdf, accessed February 8, 2017.

16. M. Kleine, "Trading Control: National Fiefdoms in International Organizations," *International Theory* 5, no. 3 (2013): 321–46; J. C. Morse and R. O. Keohane, "Contested Multilateralism," *Review of International Organizations* 9, no. 4 (2014): 385–412.

17. See contributions in H. P. Ray, ed., *Mausam: Maritime Cultural Landscapes Across the Indian Ocean* (New Delhi: Aryan Books International, 2014). Project Mausam also appeared in the Indian media, for example "Project 'Mausam' by Ministry of Culture," Simply Decoded, June 22, 2014, http://www.simplydecoded.com/

2014/06/22/project-mausam-ministry-culture, and P. Shastri and P. John, "Mausam to Link 10 Gujarat Sites to Indian Ocean World," *Times of India*, July 24, 2014, http://www.unesco.org/new/fileadmin/MULTIMEDIA/FIELD/New_Delhi/images/timesofindia_35.pdf, accessed February 12, 2017.

18. B. K. Sharma and A. Rasheed, eds., *Indian Ocean Region: Emerging Strategic Coooperation, Competition and Conflict Scenarios* (New Delhi: Vij Books India, 2015). On China's efforts, see T. Winter, "One Belt, One Road, One Heritage: Cultural Diplomacy and the Silk Road," *The Diplomat* 29 (2016): 1–5.

19. As a recent example, see UNESCO, "International Spice Route Culinary Festival and Competition," 2016, http://en.unesco.org/events/international-spice-route-culinary-festival-and-competition, accessed February 12, 2017.

20. L. M. Meskell, "Transacting UNESCO World Heritage: Gifts and Exchanges on a Global Stage," *Social Anthropology/Anthropologie Sociale* 23, no. 1 (2015): 3–21; Meskell, "World Heritage and WikiLeaks." For discussion of the concept of a resource, especially heritage as a non-renewable resource, see T. Brattli, "Managing the Archaeological World Cultural Heritage: Consensus or Rhetoric?," *Norwegian Archaeological Review* 42, no. 1 (2009): 24–39.

21. On Jamaica: "$13M Allocated Towards Designating Two Local Mountains World Heritage Sites," *Gleaner*, May 25, 2015. On Japan: "Envoys Bound for UNESCO Events to Counter Opposition Toward World Heritage Listings," *Japan Times*, May 15, 2015; Mizuho Aoki, "World Heritage Listing Has Its Price," *Japan Times*, October 4, 2011.

22. UNESCO, "World Heritage List Nominations," http://whc.unesco.org/en/nominations, accessed February 8, 2017.

23. Mixed properties are inscribed on the basis of both their natural and cultural values. Paragraph 18 of the Operational Guidelines states that "States Parties should as far as possible endeavour to include in their submissions properties which derive their outstanding universal value from a particularly significant combination of cultural and natural features."

24. B. Latour, *The Making of Law: An Ethnography of the Conseil d'Etat* (Cambridge, MA: Polity, 2010), 241.

25. S. Labadi, *UNESCO, Cultural Heritage and Outstanding Universal Value* (Walnut Creek, CA: AltaMira Press, 2013). For Nixon's speech see "48—Special Message to the Congress Proposing the 1971 Environmental Program," February 8, 1971, American Presidency Project, http://www.presidency.ucsb.edu/ws/?pid=3294, accessed February 8, 2017. Nixon goes on to say that "confronted with the pressures of population and development, and with the world's tremendously increased capacity for environmental modification, we must act together now to save for future generations the most outstanding natural areas as well as places of unique historical, archeological, architectural, and cultural value to mankind."

26. L. M. Meskell et al., "Multilateralism and UNESCO World Heritage: Decision-Making, States Parties and Political Processes," *International Journal of Heritage Studies* 21, no. 5 (2015): 423–40.

27. H. Hølleland, "Practicing World Heritage: Approaching the Changing Faces of the World Heritage Convention," Ph.D. dissertation, University of Oslo, 2013; L. M. Meskell, "The Rush to Inscribe: Reflections on the 35th Session of the World Heritage Committee, UNESCO Paris, 2011," *Journal of Field Archaeology* 37, no. 2 (2012): 145–51.

28. A. F. Vrdoljak, "Article 14: The Secretariat and Support of the World Heritage Committee," in *The 1972 World Heritage Convention: A Commentary*, ed. F. Francioni and F. Lenzerini (Oxford: Oxford University Press, 2008), 96.

29. Ibid.; J. Tabet, *Review of ICOMOS' Working Methods and Procedures for the Evaluation of Cultural and Mixed Properties Nominated for Inscription on the UNESCO World Heritage List* (Paris: ICOMOS, 2010); L. M. Meskell, "UNESCO's World Heritage Convention at 40: Challenging the Economic and Political Order of International Heritage Conservation," *Current Anthropology* 54, no. 4 (2013): 483–94; T. M. Schmitt, "Global Cultural Governance: Decision-Making Concerning World Heritage Between Politics and Science," *Erdkunde* 63, no. 2 (2009): 103–21.

30. Cited in Meskell et al., "Multilateralism and UNESCO World Heritage," 427.

31. Ibid.; L. M. Meskell, C. Liuzza, and N. Brown, "World Heritage Regionalism: UNESCO from Europe to Asia," *International Journal of Cultural Property*, 2015; E, Bertacchini, C. Liuzza, and L. Meskell, "Shifting the Balance of Power in the UNESCO World Heritage Committee: An Empirical Assessment," *International Journal of Cultural Policy*, 2015: 1–21; J. Jokilehto, "World Heritage: Observations on Decisions Related to Cultural Heritage," *Journal of Cultural Heritage Management and Sustainable Development* 1, no. 1 (2011): 61–74.

32. Meskell et al., "Multilateralism and UNESCO World Heritage."

33. Ibid.

34. W. Preston, E. S. Herman, and H. Schiller, *Hope and Folly: The United States and UNESCO 1945–1985* (Minneapolis: University of Minnesota Press, 1989), 193.

35. "UNESCO's World Heritage Sites: A Danger List in Danger," *Economist*, August 26, 2010.

36. Report by the Norwegian Delegation, "Report to the UNESCO World Heritage Committee 34th Session," Brasilia, July 25–August 3, 2010. The report stated that China established a practice of putting pressure on Committee members to garner support for decisions on the introduction on the World Heritage List for their own nominations, in advance of the Committee's treatment. Several delegations indicated informally that the situation had become uncomfortable.

37. S. Bentura, "Patrimoine: La face cachée des 1000 merveilles du monde" (Paris: Galaxie Presse, 2014). For a record of various attempts to inscribe the site of Bolgar, see UNESCO, "Bolgar Historical and Archaeological Complex,"

http://whc.unesco.org/en/list/981, accessed March 2, 2017 and Meskell et al., "Multilateralism and UNESCO World Heritage"; G. Plets, "Ethno-Nationalism, Asymmetric Federalism and Soviet Perceptions of the Past: (World) Heritage Activism in the Russian Federation," *Journal of Social Archaeology* 15, no. 1 (2015): 67–93.

38. T. Hale and D. Held, "Editor's Introduction," in *Handbook of Transnational Governance: Institutions and Innovations*, ed. T. Hale and D. Held (Cambridge: Polity, 2011), 1–36.

39. Results presented in E. Bertacchini et al., "The Politicization of UNESCO World Heritage Decision Making," *Public Choice* 167, nos. 1–2 (2016): 1–35.

40. I. Bokova, "Address by Ms Irina Bokova, UNESCO Director-General, on the Occasion of the Opening of the 36th Session of the World Heritage Committee," St. Petersburg, Russian Federation, 2012.

41. M. Batisse and G. Bolla, *The Invention of "World Heritage"* (Paris: Association of Former UNESCO Staff Members, 2005), 39. See also F. Choay, *L'allégorie du patrimoine*, vol. 271 (Paris: Seuil, 1992); F. Choay, *The Invention of the Historic Monument* (Cambridge: Cambridge University Press, 2001).

42. Y. Poria, A. Reichel, and R. Cohen, "World Heritage Site: Is It an Effective Brand Name? A Case Study of a Religious Heritage Site," *Journal of Travel Research* 50, no. 5 (2011): 482–95; C. M. Hall and R. Piggin, "World Heritage Sites: Managing the Brand," *Managing Visitor Attractions: New Directions*, 2003, 203–19; J. Ryan and S. Silvanto, "The World Heritage List: The Making and Management of a Brand," *Place Branding and Public Diplomacy* 5, no. 4 (2009): 290–300; F. Starr, *Corporate Responsibility for Cultural Heritage* (New York: Routledge, 2013).

43. UNESCO, "The Causses and the Cévennes, Mediterranean Agro-Pastoral Cultural Landscape," http://whc.unesco.org/en/list/1153, accessed February 9, 2017.

44. UNESCO, "Priority Africa," http://www.unesco.org/new/en/africa/priority-africa, accessed February 11, 2017.

45. Meskell, Liuzza, and Brown, "World Heritage Regionalism." This system is employed in other UNESCO conventions such as the 2003 convention dealing with intangible heritage.

46. Bertacchini et al., "The Politicization of UNESCO World Heritage Decision Making." Other related work on the econometrics of World Heritage includes B. S. Frey, P. Pamini, and L. Steiner, "Explaining the World Heritage List: An Empirical Study," *International Review of Economics* 60, no. 1 (2013): 1–19; B. S. Frey and L. Steiner, "World Heritage List: Does It Make Sense?," *International Journal of Cultural Policy* 17, no. 5 (2011): 555–73; Ryan and Silvanto, "The World Heritage List"; J. Ryan and S. Silvanto, "A Study of the Key Strategic Drivers of the Use of the World Heritage Site Designation as a Destination Brand," *Journal of Travel and Tourism Marketing* 31, no. 3 (2014): 327–43; B. Parenti and E. De

Simone, "Explaining Determinants of National UNESCO Tentative Lists: An Empirical Study," *Applied Economics Letters* 22, no. 15 (2015): 1193–98.

47. E. Bertacchini and D. Saccone, "Toward a Political Economy of World Heritage," *Journal of Cultural Economics* 36, no. 4 (2012): 327–52. Some of the most active and high-profile nations within the World Heritage arena from 2002 to 2013 in terms of site nominations were China (17), Iran (14), India and Italy (12), Germany (11), Mexico and Russian Federation (10), and France and Israel (9).

48. Frey, Pamini, and Steiner, "Explaining the World Heritage List."

49. UNESCO, "Decision: 33 COM 8B.24. Cultural Properties—New Nominations— A Prince Elector's Summer Residence—Garden Design and Freemasonic Allusions (Germany)," 2009, http://whc.unesco.org/en/decisions/1967, accessed February 9, 2017.

50. I am grateful to Claudia Liuzza for bringing this to my attention.

51. A full version of the debate is available at http://whc.unesco.org/en/sessions/ 36COM/records/?day=2012-07-01#tE089tABEVog81o, accessed February 9, 2017. The site was referred but has not been brought back in subsequent years and no longer appears to be an active dossier.

52. Bertacchini et al., "The Politicization of UNESCO World Heritage Decision Making."

53. UNESCO, "Frank Lloyd Wright Buildings," January 30, 2008, http://whc.unesco. org/en/tentativelists/5249, accessed February 20, 2017.

54. M. Herzfeld, *A Place in History: Social and Monumental Time in a Cretan Town* (Princeton, NJ: Princeton University Press, 1991), 66–67.

55. Bertacchini et al., "The Politicization of UNESCO World Heritage Decision Making."

56. We found that China has the largest state presence, with an average of twenty-nine official delegates per meeting, while South Africa and the Russian Federation average twenty per year. China had a 94 percent success rate for inscribing its properties.

57. For the Rules of the Procedure for the Committee, see whc.unesco.org/docu-ment/125492, accessed February 9, 2017.

58. The rules in question were 22.5, 22.6 and 22.7, and he also cites paragraph 11.6 of the Convention. Coverage of this session is available at http://whc.unesco. org/en/sessions/37COM/records/?day=2013-06-18, accessed February 11, 2017.

59. http://whc.unesco.org/en/sessions/37COM/records/?day=2013-06-24#tcyIpRz7vCJMo, accessed February 11, 2017. Estonia stated that during the meetings in Cambodia "the State Party has even been asked whether it would prefer a decision of referral or deferral and that is not good governance."

60. UNESCO, "Neolithic Site of Çatalhöyük," http://whc.unesco.org/en/list/1405, accessed February 13, 2017.

61. UNESCO, "Executive Summary: The Neolithic Site of Çatalhöyük," http://whc. unesco.org/uploads/nominations/1405.pdf, accessed February 13, 2017.

62. H. Human, "Democratising World Heritage: The Policies and Practices of Community Involvement in Turkey," *Journal of Social Archaeology* 15, no. 2 (2015): 160–83.

63. Ibid., 170.

64. L. M. Meskell, "UNESCO and the Fate of the World Heritage Indigenous Peoples Council of Experts (WHIPCOE)," *International Journal of Cultural Property* 20, no. 2 (2013): 155–74; W. Logan, "Australia, Indigenous Peoples and World Heritage from Kakadu to Cape York: State Party Behaviour under the World Heritage Convention," *Journal of Social Archaeology* 13, no. 2 (2013): 153–76. For the urban context, see S. Labadi and W. Logan, "Approaches to Urban Heritage, Development and Sustainability," in *Urban Heritage, Development and Sustainability: International Frameworks, National and Local Governance*, ed. S. Labadi and W. Logan (London: Routledge, 2016), 1–20, and the other contributions in that volume.

65. For a global study of this phenomenon, see also M. H. van den Dries, "Social Involvement as a Buzz Word in World Heritage Nominations," in *Proceedings of the 2nd International Conference on Best Practices in World Heritage: People and Communities Menorca, Spain, 29–30 April,1–2 May 2015*, ed. A. R. Castillo Mena (Madrid: Universidad Complutense de Madrid, Servicio de Publicaciones, 2015), 668–86.

66. Quoted in Human, "Democratising World Heritage," 171.

67. http://whc.unesco.org/en/sessions/36COM/records/?day=2012-07-01#tQb6x15dIskU7747, accessed February 13, 2017.

68. Human, "Democratising World Heritage," 175. Turkey confirmed that it had identified key stakeholders and that long-term financial security is under the state, per Article 63 of the Turkish Constitution.

69. See publications from the start of the project and throughout, including L. Doughty, "Training, Education, Management and Prehistory in the Mediterranean: Work in Progress on a European Union Research Project." *Conservation and Management of Archaeological Sites* 6.1 (2003): 49–53. A. Bartu Candan, G. Sert, and M. Bagdatli, "Developing Educational Programs for Prehistoric Sites: The Çatalhöyük Case," in *Mediterranean Prehistoric Heritage: Training, Education and Management*, ed. I. Hodder and L. Doughty (Cambridge: McDonald Institute for Archaeology, 2007), 95–104; I. Hodder, "Cultural Heritage Rights: From Ownership and Descent to Justice and Well-Being," *Anthropological Quarterly* 83, no. 4 (2010): 861–82; I. Hodder, "Archaeological Reflexivity and the 'Local' Voice," *Anthropological Quarterly* 76, no. 1 (2003): 55–69. For a parallel situation looking at the politics of post-inscription management in Vietnam, see W. Logan, "Making the Most of Heritage in Hanoi, Vietnam," *Historic Environment* 26, no. 3 (2014): 62–72.

70. For a selection of the work conducted between archaeologists and communities, see C. Colwell and C. Joy, "Communities and Ethics in Heritage Debates,"

in *Global Heritage: A Reader*, ed. L. M. Meskell (Oxford: Blackwell, 2015), 112–29; C. Colwell-Chanthaphonh and T. J. Ferguson, eds., *The Collaborative Continuum: Archaeological Engagements with Descendent Communities* (Thousand Oaks, CA: Altamira Press, 2007); S. Moser et al., "Transforming Archaeology Through Practice: Strategies for Collaborative Archaeology and the Community Archaeology Project at Quseir, Egypt," *World Archaeology* 34, no. 2 (2002): 220–48; S. Chirikure and G. Pwiti, "Community Involvement in Archaeology and Cultural Heritage Management: An Assessment from Case Studies in Southern Africa and Elsewhere," *Current Anthropology* 49, no. 3 (2008): 467–85; P. R. Schmidt, ed. *Postcolonial Archaeologies in Africa* (Santa Fe: SAR Press, 2009).

71. C. Luke, "The 40th World Heritage Session in Istanbul, Turkey: A Reflection on the Legacies of Heritage Policy and missed Mega-Heritage," *Journal of Field Archaeology* 41, no. 6 (2016): 641–44.

72. See Kleine, "Trading Control"; Morse and Keohane, "Contested Multilateralism"; Bertacchini, Liuzza, and Meskell, "Shifting the Balance of Power in the UNESCO World Heritage Committee: An Empirical Assessment"; Bertacchini et al., "The Politicization of UNESCO World Heritage Decision Making."

73. J. Tabet, "Some Thoughts on the Sidelines of the World Heritage Committee Meeting in Doha," unpublished paper, 2014.

CHAPTER 6

1. C. Luke, "The 40th World Heritage Session in Istanbul, Turkey: A Reflection on the Legacies of Heritage Policy and Missed Mega-Heritage," *Journal of Field Archaeology* 41, no. 6 (2016): 643.

2. This is a translation from the Turkish; see UNESCO, "40th Session of the Committee, Istanbul, Turkey, 10–20 July, UNESCO's Headquarters, 24–26 October 2016," http://whc.unesco.org/en/sessions/40com/records/?day=2016-07-17#tTf6V5Nik8-40, accessed February 19, 2017.

3. UNESCO, "Archaeological Site of Ani," http://whc.unesco.org/en/list/1518, accessed February 19, 2017. In 2008 Iran inscribed the Armenian Monastic Ensembles of Iran as "living witnesses of Armenian religious traditions through the centuries"; UNESCO, "Armenian Monastic Ensembles of Iran," http://whc.unesco.org/en/list/1262, accessed September 5, 2017.

4. See P. Balakian, "Raphael Lemkin, Cultural Destruction, and the Armenian Genocide," *Holocaust and Genocide Studies* 27, no. 1 (2013): 57–89; G. Balakian, *Armenian Golgotha: A Memoir of the Armenian Genocide*, trans. P. Balakian and A. Sevag, (New York: Alfred A. Knopf, 2009); H. Morgenthau, *Ambassador Morgenthau's Story* (New York: Doubleday, 1919); F. M. Göçek, *Denial of Violence: Ottoman Past, Turkish Present, and Collective Violence Against the Armenians, 1789–2009* (Oxford: Oxford University Press, 2014). For the Treaty of Sèvres and Turkey, see Luke, "The 40th World Heritage Session in Istanbul, Turkey."

5. After inscription, the afternoon session was then available to watch via the UNESCO website and also YouTube; see http://whc.unesco.org/en/sessions/40COM/records/?day=2016-07-15#tlfx91uOGj9Uo, accessed February 20, 2017.

6. H. Z. Watenpaugh, "Preserving the Medieval City of Ani: Cultural Heritage Between Contest and Reconciliation," *Journal of the Society of Architectural Historians* 73, no. 4 (2014): 528–55.The Bagratid dynasty, also called the Bagratuni Kingdom, was the last Armenian dynasty to hold territory within the present-day borders of Armenia.

7. There were as many as eighteen desk reviews, according to the ICOMOS coordinator.

8. Watenpaugh, "Preserving the Medieval City of Ani," 538.

9. Ibid., 543. See also A. Bilgin and S. Hakyemez, "The AKP's Engagement with Turkey's Past Crimes: An Analysis of PM Erdogan's 'Dersim Apology,'" *Dialectical Anthropology* 37, no. 1 (2013): 131–43; B. Ayata, "The Kurds in the Turkish-Armenian Reconciliation Process: Double-Bind or double-Blind?," *International Journal of Middle East Studies* 47, no. 4 (2015): 807–12; A. Erbal, "Lost in Translation: The Monument's Deconstruction," in *The Armenian Genocide Legacy*, ed. A. Demirdjian (London: Palgrave Macmillan, 2016), 212–26. Erbal also discusses the relationship between the genocide and the persecution of the Kurds as interlinked state crimes. I thank Sabrina Papazian for directing me to this literature. For memorialization among the Armenian diaspora, see S. Papazian, "The Cost of Memorializing: Analyzing Armenian Genocide Memorials and Commemorations in the Republic of Armenia and in the Diaspora," *International Journal of History, Culture and Modernity* (forthcoming).

10. Watenpaugh, "Preserving the Medieval City of Ani."

11. Article 301 is an article of the Turkish Penal Code making it illegal to insult Turkey, the Turkish nation, or Turkish government institutions. See also K. DerGhougassian, "Genocide and Identity (Geo) Politics: Bridging State Reasoning and Diaspora Activism," *Genocide Studies International* 8, no. 2 (2014): 193–207. For the murder of prominent editor and journalist Hrant Dink, see M. Freely, "Why They Killed Hrant Dink," *Index on Censorship* 36, no. 2 (2007): 15–29.

12. Morgenthau, *Ambassador Morgenthau's Story*, 307–9, 321–23.

13. Watenpaugh confirms that this listing occurred in 1996, 1998, 2000, and 2002. See the website of the World Monuments Fund, https://www.wmf.org, and Global Heritage Fund, *Saving Our Vanishing Heritage: Safeguarding Endangered Cultural Heritage Sites in the Developing World*, http://globalheritagefund.org/images/uploads/docs/GHFVanishingGlobalHeritageSitesinPeril102010.pdf, accessed May 10, 2017

14. In the nomination dossier, the State Party claims that "Ani also has a significant place for Turkish history. After it was conquered by the Great Seljuks in 1064, Anatolia adopted the Turkish culture rapidly. Great Seljuk traditions

have met with structures in Ani for the first time and spread to Anatolia from here." Ministry of Culture and Tourism (Turkey), *Ani Cultural Landscape: World Heritage Nomination File*, 2015, http://whc.unesco.org/uploads/nominations/1518.pdf, 2, accessed February 22, 2017.

15. For a discussion of the term "negative heritage" and its implications, see L. M. Meskell, "Negative Heritage and Past Mastering in Archaeology," *Anthropological Quarterly* 75, no. 3 (2002): 557–74.

16. J. Röttjer, "Safeguarding 'Negative Historical Values' for the Future? Appropriating the Past in the UNESCO Cultural World Heritage Site Auschwitz-Birkenau," *Ab Imperio* 2015, no. 4 (2015): 130–65. Röttjer describes how Michel Parent produced a UNESCO report in May 1979 that emphasized how sites to be listed may have "positive" and "negative" historical values. Parent was a major figure in ICOMOS and UNESCO and the former inspector general for historical monuments in France. While Parent acknowledged the importance of Auschwitz-Birkenau, it proved more difficult to inscribe than the Island of Gorée, for example, since it did not include architectural heritage worthy of protection from his perspective. Alternatively, Röttjer shows how Auschwitz was deemed problematic for UNESCO experts, since it did not contain built remains of independent artistic value. It is noteworthy that at the time of Hiroshima's inscription China expressed its reservations and the US delegation dissociated itself from the decision. China argued that Japan's listing potentially downplayed the fact that other Asian nations and peoples had suffered the greatest loss during the Second World War; see A. Galis, "UNESCO Documents and Procedure: The Need to Account for Political Conflict When Designating World Heritage Sites," *Georgia Journal of International and Comparative Law* 38, no. 1 (2009): 205–36. p, 205.

17. UNESCO, "The Criteria for Selection," http://whc.unesco.org/en/criteria, accessed February 18, 2017. For a recent discussion see M. Rössler, "Challenges of World Heritage Interpretation: World Heritage and Associative Values," in *International Conference on World Heritage Interpretation (November 2, 2016)* (Seoul, 2016). Previously this was set out in 2001; see UNESCO, "Report of the Rapporteur," World Heritage Committee, Twenty-Fifth Session, August 17, 2001, http://whc.unesco.org/archive/repburo1.htm, accessed March 8, 2017. In Michel Parent's 1979 report he said "Auschwitz should, it seems, remain in isolation . . . sites representing positive and negative sides of human history will only be invested with real force if we make the most remarkable into unique symbols, each one standing for the whole series of similar events. On this principle Auschwitz would be placed on the List but would not be a precedent for a whole series of similar sites" (21). See UNESCO, "Principles and Criteria for Inclusion of Properties on World Heritage List," http://whc.unesco.org/archive/1979/cc-79-conf003-11e.pdf, accessed March 6, 2017.

18. A. Witcomb, "Cross-Cultural Encounters and 'Difficult Heritage' on the Thai-Burma Railway: An Ethics of Cosmopolitanism Rather than Practices of

Exclusion," in *A Companion to Heritage Studies*, ed. W. Logan, M. N. Craith, and U. Kockel (Oxford: Blackwell, 2015), 461–78; J. Beaumont and A. Witcomb, "The Thai-Burma Railway: Asymmetrical and Transitional Memories," in *The Pacific War: Aftermaths, Remembrance and Culture*, ed. C. Twomey and E. Koh (Abingdon: Routledge, 2015), 67–88; A. B. Arrunnapaporn, "Atrocity Heritage Tourism at Thailand's "Death Railway,'" in *Contemporary Issues in Cultural Heritage Tourism*, ed. J. Kaminski, A. M. Benson, and D. Arnold (Abingdon: Routledge, 2014), 151–64.

19. Röttjer, "Safeguarding 'Negative Historical Values.'"

20. During the colonial period, more than 100,000 Koreans were forced to serve in the Imperial Japanese Army. Korean women were forced to the war front to serve the army as sexual slaves, called "comfort women."

21. UNESCO, "Sites of Japan's Meiji Industrial Revolution: Iron and Steel, Shipbuilding and Coal Mining," http://whc.unesco.org/en/list/1484, accessed February 22, 2017. Criterion (ii) refers to an important interchange of human values, over a span of time or within a cultural area of the world, whereas criterion (iv) pertains to an outstanding example of a type of building, architectural or technological ensemble, or landscape.

22. In a written statement from the Chinese delegation they said, "China has conveyed to the Committee members its opposition to Japan nominating those sites involved in forced labor while ignoring the fact and the responsibility. 23 16 Chinese altogether were forced to work under harsh conditions for years and 323 of them lost their lives in Japan. Forced labor is a crime against humanity and a violation of human rights. It's outrageous that nowadays there are still voices in Japan attempting to deny this fact."

23. Ministry of Foreign Affairs of Japan, "Extraordinary Press Conference by Foreign Minister Fumio Kishida," July 5, 2015, http://www.mofa.go.jp/press/kaiken/kaiken4e_000181.html; M. Penn, "Japan: 'Forced to Work' Isn't 'Forced Labor,'" SNA Japan, July 7, 2015, http://shingetsunewsagency.com/tokyo/?p=1383; G. Yun-hyung, "S. Korea and Japan Debate Comments About Being 'Forced to Work,'" *Hankyoreh*, July 7, 2015, http://english.hani.co.kr/arti/english_edition/e_international/699205.html, accessed February 23, 2017. This remains unresolved and was raised again in the 2017 World Heritage Committee session.

24. For numerous political intrigues around the inscription, including apologies to other groups, see "Conflict Zones: A New Spat over Japan's Wartime History Draws in the United Nations," *Economist*, May 28, 2015.

25. A. D. Smith, *Nationalism* (Cambridge: Polity, 2010), 142.

26. Ibid., 148.

27. Ibid. 150.

28. "UNESCO—World Heritage Bandarin Debrief," cable dated April 10, 2008, https://search.wikileaks.org/plusd/cables/08PARIS669_a.html,   accessed

February 18, 2017. This is a direct quote attributed to the director of the World Heritage Centre.

29. UNESCO, World Heritage Committee, "Item 7B of the Provisional Agenda: State of Conservation of World Heritage Properties Inscribed on the World Heritage List," May 29, 2009, http://whc.unesco.org/archive/2009/whc09-33com-7B-Adde.pdf, accessed March 8, 2017.

30. P. Sothirak, "Cambodia's Border Conflict with Thailand," *Southeast Asian Affairs* 2013, no. 1 (2013): 87.

31. UNESCO, "UNESCO Director-General Irina Bokova Convenes Meeting Between Cambodia and Thailand to Discuss Conservation Measures for Temple of Preah Vihear World Heritage Site," press release, May 27, 2011, http://www.unesco.org/new/en/media-services/single-view/news/unesco_director_general_irina_bokova_convenes_meeting_between_cambodia_and_thailand_to_discuss_conservation_measures_for_temple_of_preah_vihear_world_heritage_site/#.VO3ovbOsV9s, accessed February 18, 2017.

32. B. Hauser-Schäublin and S. Missling, "The Enduring Agency of Borderland Regimes: The Aftermath of Serial Regulations with Different Scopes and Temporal Scales at Preah Vihear, Cambodia," *Journal of Legal Pluralism and Unofficial Law* 46, no. 1 (2014): 79–98. p, 89.

33. T. Williams, "The Curious Tale of Preah Vihear: The Process and Value of World Heritage Nomination," *Conservation and Management of Archaeological Sites* 13, no. 1 (2011): 1–7.

34. F. Francioni, "Enforcing International Cultural Heritage Law," in *Cultural Heritage Law and Policy*, ed. F. Francioni and J. Gordley (Oxford: Oxford University Press, 2013), 17.

35. Documents submitted by China relate to Japan's bloody invasion of the southeastern Chinese city in late 1937; see J. McCurry, "Japan Threatens to Halt Unesco Funding over Nanjing Massacre Listing," *Guardian*, October 13, 2015.

36. Agence France-Presse, "Japan Halts Unesco Funding Following Nanjing Massacre Row, *Guardian*, October 14, 2016; "Japan Pays Funds for UNESCO After Halt over Nanjing Row with China," Reuters, December 21, 2016.

37. UNESCO, "Amami-Oshima Island, Tokunoshima Island, the Northern Part of Okinawa Island and Iriomote Island," http://whc.unesco.org/en/tentativelists/6160, accessed February 23, 2017.

38. Letter from the Chinese Delegation circulated at the Fortieth World Heritage Committee meeting in Paris, October 25, 2016. See also Ministry of Foreign Affairs of the People's Republic of China, "Foreign Ministry Spokesman Geng Shuang's Regular Press Conference on November 15, 2016," http://www.fmprc.gov.cn/mfa_eng/xwfw_665399/s2510_665401/t1415634.shtml, accessed February 23, 2017.

39. UNESCO, "Medium-Term Strategy, 2014–2021," 37 C/4, 2014, http://unesdoc.unesco.org/images/0022/002278/227860e.pdf, accessed February 23, 2017.

40. Galis, "UNESCO Documents and Procedure."
41. UNESCO, "Convention Concerning the Protection of the World Cultural and Natural Heritage," http://whc.unesco.org/archive/convention-en.pdf, accessed March 8, 2017.
42. Galis, "UNESCO Documents and Procedure," n. 26.
43. Ibid. Galis also discusses mechanisms by which States Parties could be held accountable. The notion of imposing a penalty for noncompliance would not be realistic, he argues, because of the "need for an international watchdog to determine whether there was a breach and then enforce the chosen penalty. In most cases, the costs of such enforcement would likely outweigh any benefits. Such preclusion might exacerbate existing tensions between state sovereignty and common heritage inherent in the concept of a World Heritage Site" (231).
44. This explains the still relatively modest rate of acceptance of the compulsory jurisdiction of the ICJ, according to A. Chechi, "Evaluating the Establishment of an International Cultural Heritage Court," *Art, Antiquity and Law* 18 (2013): 31–57. He states that this "also explains why treaties often set up 'soft' enforcement procedures such as monitoring mechanisms, committees and reporting obligations" (40). See also R. O'Keefe, "World Cultural Heritage: Obligations to the International Community as a Whole?," *International and Comparative Law Quarterly* 53, no. 1 (2004): 189–209.
45. W. W. Burke-White, "Crimea and the International Legal Order," *Survival* 56, no. 4 (2014): 65–80. p, 65.
46. UNESCO Executive Board, "Follow-up by UNESCO of the Situation in the Autonomous Republic of Crimea (Ukraine)," 194 EX/32, April 3, 2014, http://unesdoc.unesco.org/images/0022/002272/227294e.pdf, accessed March 8, 2017.
47. UNESCO, "Ancient City of Tauric Chersonese and Its Chora," http://whc.unesco.org/en/list/1411, accessed March 8, 2017.
48. "Full Text of Putin's Speech on Crimea," *Prague Post*, March 19, 2014, http://praguepost.com/eu-news/37854-full-text-of-putin-s-speech-on-crimea, accessed March 8, 2017. Putin states that "everything in Crimea speaks of our shared history and pride. This is the location of ancient Khersones, where Prince Vladimir was baptized. His spiritual feat of adopting Orthodoxy predetermined the overall basis of the culture, civilization and human values that unite the peoples of Russia, Ukraine and Belarus."
49. President of Russia, "Meeting with Young Academics and History Teachers," November 5, 2014, http://en.kremlin.ru/events/president/news/46951, accessed March 12, 2017. For a more detailed discussion of how the Kremlin has claimed to have advanced archaeology and museum practice in Crimea since annexation, see G. Plets, "Violins and Trowels for Palmyra: Post-Conflict Heritage Politics," *Anthropology Today* 33, no. 4 (2017): 18–22.

50. For Russian rebuttal of Ukraine's claims surrounding World Heritage, removal of objects, and what they call "black archaeology" or illegal excavation, see Commission of the Russian Federation, "Comment by the Information and Press Department of the Russian Ministry of Foreign Affairs Regarding the Results of the Discussion of the Decision on Crimea by UNESCO's Executive Board," 2014, http://www.unesco.ru/en/?module=news&action=print&id=556, and UNESCO Executive Board, "Follow-up of the Situation in the Autonomous Republic of Crimea."

51. UNESCO, "State of Conservation: Ancient City of Tauric Chersonese and Its Chora (Ukraine)," 2016, http://whc.unesco.org/en/soc/3483, accessed March 8, 2017.

52. Russian foreign minister Sergey Lavrov used the sixtieth anniversary of Russia's membership in UNESCO in April to hail the organization as "the generally accepted authoritative forum to protect traditional values, cultural heritage and the environment, through the deepening of a mutually respectful dialogue between civilisations and cultures." For further discussion, see L. M. Meskell, "Gridlock: UNESCO, Global Conflict and Failed Ambitions," *World Archaeology*, 2015.

53. See UNESCO Executive Board, "Part 1, Follow-up to Decisions and Resolutions Adopted by the Executive Board and the General Conference at Their Previous Sessions," 199 EX/5, March 4, 2016, http://unesdoc.unesco.org/images/0024/002439/243925e.pdf, accessed March 8, 2017. One of many claims was that during November 2015 the Bezimenna Tower No. 19 of the Sudak fortress (city of Sudak, Crimea) on the tentative list of UNESCO World Heritage sites was destroyed. For the fate of the Crimean Gold Exhibition, see R. van der Laarse, "Who Owns the Crimean Past? Conflicted Heritage and Ukrainian Identities," in *A Critical Biographical Approach of Europe's Past*, ed. D. Callebaut (Ghent: Provincie Oost-Vlaanderen, 2014), 16–53; M. Nudelman, "Who Owns the Scythian Gold: The Legal and Moral Implications of Ukraine and Crimea's Cultural Dispute," *Fordham International Law Journal* 38 (2015): 1261.

54. In a three-page report some variant of this term "sphere of competence" or "area of competence" occurs no less than a dozen times.

55. Commission of the Russian Federation, "Mitrofanova: UNESCO Properly Recognizes Russia's Stand," http://www.unesco.ru/en/?module=news&action=print&id=690, accessed March 8, 2017. For an account of heritage politics in Russia, including its stance on UNESCO, see G. Plets, "Ethno-nationalism, Asymmetric Federalism and Soviet Perceptions of the Past: (World) Heritage Activism in the Russian Federation," *Journal of Social Archaeology* 15, no. 1 (2015): 67–93.

56. J. Turtinen, *Globalising Heritage: On UNESCO and the Transnational Construction of a World Heritage* (Stockholm: Stockholm Center for Organizational Research, 2000).

57. R. Mazza, *Jerusalem: From the Ottomans to the British* (London: IB Tauris, 2009), 136.

58. Text of the Decree of Surrender of Jerusalem into British Control, http://www. firstworldwar.com/source/jerusalemdecree.htm, accessed March 13, 2017.

59. H. Bazian, "Revisiting the British Conquest of Jerusalem," Al Jazeera, December 14, 2014, http://www.aljazeera.com/indepth/opinion/2014/12/revisiting-british-conquest-je-2014121381243881138.html, accessed March 12, 2017. The "Jerusalem Operations" also included the battle of Jaffa and Nebi Samwil.

60. S. C. Tucker, *A Global Chronology of Conflict: From the Ancient World to the Modern Middle East* (Santa Barbara, CA: ABC-Clio, 2010), quoted on 1651. See also Bazian, "Revisiting the British Conquest of Jerusalem"; E. Bar-Yosef, "The Last Crusade? British Propaganda and the Palestine Campaign, 1917–18," *Journal of Contemporary History* 36, no. 1 (2001): 87–109; J. E. Kitchen, "'Khaki Crusaders': Crusading Rhetoric and the British Imperial Soldier During the Egypt and Palestine Campaigns, 1916–18," *First World War Studies* 1, no. 2 (2010): 141–60.

61. W. Preston, E. S. Herman, and H. Schiller, *Hope and Folly: The United States and UNESCO 1945–1985* (Minneapolis: University of Minnesota Press, 1989), 198. According to Larkin and Dumper, "Initial involvement by UNESCO in Jerusalem's Old City, dates back to 1967 amidst growing Arab concern over the Israeli demolition of the Mughrabi quarter and the commencement of large scale excavations or 'mythological digs' in the Jewish quarter and the southern edge of the Haram al-Sharif." C. Larkin and M. Dumper, "UNESCO and Jerusalem: Constraints, Challenges and Opportunities," *Jerusalem Quarterly* 39 (2009): 17.

62. C. De Cesari, "World Heritage and Mosaic Universalism," *Journal of Social Archaeology* 10, no. 3 (2010): 299–324. As De Cesari states, "Israel bars the Palestinian office of UNESCO from operating in East Jerusalem, and the new initiatives geared toward the protection of the endangered cultural heritage of the city are all managed from its Paris headquarters, far from Jerusalem's complex realities" (301).

63. Such consequences include the US financial withdrawals of 1977 and 2011; see L. M. Meskell, "UNESCO's World Heritage Convention at 40: Challenging the Economic and Political Order of International Heritage Conservation," *Current Anthropology* 54, no. 4 (2013): 483–94; see also R. Hoggart, *An Idea and Its Servants: UNESCO from Within* (Piscataway, NJ: Transaction, 2011); Preston, Herman, and Schiller, *Hope and Folly*; L. Blanchfield and M. Browne, *The United Nations Educational, Scientific, and Cultural Organization (UNESCO)* (Washington, DC: Congressional Research Service, 2013); J. P. Singh, "A 21st-Century UNESCO: Ideals and Politics in an Era of (Interrupted) US Re-Engagement," Briefing 23, Future United Nations Development System, Ralph Bunche Institute for International Studies, CUNY Graduate Center, New York, 2014.

64. See Galis, "UNESCO Documents and Procedure." Galis states that one "fundamental problem with expecting a UNESCO resolution of the Israel-Palestine dispute over the Jerusalem sites is that the dispute is not confined to the sites themselves, but instead is symptomatic of a much larger, historical dispute. Violence between Israel and Palestine continues today, eight years after Israel attempted to have the sites listed. The magnitude of the dispute resolution needed in this situation far exceeds the scope of the UNESCO World Heritage Convention and Guidelines. These documents were intended to protect sites of cultural and natural importance, not bring peace to war zones. Consequently, expecting those documents and procedures to resolve such a dispute is unrealistic" (225).

65. Quoted in Preston, Herman, and Schiller, *Hope and Folly*, 198.

66. UNESCO, "Statement by the Director-General of UNESCO on the Old City of Jerusalem and Its Walls, a UNESCO World Heritage Site," October 14, 2016, http://whc.unesco.org/en/news/1568, accessed March 15, 2017.

67. UNESCO, "Old City of Jerusalem and Its Walls: Documents," http://whc.unesco. org/en/list/148/documents, accessed March 13, 2017. See also the many reports to the Hague Convention Commissioners-General in Jerusalem, Mr. Reinink from the Netherlands and Mr. Brunner from Switzerland, both appointed on October 24, 1967: UNESCO Archives, Dossiers par Matière du Directeur du Cabinet, 32, Cultural Property: Jerusalem (Rapport du Prof. Lemaire), 1971–1974, CAB 7/8.

68. R. Hoggart, "UNESCO in Crisis—the Israel Resolutions," *Higher Education Quarterly* 30, no. 1 (1975): 15–23.

69. 15 C/Resolution 3.342 and 3.343, 82 EX/Decision 4.4.2, 83 EX/Decision 4.3.1, 88 EX/Decision 4.3.1, 89 EX/Decision 4.4.l, 17 C/Resolution 3.422, 18 C/Resolution 3.427 and 19 C/Resolution 4.129, all noted in the document entitled "Jerusalem and the Implementation of 20 C/Resolution 4/7.6/13." See Executive Board 107 Ex/15 Paris, 27 April 1979, unesdoc.unesco.org/images/0003/000357/035771eb. pdf, accessed March 13, 2017. As way of background, UNGA Resolution 181 (II), passed on November 29, 1947, provided for the full territorial internationalization of Jerusalem: "The City of Jerusalem shall be established as a *corpus separatum* under a special international regime and shall be administered by the United Nations." This position was restated after the 1948 Arab–Israeli War in UNGA Resolution 303(IV) from 1949.

70. Resolution 4/7.6/13 107 EX/15 Annex adopted by the General Conference at its 20th Session (1978); see http://unesdoc.unesco.org/images/0011/001140/ 114032E.pdf, 97, accessed March 8, 2017.

71. The original text stated, "Une condamnation ou une censure de l'action d'Israël paraît être inévitable si l'on tire les conséquences exactes des prémices existantes." S. Ricca, *Reinventing Jerusalem: Israel's Reconstruction of the Jewish Quarter After 1967* (London: IB Tauris, 2007), 134.

72. UN Resolution 298, September 25, 1971, http://www.un.org/en/ga/search/view_doc.asp?symbol=S/RES/298(1971), accessed March 14, 2017.

73. L. M. Meskell, C. Liuzza, and N. Brown, "World Heritage Regionalism: UNESCO from Europe to Asia," *International Journal of Cultural Property*, 2015.

74. Richard Hoggart claimed that the "more disturbing aspect of Israeli activity in the city, [was] her altering of the urban landscape, especially by high-rise building. Why was this not put at the heart of the debates? Perhaps because the archaeological charge seemed more relevant to UNESCO. Perhaps because an imputed threat to a religious site rouses feeling more quickly than most other issues. Perhaps because, if damage to a historic skyline were made an international offence, few countries would escape whipping. Perhaps because the damage to Jerusalem's skyline began before 1967; the Intercontinental Hotel, which dominates the Mount of Olives, was built by agreement with the Jordanian authorities who then ruled the city." Hoggart, "UNESCO in Crisis," 17–18.

75. Letter dated October 7, 1971, from Professor R. M. Lemaire to Director-General René Maheu, UNESCO Archives, Dossiers par Matière du Directeur du Cabinet, 32, Cultural Property: Jerusalem (Rapport du Prof. Lemaire), 1971–1974, CAB 7/8.

76. Ricca, *Reinventing Jerusalem*, 136. Lemaire was one of the authors of the Venice Charter and co-founder of ICOMOS.

77. Quoted in ibid., 143. See also the report by R. Lemaire entitled "Rapport Confidentiel a Monsieur R. Maheu Directeur General de L'UNESCO sur la Conservation des Biens Culturels à Jerusalem," UNESCO Archives, Dossiers par Matière du Directeur du Cabinet, 32, Cultural Property: Jerusalem (Rapport du Prof. Lemaire), 1971–1974, CAB 7/8. See also the Confidential Memo to the Director-General from Gérard Bolla, Department for the Cultural Heritage (CLP), June 24, 1974, Jerusalem. For more information on the nature of excavation, see 88 EX/46, "A Memorandum to be Attached to the Jordanian Report Concerning the Violations of the Hague Convention and the Resolutions Taken by UNESCO under the Numbers 15 C/Resolutions 3.343, 3.342, 83 EX/Decisions, 4.3.1 and 82 EX/Decisions, 4.4.2," 3, http://unesdoc.unesco.org/images/0011/001131/113195E.pdf, accessed March 14, 2017.

78. Quoted in Ricca, *Reinventing Jerusalem*, 143, 145.

79. Quoted in ibid., 143.

80. For a full discussion on the relationship between Israel and Palestine regarding archaeology today and past practices, see A. A. Rjoob, "The Impact of Israeli Occupation on the Conservation of Cultural Heritage sites in the Occupied Palestinian Territories: The Case of 'Salvage Excavations,'" *Conservation and Management of Archaeological Sites* 11, nos. 3–4 (2009): 214–35; C. Larkin and M. Dumper, "In Defense of Al-Aqsa: The Islamic Movement Inside Israel and the Battle for Jerusalem," *Middle East Journal* 66, no. 1 (2012): 31–52; M. Dumper and C. Larkin, "The Politics of Heritage and the Limitations of

International Agency in Contested Cities: A Study of the Role of UNESCO in Jerusalem's Old City," *Review of International Studies* 38, no. 1 (2012): 25–52; Larkin and Dumper, "UNESCO and Jerusalem"; C. De Cesari, "World Heritage and the Nation-State," in *Transnational Memory: Circulation, Articulation, Scales,* ed. C. De Cesari and A. Rigney (Berlin: de Gruyter, 2014), 247–70; N. Abu el-Haj, *Facts on the Ground: Archaeological Practice and Territorial Self-Fashioning in Israeli Society* (Chicago: University of Chicago Press, 2001); A. E. Gfeller, "Culture at the Crossroad of International Politics: UNESCO, World Heritage, and the Holy Land," *Papiers d'Actualité/Current Affairs in Perspective: Fondation Pierre du Bois* 3 (2013): 1–11. For a report detailing the long-term heritage and town planning issues produced in the 1980s, see the comprehensive report compiled by W. Logan, "Planning the Palestinian Towns Under Occupation," Working Paper 12, Australasian Midde Eastern Studies Association, Christchurch, 1989.

81. UNESCO, "Decision: 40 COM 7A.13, Old City of Jerusalem and Its Walls (Site Proposed by Jordan) (C 148 Rev)," 2016, http://whc.unesco.org/en/decisions/6818, accessed March 14, 2017.

82. Ibid.

83. UNESCO, "State of Conservation: Old City of Jerusalem and Its Walls (Jerusalem (Site Proposed by Jordan))," http://whc.unesco.org/en/soc/3342, accessed March 14, 2017. These independent evaluations, which have taken place over many years, can also be compared to reports produced by Israel as well as Jordan and Palestine, available on the same UNESCO webpage. The upsurge in reporting can be explained in some measure by "the Israeli reoccupation of the major Palestinian cities in 2002 and the ensuing widespread destruction of cultural properties—with the targeting by snipers of Bethlehem's Nativity Church becoming the iconic image of such destruction"; see De Cesari, "World Heritage and Mosaic Universalism," 303.

84. Dumper and Larkin argue that "a result of this penetration of international politics into UNESCO operations can be the influence of key players and the reluctance of UNESCO's central Headquarters in Paris to alienate its main funders. This often results in the weak implementation of Council decisions and the recommendations of its inspection teams to Jerusalem." Dumper and Larkin, "The Politics of Heritage," 27.

85. G. Murray, *From the League to the U.N.* (London: Oxford University Press, 1948), 39.

86. Ibid., 68.

87. Hoggart, "UNESCO in Crisis."

88. M. Mazower, *Governing the World: The History of an Idea* (London: Penguin, 2012), 256.

89. Ibid., 402.

90. Other team members referred to us as living "in the lion's den." In the event of an attack the security consultant had informed us that we must accept some

would die, but his job was about minimizing those numbers and buying us just twenty minutes of time before the local Jandarma (police) would arrive. We were not to congregate together or follow the road, but were to head into the fields and follow the concrete irrigation channels and wait.

91. M. Herzfeld, "Mere Symbols," *Anthropologica* 50, no. 1 (2008): 146.
92. N. Michell, *Ruins of Many Lands: A Descriptive Poem* (London: John K. Chapman, 1849).

CHAPTER 7

1. Q. Wright, "The Bombardment of Damascus," *American Journal of International Law* 20, no. 2 (1926): 263–80. See also the extensive accounts in P. S. Khoury, *Syria and the French Mandate: The Politics of Arab Nationalism, 1920–1945* (Princeton, NJ: Princeton University Press, 2014); C. Glass, *Syria Burning: A Short History of a Catastrophe* (New York: Verso Books, 2016); G. Antonius, "Syria and the French Mandate," *International Affairs (Royal Institute of International Affairs 1931–1939)* 13, no. 4 (1934): 523–39; M. Provence, *The Great Syrian Revolt and the Rise of Arab Nationalism* (Austin: University of Texas Press, 2005).
2. "The Shelling of Damascus," *Advocate of Peace Through Justice* 87, no. 12 (1925): 661.
3. S. Pedersen, *The Guardians: The League of Nations and the Crisis of Empire* (Oxford: Oxford University Press, 2015), 149.
4. Wright, "The Bombardment of Damascus," 273, 275.
5. Pedersen, *The Guardians*, 166.
6. E. Colby, "How to Fight Savage Tribes," *American Journal of International Law* 21, no. 2 (1927): 287.
7. "Russia, Syria Accused of 'War Crimes' in Aleppo Bombardment," France 24, September 26, 2016, http://www.france24.com/en/20160926-russia-syria-accused-war-crimes-aleppo-bombardment, accessed April 4, 2017; J. Borger and K. Shaheen, "Russia Accused of War Crimes in Syria at UN Security Council Session," *Guardian*, September 26, 2016.
8. J. Barr, *A Line in the Sand: Britain, France and the Struggle That Shaped the Middle East* (New York: Simon and Schuster, 2011).
9. A. Swenson, "Crusader Heritages and Imperial Preservation," *Past and Present* 226, suppl. 10 (2015): 47.
10. T. E. Lawrence, *Crusader Castles* (Oxford: Oxford University Press, 1988).
11. Editorial, "To Save Our Heritage in Stone," *UNESCO Courier* 7, (1954): 3.
12. "Praying for Palmyra: Russian Orchestra Performs Concert Honoring Victims of Syria War," YouTube, posted May 5, 2016, https://www.youtube.com/watch?v=9bohFIf4Zaw, accessed March 20, 2017.
13. Ibid.

14. A. E. Kramer and A. Higgins, "In Syria, Russia Plays Bach Where ISIS Executed 25," *New York Times*, May 5, 2016; J. Caffrey, "Shostakovich's Symphony Played by a Starving Orchestra," BBC News, January 2, 2016.

15. UNESCO, "World Heritage in Danger," http://whc.unesco.org/en/158, accessed March 20, 2017.

16. UNESCO, "The 1954 Hague Convention for the Protection of Cultural Property in the Event of Armed Conflict and Its Two (1954 and 1999) Protocols: Basic Texts," http://unesdoc.unesco.org/images/0018/001875/187580e.pdf, accessed March 20, 2017.

17. I am grateful to Ana Vrdoljak on this point. See F. A. Boyle, *Foundations of World Order: The Legalist Approach to International Relations (1898–1922)* (Durham, NC: Duke University Press, 1999); G. Best, "Peace Conferences and the Century of Total War: The 1899 Hague Conference and What Came After," *International Affairs* 75, no. 3 (1999): 619–34; A. P. Higgins, *The Hague Peace Conferences* (Cambridge: Cambridge University Press, 1909).

18. L. M. Meskell, "States of Conservation: Protection, Politics and Pacting Within UNESCO's World Heritage Committee," *Anthropological Quarterly* 87, no. 1 (2014): 267–92.

19. Quoted in S. Rosenberg, "Why Russia Sells Syria Arms," BBC News, June 29, 2012.

20. D. Trenin, "Why Russia Supports Assad," *New York Times*, February 9, 2012; H. Amos, "News Analysis: Russia Damages Image in Arab Spring," *Moscow Times*, August 25, 2011.

21. M. Mirovalev, "Syria's War: A Showroom for Russian Arms Sales," Al Jazeera, April 6, 2016.

22. B. Isakhan and J. A. González Zarandona, "Layers of Religious and Political Iconoclasm Under the Islamic State: Symbolic Sectarianism and Pre-monotheistic Iconoclasm," *International Journal of Heritage Studies* (2017): 1–16. The authors state that in "March 2015 UNESCO's Bokova issued a statement reacting to the destruction of heritage sites at the hands of the IS, referring to them as a 'war crime' . . . the following month the ISIS showed their clear disdain for such rhetoric in their Al-Hayat video filmed at the World Heritage Listed city of Hatra. The film not only shows militants using sledgehammers and assault rifles to destroy priceless reliefs engraved into the walls of the ancient fortress city, it also features a bold riposte to Bokova: 'Some of the infidel organisations say the destruction of these alleged artefacts is a war crime. We will destroy your artefacts and idols anywhere and Islamic State will rule your lands'" (10–11).

23. I. Bokova, "Preservation of Cultural Heritage: Challenges and Strategies," address at the Global Colloquium of University Presidents, "University Culture in Crisis: Diversity, Sustainability and Teaching," Yale University, New Haven, April 11, 2016, http://unesdoc.unesco.org/images/0024/002448/244824e.pdf, accessed March 23, 2017.

24. I. Bokova, "Cultural Diversity Under Attack: Protecting Heritage as a Force for Peace," The Hague, June 13, 2016, http://unesdoc.unesco.org/images/0024/002451/245151E.pdf, accessed March 29, 2017.

25. Bokova, "Preservation of Cultural Heritage."

26. Barr, *A Line in the Sand*, 18.

27. "The Bonn Declaration on World Heritage." http://whc.unesco.org/document/147735, accessed January 7, 2018.

28. "Hatra Destruction 'War Crime,' Says UN Chief in Wake of ISIL Destruction of Heritage Site," UN News Centre, March 7, 2015, http://www.un.org/apps/news/story.asp?NewsID=50273#.WNotLRKGPsk, accessed March 27, 2017.

29. I. Bokova, "Cultural Cleansing—the Imperative of Protecting Cultural Heritage and Diversity," MacCormick European Lecture, Royal Society of Edinburgh, November 30, 2016, http://unesdoc.unesco.org/images/0024/002466/246668E.pdf, accessed March 20, 2017.

30. Ibid.

31. Quoted in A. M. M'Bow, "An Age of Solidarity or an Age of Barbarism?," http://unesdoc.unesco.org/images/0004/000496/049648eo.pdf#nameddest=49643, accessed March 23, 2017.

32. Saudi Arabia is committing US$20 million, the United Arab Emirates has promised US$15 million, Kuwait US$5 million, Luxembourg US$3 million, and Morocco US$1.5 million.

33. http://www.latimes.com/world/la-fg-heritage-sites-war-zones-20170320-story.html, accessed March 23, 2017.

34. UNESCO, "People Protecting Places" website, www.peopleprotectingplaces.org, accessed March 20, 2017.

35. I. Bokova, speech at the Conférence internationale de Haut Niveau sur le Patrimoine et la Diversité culturelle en péril en Iraq et en Syrie, UNESCO, December 3, 2014, http://unesdoc.unesco.org/images/0023/002310/231070M.pdf, accessed March 20, 2017.

36. I. Bokova, speech at the opening of the Expert Meeting on Syrian Heritage, Berlin, June 2, 2016, http://unesdoc.unesco.org/images/0024/002449/244994E.pdf, accessed March 28, 2017.

37. I. Bokova, "Cultural Heritage: Extremism's New Target," speech at the Royal Institute of International Affairs, London, July 1, 2015, http://unesdoc.unesco.org/images/0023/002336/233661E.pdf, accessed March 23, 2017.

38. Bokova, "Preservation of Cultural Heritage."

39. I. Bokova, "The Protection of Cultural Heritage in Times of Conflict: Challenges and Threats," speech to the Forum for New Diplomacy, Ismaili Centre, London, October 27, 2015, http://unesdoc.unesco.org/images/0023/002351/235158e.pdf, accessed March 23, 2017.

40. UNESCO, "Eternal Sites—From Bamiyan to Palmyra, Journey to the Heart of World Heritage Sites," 2016, http://en.unesco.org/events/

eternal-sites-bamiyan-palmyra-journey-heart-world-heritage-sites-o, accessed March 29, 2017.

41. The arch also made a somewhat lackluster appearance in Florence to grace the first G7 Ministerial Meetings on Culture; see Ministero dei Beni e delle Attavità Culturali e del Turismo, "G7 Culture: The First G7 Ministerial Meeting on Culture," 2017, http://www.beniculturali.it/mibac/export/MiBAC/sito-MiBAC/Contenuti/visualizza_asset.html_1657915625.html, accessed May 3, 2017.

42. C. Voon, "Slick Replica of Palmyra's Triumphal Arch Arrives in New York, Prompting Questions [Updated]," *Hyperallergic*, September 21, 2016, https://hyperallergic.com/323978/slick-replica-of-palmyras-triumphal-arch-arrives-in-new-york-prompting-questions, accessed March 29, 2017.

43. S. Eastaugh, "Palmyra's Ancient Triumphal Arch Resurrected in London's Trafalgar Square," CNN, April 19, 2016. http://edition.cnn.com/2016/04/19/architecture/palmyra-triumphal-arch-replica-london, accessed March 29, 2017.

44. UNESCO, "International Conference 'World Heritage and Museums,'" October 24, 2016, http://en.unesco.org/news/international-conference-world-heritage-and-museums, accessed March 29, 2017.

45. B. Latour, *We Have Never Been Modern*, trans. C. Porter (Cambridge, MA: Harvard University Press, 1991), 70.

46. Ibid.

47. T. Allbeson, "Photographic Diplomacy in the Postwar World: Unesco and the Conception of Photography as a Universal Language, 1946–1956," *Modern Intellectual History* 12, no. 2 (2015): 383–415.

48. UNESCO, "Old City of Sana'a," http://whc.unesco.org/en/list/385; "Archaeological Site of Marib," http://whc.unesco.org/en/tentativelists/1717; and "Historic City of Saada," http://whc.unesco.org/en/tentativelists/1718, accessed May 7, 2017.

49. http://old.theartnewspaper.com/news/news/yemen-battles-to-save-ancient-heritage-from-destruction/, accessed December 21, 2017; for an archaeological, museums, and world heritage perspective, see L. Khalidi, "Yemeni Heritage, Saudi Vandalism," *New York Times*, June 26, 2015.

50. M. bin Nawaf bin Abdulaziz, "Saudi Arabia Is Bombing in Yemen to Bring Peace and Stability," *Telegraph*, February 29, 2016.

51. UNESCO, "#Unite4Heritage Campaign Launched by UNESCO Director-General in Baghdad," March 28, 2015, http://whc.unesco.org/en/news/1254, accessed March 29, 2017.

52. UNESCO, "#Unite4Heritage: United Nations University Joins UNESCO Campaign to Protect Heritage in Danger," May 6, 2015, http://whc.unesco.org/en/news/1272, accessed April 1, 2017.

53. Isakhan and González Zarandona, "Layers of Religious and Political Iconoclasm."

54. Ibid.

55. C. De Cesari, "Post-colonial Ruins: Archaeologies of Political Violence and IS," *Anthropology Today* 31, no. 6 (2015): 22–26; B. Isakhan, "Targeting the Symbolic Dimension of Baathist Iraq: Cultural Destruction, Historical Memory, and National Identity," *Middle East Journal of Culture and Communication* 4, no. 3 (2011): 257–81.

56. V. Azam, "Middle East Cultural Liaison Office Proposed," *UNESCO Courier*, November 1948, 2, http://unesdoc.unesco.org/images/0007/000738/073867eo.pdf#nameddest=73867, accessed March 30, 2017.

57. J. Huxley, "The Advance of World Civilization," *UNESCO Courier*, November 1948, 1, http://unesdoc.unesco.org/images/0007/000738/073867eo.pdf#nameddest=73867, accessed March 30, 2017.

58. M. Hojjat, "Cultural Identity in Danger," in *The Iran-Iraq War: The Politics of Aggression*, ed. F. Rajaee (Gainesville: University Press of Florida, 1993), 41–46; "Iran's Cultural Heritages Destroyed by Iraqi Invasion," IRIB World Service, September 23, 2013, http://english.irib.ir/radioculture/iran/history/item/151069-iran%E2%80%99s-cultural-heritages-destroyed-by-iraqi-invasion, accessed April 4, 2017.

59. See I. D. Putra and M. Hitchcock, "Pura Besakih: A World Heritage Site Contested," *Indonesia and the Malay World* 33, no. 96 (2005): 225–38; M. Bloembergen and M. Eickhoff, "Decolonizing Borobudur: Moral Engagements and the Fear of Loss," in *Sites, Bodies and Stories: Imagining Indonesian History*, ed. S. Legêne, B. Purwato, and H. Shulte Nordholt (Singapore: NUS Press, 2015), 33–66; M. Nagaoka, "'European' and 'Asian' Approaches to Cultural Landscapes Management at Borobudur, Indonesia in the 1970s," *International Journal of Heritage Studies* 21, no. 3 (2014): 232–49; T. Rico, "The Heritage of Aftermath: Making 'Heritage at Risk' in Post-Tsnumai Banda Aceh," Ph.D. dissertation, Department of Anthropology, Stanford University, 2011.

60. D. A. Tanudirjo, "Changing Perspectives on the Relationship Between Heritage Landscape and Local Communities: A Lesson from Borobudur," in *Transcending the Culture-Nature Divide in Cultural Heritage: Views from the Asia-Pacific Region*, ed. S. Brockwell, S. O'Connor, and D. Byrne (Canberra: ANU Press, 2013), 65–81.

61. A. F. Vrdoljak, "Intentional Destruction of Cultural Heritage and International Law," in *Multiculturalism and International Law, XXXV Thesaurus Acroasium*, ed. K. Koufa (Thessaloniki: Sakkoulas Publications, 2007), 377–96.

62. See also S. Barakat, J. Calame, and E. Charlesworth, eds., *Urban Triumph or Urban Disaster? Dilemmas of Contemporary Post-war Reconstruction* (York: University of York Press, 1998).

63. H. Walasek, *Bosnia and the Destruction of Cultural Heritage* (Abingdon: Routledge, 2016). Also known as Stari Most, the Ottoman bridge was originally built in the sixteenth century. Walasek documents the negative perception of UNESCO by local authorities since requests for missions were either ignored or denied on the basis of the security situation. In April 1995 UNESCO opened a local

office in Mostar and relations appeared to improve. See also "The Situation of the Cultural and Architectural Heritage as Well as of Educational and Cultural Institutions in Bosnia and Herzegovina," UNESCO Executive Board, 144 ex/ 34, Paris, April 19, 1994, http://unesdoc.unesco.org/images/0009/000969/ 096973eo.pdf, accessed April 12, 2017. The proposal was submitted by Egypt, Pakistan, and Turkey.

64. UNESCO, "Old Bridge Area of the Old City of Mostar," http://whc.unesco.org/ en/list/946, accessed April 4, 2017.

65. It was inscribed on the basis of criterion (vi); see ibid. In a 2010 speech UNESCO Director-General Irina Bokova claimed that "the rebuilding of the Old Bridge of Mostar under UNESCO's stewardship in Bosnia and Herzegovina to restore dialogue between former belligerents; the reinstallation of the Aksum Obelisk returned by Ethiopia in 2005; the preservation of the Old City of Jerusalem— all of these UNESCO-led projects are ways to bring humanity and individual human beings closer together. See I. Bokova, "A New Humanism for the 21st Century," October 7, 2010, http://unesdoc.unesco.org/images/0018/001897/ 189775e.pdf, accessed April 4, 2017.

66. M. B. Ulengin and Ö. Ulengin, "A New Layer in a World Heritage Site: The Post-War Reconstruction of Mostar's Historic Core," *Megaron* 10, no. 3 (2015): 332– 42; S. Forde, "The Bridge on the Neretva: Stari Most as a Stage of Memory in Post-Conflict Mostar, Bosnia–Herzegovina," *Cooperation and Conflict* 51, no. 4 (2016): 467–83; A. Connor, "Heritage in an Expanded Field: Reconstructing Bridge-ness in Mostar," in *A Companion to Heritage Studies*, ed. W. Logan, M. N. Craith, and U. Kockel (New York: John Wiley & Sons, 2016), 254–67. See also I. Traynor, "Bridge Opens but Mostar Remains a Divided City," *Guardian*, July 4, 2006. I thank Sophia Labadi for drawing my attention to this article.

67. UNESCO, "Sacred City of Kandy," http://whc.unesco.org/en/list/450, accessed April 4, 2017. See also R. Coningham and N. Lewer, "Paradise Lost: The Bombing of the Temple of the Tooth—a UNESCO World Heritage site in Sri Lanka," *Antiquity* 73, no. 282 (1999): 857–66.

68. G. Wijesuriya, "Conserving the Temple of the Tooth Relic, Sri Lanka," *Public Archaeology* 1, no. 2 (2000): 99–108; G. Wijesuriya, "Conservation in Context," in *Conservation and Preservation Interactions Between Theory and Practice: in Memoriam Alois Riegl (1858–1905). Proceedings of the International Conference of the ICOMOS International Scientific Committee for the Theory and the Philosophy of Conservation and Restoration*, ed. M. Falser, W. Lipp, and A. Tomaszewski (Florence: Edizioni Polistampa, 2010), 233–47.

69. Coningham and Lewer, "Paradise Lost"; A. Pieris, "From Colombo to Sri Jayewardenepura: National Heritage and the Capricious Subjectivities of Postcolonial Capitals," *Historic Environment* 26, no. 3 (2014): 74–85.

70. UNESCO, *Protection of Mankind's Cultural Heritage: Sites and Monuments* (Paris: UNESCO, 1970).

71. L. M. Meskell, "Negative Heritage and Past Mastering in Archaeology," *Anthropological Quarterly* 75, no. 3 (2002): 557–74. See also D. Gamboni, "World Heritage: Shield or Target?," *Getty Conservation Institute Newsletter* 16, no. 2 (2001): 5–11; C. Colwell-Chanthaphonh, "Dismembering/Disremembering the Buddhas: Renderings on the Internet During the Afghan Purge of the Past," *Journal of Social Archaeology* 3, no. 1 (2003): 75–98; M. Lostal, *International Cultural Heritage Law in Armed Conflict: Case-Studies of Syria, Libya, Mali, the Invasion of Iraq, and the Buddhas of Bamiyan* (Cambridge: Cambridge University Press, 2017); S. Reza Husseini, "Destruction of Bamiyan Buddhas: Taliban Iconoclasm and Hazara Response," *Himalayan and Central Asian Studies* 16, no. 2 (2012): 15–50.

72. Meskell, "Negative Heritage and Past Mastering in Archaeology."

73. F. Francioni and F. Lenzerini, "The Destruction of the Buddhas of Bamiyan and International Law," *European Journal of International Law* 14, no. 4 (2003): 619–51. See also K. Kornegay, "Destroying the Shrines of Unbelievers: The Challenge of Iconoclasm to the International Framework for the Protection of Cultural Property," *Military Law Review* 221 (2014): 153–82.

74. Francioni and Lenzerini, "The Destruction of the Buddhas of Bamiyan and International Law."

75. Isakhan, "Targeting the Symbolic Dimension of Baathist Iraq," 270. See also P. Stone, "Protecting Cultural Heritage in Times of Conflict: Lessons from Iraq," *Archaeologies* 5, no. 1 (2009): 32–38; P. G. Stone and J. F. Bajjaly, eds., *The Destruction of Cultural Heritage in Iraq* (Woodbridge: Boydell & Brewer, 2008).

76. B. Isakhan, "Heritage Destruction and Spikes in Violence: The Case of Iraq," in *Cultural Heritage in the Crosshairs: Protecting Cultural Property during Conflict*, ed. J. D. Kila and J. A. Zeidler (Leiden: Brill, 2013), 232.

77. B. Isakhan, "The Iraq Legacies and the Roots of the 'Islamic State,'" in *The Legacy of Iraq: From the 2003 War to the "Islamic State,"* ed. B. Isakhan (Edinburgh: Edinburgh University Press, 2015), 228. See also Isakhan, "Targeting the Symbolic Dimension of Baathist Iraq; Isakhan, "Heritage Destruction and Spikes in Violence."

78. UNESCO, "Iraq," http://whc.unesco.org/en/statesparties/iq, accessed May 22, 2017.

79. Isakhan, "Heritage Destruction and Spikes in Violence," 239. At the time of writing the Iraq Body Count, a website documenting deaths since the 2003 invasion, records some 268,000 people, including combatants. However, almost 200,000 are civilians; see https://www.iraqbodycount.org, accessed May 22, 2017.

80. UNESCO, "Timbuktu," http://whc.unesco.org/en/list/119; UNESCO, "Tomb of Askia," http://whc.unesco.org/en/list/1139, accessed April 5, 2017. See also A. O. Sidi, "Maintaining Timbuktu's Unique Tangible and Intangible Heritage," *International Journal of Heritage Studies* 18, no. 3 (2012): 324–31.

81. UNESCO, "International Experts and Decision Makers Gathered at UNESCO Adopt Action Plan for Mali's Cultural Heritage and Manuscripts," February 19, 2013, http://whc.unesco.org/en/news/987, accessed May 28, 2014.

82. C. Joy, "'UNESCO Is What?' World Heritage, Militant Islam and the Search for a Common Humanity in Mali," in *World Heritage on the Ground: Ethnographic Perspectives*, ed. C. Brumann and D. Berliner (Oxford: Berghahn, 2016), 69.

83. "Timbuktu Shrines Damaged by Mali Ansar Dine Islamists," BBC News, June 30, 2012, cited in L. M. Meskell, "Gridlock: UNESCO, Global Conflict and Failed Ambitions," *World Archaeology*, 2015.

84. Joy, "'UNESCO Is What?'"

85. UNESCO, "State of Conservation: Hatra (Iraq)," http://whc.unesco.org/en/soc/3328; "Samarra Archaeological City," http://whc.unesco.org/en/list/276; "State of Conservation: Samarra Archaeological City (Iraq)," http://whc.unesco.org/en/soc/3340, accessed April 5, 2017. See specifically the report of the Republic of Iraq, Ministry of Culture State Board of Antiquities and Heritage, World Heritage Department, The High Commission for Managing World Heritage Sites in Iraq (Hatra-Ashur- Samarra), "State of Conservation Report 2016," prepared by Abdul Razzak Aboudi and Dr. Ayad Kadhum Dawood. See also Isakhan, "Targeting the Symbolic Dimension of Baathist Iraq."

86. Republic of Iraq, "State of Conservation Report 2016," 21.

87. H. Z. Watenpaugh, "Cultural Heritage and the Arab Spring: War over Culture, Culture of War and Culture War," *International Journal of Islamic Architecture* 5, no. 2 (2016): 245–63; N. Rabbat, "Heritage as a Right: Heritage and the Arab Spring," *International Journal of Islamic Architecture* 5, no. 2 (2016): 267–78.

88. For research into the 1954 Hague Convention, see S. Van der Auwera, "'Culture for Development' and the UNESCO Policy on the Protection of Cultural Property During Armed Conflict," *International Journal of Cultural Policy* 20, no. 3 (2014): 245–60; S. Van der Auwera, "UNESCO and the Protection of Cultural Property During Armed Conflict," *International Journal of Cultural Policy* 19, no. 1 (2013): 1–19; A. F. Vrdoljak, "Challenges for International Cultural Heritage Law," in *Blackwell Companion to the New Heritage Studies*, ed. W. Logan, M. N. Craith, and U. Kockel (New York: Wiley Blackwell, 2016); M. Frulli, "The Criminalization of Offences Against Cultural Heritage in Times of Armed Conflict: The Quest for Consistency," *European Journal of International Law* 22, no. 1 (2011): 203–17; P. Gerstenblith, "Beyond the 1954 Hague Convention," in *Cultural Awareness in the Military: Developments and Implications for Future Humanitarian Cooperation*, ed. R. Albro and B. Ivey (New York: Palgrave Macmillan, 2014), 83–98.

89. C54/16/11.Com/5 Paris, 22 November 2016, Committee for the Protection of Cultural Property in the Event of Armed Conflict, Eleventh Meeting, UNESCO Headquarters, Paris 8–9 December 2016.

90. UNESCO, "Tomb of Askia," http://whc.unesco.org/en/list/1139, accessed April 3, 2017.

91. On the earlier events, see F. Valderrama, *A History of UNESCO* (Paris: UNESCO, 1995), 246. In 2011 the vote to extend UNESCO membership to Palestine was passed 107 to 14, with 52 abstentions.

92. C. De Cesari, "World Heritage and the Nation-State," in *Transnational Memory: Circulation, Articulation, Scales,* ed. C. De Cesari and A. Rigney (Berlin: de Gruyter, 2014), 252.

93. UNESCO, "Birthplace of Jesus: Church of the Nativity and the Pilgrimage Route, Bethlehem," http://whc.unesco.org/en/list/1433, accessed April 3, 2017. Dual listing ensures more immediate international technical and financial assistance for properties under threat. This step was also taken with Angkor Wat, Cambodia; the Minaret and Archaeological Remains of Jam, Afghanistan; Cultural Landscape and Archaeological Remains of the Bamiyan Valley, Afghanistan; and Bam and Its Cultural Landscape, Iran.

94. Palestine ICOMOS, "Palestine: Destruction in the West Bank, April 2002," *Heritage at Risk* 2002/2003 (2015): 157–60.

95. Between 1997 and 2000, Bethlehem was the focus of a major restoration project known as Bethlehem 2000. Over US $100 million was invested by more than a dozen countries, international organizations, including the World Bank and the United Nations Development Programme, and other donors, to refurbish buildings, restore archaeological sites, pave streets and squares, rehabilitate water lines and sewage systems, and develop tourism.

96. De Cesari, "World Heritage and the Nation-State," 248.

97. UNESCO Office in Ramallah, "Cultural Heritage," http://www.unesco.org/new/en/ramallah/culture/cultural-heritage, accessed April 2, 2017.

98. Jerusalem Southern Terraced Landscape World Heritage Site Emergency Nomination, Ministry of Tourism and Antiquities, Department of Antiquities and Cultural Heritage, Palestine, 2012.

99. W. Logan, "Planning the Palestinian Towns Under Occupation," Working Paper 12, Australasian Midde Eastern Studies Association, Christchurch, 1989.

100. R. Barnard and H. Muamer, "Ongoing Dispossession and a Heritage of Resistance," in *The Politics and Power of Tourism in Palestine,* ed. R. K. Isaac, C. M. Hall, and F. Higgins-Desbiolles (Abingdon: Routledge, 2015), 63; K. Reynolds, "Palestinian Agriculture and the Israeli Separation Barrier: The Mismatch of Biopolitics and Chronopolitics with the Environment and Human Survival," *International Journal of Environmental Studies* 72, no. 2 (2015): 237–55.

101. De Cesari, "World Heritage and the Nation-State," 250–51.

102. In the report ICOMOS refers initially to a wall or separation wall, then a "wall/fence," then more frequently a "fence." The word fence is used 32 times. ICOMOS state that it "was confirmed that the barrier would be a Fence rather

than a Wall." See the Advisory Body evaluation, http://whc.unesco.org/en/list/ 1492/documents, accessed May 21, 2017.

103. UNESCO, "38th Session of the Committee, Doha, Qatar, 15–25 June 2014," http://whc.unesco.org/en/sessions/38COM/records/?day=2014-06-20#tr9DHtAPostU4876, accessed April 2, 2017.

104. UNESCO, "Palestine: Land of Olives and Vines—Cultural Landscape of Southern Jerusalem, Battir," http://whc.unesco.org/en/list/1492, accessed April 2, 2017.

105. M. T. Obidallah, "Saving the Roman Water System and the Terraced Landscape of Battir, Palestine," in *The UNESCO World Heritage and the Role of Civil Society. Proceedings of the International Conference Bonn 2015*, ed. S. Doempke (Berlin: World Heritage Watch, 2015), 136–39.

106. Letter from the Delegation of Palestine to the Director-General of the World Heritage Center, March 9, 2017, Hebron/Al-Khalil Old Town (Palestine), request for changing the procedure of submission of its nomination dossier.

107. "UNESCO Chief Regrets United States Decision to Withhold Funding," UN News Centre, November 2, 2011, http://www.un.org/apps/news/story. asp?NewsID=40286#.WOJiFhJ97sk, accessed April 2, 2017. Quoting the State Department, she recalled that "US engagement with UNESCO serves a wide range of our national interests on education, science, culture and communications issues . . . we will work with Congress to ensure that US interests and influence are preserved."

108. Two aspects of federal law obliged the State Department to terminate its funding to UNESCO. The first is a 1990 law that bans the appropriation of funds "for the United Nations or any specialized agency thereof which accords the Palestine Liberation Organization the same standing as a member state." The second is a 1994 law barring Congress from funding "any affiliated organization of the United Nations which grants full membership as a state to any organization or group that does not have the internationally recognized attributes of statehood."

109. W. H. C. Laves and C. A. Thomson, *UNESCO: Purpose, Progress, Prospects* (Bloomington: University of Indiana Press, 1957), 330.

110. Back in 1947 the CIA was secretly investigating UNESCO activities. In one top secret document dated February 7, 1947, the CIA alleged that British UNESCO official Professor Joseph Needham (Huxley's colleague from Cambridge) was working to establish "listening posts" to record classified discussions "with respect to developments in nuclear science." See C. Dorn and K. Ghodsee, "The Cold War Politicization of Literacy: Communism, UNESCO, and the World Bank," *Journal of the Society for Historians of American Foreign Relations* 36, no. 2 (2012): 373–98. Extensive coverage can be found in W. Preston, E. S. Herman, and H. Schiller, *Hope and Folly: The United States and UNESCO 1945–1985* (Minneapolis: University of Minnesota Press, 1989).

111. Valderrama, *A History of UNESCO*, 294.

112. Preston, Herman, and Schiller, *Hope and Folly*, 198.

113. Address by Amadou-Mahtar M'Bow at the ceremony for the award of the Insignia of Grand Cross of the Ordre du Mérite Diplomatique by the Institut des Relations Diplomatiques, Brussels, 12 June 1987, UNESCO DG/87/21, http://unesdoc.unesco.org/images/0007/000752/075278eb.pdf,   accessed January 14, 2017.

114. B. Hocking, "Words and Deeds: Why America Left Unesco," *The World Today* 41, no. 4 (1985): 75–78. For the original US report, see Committee on Foreign Affairs, *Assessment of US-UNESCO Relations, 1984: Report of a Staff Study Mission to Paris-UNESCO to the Committee on Foreign Affairs House of Representatives* (Washington: GPO, 1985).

115. T. L. Hughes, "The Twilight of Internationalism," *Foreign Policy*, no. 61 (1985): 25–48. p, 25.

116. General Smuts made this comment to reporters this after the 1945 San Francisco Conference where the United Nations Declaration was signed by forty-six nations; cited in G. Murray, *From the League to the U.N.* (London: Oxford University Press, 1948), 160.

117. W. Y. Adams, "The Nubian Archaeological Campaigns of 1959–1969: Myths and Realities, Successes and Failures," in *Etudes nubiennes. Conférence de Geneve. Actes du VIIe Congres International d'Etudes Nubiennes* (Geneva, 1992), 4. Adams suggested that we had to "set aside the carefully nurtured public images as well as the accidentally nurtured misconceptions, and to consider what really did happen between 1959 and 1969; also why and how it happened."

118. M. Herzfeld, "Mere Symbols," *Anthropologica* 50, no. 1 (2008): 141–55. For an example of Japanese heritage understandings as oppositional to UNESCO, see J. Sand, "Japan's Monument Problem: Ise Shrine as Metaphor," *Past and Present* 226, suppl. 10 (2015): 126–52.

CHAPTER 8

1. Rome Statute of the International Criminal Court, http://legal.un.org/icc/statute/99_corr/cstatute.htm, accessed April 25, 2017.

2. Human Rights Watch, "Mali: Abuses Spread South," February 19, 2016, https://www.hrw.org/news/2016/02/19/mali-abuses-spread-south;   FIDH, "War Crimes in North Mali," https://www.fidh.org/IMG/pdf/mali592ang.pdf, accessed April 26, 2017.

3. For discussion, see F. Francioni and F. Lenzerini, "The Destruction of the Buddhas of Bamiyan and International Law," *European Journal of International Law* 14, no. 4 (2003): 619–51; F. Lenzerini, "The UNESCO Declaration Concerning the Intentional Destruction of Cultural Heritage: One Step Forward and Two Steps Back," *Italian Yearbook of International Law* 13

(2003): 131–45; J. Brosché et al., "Heritage Under Attack: Motives for Targeting Cultural Property During Armed Conflict," *International Journal of Heritage Studies* 23, no. 3 (2017): 248–60; B. Drazewska, "The Human Dimension of the Protection of the Cultural Heritage from Destruction During Armed Conflicts," *International Journal of Cultural Property* 22, no. 2-3 (2015): 205–28; A. F. Vrdoljak, "Challenges for International Cultural Heritage Law," in *Blackwell Companion to the New Heritage Studies*, ed. W. Logan, M. N. Craith, and U. Kockel (New York: Wiley Blackwell, 2015); P. Gerstenblith, "The Destruction of Cultural Heritage: A Crime Against Property or a Crime Against People?," *John Marshall Review of Intellectual Property Law* 15, no. 3 (2016): 337–93.

4. B. Isakhan, "The Iraq Legacies and the Roots of the 'Islamic State,'" in *The Legacy of Iraq: From the 2003 War to the "Islamic State,"* ed. B. Isakhan (Edinburgh: Edinburgh University Press, 2015), 223.

5. J. Barr, *A Line in the Sand: Britain, France and the Struggle that Shaped the Middle East* (New York: Simon and Schuster, 2011), 12. For an excellent account of ISIS and its history, see F. A. Gerges, *Isis: A History* (Princeton, NJ: Princeton University Press, 2017).

6. T. A. Benjaminsen and G. Berge, "Myths of Timbuktu: From African El Dorado to Desertification," *International Journal of Political Economy* 34, no. 1 (2004): 31–59.

7. Quoting Erica Bussey, senior legal advisor at Amnesty International; see Amnesty International UK, "Landmark ICC Verdict Must Be First Step to Broader Justice in Mali Conflict," September 26, 2016, https://www.amnesty.org.uk/press-releases/landmark-icc-verdict-must-be-first-step-broader-justice-mali-conflict, accessed April 23, 2017.

8. See the many speeches by UNESCO Director-General Irina Bokova: "Cultural Heritage: Extremism's New Target," London, July 1, 2015; "Culture and Countering Violent Extremism," New York, September 28, 2015; "Protecting Cultural Heritage in Times of Conflict," The Hague, June 13, 2016; "Preservation of Cultural Heritage: Challenges and Strategies," New Haven, CT, April 11, 2016.

9. UNESCO, "Timbuktu," http://whc.unesco.org/en/list/119, accessed April 23, 2017.

10. UNESCO, "Timbuktu: Documents," esp. Document 119rev-ICOMOS-131-en.pdf, at http://whc.unesco.org/en/list/119/documents, accessed April 23, 2017.

11. See the UNESCO site nomination for a fuller description of building, demolition and rebuilding practices, such as the following: "Built in the 14th century, the Sankore Mosque was, like the Djingareyber Mosque, restored by the Imam Al Aqib between 1578 and 1582. He had the sanctuary demolished and rebuilt according to the dimensions of the Kaaba of the Mecca." UNESCO, "Timbuktu."

12. A consultant stated that the "voluntary system in force contributes to the rapid degradation of traditional technology. The poor quality of the mud construction materials ('banco') prepared and applied each year by inexpert hands causes water infiltration and attack by micro-organisms, and this attempt at creating a protective coating for the building also tends to weaken its structure." The report recommends a method of intervention involving the local population that, since the construction of the mosques, has been responsible for their upkeep, thus perpetuating a living religious culture. See UNESCO, "Decision: CONF 001 VI.B, Timbuktu (Mali)," 1994, http://whc.unesco.org/en/decisions/5439, accessed April 27, 2017.

13. UNESCO, "Tomb of Askia," http://whc.unesco.org/en/list/1139, accessed April 27, 2017.

14. UNESCO, "Decision: 36 COM 7B.106, Mali World Heritage Properties (Mali)," 2012, http://whc.unesco.org/en/decisions/4767, accessed April 27, 2017.

15. T. Pakenham, *The Scramble for Africa* (New York: Avon Books, 1992).

16. UNESCO compounded this scenario when it embarked on its global "missions for monuments" in 1970 by only identifying three African projects: two in Cameroon and one in Ethiopia. See UNESCO, *Protection of Mankind's Cultural Heritage: Sites and Monuments* (Paris: UNESCO, 1970).

17. M. Lostal, *International Cultural Heritage Law in Armed Conflict: Case-Studies of Syria, Libya, Mali, the Invasion of Iraq, and the Buddhas of Bamiyan* (Cambridge: Cambridge University Press, 2017).

18. He was held criminally responsible under Article 25(3)(a) as a direct co-perpetrator, Article 25(3)(b) for soliciting and inducing the commission of the crime, Article 25(3)(c) for facilitating the commission of such a crime by aiding, abetting or otherwise assisting, and Article 25(3)(d) for contributing in any other way to the commission of such a crime by a group of persons acting with a common purpose. Those historic monuments include the Sidi Mahmoud Ben Omar Mohamed Aquit Mausoleum, the Sheikh Mohamed Mahmoud Al Arawani Mausoleum, the Sheikh Sidi El Mokhtar Ben Sidi Mouhammad Al Kabir Al Kounti Mausoleum, the Alpha Moya Mausoleum, the Sheikh Muhammad El Micky Mausoleum, the Sheikh Abdoul Kassim Attouaty Mausoleum, the Sheikh Sidi Ahmed Ben Amar Arragadi Mausoleum, the Sidi Yahia Mosque (the door), and the Bahaber Babadié Mausoleum and the Ahamed Fulane Mausoleum, both adjoining the Djingareyber Mosque. ICC-01/12-01/15, Trial Chamber VIII, "Situation in the Republic of Mali in the Case of the Prosecutor v. Ahmad Al Faqi Al Mahdi."

19. ICC, "Summary of the Judgment and Sentence in the Case of the Prosecutor v. Ahmad Al Faq Al Mahdi," https://www.icc-cpi.int/itemsDocuments/160926Al-MahdiSummary.pdf, accessed April 27, 2017.

20. ICC, "Al Mahdi Case: Opening Statement, ICC Prosecutor Fatou Bensouda, 22 August 2016," YouTube, posted August 22, 2016, https://www.youtube.com/wat

ch?v=b69iOzQoFBY&index=23&list=PLz3-Py_E3klC-PQD5bevpop6kgwvaYn-Q, accessed April 22, 2017.

21. Agreement, ICC-01/12-01/15-78-Anx1-tENG-Red, paras. 66–72; ICC-01/12-01/15, Trial Chamber VIII, "Situation in the Republic of Mali in the Case of the Prosecutor v. Ahmad Al Faqi Al Mahdi: Public Judgment and Sentence," September 27, 2016, https://www.icc-cpi.int/CourtRecords/CR2016_07244. PDF, accessed April 23, 2017.

22. M. Douglas, *Purity and Danger: An Analysis of the Concepts of Pollution and Taboo* (London: Routledge, 1966), 36. For a discussion of these ideas in relation to space and architecture, see B. Campkin, "Placing 'Matter Out of Place': Purity and Danger as Evidence for Architecture and Urbanism," *Architectural Theory Review* 18, no. 1 (2013): 46–61.

23. Douglas, *Purity and Danger*, 40.

24. For different responses in the community, see A. O. Sidi, "Maintaining Timbuktu's Unique Tangible and Intangible Heritage," *International Journal of Heritage Studies* 18, no. 3 (2012): 324–31.

25. Douglas, *Purity and Danger*, 38, 164.

26. According to Isakahan and Gonzalez Zarandona, the Wahhabi sect subscribes to the broader Islamic belief in *tawhid* (monotheism). In the most extreme iterations this belief can be used to justify targeting the *kuffar* (unbeliever), including those who commit *shirk* (idolatry) or are accused of practicing *mushrikin* (those who associate others with God, such as polytheists). Several extremist Salafi/Wahhabi movements have sought to eradicate any rival sect within Islam (Sufi, Shia), alternative religions, or pre-monotheistic cults. This is heightened when such beliefs include the active worship of images or structures, as in the case of Timbuktu, that undermine the oneness of God and ultimately lead to the grave sin of idolatry. B. Isakhan and J. A. González Zarandona, "Layers of Religious and Political Iconoclasm Under the Islamic State: Symbolic Sectarianism and Pre-monotheistic Iconoclasm," *International Journal of Heritage Studies* (2017): 1–16.

27. Taken from line 274 of the transcript to line 275. August 23, 2016, CR2016_05772.

28. Taken from transcript ICC-01/12-01/15, August 22, 2016, Trial Chamber VIII, "Situation in the Republic of Mali in the Case of the Prosecutor v. Ahmad Al Faqi Al Mahdi," https://www.icc-cpi.int/Transcripts/CR2016_05767.PDF, accessed April 26, 2017.

29. M. E. Badar, "Islamic Law (Shari'a) and the Jurisdiction of the International Criminal Court," *Leiden Journal of International Law* 24, no. 2 (2011): 411. See also A. E. Nassar, "The International Criminal Court and the Applicability of International Jurisdiction Under Islamic Law," *Chicago Journal of International Law* 4, no. 2 (2003): 587–96; D. J. Veintimilla, "Islamic Law and War Crimes

Trials: The Possibility and Challenges of a War Crimes Tribunal Against the Assad Regime and ISIL," *Cornell International Law Journal* 49 (2016): 497–519.

30. ICC-01/12-01/15, Trial Chamber VIII, "Situation in the Republic of Mali in the Case of the Prosecutor v. Ahmad Al Faqi Al Mahdi," August 22, 2016, https://www.icc-cpi.int/Transcripts/CR2016_05767.PDF, accessed April 26, 2017.

31. Cited in L. M. Meskell, "Gridlock: UNESCO, Global Conflict and Failed Ambitions," *World Archaeology* (2015); C. Joy, "'UNESCO Is What?' World Heritage, Militant Islam and the Search for a Common Humanity in Mali," in *World Heritage on the Ground: Ethnographic Perspectives,* ed. C. Brumann and D. Berliner (Oxford: Berghahn, 2016), 60–77. See also "Timbuktu Shrines Damaged by Mali Ansar Dine Islamists," BBC News, June 30, 2012, http://www.bbc.co.uk/news/world-africa-18657463, accessed April 26, 2017.

32. According to Casaly, the Office of the Prosecutor mentioned the World Heritage status of the Timbuktu sites in its analysis of three out of the four factors for gravity of the crimes (scale, nature, manner of commission of the crimes, and their impact), indicating a universalist approach; see P. Casaly, "Al Mahdi Before the ICC: Cultural Property and World Heritage in International Criminal Law," *Journal of International Criminal Justice* 14, no. 5 (2016): 1199–220.

33. UNESCO, "900-Year-Old Consecration Ceremony Held for the Timbuktu Mausoleums," press release, February 4, 2016, http://whc.unesco.org/en/news/1430, accessed April 27, 2017.

34. See the Unite4Heritage booklet *UNESCO's Response to Protect Culture in Crises* (Paris: UNESCO, 2016), http://unesdoc.unesco.org/images/0024/002449/244984e.pdf, accessed April 28, 2017.

35. The Malian delegate did explain that the French NGO CRAterre, with expertise in earthen architecture, makes site visits every two months.

36. See UNESCO, "40th World Heritage Committee in Istanbul, Tuesday 12 July, 9h30–13h," YouTube, posted July 12, 2016, https://www.youtube.com/watch?v=1TNiUlj3U3Q, accessed May 6, 2017.

37. The sentence carries with it a maximum of thirty years in prison. Yet an agreement struck between prosecution and defense teams sought a range of nine to eleven years, and in many ways this may have been a signal that the severity of this crime was not that of other war crimes: a crime against property, Prosecutor Fatou Bensouda stated, was not as severe as one against persons.

38. A. Herscher and A. J. Riedlmayer, "The Destruction of Cultural Heritage in Kosovo, 1998–1999: A Post-War Survey, Prosecution Submission," in Prosecutor v. Slobodan Milosevic, case no. IT-02-54-T, International Criminal Tribunal for the Former Yugloslavia, February 28, 2002.

39. Fatou Bensouda also referred to the Serbian destruction of mosques in Bosnia that later precipitated revisionist histories that there had never been any mosques in the past, leading to further religious and ethnic tension.

40. The ICC defines "genocide" as criminal acts committed with intent to destroy, in whole or in part, a national, ethnical, racial, or religious group. A "crime against humanity" pertains to acts committed as part of a widespread or systematic attack directed against any civilian population, with knowledge of the attack. A "war crime" is defined by a breach of the Geneva Conventions of August 12, 1949, against persons or property protected under the provisions of the relevant Geneva Convention.

41. According to Chechi, "Humankind is a difficult entity to deal with when discussing the issues of dispute prevention and dispute resolution." It is "generally depicted as a sort of legitimate repository of interests that transcend individual States or supranational authorities." A. Chechi, *The Settlement of International Cultural Heritage Disputes* (Oxford: Oxford University Press, 2014), 37.

42. ICC-01/12-01/15, Trial Chamber VIII, Situation in the Republic of Mali in the Case of the Prosecutor v. Ahmad Al Faqi Al Mahdi, Testimony from Witness: MLI-OTP-P-0151, 60–61, August 23, 2016, https://www.icc-cpi.int/Transcripts/CR2016_05772.PDF, accessed August 27, 2017.

43. Ibid.

44. ICC-01/12-01/15, Trial Chamber VIII, Situation in the Republic of Mali in the Case of the Prosecutor v. Ahmad Al Faqi Al Mahdi, Public Reparations Order, August 17, 2017, https://www.icc-cpi.int/CourtRecords/CR2017_05117.PDF, accessed August 27, 2017.

45. Chechi argues that, while useful, the common humanity "concept can carry only a purely philosophical or political meaning: it can only emphasize that there is a general interest of the international community in the conservation and enjoyment of cultural heritage . . . [and] might appear useful only with a view to stopping destruction, looting, decay"; see Chechi, *The Settlement of International Cultural Heritage Disputes*.

46. Casaly, "Al Mahdi Before the ICC," 1200.

47. J. Petrovic, "What Next for Endangered Cultural Treasures: The Timbuktu Crisis and the Responsibility to Protect," *New Zealand Journal of Public and International Law* 11 (2013): 381–426. She goes as far as stating that "cultural property belongs to everyone and to no one in particular, and because we are all only its custodians, the international community has the responsibility to protect it irrespective of state borders" (425).

48. C. Joy, *The Politics of Heritage Management in Mali: From UNESCO to Djenné* (Walnut Creek: Left Coast Press, 2012), 64. For this comprehensive work, see also C. Joy, "Negotiating Material Identities: Young Men and Modernity in Djenné," *Journal of Material Culture* 16, no. 4 (2011): 389–400.

49. E. Cunliffe, N. Muhesen, and M. Lostal, "The Destruction of Cultural Property in the Syrian Conflict: Legal Implications and Obligations," *International Journal of Cultural Property* 23, no. 1 (2016): 1–31. Here the authors argue that without ratification of the Rome Statute "or unless Syria declares acceptance of

the ICC's jurisdiction, the ICC will only have authority if the issue is referred to them by the UN Security Council. Given the divisions surrounding Syria in the UN Security Council, such unified action is unlikely. In 2013, 58 countries sent a letter to the UN Security Council requesting that the ICC begin an investigation into war crimes in Syria (referring to human rights abuses, not cultural war crimes). The referral was blocked by some Security Council permanent members, who stated that it might destabilize chances for a peaceful solution" (18).

50. Resolution 2347 (2017) adopted by the Security Council at its 7907th meeting, on March 24, 2017.

51. Cunliffe, Muhesen, and Lostal, "The Destruction of Cultural Property in the Syrian Conflict," 19.

52. C. Power, "Saudi Arabia Bulldozes over Its Heritage," *Time*, November 14, 2014; O. Beranek and P. Tupek, "From Visiting Graves to Their Destruction: The Question of Ziyara Through the Eyes of Salafis," Crown Paper 2, Crown Center for Middle East Studies, 2009, http://www.islamicpluralism.org/documents/1374.pdf; Islamic Human Rights Commission, "Whose Hajj Is It Anyway?," IHRC, 2016, http://www.ihrc.org.uk/publications/briefings/11763-whose-hajj-is-it-anyway).

53. http://old.theartnewspaper.com/comment/why-is-saudi-arabia-destroying-the-cultural-heritage-of-mecca-and-medina, accessed December 21, 2017; "Making Way for Pilgrims: The Destruction of Mecca," *Economist*, March 2, 2017.

54. UNESCO, "Convention Concerning the Protection of the World Cultural and Natural Heritage: Complete Text," 1972, http://whc.unesco.org/en/conventiontext, accessed May 23, 2017.

55. Drazewska, "The Human Dimension of the Protection of the Cultural Heritage."

56. UNESCO, "UNESCO Director-General Welcomes the Liberation of Hatra and Will Send Emergency Assessment Mission 'As Soon as Possible,'" press release, April 28, 2017, http://whc.unesco.org/en/news/1658, accessed May 7, 2017.

57. Petrovic, "What Next for Endangered Cultural Treasures: The Timbuktu Crisis and the Responsibility to Protect."

58. C. De Cesari, "Post-Colonial Ruins: Archaeologies of Political Violence and IS," *Anthropology Today* 31, no. 6 (2015): 22–26; Ö. Harmanşah, "ISIS, Heritage, and the Spectacles of Destruction in the Global Media," *Near Eastern Archaeology* 78, no. 3 (2015): 170–77; L. M. Meskell, "Negative Heritage and Past Mastering in Archaeology," *Anthropological Quarterly* 75, no. 3 (2002): 557–74; "Gridlock: UNESCO, Global Conflict and Failed Ambitions."

59. See the address by Irina Bokova on the occasion of the opening of the 39th Session of the World Heritage Committee, Bonn, June 28, 2015; also the Bonn Declaration on World Heritage, http://www.39whcbonn2015.de/fileadmin/media/Dateien/Bonn_Declaration_on_World_Heritage_REV.en.pdf, accessed May 7, 2017.

60. M. Lamprakos, *Building a World Heritage City: Sanaa, Yemen* (Farnham: Ashgate, 2015).

61. http://old.theartnewspaper.com/news/news/yemen-battles-to-save-ancient-heritage-from-destruction, accessed May 8, 2017.

62. Letter from Trygve Lie and read aloud in Item 8: Authorisation of the Executive Secretary and his staff to perform the function of the Director-General, acting as Secretary-General of the Conference, and of the Secretariat, pending the appointment of the Director-General. UNESCO General Conference, First Session, held at UNESCO House, Paris, from 20 November to 10 December 1946.

63. B. Urquhart, "Character Sketches: Trygve Lie," UN News Centre, http://www.un.org/apps/news/infocus/trygvie-lie.asp#.WRGOk7zyvsk,   accessed   May 9, 2017.

64. R.-P. Droit, *Humanity in the Making: Overview of the Intellectual History of UNESCO 1945–2005* (Paris: UNESCO, 2005), 21.

65. Ibid., 23.

66. For UNESCO's Constitution, see http://portal.unesco.org/en/ev.php-URL_ID=15244&URL_DO=DO_TOPIC&URL_SECTION=201.html, accessed May 7, 2017.

67. UNESCO, "The Constitution," http://www.unesco.org/new/en/unesco/about-us/who-we-are/history/constitution, accessed May 10, 2017.

68. See ICOMOS Norge, "World Heritage and Rights-Based Approaches," last updated March 15, 2017, www.icomos.no/whrba/whrba, accessed May 8, 2017. See also M. H. van den Dries, "Social Involvement as a Buzz Word in World Heritage Nominations," in *Proceedings of the 2nd International Conference on Best Practices in World Heritage: People and Communities Menorca, Spain, 29–30 April, 1–2 May 2015*, ed. A. R. Castillo Mena (Madrid: Universidad Complutense de Madrid, Servicio de Publicaciones, 2015), 668–86. The IUCN has also embarked on a similar project to consider rights-based approaches in conjunction with ICOMOS.

69. ICOMOS, "Human Rights and World Heritage," http://www.icomos.org/en/what-we-do/image-what-we-do/154-human-rights-and-world-heritage. See also S. Ekern et al., "Human Rights and World Heritage: Preserving Our Common Dignity Through Rights-Based Approaches to Site Management," *International Journal of Heritage Studies* 18, no. 3 (2012): 213–25; S. Ekern et al., eds., *World Heritage Management and Human Rights* (Abingdon: Routledge, 2015); S. Disko and H. Tugendhat, *World Heritage Sites and Indigenous Peoples' Rights* (Copenhagen: IWGIA, 2014).

70. A. F. Vrdoljak, "Indigenous Peoples and Protection of Cultural Heritage in International Law" (in press).

71. UN, Division for Social Policy and Development, Indigenous Peoples, "United Nations Declaration on the Rights of Indigenous Peoples," A/RES/61/295, 2007, https://www.un.org/development/desa/indigenouspeoples/declaration-on-the-rights-of-indigenous-peoples.html, accessed May 10, 2017.

72. See A/HRC/30/53, "Promotion and Protection of the Rights of Indigenous Peoples with Respect to their Cultural Heritage," Human Rights Council, Thirtieth Session, Agenda Item 5, "Human Rights Bodies and Mechanisms," August 9, 2015.

73. Vrdoljak, "Indigenous Peoples and Protection of Cultural Heritage in International Law." See WHC-15/39.COM/13A, "Working Methods of the Evaluation and Decision-making Process of Nomination: Report of the Ad-hoc Working Group," http://whc.unesco.org/en/sessions/39com/documents, accessed May 10, 2017.

74. See Vrdoljak, "Indigenous Peoples and Protection of Cultural Heritage in International Law," for a full discussion, where she states that "UNESCO, as the specialist UN agency in the field of culture, must work closely with indigenous representatives, including the UN mechanisms, to facilitate the finalization and adoption of these principles and guidelines."

75. W. Logan, "Australia, Indigenous Peoples and World Heritage from Kakadu to Cape York: State Party Behaviour Under the World Heritage Convention," *Journal of Social Archaeology* 13, no. 2 (2013): 153–76; L. M. Meskell, "UNESCO and the Fate of the World Heritage Indigenous Peoples Council of Experts (WHIPCOE)," *International Journal of Cultural Property* 20, no. 2 (2013): 155–74.

76. See WHC.16/01, Operational Guidelines for the Implementation of the World Heritage Convention, October 26, 2016, http://whc.unesco.org/document/156250, accessed May 8, 2017. Specifically, see paragraph 123: "Participation in the nomination process of local communities, indigenous peoples, governmental, non-governmental and private organizations and other stakeholders is essential to enable them to have a shared responsibility with the State Party in the maintenance of the property."

77. See studies including I. Anatole-Gabriel, *La fabrique du patrimoine de l'humanité, L'UNESCO et la protection patrimoniale (1945-1992)* (Paris: FMSH Editions, 2016); D. Berliner and C. Bortolotto, "Introduction. Le monde selon l'Unesco," *Gradhiva*, no. 2 (2013): 4–21; S. Disko, "World Heritage Sites in Indigenous Peoples' Territories: Ways of Ensuring Respect for Indigenous Cultures, Values and Human Rights," in *World Heritage and Cultural Diversity*, ed. D. Offenhäußer, W. Zimmerli, and M.-T. Alberts (Cottbus: German Commission for UNESCO, 2010), 167–77; S. Labadi, *UNESCO, Cultural Heritage and Outstanding Universal Value* (Walnut Creek, CA: AltaMira Press, 2013); V. Hafstein, "Intangible Heritage as a List: From Masterpieces to Representation," in *Intangible Heritage*, ed. L.-J. Smith and N. Akagawa (London: Routledge, 2009), 93–111; W. Logan, "Playing the Devil's Advocate: Protecting Intangible Cultural Heritage and the Infringement of Human Rights," *Historic Environment* 22, no. 3 (2009): 14–18; P. J. M. Nas, "Masterpieces of Oral and Intangible Culture," *Current Anthropology* 43, no. 1 (2002): 139–48; T. M. Schmitt, "The UNESCO Concept of Safeguarding Intangible Cultural Heritage: Its Background and *Marrakchi* Roots," *International*

Journal of Heritage Studies 14, no. 2 (2008): 95–111; L.-J. Smith and N. Akagawa, eds., *Intangible Heritage* (London: Routledge, 2009).

78. UNESCO, "Convention on the Protection and Promotion of the Diversity of Cultural Expressions 2005," http://portal.unesco.org/en/ev.php-URL_ID=31038&URL_DO=DO_TOPIC&URL_SECTION=201.html, accessed May 7, 2017.

79. F. Francioni, "Enforcing International Cultural Heritage Law," in *Cultural Heritage Law and Policy*, ed. F. Francioni and J. Gordley (Oxford: Oxford University Press, 2013), 16.

80. According to Petrovic, the original "concept of R2P was conceived as a response to legal ambiguities surrounding the concept of humanitarian intervention. The 1999 NATO Kosovo intervention raised the question of whether a norm of humanitarian intervention existed and, if so, whether it could be invoked only by the Security Council or by individual states as well. While there are fears, for example, that the concept might be exploited by powerful states to advance their interests and that intervention in weaker states can lead to neo-imperialism, there are compelling reasons as to why to rescue population from oppression and mass suffering." Petrovic, "What Next for Endangered Cultural Treasures," 407.

81. See A/HRC/31/59, Report of the Special Rapporteur in the Field of Cultural Rights, Human Rights Council, Thirty-First Session, Agenda Item 3, "Promotion and Protection of All Human Rights, Civil, Political, Economic, Social and Cultural Rights, Including the Right to Development," February 3, 2016.

82. Chechi, *The Settlement of International Cultural Heritage Disputes*, 15.

83. M. Rössler, "Applying Authenticity to Cultural Landscapes," *Association for Preservation Technology International Bulletin* 39, nos. 2–3 (2008): 47–52; G. Aplin, "World Heritage Cultural Landscapes," *International Journal of Heritage Studies* 13, no. 6 (2007): 427–46; P. J. Fowler, *World Heritage Cultural Landscapes 1992–2002: World Heritage Papers 6* (Paris: UNESCO World Heritage Centre, 2003).

84. J. Rodriguez, "Cleaning up Bodhgaya: Conflicts over Development and the Worlding of Buddhism," *City and Society* 29, no. 1 (2017): 59–81; J. Kinnard, "The Ambiguities of Preservation: Bodhgayā, UNESCO, and the Making of a World Heritage Site," in *Religious Representation in Place*, ed. M. K. George and D. Pezzoli-Olgiati (New York: Springer, 2014), 235–50.

85. P. West, J. Igoe, and D. Brockington, "Parks and People: The Social Impacts of Protected Areas," *Annual Review of Anthropology* 35 (2006): 251–77; D. Brockington, *Fortress Conservation: The Preservation of the Mkomazi Game Reserve, Tanzania* (Bloomington: Indiana University Press, 2004); D. Brockington and J. Igoe, "Eviction for Conservation: A Global Overview," *Conservation and Society* 4 (2006): 424–70; L. M. Meskell, *The Nature of Heritage: The New South Africa* (Oxford: Blackwell, 2011); M. Dowie, *Conservation Refugees: The Hundred-Year Conflict between Global Conservation and Native Peoples* (Cambridge, MA: MIT Press, 2009).

86. Appeal by Vittorino Veronese, Director-General of UNESCO, cited in T. Säve-Söderbergh, *Temples and Tombs of Ancient Nubia: The International Rescue Campaign at Abu Simbel, Philae and Other Sites* (London: Thames and Hudson, 1987), 76.

87. Testimony given by Francesco Bandarin, Assistant Director-General for Culture at UNESCO; see ICC-01/12-01/15, Trial Chamber VIII, Situation in the Republic of Mali in the Case of the Prosecutor v. Ahmad Al Faqi Al Mahdi, Testimony from witness, MLI-OTP-P-0151, 60–61, August 23, 2016, https://www.icc-cpi.int/Transcripts/CR2016_05772.PDF, accessed May 7, 2017.

88. For some recent examples, including the site of Bolgar for Russia, see G. Plets, "Ethno-nationalism, Asymmetric Federalism and Soviet Perceptions of the Past: (World) Heritage Activism in the Russian Federation," *Journal of Social Archaeology* 15, no. 1 (2015): 67–93; L. M. Meskell et al., "Multilateralism and UNESCO World Heritage: Decision-making, States Parties and Political Processes," *International Journal of Heritage Studies* 21, no. 5 (2015): 423–40. For Tibet and China, see R. Shepherd, "UNESCO and the Politics of Cultural Heritage in Tibet," *Journal of Contemporary Asia* 36, no. 2 (2006): 243–57; "Cultural Heritage, UNESCO, and the Chinese State," *Heritage Management* 2, no. 1 (2009): 55–79; A. Sinding-Larsen, "Lhasa Community, World Heritage and Human Rights," *International Journal of Heritage Studies* 18, no. 3 (2012): 297–306. Concerning Brazil, see J. Collins, "'But What if I Should Need to Defecate in Your Neighborhood, Madame? Empire, Redemption, and the 'Tradition of the Oppressed' in a Brazilian World Heritage Site," *Cultural Anthropology* 23, no. 2 (2008): 279–328. For Indonesia, see M. Bloembergen and M. Eickhoff, "Decolonizing Borobudur: Moral Engagements and the Fear of Loss," in *Sites, Bodies and Stories: Imagining Indonesian History*, ed. S. Legêne, B. Purwato, and H. Shulte Nordholt (Singapore: NUS Press, 2015), 33–66; M. Nagaoka, "'European' and 'Asian' Approaches to Cultural Landscapes Management at Borobudur, Indonesia in the 1970s," *International Journal of Heritage Studies* 21, no. 3 (2014): 232–49; D. A. Tanudirjo, "Changing Perspectives on the Relationship Between Heritage Landscape and Local Communities: A Lesson from Borobudur," in *Transcending the Culture-Nature Divide in Cultural Heritage: Views from the Asia-Pacific Region*, ed. S. Brockwell, S. O'Connor, and D. Byrne (Canberra: ANU Press, 2013), 65–81.

89. G. Sluga, *Internationalism in the Age of Nationalism* (Philadelphia: University of Pennsylvania Press, 2013), 111.

90. UK Government, "Key to the MDR One Page Assessment Summaries," https://www.gov.uk/government/uploads/system/uploads/attachment_data/file/573494/United-Nations-Educational-Scientific-Cultural-Org-Review.pdf followed by UNESCO, "UNESCO Rejects Findings of the 2016 UK Multilateral Development Review," December 1, 2016, http://en.unesco.org/news/

unesco-rejects-findings-2016-uk-multilateral-development-review, accessed May 7, 2017. For an early study of UNESCO in relation to modernism, see W. Logan, "Globalizing Heritage: World Heritage as a Manifestation of Modernism, and Challenges from the Periphery," paper presented at the Twentieth Century Heritage: Our Recent Cultural Legacy, Australia ICOMOS National Conference, 2001, University of Adelaide, Adelaide.

91. M. Askew, "The Magic List of Global Status: UNESCO, World Heritage and the Agendas of States," in *Heritage and Globalisation*, ed. S. Labadi and C. Long (London: Routledge, 2010), 20.

92. M. Herzfeld, "Mere Symbols," *Anthropologica* 50, no. 1 (2008): 141–55.

93. G. Murray, *From the League to the U.N.* (London: Oxford University Press, 1948), 2.

94. Quotes from Fatou Bensouda, head of prosecution in the Al Mahdi case.

95. UNESCO, "Protection of Mankind's Cultural Heritage: Sites and Monuments."

96. V. Pavone, "From Intergovernmental to Global: UNESCO's Response to globalization," *Review of International Organizations* 2, no. 1 (2007): 77–95.

97. A. Guterres, "U.N. Secretary-General António Guterres: My Vision for Revitalizing the United Nations," *Newsweek*, January 9, 2017.

98. W. Preston, E. S. Herman, and H. Schiller, *Hope and Folly: The United States and UNESCO 1945–1985* (Minneapolis: University of Minnesota Press, 1989), 5. See also L. Fasulo, *An Insider's Guide to the UN* (New Haven, CT: Yale University Press, 2009).

99. Preston, Herman, and Schiller, *Hope and Folly*, 5.

Bibliography

Abu el-Haj, N. *Facts on the Ground: Archaeological Practice and Territorial Self-Fashioning in Israeli Society*. Chicago: University of Chicago Press, 2001.

Adams, W. Y. "A Century of Archaeological Salvage, 1907–2007." *Sudan and Nubia* 11 (2007): 48–56.

———. *Nubia: Corridor to Africa*. London: Allen Lane, 1977.

———. "The Nubian Archaeological Campaigns of 1959–1969: Myths and Realities, Successes and Failures." *Actes du VIIe Congrès International d'Études Nubiennes* (Geneva: Société d'Études Nubiennes, 1992).

———. "Organizational Problems in International Salvage Archaeology." *Anthropological Quarterly* 41, no. 3 (1968): 110–21.

Allais, L. "The Design of the Nubian Desert: Monuments, Mobility, and the Space of Global Culture." In *Governing by Design: Architecture, Economy, and Politics in the Twentieth Century*, edited by Aggregate, 179–215. Pittsburgh: University of Pittsburgh Press, 2012.

———. "Integrities: The Salvage of Abu Simbel." *Grey Room* 50 (2013): 6–45.

Allbeson, T. "Photographic Diplomacy in the Postwar World: Unesco and the Conception of Photography as a Universal Language, 1946–1956." *Modern Intellectual History* 12, no. 2 (2015): 383–415.

Amrith, S., and G. Sluga. "New Histories of the United Nations." *Journal of World History* 19, no. 3 (2008): 251–74.

Anatole-Gabriel, I. *La fabrique du patrimoine de l'humanité, L'UNESCO et la protection patrimoniale (1945–1992)*. Paris: FMSH Editions, 2016.

Antonius, G. "Syria and the French Mandate." *International Affairs (Royal Institute of International Affairs 1931–1939)* 13, no. 4 (1934): 523–39.

Aplin, G. "World Heritage Cultural Landscapes." *International Journal of Heritage Studies* 13, no. 6 (2007): 427–46.

Arizpe, L. "The Intellectual History of Culture and Development Institutions." In *Culture, Diversity and Heritage: Major Studies*, edited by L. Arizpe, 58–81. New York: Springer, 2015.

Arroyo, S. I. "El plan maestro del Conjunto monumental de Panamá Viejo: Diez años
   después." *Canto Rodado* 5 (2011): 185–212.
Arrunnapaporn, A. B. "Atrocity Heritage Tourism at Thailand's 'Death Railway.'" In
   Contemporary Issues in Cultural Heritage Tourism, edited by J. Kaminski, A. M.
   Benson, and D. Arnold, 151–64. Abingdon: Routledge, 2014.
Askew, M. "The Magic List of Global Status: UNESCO, World Heritage and the
   Agendas of States." In *Heritage and Globalisation*, edited by S. Labadi and C. Long,
   19–44. London: Routledge, 2010.
————. "The Rise of 'Moradok' and the Decline of the 'Yarn': Heritage and Cultural
   Construction in Urban Thailand." *Sojourn: Journal of Social Issues in Southeast
   Asia* 11, no. 2 (1996): 183–210.
Audouze, F., and A. Leroi-Gourhan. "France: A Continental Insularity." *World
   Archaeology* 13, no. 2 (1981): 170–89.
Ayán Vila, X., and A. González-Ruibal. "Spanish Archaeology Abroad." In *European
   Archaeology Abroad: Global Settings, Comparative Perspectives*, edited by S. van
   de Linde, M. H. van de Dries, N. Schlanger, and C. G. Slappendel, 85–104.
   Leiden: Sidestone Press, 2012.
Ayata, B. "The Kurds in the Turkish-Armenian Reconciliation Process: Double-
   Bind or Double-Blind?" *International Journal of Middle East Studies* 47, no. 4
   (2015): 807–12.
Badar, M. E. "Islamic Law (Shari'a) and the Jurisdiction of the International Criminal
   Court." *Leiden Journal of International Law* 24, no. 2 (2011): 411–33.
Bahnassi, A. "Le sauvetage des vestiges de la zone de submersion du barrage de
   tabqa sur l'euphrate." *Monumentum* 17 (1978): 57–70.
Baker, C. J. *Protecting Siam's Heritage*. Chiang Mai: Siam Society Under Royal
   Patronage, 2013.
Balakian, G. *Armenian Golgotha: A Memoir of the Armenian Genocide*, translated by
   P. Balakian and A. Sevag. New York: Alfred A. Knopf, 2009.
Balakian, P. "Raphael Lemkin, Cultural Destruction, and the Armenian Genocide."
   Holocaust and Genocide Studies 27, no. 1 (2013): 57–89.
Bar-Yosef, E. "The Last Crusade? British Propaganda and the Palestine Campaign,
   1917–18." *Journal of Contemporary History* 36, no. 1 (2001): 87–109.
Barakat, S., J. Calame, and E. Charlesworth, eds. *Urban Triumph or Urban Disaster?
   Dilemmas of Contemporary Post-war Reconstruction*. York: University of York
   Press, 1998.
Barnard, R., and H. Muamer. "Ongoing Dispossession and a Heritage of Resistance."
   In *The Politics and Power of Tourism in Palestine*, edited by R. K. Isaac, C. M. Hall,
   and F. Higgins-Desbiolles, 63. Abingdon: Routledge, 2015.
Barnett, M. "Cambodia v. Thailand: A Case Study on the Use of Provisional Measures
   to Protect Human Rights in International Border Disputes." *Brooklyn Journal of
   International Law* 38 (2012): 269.

Barr, J. *A Line in the Sand: Britain, France and the Struggle That Shaped the Middle East.* New York: Simon and Schuster, 2011.

Bartu Candan, A., G. Sert, and M. Bagdatli. "Developing Educational Programs for Prehistoric Sites: The Çatalhöyük Case." In *Mediterranean Prehistoric Heritage: Training, Education and Management,* edited by I. Hodder and L. Doughty, 95–104. Cambridge: McDonald Institute for Archaeology, 2007.

Batisse, M., and G. Bolla. *The Invention of "World Heritage."* Paris: Association of Former UNESCO Staff Members, 2005.

Beaumont, J., and A. Witcomb. "The Thai-Burma Railway: Asymmetrical and Transitional Memories." In *The Pacific War: Aftermaths, Remembrance and Culture,* edited by C. Twomey and E. Koh, 67–88. Abingdon: Routledge, 2015.

Bendix, R. "The Power of Perseverance: Exploring the Negotiation Dynamics at the World Intellectual Property Organization." In *The Gloss of Harmony: The Politics of Policy-Making in Multilateral Organisations,* edited by B. Müller, 23–45. London: Pluto Press, 2013.

Benjaminsen, T. A., and G. Berge. "Myths of Timbuktu: From African El Dorado to Desertification." *International Journal of Political Economy* 34, no. 1 (2004): 31–59.

Bentura, S. "Patrimoine: La face cachée des 1000 merveilles du monde." Paris: Galaxie Presse, 2014.

Beranek, O., and P. Tupek. "From Visiting Graves to Their Destruction: The Question of Ziyara Through the Eyes of Salafis." Crown Paper 2, Crown Center for Middle East Studies, 2009.

Berliner, D. "Multiple Nostalgias: The Fabric of Heritage in Luang Prabang (Lao PDR)." *Journal of the Royal Anthropological Institute* 18, no. 4 (2012): 769–86.

Berliner, D., and C. Bortolotto. "Introduction. Le monde selon l'Unesco." *Gradhiva* 2 (2013): 4–21.

Bertacchini, E., C. Liuzza, and L. M. Meskell. "Shifting the Balance of Power in the UNESCO World Heritage Committee: An Empirical Assessment." *International Journal of Cultural Policy* (2015): 1–21.

Bertacchini, E., C. Liuzza, L. M. Meskell, and D. Saccone. "The Politicization of UNESCO World Heritage Decision Making." *Public Choice* 167, nos. 1–2 (2016): 1–35.

Bertacchini, E., and D. Saccone. "Toward a Political Economy of World Heritage." *Journal of Cultural Economics* 36, no. 4 (2012): 327–52.

Best, G. "Peace Conferences and the Century of Total War: The 1899 Hague Conference and What Came After." *International Affairs* 75, no. 3 (1999): 619–34.

Betts, P. "Humanity's New Heritage: Unesco and the Rewriting of World History." *Past and Present* 228, no. 1 (2015): 249–85.

———. "The Warden of World Heritage: UNESCO and the Rescue of the Nubian Monuments." *Past and Present* 226, suppl. 10 (2015): 100–25.

Betts, P., and C. Ross. "Modern Historical Preservation—Towards a Global Perspective." *Past and Present* 226, suppl 10. (2015): 7–26.

Bilgin, A., and S. Hakyemez. "The AKP's Engagement with Turkey's Past Crimes: An Analysis of PM Erdogan's 'Dersim Apology.'" *Dialectical Anthropology* 37, no. 1 (2013): 131–43.

Blanchfield, L., and M. Browne. *The United Nations Educational, Scientific, and Cultural Organization (UNESCO)*. Washington, DC: Congressional Research Service, 2013.

Blanck, H. "The Instituto di Corrispondenza Archeologica." *Fragmenta* 2 (2008): 63–78.

Bloch, N. "Evicting Heritage: Spatial Cleansing and Cultural Legacy at the Hampi UNESCO Site in India." *Critical Asian Studies* 48, no. 4 (2016): 556–78.

Bloembergen, M., and M. Eickhoff. "Decolonizing Borobudur: Moral Engagements and the Fear of Loss." In *Sites, Bodies and Stories: Imagining Indonesian History*, edited by S. Legêne, B. Purwato, and H. Shulte Nordholt, 33–66. Singapore: NUS Press, 2015.

Bokova, I. "Address by Ms. Irina Bokova, UNESCO Director-General, on the Occasion of the Opening of the 36th Session of the World Heritage Committee." St. Petersburg, Russian Federation, June 24, 2012.

Boyle, F. A. *Foundations of World Order: The Legalist Approach to International Relations (1898–1922)*. Durham, NC: Duke University Press, 1999.

Brattli, T. "Managing the Archaeological World Cultural Heritage: Consensus or Rhetoric?" *Norweigian Archaeological Review* 42, no. 1 (2009): 24–39.

Brenneis, D. L. "Sand, Stability and Stakeholders." In *Heritage Regimes and the State*, edited by R. Bendix, A. Eggert, and A. Peselmann, 376–74. Göttingen: Universitätsverlag Göttingen, 2013.

Brew, J. O. "Emergency Archaeology: Salvage in Advance of Technological Progress." *Proceedings of the American Philosophical Society* 105, no. 1 (1961): 1–10.

Brockington, D. *Fortress Conservation: The Preservation of the Mkomazi Game Reserve, Tanzania*. Bloomington: Indiana University Press, 2004.

Brockington, D., and J. Igoe. "Eviction for Conservation: A Global Overview." *Conservation and Society* 4 (2006): 424–70.

Brosché, J., M. Legnér, J. Kreutz, and A. Ijla. "Heritage Under Attack: Motives for Targeting Cultural Property During Armed Conflict." *International Journal of Heritage Studies* 23, no. 3 (2017): 248–60.

Brumann, C. "Heritage Agnosticism: A Third Path for the Study of Cultural Heritage." *Social Anthropology* 22, no. 2 (2014): 173–88.

———. "Multilateral Ethnography: Entering the World Heritage Arena." Max Planck Institute for Social Anthropology, Working Paper 136, 2012.

———. "Shifting Tides of World-Making in the UNESCO World Heritage Convention: Cosmopolitanisms Colliding." *Ethnic and Racial Studies* 37, no. 12 (2014): 2176–92.

Burke-White, W. W. "Crimea and the International Legal Order." *Survival* 56, no. 4 (2014): 65–80.

Byrne, D. "Buddhist Stupa and Thai Social Practice." *World Archaeology* 27, no. 2 (1995): 266–81.

———. *Counterheritage: Critical Perspectives on Heritage Conservation in Asia.* London: Routledge, 2014.

———. *Surface Collection: Archaeological Travels in Southeast Asia.* Walnut Creek, CA: AltaMira, 2007.

———. "Western Hegemony in Archaeological Heritage Management." *History and Anthropology* 5 (1991): 269–76.

Cameron, C., and M. Rössler. *Many Voices, One Vision: The Early Years of the World Heritage Convention.* Surrey: Ashgate, 2013.

Campkin, B. "Placing 'Matter Out of Place': Purity and Danger as Evidence for Architecture and Urbanism." *Architectural Theory Review* 18, no. 1 (2013): 46–61.

Carr, E. H. *The Twenty Years' Crisis, 1919–1939: An Introduction to the Study of International Relations.* London: Macmillan, 1946.

Carruthers, W. "Multilateral Possibilities: Decolonization, Preservation and the Case of Egypt." *Future Anterior: Journal of Historic Preservation History Theory and Criticism* 13, no. 1 (2016): 36–48.

Casaly, P. "Al Mahdi Before the ICC: Cultural Property and World Heritage in International Criminal Law." *Journal of International Criminal Justice* 14, no. 5 (2016): 1199–220.

Chachavalpongpun, P. "Temple of Doom: Hysteria About the Preah Vihear Temple in the Thai Nationalist Discourse." In *Legitimacy and Crisis in Thailand,* edited by M. Askew, 83–118. Chiang Mai: Silkworm Books, 2010.

Chechi, A. "Evaluating the Establishment of an International Cultural Heritage Court." *Art, Antiquity and Law* 18 (2013): 31–57.

———. *The Settlement of International Cultural Heritage Disputes.* Oxford: Oxford University Press, 2014.

Chesterman, S. "The International Court of Justice in Asia: Interpreting the Temple of Preah Vihear Case." *Asian Journal of International Law* 5, no. 1 (2015): 1–6.

Chirikure, Shadreck, and Gilbert Pwiti. "Community Involvement in Archaeology and Cultural Heritage Management: An Assessment from Case Studies in Southern Africa and Elsewhere." *Current Anthropology* 49, no. 3 (2008): 467–85.

Choay, F. *The Invention of the Historic Monument.* Cambridge: Cambridge University Press, 2001.

———. *L'allégorie du patrimoine.* Vol. 271. Paris: Seuil, 1992.

Ciorciari, J. D. "Request for Interpretation of the Judgment of 15 June 1962 in the Case Concerning the Temple of Preah Vihear (Cambodia v. Thailand)." *American Journal of International Law* 108, no. 2 (2014): 288–95.

Claudi, I. B. "The New Kids on the Block: BRICs in the World Heritage Committee." M.A. thesis, Department of Political Science, University of Oslo, Norway, 2011.

Cleere, H. "The 1972 UNESCO World Heritage Convention." *Heritage and Society* 4, no. 2 (2011): 173–86.

Cleuziou, S., A. Coudart, J.-P. Demoule, and A. Schnapp. "The Use of Theory in French Archaeology." In *Archaeological Theory in Europe: The Last Three Decades*, edited by I. Hodder, 91–128. London: Routledge, 1991.

Colby, E. "How to Fight Savage Tribes." *American Journal of International Law* 21, no. 2 (1927): 279–88.

Collins, J. " 'But What if I Should Need to Defecate In Your Neighborhood, Madame? Empire, Redemption, and the 'Tradition of the Oppressed' in a Brazilian World Heritage Site." *Cultural Anthropology* 23, no. 2 (2008): 279–328.

Colwell, C., and C. Joy. "Communities and Ethics in Heritage Debates." In *Global Heritage: A Reader*, edited by L. M. Meskell, 112–29. Oxford: Blackwell, 2015.

Colwell-Chanthaphonh, C. "Dismembering/Disremembering the Buddhas: Renderings on the Internet During the Afghan Purge of the Past." *Journal of Social Archaeology* 3, no. 1 (2003): 75–98.

Colwell-Chanthaphonh, C., and T. J. Ferguson, eds. *The Collaborative Continuum: Archaeological Engagements with Descendent Communities*. Thousand Oaks, CA: Altamira Press, 2007.

Committee on Foreign Affairs. "Assessment of U.S.-UNESCO Relations, 1984. Report of a Staff Study Mission to Paris-UNESCO to the Committee on Foreign Affairs House of Representatives." Washington, DC: GPO, 1985.

Coningham, R., and N. Lewer. "Paradise Lost: The Bombing of the Temple of the Tooth—a UNESCO World Heritage Site in Sri Lanka." *Antiquity* 73, no. 282 (1999): 857–66.

Connor, A. "Heritage in an Expanded Field: Reconstructing Bridge-ness in Mostar." In *A Companion to Heritage Studies*, edited by W. Logan, M. N. Craith, and U. Kockel, 254–67. New York: John Wiley & Sons, 2016.

Cunliffe, E., N. Muhesen, and M. Lostal. "The Destruction of Cultural Property in the Syrian Conflict: Legal Implications and Obligations." *International Journal of Cultural Property* 23, no. 1 (2016): 1–31.

Cuno, J. *Who Owns Antiquity? Museums and the Battle over Our Ancient Heritage*. New Jersey: Princeton, 2008.

de Arango, J. "El sitio de Panamá Viejo. Un ejemplo de gestión patrimonial." *Canto Rodado* 1 (2006): 1–15.

De Cesari, C. "Post-Colonial Ruins: Archaeologies of Political Violence and IS." *Anthropology Today* 31, no. 6 (2015): 22–26.

———. "World Heritage and Mosaic Universalism." *Journal of Social Archaeology* 10, no. 3 (2010): 299–324.

———. "World Heritage and the Nation-State." In *Transnational Memory: Circulation, Articulation, Scales*, edited by C. De Cesari and A. Rigney, 247–70. Berlin: de Gruyter, 2014.

Deese, R. S. "Twilight of Utopias: Julian and Aldous Huxley in the Twentieth Century." *Journal for the Study of Religion, Nature and Culture* 5, no. 2 (2011): 210–40.

———. *We Are Amphibians: Julian and Aldous Huxley on the Future of Our Species.* Berkeley: University of California Press, 2014.

Demoule, J.-P. "Rescue Archaeology: A European View." *Annual Review of Anthropology* 41 (2012): 611–26.

DerGhougassian, K. "Genocide and Identity (Geo) Politics: Bridging State Reasoning and Diaspora Activism." *Genocide Studies International* 8, no. 2 (2014): 193–207.

Disko, S. "World Heritage Sites in Indigenous Peoples' Territories: Ways of Ensuring Respect for Indigenous Cultures, Values and Human Rights." In *World Heritage and Cultural Diversity*, edited by D. Offenhäußer, W. Zimmerli and M.-T. Alberts, 167–77. Cottbus: German Commission for UNESCO, 2010.

Disko, S., and H. Tugendhat. *World Heritage Sites and Indigenous Peoples' Rights.* Copenhagen: IWGIA, 2014.

Dorn, C., and K. Ghodsee. "The Cold War Politicization of Literacy: Communism, UNESCO, and the World Bank." *The Journal of the Society for Historians of American Foreign Relations* 36, no. 2 (2012): 373–98.

Doughty, L. "Training, Education, Management and Prehistory in the Mediterranean: Work in Progress on a European Union Research Project." *Conservation and Management of Archaeological Sites* 6.1 (2003): 49–53.

Douglas, M. *Purity and Danger: An Analysis of the Concepts of Pollution and Taboo.* London: Routledge, 1966.

Dowie, M. *Conservation Refugees: The Hundred-Year Conflict between Global Conservation and Native Peoples* Cambridge: MIT Press, 2009.

Drazewska, B. "The Human Dimension of the Protection of the Cultural Heritage from Destruction During Armed Conflicts." *International Journal of Cultural Property* 22, no. 2–3 (2015): 205–28.

Droit, R.-P. *Humanity in the Making: Overview of the Intellectual History of UNESCO 1945–2005.* Paris: UNESCO, 2005.

Duedahl, P., ed. *A History of UNESCO: Global Actions and Impacts.* New York: Palgrave Macmillan, 2016.

———. "Selling Mankind: UNESCO and the Invention of Global History, 1945–1976." *Journal of World History* 22, no. 1 (2011): 101–33.

Dumper, M., and C. Larkin. "The Politics of Heritage and the Limitations of International Agency in Contested Cities: A Study of the Role of UNESCO in Jerusalem's Old City." *Review of International Studies* 38, no. 1 (2012): 25–52.

Dutt, S. *The Politicization of the United Nations Specialized Agencies: A Case Study of UNESCO.* Lewiston, ME: Edwin Mellen Press, 1995.

———. "Striving to Promote Shared Values UNESCO in the Troubled World of the Twenty-First Century." *India Quarterly: A Journal of International Affairs* 65, no. 1 (2009): 83–95.

The Economist. "UNESCO's World Heritage Sites: A Danger List in Danger." August 26, 2010.

Ekern, S., W. Logan, B. Sauge, and A. Sinding-Larsen. "Human Rights and World Heritage: Preserving Our Common Dignity Through Rights-Based Approaches to Site Management." *International Journal of Heritage Studies* 18, no. 3 (2012): 213–25.

———. *World Heritage Management and Human Rights.* Abingdon: Routledge, 2015.

El-Khatib, M. "The Syrian Tabqa Dam: Its Development and Impact." *The Geographical Bulletin* 26 (1984): 19.

Elliott, M. A., and V. Schmutz. "World Heritage: Constructing a Universal Cultural Order." *Poetics* 40, no. 3 (2012): 256–77.

Erbal, A. "Lost in Translation: The Monument's Deconstruction." In *The Armenian Genocide Legacy*, edited by A. Demirdjian, 212–26. London: Palgrave Macmillan UK, 2016.

Eriksen, T. H. "Between Universalism and Relativism: A Critique of the UNESCO Concept of Culture." In *Human Rights: An Anthropological Reader*, edited by M. Goodale, 356–71. Malden: Wiley-Blackwell, 2009.

Fahim, H. M. *Dams, People and Development: The Aswan High Dam Case.* Burlington, VT: Elsevier, 2015.

Falser, M. "Cultural Heritage as Civilizing Mission: Methodological Considerations." In *Cultural Heritage as Civilizing Mission*, edited by M. Falser, 1–32. New York: Springer, 2015.

———. "Epilogue: Clearing the Path Towards Civilization: 150 Years of 'Saving Angkor.'" In *Cultural Heritage as Civilizing Mission*, edited by M. Falser, 279–346. New York: Springer, 2015.

———. "Representing Heritage Without Territory: The Khmer Rouge at the UNESCO in Paris During the 1980s and Their Political Strategy for Angkor." In *Cultural Heritage as Civilizing Mission*, edited by M. Falser, 225–49. New York: Springer, 2015.

Falser, M., M. Juneja, and P. Pichard. "Today's Pagan: Conservation Under the Generals." In *"Archaeologizing" Heritage?*, edited by M. Falser and M. Juneja., 235–49. Berlin: Springer, 2013.

Fasulo, L. *An Insider's Guide to the UN.* New Haven, CT: Yale University Press, 2009.

Fletcher, C., and J. Da Mosto. *The Science of Saving Venice.* Turin: Umberto Allenamandi, 2004.

Forde, S. "The Bridge on the Neretva: Stari Most as a Stage of Memory in Post-Conflict Mostar, Bosnia-Herzegovina." *Cooperation and Conflict* 51, no. 4 (2016): 467–83.

Foucault, M. "The Subject and Power." *Critical Inquiry* 8, no. 4 (1982): 777–95.

Fowler, P. J. *World Heritage Cultural Landscapes 1992–2002: World Heritage Papers 6.* Paris: UNESCO World Heritage Centre, 2003.

Francioni, F. "Enforcing International Cultural Heritage Law." In *Cultural Heritage Law and Policy*, edited by F. Francioni and J. Gordley, 9–21. Oxford: Oxford University Press, 2013.

Francioni, F., and F. Lenzerini. *The 1972 World Heritage Convention: A Commentary.* Oxford: Oxford University Press, 2008.

———. "The Destruction of the Buddhas of Bamiyan and International Law." *European Journal of International Law* 14, no. 4 (2003): 619–51.

Freely, M. "Why They Killed Hrant Dink." *Index on Censorship* 36, no. 2 (2007): 15–29.

Fresia, M. "The Making of Global Consensus: Constructing Norms on Refugee Protection at UNHCR." In *The Gloss of Harmony: The Politics of Policy-Making in Multilateral Organisations*, edited by B. Müller. London: Pluto Press, 2013.

Frey, B. S., P. Pamini, and L. Steiner. "Explaining the World Heritage List: An Empirical Study." *International Review of Economics* 60, no. 1 (2013): 1–19.

Frey, B. S., and L. Steiner. "World Heritage List: Does It Make Sense?" *International Journal of Cultural Policy* 17, no. 5 (2011): 555–73.

Fritz, J. M., and G. Michell. "Living Heritage at Risk: Searching for a New Approach to Development, Tourism, and Local Needs at the Grand Medieval City of Vijayanagara." *Archaeology* 65, no. 6 (2012): 55–62.

Frulli, M. "The Criminalization of Offences Against Cultural Heritage in Times of Armed Conflict: The Quest for Consistency." *European Journal of International Law* 22, no. 1 (2011): 203–17.

Galis, A. "UNESCO Documents and Procedure: The Need to Account for Political Conflict When Designating World Heritage Sites." *Georgia Journal of International and Comparative Law* 38, no. 1 (2009): 205–36.

Gamboni, D. "World Heritage: Shield or Target?" *Getty Conservation Institute Newsletter* 16, no. 2 (2001): 5–11.

García y García, L. "Danni di guerra a Pompei: una dolorosa vicenda quasi dimenticata: con numerose notizie sul 'museo Pompeiano' distrutto nel 1943." Rome: L'Erma di Bretschneider, 2006.

Gasparoli, P., and F. Trovo. *Fragile Venice.* Venice: Altralinea Edizioni, 2014.

Gerges, F. A. *ISIS: A History.* Princeton, NJ: Princeton University Press, 2017.

Gerstenblith, P. "Beyond the 1954 Hague Convention." In *Cultural Awareness in the Military: Developments and Implications for Future Humanitarian Cooperation*, edited by R. Albro and B. Ivey, 83–98. New York: Palgrave Macmillan, 2014.

———. "The Destruction of Cultural Heritage: A Crime Against Property or a Crime Against People?" *John Marshall Review of Intellectual Property Law* 15, no. 3 (2016): 337–93.

Gfeller, A. E. "Culture at the Crossroad of International Politics: UNESCO, World Heritage, and the Holy Land." *Papiers d'Actualité/Current Affairs in Perspective: Fondation Pierre du Bois* 3 (2013): 1–11.

Gfeller, A. E., and J. Eisenberg. "UNESCO and the Shaping of Global Heritage." In *A History of UNESCO*, edited by P. Duedahl, 279–99. New York: Springer, 2016.

Gilmore, C. "Speaking Through the Silence." In *Development-Induced Displacement and Resettlement: New Perspectives on Persisting Problems,* edited by I. Satiroglu and N. Choi, 199–211. Abingdon: Routledge, 2015.

Glass, C. *Syria Burning: A Short History of a Catastrophe.* New York: Verso Books, 2016.

Goçek, F. M. *Denial of Violence: Ottoman Past, Turkish Present, and Collective Violence Against the Armenians, 1789–2009.* Oxford: Oxford University Press, 2014.

Grant Ross, H. "The Civilizing Vision of an Enlightened Dictator: Norodom Sihanouk and the Cambodian Post-Independence Experiment (1953–1970)." In *Cultural Heritage as Civilizing Mission,* edited by M. Falser, 149–78. New York: Springer, 2015.

Guidi, A. "Nationalism Without a Nation: The Italian Case." In *Nationalism and Archaeology in Europe,* edited by M. Díaz-Andreu and T. Champion, 108–18. London: Routledge, 1996.

Guitton, J. "N'en déplaise à quelques tenants de l'esprit pur . . ." In *L'UNESCO racontée par ses anciens,* 29–31. Paris: UNESCO, 2006.

Hafsaas-Tsakos, H. "Ethical Implications of Salvage Archaeology and Dam Building: The Clash Between Archaeologists and Local People in Dar al-Manasir, Sudan." *Journal of Social Archaeology* 11, no. 1 (2011): 49–76.

Hafstein, V. "Intangible Heritage as a List: From Masterpieces to Representation." In *Intangible Heritage,* edited by L.-J. Smith and N. Akagawa, 93–111. London: Routledge, 2009.

Hale, T., and D. Held. "Editor's Introduction." In *Handbook of Transnational Governance: Institutions and Innovations,* edited by T. Hale and D. Held, 1–36. Cambridge: Polity, 2011.

Hall, C. M., and R. Piggin. "World Heritage Sites: Managing the Brand." *Managing Visitor Attractions: New Directions,* 2003, 203–19.

Harmanşah, Ö. "ISIS, Heritage, and the Spectacles of Destruction in the Global Media." *Near Eastern Archaeology* 78, no. 3 (2015): 170–77.

Harvey, D. C. "Heritage Pasts and Heritage Presents: Temporality, Meaning and the Scope of Heritage Studies." *International Journal of Heritage Studies* 7, no. 4 (2001): 319–38.

Hassan, F. A. "The Aswan High Dam and the International Rescue Nubia Campaign." *African Archaeological Review* 24, nos. 3–4 (2007): 73–94.

Hauser-Schäublin, B. "Preah Vihear: From Object of Colonial Desire to a Contested World Heritage Site." In *World Heritage Angkor and Beyond: Circumstances and Implications of UNESCO Listings in Cambodia,* edited by B. Hauser-Schäublin, 33–56. Göttingen: Göttingen Studies in Cultural Property, 2011.

———, ed. *World Heritage Angkor and Beyond: Circumstances and Implications of UNESCO Listings in Cambodia.* Göttingen: Universitätsverlag Göttingen, 2011.

Hauser-Schäublin, B., and S. Missling. "The Enduring Agency of Borderland Regimes: The Aftermath of Serial Regulations with Different Scopes and

Temporal Scales at Preah Vihear, Cambodia." *Journal of Legal Pluralism and Unofficial Law* 46, no. 1 (2014): 79–98.

Hawkes, J. "Adventures in Archaeology: The Biography of Sir Mortimer Wheeler." New York: St. Martins Press, 1982.

Hawkes, J., and L. Woolley. *Prehistory and the Beginnings of Civilization.* Vol. 1. New York: Harper & Row, 1963.

Heinich, N. *La fabrique du patrimoine: de la cathédrale à la petite cuillère.* Paris: Éditions de la MSH, 2009.

Heller, P. B. *The United Nations Under Dag Hammarskjold, 1953–1961.* Lanham, MD: Scarecrow Press, 2001.

Herscher, A., and A. J. Riedlmayer. "The Destruction of Cultural Heritage in Kosovo, 1998–1999: A Post-War Survey, Prosecution Submission." In *Prosecutor v. Slobodan Milosevic,* case no. IT-02-54-T. International Criminal Tribunal for the Former Yugloslavia, February 28, 2002.

Herzfeld, M. *Anthropology: Theoretical Practice in Culture and Society.* Paris: UNESCO, 2000.

——. "Mere Symbols." *Anthropologica* 50, no. 1 (2008): 141–55.

——. *A Place in History: Social and Monumental Time in a Cretan Town.* Princeton, NJ: Princeton University Press, 1991.

——. *Siege of the Spirits: Community and Polity in Bangkok.* Chicago: University of Chicago Press, 2016.

——. *The Social Production of Indifference.* Chicago: University of Chicago Press, 1993.

——. "Spatial Cleansing: Monumental Vacuity and the Idea of the West." *Journal of Material Culture* 11, nos. 1–2 (2006): 127–49.

Higgins, A. P. *The Hague Peace Conferences.* Cambridge: Cambridge University Press, 1909.

Hocking, B. "Words and Deeds: Why America Left Unesco." *The World Today* 41, no. 4 (1985): 75–78.

Hodder, I. "Archaeological Reflexivity and the 'Local' Voice." *Anthropological Quarterly* 76, no. 1 (2003): 55–69.

——. "Cultural Heritage Rights: From Ownership and Descent to Justice and Well-being." *Anthropological Quarterly* 83, no. 4 (2010): 861–82.

Hodge, J. M. *Triumph of the Expert: Agrarian Doctrines of Development and the Legacies of British Colonialism.* Athens: Ohio University Press, 2007.

Hoggart, R. *An Idea and Its Servants: UNESCO from Within.* Piscataway, NJ: Transaction, 2011.

——. "UNESCO in Crisis—the Israel Resolutions." *Higher Education Quarterly* 30, no. 1 (1975): 15–23.

Hojjat, M. "Cultural Identity in Danger." In *The Iran-Iraq War: The Politics of Aggression,* edited by F. Rajaee, 41–46. Gainesville: University Press of Florida, 1993.

Hølleland, H. "Practicing World Heritage. Approaching the Changing Faces of the World Heritage Convention." Ph.D. dissertation, University of Oslo, 2013.

Hopkins, N. S., and S. R. Mehanna. *Nubian Encounters: The Story of the Nubian Ethnological Survey 1961–1964.* Oxford: Oxford University Press, 2011.

Hudson, B. "Restoration and Reconstruction of Monuments at Bagan (Pagan), Myanmar (Burma)." *World Archaeology* 40, no. 4 (2008): 553–71.

Hüfner, K. *What Can Save UNESCO?* Berlin: Frank & Timme, 2015.

Hughes, T. L. "The Twilight of Internationalism." *Foreign Policy*, no. 61 (1985): 25–48.

Hull, M. S. "Documents and Bureaucracy." *Annual Review of Anthropology* 41 (2012): 251–67.

Human, H. "Democratising World Heritage: The Policies and Practices of Community Involvement in Turkey." *Journal of Social Archaeology* 15, no. 2 (2015): 160–83.

Huxley, J. *From an Antique Land: Ancient and Modern in the Middle East.* Boston: Beacon Press, 1966.

———. *TVA: Adventure in Planning.* Surrey: Architectural Press, 1943.

———. *UNESCO: Its Purpose and Its Philosophy.* Washington, DC: Public Affairs Press, 1947.

INTACH. "Charter for the Conservation of Unprotected Architectural Heritage and Sites in India." Indian National Trust for Art and Cultural Heritage, New Delhi, 2004.

International Museums Office, ed. *Manual on the Technique of Archaeological Excavations.* Paris: International Institute of Intellectual Cooperation, 1940.

Iriye, A. *Global Community: The Role of International Organizations in the Making of the Contemporary World.* Berkeley: University of California Press, 2002.

Isakhan, B. "Heritage Destruction and Spikes in Violence: The Case of Iraq." In *Cultural Heritage in the Crosshairs: Protecting Cultural Property During Conflict,* edited by J. D. Kila and J. A. Zeidler, 219–47. Leiden: Brill, 2013.

———. "Targeting the Symbolic Dimension of Baathist Iraq: Cultural Destruction, Historical Memory, and National Identity." *Middle East Journal of Culture and Communication* 4, no. 3 (2011): 257–81.

Isakhan, B., and J. A. González Zarandona. "Layers of Religious and Political Iconoclasm Under the Islamic State: Symbolic Sectarianism and Pre-monotheistic Iconoclasm." *International Journal of Heritage Studies* (2017): 1–16.

Isakhan, B. "The Iraq Legacies and the Roots of the 'Islamic State.'" In *The Legacy of Iraq: From the 2003 War to the "Islamic State,"* edited by B. Isakhan, 223–35. Edinburgh: Edinburgh University Press, 2015.

Isar, Y. R. "UNESCO and Heritage: Global Doctrine and Global Practice." In *Cultures and Globalization: Heritage, Memory and Identity,* edited by H. K. Anheier and Y. R. Isar, 39–52. London: Sage, 2011.

Islamic Human Rights Commission. "Whose Hajj Is It Anyway?" IHRC, 2016.

Jameson, F. *Archaeologies of the Future: The Desire called Utopia and Other Science Fictions*. New York: Verso, 2005.

Janmyr, M. "Human Rights and Nubian Mobilisation in Egypt: Towards Recognition of Indigeneity." *Third World Quarterly* 38, no. 3 (2017): 717–33.

Johansson, C. "Digital Reconstruction of the Archaeological Landscape in the Concession Area of the Scandinavian Joint Expedition to Sudanese Nubia (1961–1964)." M.A. thesis, Uppsala University, 2014.

Jokilehto, J. "World Heritage: Observations on Decisions Related to Cultural Heritage." *Journal of Cultural Heritage Management and Sustainable Development* 1, no. 1 (2011): 61–74.

Jokilehto, J., and C. Cameron. *The World Heritage List: What Is OUV? Defining the Outstanding Universal Value of Cultural World Heritage Properties*. Berlin: Bässler Verlag, 2008.

Joy, C. "Negotiating Material Identities: Young Men and Modernity in Djenné." *Journal of Material Culture* 16, no. 4 (2011): 389–400.

———. *The Politics of Heritage Management in Mali: From UNESCO to Djenné*. Walnut Creek, CA: Left Coast Press, 2012.

———. "'UNESCO Is What?' World Heritage, Militant Islam and the Search for a Common Humanity in Mali." In *World Heritage on the Ground: Ethnographic Perspectives*, edited by C. Brumann and D. Berliner, 60–77. Oxford: Berghahn, 2016.

Källén, A. "The Invisible Archaeologist: Letters from the UNESCO Secretariat 1946–1947." *Journal of Social Archaeology* 14, no. 3 (2014): 383–405.

Kasetsiri, C., P. Sothirak, and P. Chachavalpongpun. *Preah Vihear: A Guide to the Thai-Cambodian Conflict and its Solutions*. Bangkok: White Lotus Press, 2013.

Kersel, M. M., and C. Luke. "Diplomacy and Neo-imperialism." In *Global Heritage: A Reader*, edited by L. Meskell, 70–93. Oxford: Wiley Blackwell, 2015.

Kersel, M. M., and C. Luke. "A Crack in the Diplomatic Armor: The United States and the Palestinian Authority's Bid for UNESCO Recognition." *Journal of Field Archaeology* 37, no. 2 (2012): 143–44.

Khoury, P. S. *Syria and the French Mandate: The Politics of Arab Nationalism, 1920–1945*. Princeton, NJ: Princeton University Press, 2014.

Kinnard, J. "The Ambiguities of Preservation: Bodhgayā, UNESCO, and the Making of a World Heritage Site." In *Religious Representation in Place*, edited by M. K. George and D. Pezzoli-Olgiati, 235–50. New York: Springer, 2014.

Kitchen, J. E. "'Khaki Crusaders': Crusading Rhetoric and the British Imperial Soldier During the Egypt and Palestine Campaigns, 1916–18." *First World War Studies* 1, no. 2 (2010): 141–60.

Kleine, M. "Trading Control: National Fiefdoms in International Organizations." *International Theory* 5, no. 3 (2013): 321–46.

Kleinitz, C. "Between Valorisation and Devaluation: Making and Unmaking (World) Heritage in Sudan." *Archaeologies* 9, no. 3 (2013): 427–69.

Kleinitz, C., and C. Näser. "The Loss of Innocence: Political and Ethical Dimensions of the Merowe Dam Archaeological Salvage Project at the Fourth Nile Cataract (Sudan)." *Conservation and Management of Archaeological Sites* 13, no. 2–3 (2011): 253–80.

Klimowicz, A., and P. Klimowicz. "The Socio-political Context of Polish Archaeological Discoveries in Faras, Sudan." In *European Archaeology Abroad: Global Settings, Comparative Perspectives,* edited by S. van de Linde, M. H. van de Dries, N. Schlanger, and C. G. Slappendel, 287. Leiden: Sidestone Press, 2012.

Kornegay, K. "Destroying the Shrines of Unbelievers: The Challenge of Iconoclasm to the International Framework for the Protection of Cultural Property." *Military Law Review* 221 (2014): 153–82.

Kowalski, A. "When Cultural Capitalization Became Global Practice." In *The Cultural Wealth of Nations,* edited by N. Bandelj and F. F. Wherry, 73–89. Stanford: Stanford University Press, 2011.

Krairiksh, P. "A Brief History of Heritage Protection in Thailand." In *Protecting Siam's Heritage,* edited by C. Baker, 15–40. Chiang Mai: Siam Society under Royal Patronage, 2013.

Kunz, D. B. "When Money Counts and Doesn't: Economic Power and Diplomatic Objectives." *Diplomatic History* 18, no. 4 (1994): 451–62.

Labadi, S. "The Impacts of Culture and Heritage-Led Development Programmes: The Cases of Liverpool (UK) and Lille (France)." In *Urban Heritage, Development and Sustainability: International Frameworks, National and Local Governance,* edited by S. Labadi and W. Logan, 137–50. Abingdon: Routledge, 2016.

———. "Representations of the Nation and Cultural Diversity in Discourses on World Heritage." *Journal of Social Archaeology* 7, no. 2 (2007): 147–70.

———. "A Review of the Global Strategy for a Balanced, Representative and Credible World Heritage List 1994–2004." *Conservation and Management of Archaeological Sites* 7, no. 2 (2005): 89–102.

———. *UNESCO, Cultural Heritage and Outstanding Universal Value.* Walnut Creek, CA: AltaMira Press, 2013.

———. "The Upstream Process: The Way Forward for the World Heritage Convention?" *Heritage and Society* 7, no. 1 (2014): 57–58.

Labadi, S., and F. Bandarin. *World Heritage: Challenges for the Millennium.* Paris: UNESCO, 2007.

Labadi, S., and W. Logan. "Approaches to Urban Heritage, Development and Sustainability." In *Urban Heritage, Development and Sustainability: International Frameworks, National and Local Governance,* edited by S. Labadi and W. Logan, 1–20. London: Routledge, 2016.

Lafrenz Samuels, K. "Trajectories of Development: International Heritage Management of Archaeology in the Middle East and North Africa." *Archaeologies* 5, no. 1 (2009): 68–91.

Lal, B. B. "Expeditions Outside India." *Indian Archaeology* 1961–2 (1964): 64–70.

Lamprakos, M. *Building a World Heritage City: Sanaa, Yemen.* Farnham: Ashgate, 2015.

Larkin, C., and M. Dumper. "In Defense of Al-Aqsa: The Islamic Movement Inside Israel and the Battle for Jerusalem." *Middle East Journal* 66, no. 1 (2012): 31–52.

———. "UNESCO and Jerusalem: Constraints, Challenges and Opportunities." *Jerusalem Quarterly* 39 (2009): 16–28.

Larsen, P. B. "The Politics of Technicality: Guidance Culture in Environmental Governance." In *The Gloss of Harmony: The Politics of Policymaking in Multilateral Organisations,* edited by B. Müller, 75–100. London: Pluto Press, 2013.

Latour, B. *The Making of Law: An Ethnography of the Conseil d'Etat.* Cambridge, MA: Polity, 2010.

———. *We Have Never Been Modern.* Translated by C. Porter. Cambridge, MA: Harvard University Press, 1991.

Laves, W. H. C., and C. A. Thomson. *UNESCO: Purpose, Progress, Prospects.* Bloomington: University of Indiana Press, 1957.

Lawrence, T. E. *Crusader Castles.* Oxford: Oxford University Press, 1988.

Lee, S. K. "Siam Mismapped: Revisiting the Territorial Dispute over the Preah Vihear Temple." *South East Asia Research* 22, no. 1 (2014): 39–55.

Lenzerini, F. "Articles 15–16 World Heritage Fund." In *The 1972 World Heritage Convention: A Commentary,* edited by F. Francioni and F. Lenzerini, 269–88. Oxford: Oxford University Press, 1972.

———. "The UNESCO Declaration Concerning the Intentional Destruction of Cultural Heritage: One Step Forward and Two Steps Back." *Italian Yearbook of International Law* 13 (2003): 131–45.

Leturcq, J.-G. "Heritage-Making and Policies of Identity in the 'Post-Conflict Reconstruction' of Sudan." *Égypte/Monde Arabe,* nos. 5–6 (2009): 295–328.

Liljeblad, J. "The Pyu Ancient Cities World Heritage Application: Lessons from Myanmar on Transnational Advocacy Networks." *Journal of Civil Society* (2016): 1–17.

Locard, H. "The Myth of Angkor as an Essential Component of the Khmer Rouge Utopia." In *Cultural Heritage as Civilizing Mission,* edited by M. Falser, 201–22. New York: Springer, 2015.

Logan, W. "Australia, Indigenous Peoples and World Heritage from Kakadu to Cape York: State Party Behaviour Under the World Heritage Convention." *Journal of Social Archaeology* 13, no. 2 (2013): 153–76

———. "Closing Pandora's Box: Human Rights Conudrums in Cultural Heritage Protection." In *Cultural Heritage and Human Rights,* edited by H. Silverman and Fairchild Ruggles, 33–52. New York: Springer, 2008.

———. "Cultural Diversity, Cultural Heritage and Human Rights: Towards Heritage Management as Human Rights-Based Cultural Practice." *International Journal of Heritage Studies* 18, no. 3 (2012/04/29 2012): 231–44.

———. "Ethnicity, Heritage, Human Rights and Governance in the Union of Myanmar." In Cultural Contestation: Heritage, Identity and the Role of Government, edited by J. Rodenberg and P. Wagenaar, New York: Palgrave-Macmillan, forthcoming.

————. "Globalizing Heritage: World Heritage as a Manifestation of Modernism, and Challenges from the Periphery." In *Proceedings of the Australia ICOMOS National Conference*, 51–57. Adelaide: University of Adelaide/ICOMOS, 2002.

————. "Heritage in Times of Rapid Transformation: A Tale of Two Cities—Yangon and Hanoi." In *Asian Cities: Colonial to Global*, edited by G. Bracken, 279–300. Amsterdam: Amsterdam University Press, 2015.

————. "Making the Most of Heritage in Hanoi, Vietnam." *Historic Environment* 26, no. 3 (2014): 62–72.

————. "Planning the Palestinian Towns Under Occupation." Working Paper 12. Australasian Midde Eastern Studies Association, Christchurch, 1989.

————. "Playing the Devil's Advocate: Protecting Intangible Cultural Heritage and the Infringement of Human Rights." *Historic Environment* 22, no. 3 (2009): 14–18.

Lostal, M. *International Cultural Heritage Law in Armed Conflict: Case-Studies of Syria, Libya, Mali, the Invasion of Iraq, and the Buddhas of Bamiyan.* Cambridge: Cambridge University Press, 2017.

Luke, C. "The 40th World Heritage Session in Istanbul, Turkey: A Reflection on the Legacies of Heritage Policy and Missed Mega-Heritage." *Journal of Field Archaeology* 41, no. 6 (2016): 641–44.

Luke, C., and M. M. Kersel. *U.S. Cultural Diplomacy and Archaeology: Soft Power, Hard Heritage.* London: Routledge, 2013.

Mann, T. *Death in Venice.* Mineola, NY: Dover Publications, 1995 [1912].

Martín, J. G., and B. Rovira. "The Panamá Viejo Archaeological Project: More than a Decade of Research and Management of Heritage Resources." *Historical Archaeology* 46, no. 3 (2012): 16–26.

Marx, K., and J. O'Malley. *Critique of Hegel's "Philosophy of Right."* Cambridge: Cambridge University Press, 1977.

Maurel, C. *Histoire de l'UNESCO.* Paris: Editions L'Harmattan, 2010.

————. "Le sauvetage des monuments de Nubie par l'Unesco (1955–1968)." *Égypte/ Monde arabe*, no. 10 (2013).

Mauss, M. *The Gift: The Form and Reason for Exchange in Archaic Societies.* Translated by W. D. Halls. New York: W. W. Norton, 1990.

Mayor, F. *The New Page.* Paris: UNESCO, 1999.

Mazower, M. "The End of Eurocentrism." *Critical Inquiry* 40, no. 4 (2014): 298–313.

————. *Governing the World: The History of an Idea.* London: Penguin, 2012.

————. *No Enchanted Palace: The End of Empire and the Ideological Origins of the United Nations.* Princeton, NJ: Princeton University Press, 2009.

Mazza, R. *Jerusalem: From the Ottomans to the British.* London: IB Tauris, 2009.

McAlexander, R. J. "Couscous Mussolini: US Perceptions of Gamal Abdel Nasser, the 1958 Intervention in Lebanon and the Origins of the US–Israeli Special Relationship." *Cold War History* 11, no. 3 (2011): 363–85.

McNamara, R. *Britain, Nasser and the Balance of Power in the Middle East, 1952– 1977: From the Egyptian Revolution to the Six Day War.* London: Routledge, 2004.

Meskell, L. M. "From Paris to Pontdrift: UNESCO Meetings, Mapungubwe and Mining." *South African Archaeological Bulletin* 66, no. 194 (2011): 149–56.

——, ed. *Global Heritage: A Reader*. Oxford: Wiley Blackwell, 2015.

——. "Gridlock: UNESCO, Global Conflict and Failed Ambitions." *World Archaeology* 47, no. 2 (2015): 225–238.

——. *The Nature of Heritage: The New South Africa*. Oxford: Blackwell, 2011.

——. "Negative Heritage and Past Mastering in Archaeology." *Anthropological Quarterly* 75, no. 3 (2002): 557–74.

——. "The Rush to Inscribe: Reflections on the 35th Session of the World Heritage Committee, UNESCO Paris, 2011." *Journal of Field Archaeology* 37, no. 2 (2012): 145–51.

——. "States of Conservation: Protection, Politics and Pacting Within UNESCO's World Heritage Committee." *Anthropological Quarterly* 87, no. 1 (2014): 267–92.

——. "Transacting UNESCO World Heritage: Gifts and Exchanges on a Global Stage." *Social Anthropology/Anthropologie Sociale* 23, no. 1 (2015): 3–21

——. "UNESCO and the Fate of the World Heritage Indigenous Peoples Council of Experts (WHIPCOE)." *International Journal of Cultural Property* 20, no. 2 (2013): 155–74.

——. "UNESCO's World Heritage Convention at 40: Challenging the Economic and Political Order of International Heritage Conservation." *Current Anthropology* 54, no. 4 (2013): 483–94.

——. "World Heritage and WikiLeaks: Territory, Trade and Temples on the Thai-Cambodian Border." *Current Anthropology* 57, no. 1 (2016): 72–95.

Meskell, L. M., and C. Brumann. "UNESCO and New World Orders." In *Global Heritage: A Reader*, 22–42. Oxford: Wiley Blackwell, 2015.

Meskell, L. M., C. Liuzza, E. Bertacchini, and D. Saccone. "Multilateralism and UNESCO World Heritage: Decision-Making, States Parties and Political Processes." *International Journal of Heritage Studies* 21, no. 5 (2015): 423–40.

Meskell, L. M., C. Liuzza, and N. Brown. "World Heritage Regionalism: UNESCO from Europe to Asia." *International Journal of Cultural Property* (2015).

Métraux, A. "UNESCO and Anthropology." *American Anthropologist* 53, no. 2 (1951): 294–300.

Michell, N. *Ruins of Many Lands: A Descriptive Poem*. London: John K. Chapman, 1849.

Mills, A. J. "The Reconnaissance Survey from Gemai to Dal: A Preliminary Report for 1963–64." *Kush* 15 (1967–68): 200–210.

Mitchell, T. *Rule of Experts*. Berkeley: University of California Press, 2002.

Mitrany, D. *A Working Peace System*. Chicago: Quadrangle Books, 1966.

Miura, K. "Discourses and Practices Between Traditions and World Heritage Making in Angkor After 1990." In *Cultural Heritage as Civilizing Mission: From Decay to Recovery.*, edited by M. Falser, 251–78. New York: Springer, 2015.

——. "World Heritage Making in Angkor. Global, Regional, National and Local Actors, Interplays and Implications." In *World Heritage Angkor and*

Beyond: Circumstances and Implications of UNESCO Listings in Cambodia, edited by B. Hauser-Schäublin, 9–33. Göttingen: Universitätsverlag Göttingen, 2011.

Moore, E. H., and W. Maung. "The Social Dynamics of Pagoda Repair in Upper Myanmar." *Journal of Burma Studies* 20, no. 1 (2016): 149–98.

More, T. *Utopia*. http://history-world.org/Utopia_T.pdf, [1516].

Morgenthau, H. *Ambassador Morgenthau's Story*. New York: Doubleday, 1919.

Morse, J. C., and R. O. Keohane. "Contested Multilateralism." *The Review of International Organizations* 9, no. 4 (2014): 385–412.

Moser, S., D. Glazier, S. Ballard, J. Phillips, L. N. el Nemer, M. S. Mousa, S. Richardson, A. Conner, and M. Seymour. "Transforming Archaeology Through Practice: Strategies for Collaborative Archaeology and the Community Archaeology Project at Quseir, Egypt." *World Archaeology* 34, no. 2 (2002): 220–48.

Mosse, D. "Politics and Ethics: Ethnographies of Expert Knowledge and Professional Identities." In *Policy Worlds: Anthropology and the Analysis of Contemporary Power*, edited by C. Shore, S. Wright, and D. Però, 50–67. Oxford: Berghahn, 2011.

Müller, B. "Lifting the Veil of Harmony: Anthropologists Approach International Organizations." In *The Gloss of Harmony: The Politics of Policy-Making in Multilateral Organisations*, edited by B. Müller, 1–20. London: Pluto Press, 2013.

Murray, G. *From the League to the U.N.* London: Oxford University Press, 1948.

Musitelli, J. "World Heritage, Between Universalism and Globalization." *International Journal of Cultural Property* 11, no. 2 (2002): 323–36.

Nagaoka, M. "'European' and 'Asian' Approaches to Cultural Landscapes Management at Borobudur, Indonesia in the 1970s." *International Journal of Heritage Studies* 21, no. 3 (2014): 232–49.

Nas, P. J. M. "Masterpieces of Oral and Intangible Culture." *Current Anthropology* 43, no. 1 (2002): 139–48.

Nassar, A. E. "The International Criminal Court and the Applicability of International Jurisdiction Under Islamic Law." *Chicago Journal of International Law* 4, no. 2 (2003): 587–96.

Ndoro, W., and G. Wijesuriya. "Heritage Management and Conservation: From Colonization to Globalization." In *Global Heritage: A Reader*, edited by L. M. Meskell, 131–49. Oxford: Blackwell, 2015.

Newsroom Panama. "Concerns Linger over Route of Third Stage of Cinta Costera." Newsroom Panama, 2011.

Niebuhr, R. "The Theory and Practice of UNESCO." *International Organization* 4, no. 1 (1950): 3–11.

Nielsen, B. "L'Unesco et le culturellement correct." *Gradhiva* 2 (2013): 74–97.

———. "UNESCO and the 'Right' Kind of Culture: Bureaucratic Production and Articulation." *Critique of Anthropology* 31, no. 4 (2011): 273–92.

Nordström, H.-Å. *The West Bank Survey from Faras to Gemai I: Sites of Early Nubian, Middle Nubian and Pharaonic Age*. Oxford: Archaeopress, 2014.

Nudelman, M. "Who Owns the Scythian Gold—The Legal and Moral Implications of Ukraine and Crimea's Cultural Dispute." *Fordham International Law Journal* 38 (2015): 1261.

O'Keefe, R. "World Cultural Heritage: Obligations to the International Community as a Whole?" *International and Comparative Law Quarterly* 53, no. 1 (2004): 189–209.

Obidallah, M. T. "Saving the Roman Water System and the Terraced Landscape of Battir, Palestine." In *The UNESCO World Heritage and the Role of Civil Society. Proceedings of the International Conference Bonn 2015*, edited by S. Doempke, 136–39. Berlin: World Heritage Watch, 2015.

Okasha, S. "Address by H. E. Dr. Sarwat Okasha, Minister of Culture of the United Arab Republic." In *Abu Simbel: Addresses Delivered at the Ceremony to Mark the Completion of the Operations for Saving the Two Temples*, 7–19. Paris: UNESCO, 1968.

———. "Rameses Recrowned: The International Campaign to Preserve the Monuments of Nubia, 1959–68." In *Offerings to the Discerning Eye*, edited by S. H. D'Auria, 223–44. Leiden: Brill, 2009.

Osorio Ugarte, K. "Los atributos del Valor Universal Excepcional de una propiedad considerada Patrimonio Mundial." *Canto Rodado* 7 (2012): 1–27.

Pakenham, T. *The Scramble for Africa*. New York: Avon Books, 1992.

Palestine ICOMOS. "Palestine: Destruction in the West Bank, April 2002." *Heritage at Risk* 2002/2003 (2015): 157–60.

Papazian, S. "The Cost of Memorializing: Analyzing Armenian Genocide Memorials and Commemorations in the Republic of Armenia and in the Diaspora." *International Journal of History, Culture and Modernity* (forthcoming).

Parenti, B., and E. De Simone. "Explaining Determinants of National UNESCO Tentative Lists: An Empirical Study." *Applied Economics Letters* 22, no. 15 (2015): 1193–98.

Pavone, V. "From Intergovernmental to Global: UNESCO's Response to Globalization." *Review of International Organizations* 2, no. 1 (2007): 77–95.

———. *From the Labyrinth of the World to the Paradise of the Heart: Science and Humanism in UNESCO's Approach to Globalization*. New York: Lexington, 2008.

Pedersen, S. "Empires, States and the League of Nations." In *Internationalisms: A Twentieth-Century History*, edited by G. Sluga and P. Clavin, 113–38. Cambridge: Cambridge University Press, 2017.

———. *The Guardians: The League of Nations and the Crisis of Empire*. Oxford: Oxford University Press, 2015.

Peleggi, M. *The Politics of Ruins and the Business of Nostalgia*. Bangkok: White Lotus Press, 2002.

Pendergast, W. R. "UNESCO and French Cultural Relations 1945–1970." *International Organization* 30, no. 3 (1976): 453–83.

Petrovic, J. "What Next for Endangered Cultural Treasures: The Timbuktu Crisis and the Responsibility to Protect." *New Zealand Journal of Public and International Law* 11 (2013): 381–426.

Peycam, P. "The International Coordinating Committee for Angkor: A World Heritage Site as an Arena of Competition, Connivance and State(s) Legitimation." *SOJOURN: Journal of Social Issues in Southeast Asia* 31, no. 3 (2016): 743–85.

Philp, J. "The Political Appropriation of Burma, Cultural Heritage and Its Implications for Human Rights." In *Cultural Diversity, Heritage, and Human Rights: Intersections in Theory and Practice*, edited by M. Langfield, W. Logan, and M. N. Craith, 83–100. London: Routledge, 2009.

Pichard, P. "Today's Pagan: Conservation Under the Generals." In *"Archaeologizing" Heritage?*, edited by M. Falser and M. Juneja, 235–49. Berlin: Springer, 2013.

Pieris, A. "From Colombo to Sri Jayewardenepura: National Heritage and the Capricious Subjectivities of Postcolonial Capitals." *Historic Environment* 26, no. 3 (2014): 74–85.

Plets, G. "Ethno-nationalism, Asymmetric Federalism and Soviet Perceptions of the Past: (World) Heritage Activism in the Russian Federation." *Journal of Social Archaeology* 15, no. 1 (2015): 67–93.

———. "Violins and Trowels for Palmyra: Post-conflict Heritage Politics." *Anthropology Today* 33, no. 4 (2017): 18–22.

Poria, Y., A. Reichel, and R. Cohen. "World Heritage Site: Is It an Effective Brand Name? A Case Study of a Religious Heritage Site." *Journal of Travel Research* 50, no. 5 (2011): 482–95.

Power, C. "Saudi Arabia Bulldozes over Its Heritage." *Time*, November 14, 2014.

Pressouyre, L. *The World Heritage Convention, Twenty Years Later*. Paris: UNESCO Publishing, 1996.

Preston, W., E. S. Herman, and H. Schiller. *Hope and Folly: The United States and UNESCO 1945–1985*. Minneapolis: University of Minnesota Press, 1989.

Prott, L. "From Admonition to Action: UNESCO's Role in the Protection of Cultural Heritage." *Nature and Resources* 28, no. 3 (1992): 4–11.

Provence, M. *The Great Syrian Revolt and the Rise of Arab Nationalism*. Austin: University of Texas Press, 2005.

Putra, I. D., and M. Hitchcock. "Pura Besakih: A World Heritage Site Contested." *Indonesia and the Malay World* 33, no. 96 (2005): 225–38.

Rabbat, N. "Heritage as a Right: Heritage and the Arab Spring." *International Journal of Islamic Architecture* 5, no. 2 (2016): 267–78.

Rao, K. "A New Paradigm for the Identification, Nomination and Inscription of Properties on the World Heritage List." *International Journal of Heritage Studies* 16, no. 3 (2010): 161–72.

Ray, H. P. *Colonial Archaeology in South Asia: The Legacy of Sir Mortimer Wheeler*. New Delhi: Oxford University Press, 2008.

Ray, H. P., ed. *Mausam: Maritime Cultural Landscapes Across the Indian Ocean*. New Delhi: Aryan Books International, 2014.

Reid, D. M. *Contesting Antiquity in Egypt: Archaeologies, Museums, and the Struggle for Identities from World War I to Nasser*. Cairo: American University in Cairo Press, 2015.

———. "Indigenous Egyptology: The Decolonization of a Profession?" *Journal of the American Oriental Society* 105, no. 2 (1985): 233–46.

Report by the Norwegian Delegation. "Report to the UNESCO World Heritage Committee 34th Session." Brasilia July 25–August 3, 2010.

Reyes, V. "The Production of Cultural and Natural Wealth: An Examination of World Heritage Sites." *Poetics* 44 (2014): 42–63.

Reynolds, K. "Palestinian Agriculture and the Israeli Separation Barrier: The Mismatch of Biopolitics and Chronopolitics with the Environment and Human Survival." *International Journal of Environmental Studies* 72, no. 2 (2015): 237–55.

Reynolds, N. Y. "City of the High Dam: Aswan and the Promise of Postcolonialism in Egypt." *City and Society* 29, no. 1 (2017): 213–35.

Reza Husseini, S. "Destruction of Bamiyan Buddhas: Taliban Iconoclasm and Hazara Response." *Himalayan and Central Asian Studies* 16, no. 2 (2012): 15–50.

Ricca, S. *Reinventing Jerusalem: Israel's Reconstruction of the Jewish Quarter After 1967.* London: IB Tauris, 2007.

Richardson, L. "Avoiding and Incurring Losses: Decision-making in the Suez Crisis." *International Journal* 47, no. 2 (1992): 370–401.

Rico, T. "Heritage at Risk: The Authority and Autonomy of a Dominant Preservation Framework." In *Heritage Keywords: Rhetoric and Redescription in Cultural Heritage,* edited by K. Lafrenz Samuels and T. Rico, 147–62. Boulder: University Press of Colorado, 2015.

———. "The Heritage of Aftermath: Making 'Heritage at Risk' in Post-Tsnumai Banda Aceh." Ph.D. dissertation, Department of Anthropology, Stanford University, 2011.

———. "The Limits of a 'Heritage at Risk' Framework: The Construction of Post-Disaster Cultural Heritage in Banda Aceh, Indonesia." *Journal of Social Archaeology* 14, no. 2 (2014): 157–76.

———. "Stakeholder in Practice: 'Us,' 'Them' and the Problem of Expertise." In *Archaeologies of "Us" and "Them": Debating History, Heritage and Indigeneity,* edited by C. Hillerdal, A. Karlström, and C.-G. Ojala. London: Routledge, 2017.

———. "Technologies, Technocracy, and the Promise of 'Alternative' Heritage Values." In *Heritage in Action,* edited by H. Silverman, E. Waterton, and S. Watson, 217–30. New York: Springer, 2017.

Riles, A. "Infinity Within the Brackets." *American Ethnologist* 25, no. 3 (1998): 378–98.

Rjoob, A. A. "The Impact of Israeli Occupation on the Conservation of Cultural Heritage Sites in the Occupied Palestinian Territories: The Case of 'Salvage Excavations.'" *Conservation and Management of Archaeological Sites* 11, nos. 3–4 (2009): 214–35.

Rodriguez, J. "Cleaning up Bodhgaya: Conflicts over Development and the Worlding of Buddhism." *City and Society* 29, no. 1 (2017): 59–81.

Rosamond, B. *Theories of European Integration.* New York: Palgrave Macmillan, 2000.

Rössler, M. "Applying Authenticity to Cultural Landscapes." *Association for Preservation Technology International Bulletin* 39, no. 2/3 (2008): 47–52.

———. "Challenges of World Heritage Interpretation: World Heritage and Associative Values." In *International Conference on World Heritage Interpretation (November 2, 2016)*. Seoul, 2016.

Rothschild, E. "The Archives of Universal History." *Journal of World History* 19, no. 3 (2008): 375–401.

Röttjer, J. "Safeguarding 'Negative Historical Values' for the Future? Appropriating the Past in the UNESCO Cultural World Heritage Site Auschwitz-Birkenau." *Ab Imperio* 2015, no. 4 (2015): 130–65.

Ryan, J., and S. Silvanto. "The World Heritage List: The Making and Management of a Brand." *Place Branding and Public Diplomacy* 5, no. 4 (2009): 290–300.

———. "A Study of the Key Strategic Drivers of the Use of the World Heritage Site Designation as a Destination Brand." *Journal of Travel and Tourism Marketing* 31, no. 3 (2014): 327–43.

Sand, J. "Japan's Monument Problem: Ise Shrine as Metaphor." *Past and Present* 226, suppl. 10 (2015): 126–52.

Sassen, S. *Territory, Authority, Rights: From Medieval to Global Assemblages*. Princeton, NJ: Princeton University Press, 2006.

Sathyamurthy, T. V. *The Politics of International Cooperation: Contrasting Conceptions of UNESCO*. Geneva: Librairie Droz, 1964.

Säve-Söderbergh, T. "The International Nubia Campaign: Two Perspectives." *Actes du VIIe Congres International d'Etudes Nubiennes*. Geneva: Sociéte d'Etudes Nubiennes, 1992.

———. "International Salvage Archaeology: Some Organizational and Technical Aspects of the Nubian Campaign." *Annals of the Royal Science Academy* 15–16 (1972): 116–40.

———. *Temples and Tombs of Ancient Nubia: The International Rescue Campaign at Abu Simbel, Philae and Other Sites*. London: Thames and Hudson, 1987.

Schmidt, P. R., ed. *Postcolonial Archaeologies in Africa*. Santa Fe: SAR Press, 2009.

Schmitt, T. M. *Cultural Governance: Zur Kulturgeographie Des UNESCO-Welterberegimes*. Wiesbaden: Franz Steiner Verlag, 2012.

———. "Global Cultural Governance: Decision-Making Concerning World Heritage Between Politics and Science." *Erdkunde* 63, no. 2 (2009): 103–21.

———. "The UNESCO Concept of Safeguarding Intangible Cultural Heritage: Its Background and Marrakchi Roots." *International Journal of Heritage Studies* 14, no. 2 (2008): 95–111.

Schnapp, A. "Archéologie et tradition académique en Europe aux XVIIIe et XIXe siècles." *Annales, Histoire, Sciences Sociales* 37, nos. 5–6 (1982): 760–77.

Schofield, C. H., and M. Tan-Mullins. "Maritime Claims, Conflicts and Cooperation in the Gulf of Thailand." *Ocean Yearbook Online* 22, no. 1 (2008): 75–116.

Scudder, T. "Aswan High Dam Resettlement of Egyptian Nubians." In *Aswan High Dam Resettlement of Egyptian Nubians*, 1–52. Singapore: Springer, 2016.

Settis, S. *If Venice Dies*. New York: New Vessel Press, 2015.

Sewell, J. P. *UNESCO and World Politics.* Princeton, NJ: Princeton University Press, 1975.

Shabab, Q. U. "Address of Welcome." In *Proceedings of International Symposium on Moenjodaro, 1973,* edited by A. N. Khan. Karachi: National Book Foundation, 1975.

Sharma, B. K., and A. Rasheed, eds. *Indian Ocean Region: Emerging Strategic Coooperation, Competition and Conflict Scenarios.* New Delhi: Vij Books India, 2015.

"The Shelling of Damascus." *Advocate of Peace Through Justice* 87, no. 12 (1925): 659–62.

Shemesh, M., and S. I. Troen, eds. *The Suez-Sinai Crisis: A Retrospective and Reappraisal.* London: Routledge, 2005.

Shepherd, R. "Cultural Heritage, UNESCO, and the Chinese State." *Heritage Management* 2, no. 1 (2009): 55–79.

———. "UNESCO and the Politics of Cultural Heritage in Tibet." *Journal of Contemporary Asia* 36, no. 2 (2006): 243–57.

Shinnie, P. L. *Ancient Nubia.* London: Kegan Paul, 1996.

Shinnie, P. L., and M. Shinnie. *Debeira West. A Mediaeval Nubian Town.* Warminster: Aris and Phillips, 1978.

Shokr, A. "Hydropolitics, Economy, and the Aswan High Dam in Mid-Century Egypt." *Arab Studies Journal* 17, no. 1 (2009): 9–31.

Shore, C. "European Integration in Anthropological Perspective: Studying the 'Culture' of the EU Civil Service." In *Observing Government Elites: Up Close and Personal,* edited by R. A. W. Rhodes, P. 't Hart, and M. Noordegraaf, 180–205. New York: Palgrave Macmillan, 2007.

Sidi, A. O. "Maintaining Timbuktu's Unique Tangible and Intangible Heritage." *International Journal of Heritage Studies* 18, no. 3 (2012): 324–31.

Sinding-Larsen, A. "Lhasa Community, World Heritage and Human Rights." *International Journal of Heritage Studies* 18, no. 3 (2012): 297–306.

Singh, J. P. *United Nations Educational, Scientific and Cultural Organization (UNESCO): Creating Norms for a Complex World.* London: Routledge, 2011.

———. "A 21st-Century UNESCO: Ideals and Politics in an Era of (Interrupted) US Re-engagement." Briefing 23, Future United Nations Development System, Ralph Bunche Institute for International Studies, CUNY Graduate Center, New York, 2014.

———. "Global Institutions and Deliberations: Is the World Trade Organization More Participatory than UNESCO?" In *Deliberation and Development: Rethinking the Role of Voice and Collective Action in Unequal Societies,* edited by P. Heller and V. Rao, 193–222. Washington, DC: World Bank Group, 2015.

Sluga, G. "Editorial—The Transnational History of International Institutions." *Journal of Global History* 6, no. 2 (2011): 219–22.

———. "Imagining Internationalism." *Arts: The Journal of the Sydney University Arts Association* 32 (2012): 55–68.

———. *Internationalism in the Age of Nationalism.* University of Pennsylvania Press, 2013.

———. "UNESCO and the (One) World of Julian Huxley." *Journal of World History* 21, no. 3 (2010): 393–418.

Smith, A. D. *Nationalism.* Cambridge: Polity, 2010.

Smith, L.-J., and N. Akagawa, eds. *Intangible Heritage.* London: Routledge, 2009.

Sothirak, P. "Cambodia's Border Conflict with Thailand." *Southeast Asian Affairs* 2013, no. 1 (2013): 87–100.

Standish, D. *Venice in Environmental Peril? Myth and Reality.* Lanham, MD: University Press of America, 2011.

Starr, F. *Corporate Responsibility for Cultural Heritage.* New York: Routledge, 2013.

Stone, P. "Protecting Cultural Heritage in Times of Conflict: Lessons from Iraq." *Archaeologies* 5, no. 1 (2009): 32–38.

Stone, P. and J. F. Bajjaly, eds. *The Destruction of Cultural Heritage in Iraq.* Woodbridge: Boydell & Brewer, 2008.

Stott, P. "The World Heritage Convention and the National Park Service, 1962–1972." *George Wright Forum* 28 (2011): 279–90.

Strasser, P. " 'Putting Reform into Action'—Thirty Years of the World Heritage Convention: How to Reform a Convention Without Changing Its Regulations." *International Journal of Cultural Property* 11 (2002): 215–66.

Strate, S. "A Pile of Stones? Preah Vihear as a Thai Symbol of National Humiliation." *South East Asia Research* 21, no. 1 (2013): 41–68.

Suková, L. "Pictures in Place: A Case Study from Korosko (Lower Nubia)." *Studies in African Archaeology (Poznań Archaeological Museum)* 14 (2015): 119–43.

Swenson, A. "Crusader Heritages and Imperial Preservation." *Past and Present* 226, suppl. 10 (2015): 27–56.

———. "The First Heritage International(s): Rethinking Global Networks Before UNESCO." *Future Anterior: Journal of Historic Preservation History Theory and Criticism* 13, no. 1 (2016): 1–16.

———. *The Rise of Heritage: Preserving the Past in France, Germany and England, 1789–1914.* Cambridge: Cambridge University Press, 2013.

Tabet, J. *Review of ICOMOS' Working Methods and Procedures for the Evaluation of Cultural and Mixed Properties Nominated for Inscription on the UNESCO World Heritage List.* Paris: ICOMOS, 2010.

———. "Some Thoughts on the Sidelines of the World Heritage Committee Meeting in Doha." Unpublished paper, 2014.

Tanudirjo, D. A. "Changing Perspectives on the Relationship Between Heritage Landscape and Local Communities: A Lesson from Borobudur." In *Transcending the Culture-Nature Divide in Cultural Heritage: Views from the Asia-Pacific Region*, edited by S. Brockwell, S. O'Connor, and D. Byrne, 65–81. Canberra: ANU Press, 2013.

Toye, J., and R. Toye. "One World, Two Cultures? Alfred Zimmern, Julian Huxley and the Ideological Origins of UNESCO." *History* 95, no. 319 (2010): 308–31.

Tucker, S. C. *A Global Chronology of Conflict: From the Ancient World to the Modern Middle East: From the Ancient World to the Modern Middle East.* Santa Barbara, CA: ABC-Clio, 2010.

Turtinen, J. *Globalising Heritage: On UNESCO and the Transnational Construction of a World Heritage.* Stockholm: Stockholm Center for Organizational Research, 2000.

Ulengin, M. B., and Ö. Ulengin. "A New Layer in a World Heritage Site: The Post-war Reconstruction of Mostar's Historic Core." *Megaron* 10, no. 3 (2015): 332–42.

UNESCO. *A Common Trust: The Preservation of the Ancient Monuments of Nubia.* Paris: UNESCO 1960.

———. "Our Creative Diversity. Report of the World Commission on Culture and Development." Paris: UNESCO, 1995.

———. "Protection of Mankind's Cultural Heritage: Sites and Monuments." Paris: UNESCO, 1970.

Valderrama, F. *A History of UNESCO.* Paris: UNESCO, 1995.

van den Dries, M. H. "Social Involvement as a Buzz Word in World Heritage Nominations." In *Proceedings of the 2nd International Conference on Best Practices in World Heritage: People and Communities Menorca, Spain, 29–30 April, 1–2 May 2015*, edited by A. R. Castillo Mena, 668–86. Madrid: Universidad Complutense de Madrid, Servicio de Publicaciones, 2015.

Van der Aa, B. "Preserving the Heritage of Humanity? Obtaining World Heritage Status and the Impacts of Listing." Ph.D. dissertation, Netherlands Organisation for Scientific Research, 2005.

Van der Auwera, S. "'Culture for Development' and the UNESCO Policy on the Protection of Cultural Property During Armed Conflict." *International Journal of Cultural Policy* 20, no. 3 (2014): 245–60.

———. "UNESCO and the Protection of Cultural Property During Armed Conflict." *International Journal of Cultural Policy* 19, no. 1 (2013): 1–19.

van der Laarse, R. "Who Owns the Crimean Past? Conflicted Heritage and Ukrainian Identities." In *A Critical Biographical Approach of Europe's Past*, edited by D. Callebaut, 16–53. Ghent: Provincie Oost-Vlaanderen, 2014.

Veintimilla, D. J. "Islamic Law and War Crimes Trials: The Possibility and Challenges of a War Crimes Tribunal Against the Assad Regime and ISIL." *Cornell International Law Journal* 49 (2016): 497–519.

Vianello, M. "The No Grandi Navi Campaign." In *Protest and Resistance in the Tourist City*, edited by C. Colomb and J. Novy, 171–90. London: Routledge, 2016.

von Droste, B. "The Concept of Outstanding Universal Value and Its Application: 'From the Seven Wonders of the Ancient World to the 1,000 World Heritage Places Today.'" *Journal of Cultural Heritage Management and Sustainable Development* 1, no. 1 (2011): 26–41.

Vrdoljak, A. F. "Article 14: The Secretariat and Support of the World Heritage Committee." In *The 1972 World Heritage Convention: A Commentary*, edited by F. Francioni and F. Lenzerini, 243–68. Oxford: Oxford University Press, 2008.

———. "Challenges for International Cultural Heritage Law." In *Blackwell Companion to the New Heritage Studies*, edited by W. Logan, M. N. Craith, and U. Kockel, 541–556. New York: Wiley Blackwell, 2015.

———. "Indigenous Peoples and Protection of Cultural Heritage in International Law." (in press).

———. "Intentional Destruction of Cultural Heritage and International Law." In *Multiculturalism and International Law, XXXV Thesaurus Acroasium*, edited by K. Koufa, 377–96. Thessaloniki: Sakkoulas Publications, 2007.

———. "International Exchange and Trade in Cultural Objects." In *Culture and International Economic Law*, edited by V. Vadi and B. de Witte, 124–42. London: Routledge, 2015.

———. *International Law, Museums, and the Return of Cultural Objects*. Cambridge: Cambridge University Press, 2006.

———. "Self-Determination and Cultural Rights." In *Cultural Human Rights*, edited by F. Francioni and M. Scheinin, 41–78. Leiden: Brill, 2008.

Walasek, H. *Bosnia and the Destruction of Cultural Heritage*. Abingdon: Routledge, 2016.

Wanner, R. E. *UNESCO's Origins, Achievements, Problems and Promises: An Inside/Outside Perspective from the US*. Hong Kong: Comparative Education Research Center, 2015.

Watenpaugh, H. Z. "Cultural Heritage and the Arab Spring: War over Culture, Culture of War and Culture War." *International Journal of Islamic Architecture* 5, no. 2 (2016): 245–63.

———. "Preserving the Medieval City of Ani: Cultural Heritage Between Contest and Reconciliation." *Journal of the Society of Architectural Historians* 73, no. 4 (2014): 528–55.

Weber, M. *Economy and Society: An Outline of Interpretive Sociology*. Berkeley: University of California Press, 1978.

Weickert, C. "Zur Geschichte des Deutschen Archäologischen Institute." *Archäologischer Anzeiger* 70 (1955): 127–56.

Weiner, A. *Inalienable Possessions: The Paradox of Keeping-While-Giving*. Berkeley: University of California Press, 1992.

Wendorf, F. "The Campaign for Nubian Prehistory." In *Etudes Nubiennes: Conférence de Geneve. Actes du VIIe Congres International d'Etudes Nubiennes*, edited by C. Bonnet, 43–54. Geneva: J. G. Cecconi, 1992.

———. *The Prehistory of Nubia*. Dallas: Southern Methodist University Press, 1968.

West, P., J. Igoe, and D. Brockington. "Parks and People: The Social Impacts of Protected Areas." *Annual Review of Anthropology* 35 (2006): 251–77.

Wijesuriya, G. "Conservation in Context." In *Conservation and Preservation Interactions Between Theory and Practice: In Memoriam Alois Riegl (1858–1905). Proceedings of the International Conference of the ICOMOS International Scientific Committee for the Theory and the Philosophy of Conservation and Restoration*, edited by M. Falser, W. Lipp, and A. Tomaszewski, 233–47. Florence: Edizioni Polistampa, 2010.

————. "Conserving the Temple of the Tooth Relic, Sri Lanka." *Public Archaeology* 1, no. 2 (2000): 99–108.

Wilkinson, T., N. Miller, C. Reichel, and D. Whitcomb. *On the Margin of the Euphrates: Settlement and Land Use at Tell es-Sweyhat and in the Upper Lake Assad Area, Syria.* Chicago: Oriental Institute, 2004.

Williams, T. "The Curious Tale of Preah Vihear: The Process and Value of World Heritage Nomination." *Conservation and Management of Archaeological Sites* 13, no. 1 (2011): 1–7.

Wilson, J. A. "The Nubian Campaign: An Exercise in International Archaeology." *Proceedings of the American Philosophical Society* 111, no. 5 (1967): 268–71.

Winter, T. "One Belt, One Road, One Heritage: Cultural Diplomacy and the Silk Road." *The Diplomat* 29 (2016): 1–5.

Witcomb, A. "Cross-Cultural Encounters and 'Difficult Heritage' on the Thai-Burma Railway: An Ethics of Cosmopolitanism Rather than Practices of Exclusion." In *A Companion to Heritage Studies*, edited by W. Logan, M. N. Craith, and U. Kockel, 461–78. Oxford: Blackwell, 2015.

Woolf, L. S. *International Government* Westminster: Fabian Society, 1916.

Wright, Q. "The Bombardment of Damascus." *American Journal of International Law* 20, no. 2 (1926): 263–80.

Yoosuk, U. "The Preah Vihear Temple: Roots of Thailand-Cambodia Border Dispute." *International Journal of Asian Social Science* 3, no. 4 (2013): 921–29.

Yusuf, A. A. "Article 1: Definition of Cultural Heritage." In *The 1972 World Heritage Convention: A Commentary*, edited by F. Francioni and F. Lenzerini, 23–50. Oxford: Oxford University Press, 2008.

Zacharias, D. "The UNESCO Regime for the Protection of World Heritage as Prototype of an Autonomy-Gaining International Institution." In *The Exercise of Public Authority by International Institutions*, edited by A. von Bogdandy, 301–36. Berlin: Springer, 2010.

Zuringa, S. "The Spanish Nubian Salvage Campaign Through the Media and Official Archives." In *The Kushite World: Proceeedings of the 11th International Conference for Meroitic Studies*, edited by M. H. Zach, 613–22. Vienna: Verein der Förderer der Sudanforschung, 2008.

Index